OXFORD CLASSICAL MONOGRAPHS

Published under the supervision of a Committee of the Faculty of Classics in the University of Oxford

The aim of the Oxford Classical Monographs series (which replaces the Oxford Classical and Philosophical Monographs) is to publish books based on the best theses on Greek and Latin literature, ancient history, and ancient philosophy examined by the Faculty Board of Classics.

Imperial Power, Provincial Government, and the Emergence of Roman Asia, 133 BCE–14 CE

BRADLEY JORDAN

OXFORD
UNIVERSITY PRESS

Great Clarendon Street, Oxford, OX2 6DP,
United Kingdom

Oxford University Press is a department of the University of Oxford.
It furthers the University's objective of excellence in research, scholarship,
and education by publishing worldwide. Oxford is a registered trade mark of
Oxford University Press in the UK and in certain other countries

Published in the United States of America by Oxford University Press
198 Madison Avenue, New York, NY 10016, United States of America

British Library Cataloguing in Publication Data
Data available

Library of Congress Control Number: 2023942431

ISBN 978–0–19–888706–5

DOI: 10.1093/oso/9780198887065.001.0001

Printed and bound by
CPI Group (UK) Ltd, Croydon, CR0 4YY

meis amicis, qui se agnoscant

Acknowledgements

It is a delight to be able to acknowledge the numerous people who have helped to shepherd this manuscript from vaguely conceived doctoral project into print. First, I owe a particular debt of gratitude to my graduate supervisor, Georgy Kantor. His kindness in offering copious, perceptive, and swift feedback on my many (many) drafts and enlightening an unsophisticated provincial as to the peculiarities of Oxford would require many lifetimes to repay. He remains a crucial source of insightful comments, unending encouragement, and inspiration.

The original thesis was examined by Federico Santangelo and Ed Bispham, whose sympathetic, yet incisive, comments and recommendations have immeasurably improved the published version. The observations of Andy Meadows were invaluable in producing the final text. Each has given substantial time and effort to help me produce the published volume and I sincerely thank them for that. The two anonymous reviewers for the press offered an indispensable critique of the work at an early stage, which I genuinely appreciate.

My graduate work and subsequent research would not have been possible without the generous financial support of the Clarendon Fund, Oxford-Australia Scholarships Fund, and Merton College. I would also like to acknowledge the support of Walter Ameling and the Alfried Krupp von Halbach und Bohlen Stiftung during a fellowship at the University of Cologne, sadly disrupted by Covid-19. I am grateful to the British Institute at Ankara for supporting an especially productive Fellowship in Turkey, and I would like to thank the staff and visitors for their help, support, and valuable conversations. The generosity of the Classical Association made possible an exceptionally valuable research trip to the idyllic library of the Fondation Hardt in Vandœuvres during my DPhil. It was a joy to be able to return thanks to the Fondation's own generosity in 2022, to put the finishing touches to this manuscript, and I am grateful for the support, kindness, and interesting discussions of the staff and other visitors.

During my time at Oxford, the suggestions and advice of Nicholas Purcell, Jonathan Prag, and Peter Thonemann proved extremely helpful and guided my research on several key points. I also must acknowledge the community of scholars in Australia, which nurtured my nascent interest in the ancient world and pushed me to pursue research to the highest standard, especially Frederik Vervaet, Kathryn Welch, Glenys Wooton, and Michael Champion. Others, too many to list here, have offered help, advice, and encouragement for which I am infinitely grateful: Lina Girdvainyte, Dylan James, Harry Morgan, Lewis Webb, Marcus Chin, David Rafferty, Leah Lazar, Tobi Menzel, Anna McGlade, and many more.

Finally, and most of all, I must thank Kim Webb, who has now read and commented more drafts than I can count with insight, acuity, and perceptiveness. She offered crucial support throughout the slow descent into academia and without that, this book would certainly not exist. Accordingly, I offer eternal, heartfelt thanks.

Contents

Abbreviations

Ancient authors and texts are referenced in the style of *Oxford Classical Dictionary*, 5th edition. Periodicals follow the conventions of *L'Année Philologique* with occasional self-evident modifications. All dates are BCE unless otherwise stated. Other abbreviations are as follows:

AÉ	1888–, *L'année épigraphique*, Paris.
ANRW	Haase, W. & Temporini, H. (eds), 1972–, *Aufstieg und Niedergang der römischen Welt: Geschichte und Kultur Roms im Spiegel der neueren Forschung*, Berlin.
AvP	1885– *Altertümer von Pergamon*, Berlin.
BÉ	'*Bulletin épigraphique*', appearing annually in *Revue des études grecques*.
BMC	*British Museum Catalogue.*
Carie	Robert, L., 1954, *La Carie: histoire et géographie historique avec le recueil des inscriptions antiques*, Paris.
CIL	Henzen, W., Hülsen, C., & Mommsen, T. (eds), *Corpus Inscriptionum Latinarum*, Rome.
FGrH	Jacoby, F. (ed.), 1923–, *Die Fragmente der Griechischen Historiker*, Berlin.
IAph2007	Reynolds, J., Rouché, C., & Bodard, G. (eds), 2007, *Inscriptions of Aphrodisias*, available <https://insaph.kcl.ac.uk/insaph/iaph2007/>.
I.Cos	Segre, M. (ed.), 1993, *Iscrizioni di Cos*, 2 vols, Rome.
I.Délos	Dürrbach, F. (ed.), *Inscriptions de Délos*, Paris.
I.Didyma	Rehm, A., 1958, in Wiegnand, T. (ed.), *Didyma*, vol. 2, Berlin.
I.Eph.	1979–1984, *Die Inschriften von Ephesos*, 8 vols, Bonn.
IG	1873– *Inscriptiones Graecae*, Berlin.
IGR	Cagnat, R. (ed.), 1906–27, *Inscriptiones graecae ad res romanas pertinentes*, Paris.
I.Ilion	Frisch, P. (ed.), 1975, *Inschriften von Ilion*, Bonn.
ILS	Dessau, H. (ed.), 1892–1916, *Inscriptiones Latinae Selectae*, Berlin.
I.Kaunos	Marek, C. (ed.), 2006, *Die Inschriften von Kaunos*, Munich.
I.Keramos	Varinioğlu, E. (ed.), 1986, *Die Inschriften von Keramos*, Bonn.
I.Kyme	Engelmann, H. (ed.), 1976, *Die Inscriften von Kyme*, Bonn.
I.Labraunda	Crampa, J., 1969–72, *Labraunda: Swedish Excavations and Researches*, vol. 3, Lund.
I.Magnesia	Kern, O. (ed.), 1900, *Die Inschriften von Magnesia am Maeander*, Berlin.
I.Magnesia Sipylos	Ihnken, T. (ed.), 1978, *Die Inschriften von Magnesia am Sipylos*, Bonn.
I.Metropolis	Dreyer, B. (ed.), 2003–, *Die Inschriften von Metropolis*, Bonn.
I.Mylasa	Blümel, W. (ed.), 1987–8, *Die Inschriften von Mylasa*, 2 vols, Bonn.
Inscr. It.	1937–1963, *Inscriptiones Italiae*, Rome.

I.Priene[2]	Blümel, W. & Merkelbach, R. (eds), 2014, *Inschriften von Priene*, 2nd edn, 2 vols, Bonn.
I.Sagalassos	Eich, A., Eich, P., & Eck, W. (eds), 2018–, *Die Inschriften von Sagalassos*, Bonn.
I.Sestos	Krauss, J. (ed.), 1980, *Die Inschriften von Sestos und der thrakischen Chersones*, Bonn.
I.Smyrna	Petzl, G. (ed.), 1982–90, *Die Inschriften von Smyrna*, 2 vols, Bonn.
I.Stratonikeia	Şahin, M.Ç. (ed.), 1981–2010, *Die Inschriften von Stratonikeia*, 3 vols, Bonn.
I.Sultan Dağı	Jonnes, L. (ed.), 2002–, *The Inscriptions of Sultan Dağı*, Bonn.
I.Tralleis	1989–2019, *Die Inschriften von Tralleis und Nysa*, 2 vols, Bonn.
MAMA	Calder, W.M. (ed.), 1928–62, *Monumenta Asiae Minoris antiqua*, Manchester.
Milet	1997–, *Inschriften von Milet*, Berlin.
MRR	Broughton, T.R.S., 1951–60, *The Magistrates of the Roman Republic*, 3 vols, New York.
OGIS	Dittenberger, W. (ed.), 1903–5, *Orientis graeci inscriptiones selectae: supplementum sylloges inscriptionum graecarum*, Leipzig.
Opramoas	Kokkinia, C., 2000, *Die Opramoas-Inschrift von Rhodiapolis: Euergetismus und soziale Elite in Lykien*, Bonn.
RDGE	Sherk, R.K., 1969, *Roman Documents from the Greek East: Senatus Consulta and Epistulae to the Age of Augustus*, Baltimore.
RIC	1923–, *The Roman Imperial Coinage*, London.
RPC	Burnett, A.M., Amandry, M., & Ripollès Alegre, P.P. (eds), 1992–, *Roman Provincial Coinage*, London.
RRC	Crawford, M.H., 1974, *Roman Republican Coinage*, 2 vols, London.
RS	Crawford, M.H. et al. (eds), 1996, *Roman Statutes*, 2 vols, London.
Sardis	Robinson, D.M. & Buckler, W.H. (eds), *Sardis VII: Greek and Latin Inscriptions*, Leiden.
SEG	1923–, *Supplementum Epigraphicum Graecum*, Amsterdam.
Syll.[3]	Dittenberger, W. (ed.), 1915–24, *Sylloge inscriptioum graecarum*, 3rd edn, 4 vols, Leipzig.
TAM	1901–, *Tituli Asiae Minoris*, Vienna.
ZPE	1967–, *Zeitschrift für Papyrologie und Epigraphik*, Bonn.

Introduction

In 9/8 BCE, Paullus Fabius Maximus, the proconsul of Asia, issued an edict proposing that henceforth the cities of the Roman province of Asia begin their civic calendars on the birthday of Augustus. This is one of the most widely attested decrees ever issued by a Roman magistrate: fragmentary inscribed copies appear at Priene, Metropolis, Maeonia, Apamea, Eumenea, and Dorylaeum.[1] However, alongside Paullus' edict we find a decree solicited by him from a body described as the κοινόν of Asia.[2] The Greeks in Asia (*οἱ ἐπὶ τῆς Ἀσίας Ἕλληνες*) wholeheartedly endorsed the proconsul's suggestion and granted him significant honours. While, for the most part, the *koinon*'s decree corresponds with Paullus' instructions, some subtle differences emerge, most notably regarding the publication and memorialization of the act. Where the proconsul required only that the text of his edict and the subsequent decree of the *koinon* be inscribed at the temple for Roma and Augustus in Pergamum, the *koinon* decreed, in addition, that these should be inscribed in the temples of Caesar in the cities heading judicial districts, the Roman *conventus*. Notably, none of the sites which preserve copies, except for Apamea, was a *conventus* centre. The communities themselves, unbidden, chose to commemorate this weighty occasion through the inscription of these normative documents.[3] This example illustrates the complex interplay between imperial, provincial, and local institutions and actors in the Greek-speaking East. In turn, it raises important questions about the aims of Roman provincial government.

What ambitions lay behind Roman provincial governance? How did these change over time and in response to local conditions? To what extent did local agents facilitate and contribute to the creation of imperial administrative institutions? The answers to these questions shape our understanding of how the Roman empire established and maintained hegemony within its provinces. This issue is particularly acute for the period during which the political apparatus of the Roman Republic was itself in crisis and flux—precisely the period in which many provinces first came under Roman control. This work takes up the challenge by focusing closely on the formation and evolution of the administrative institutions of the Roman empire through a case study of the province of Asia. Comparatively well excavated, Asia's rich epigraphy lends itself to detailed

[1] *RDGE* 65; *I.Priene*² 14; *SEG* 56.1233 with Laffi 1967; Dreyer & Engelmann 2006; Thonemann 2015, 123. On the date: Stern 2012, 274–6 contra Buxton & Hannah 2005, 290–306.
[2] *RDGE* 65 a.26–30. [3] *RDGE* 65 d.62–67.

Imperial Power, Provincial Government, and the Emergence of Roman Asia, 133 BCE–14 CE. Bradley Jordan, Oxford University Press. © Bradley Jordan 2023. DOI: 10.1093/oso/9780198887065.003.0001

study, while the region's long history of autonomous civic diplomacy and engagement with a range of Roman actors provide important evidence for assessing the ways in which Roman empire and hegemony affected conditions on the ground in the province. Most significantly, its unique history, moving from allied kingdom to regularly assigned *provincia* and, after the First Mithridatic War (*c.*89–85), to a reconquered and reorganized territory, offers an insight into the complex mechanics of institutional formation during this crucial transition.

Scholarly literature focusing on Roman *provincia Asia* touches on a wide range of topics and is correspondingly vast. Beginning with Foucart and Chapot in the early twentieth century, accounts of its formation have generally focused on political history, as guided by the Republican historiographical sources. Scholarship on the governance of *provincia Asia* during the Republican period has tended to fit within this well-worn tradition.[4] However, a slew of recent, substantial studies have emerged treating the interaction between local elites at Ephesus and Pergamum and the Roman state, alongside volumes tackling issues as diverse as citizenship, property ownership, and civic honours.[5] Scholarship on the so-called *koinon* of Asia has moved forward substantially in the last decade and its links to the imperial cult under Augustus and his successors have been the subject of extensive investigation.[6] Simply put, in light of these recent publications, it is desirable to reassess the mechanisms through which Rome established its power over the communities of the region. Revisiting the unique status of Asia in the late second century as an inherited, rather than conquered, addition to the empire can only be beneficial.[7] In light of this flurry of interest, Asia offers an excellent target for detailed analysis of Roman administrative objectives, outcomes, and local responses.

Typically, scholarship on provincial governance during the late Republic has been grounded in approaches to the expansion of Roman power in the Mediterranean. In his seminal *Foreign Clientelae (264–70 BC)*, Badian believed that when communities submitted to Rome through the process of *deditio* or were named *amici et socii*—that is, they were integrated into a Roman province—they became *clientes* of the Roman people and of the magistrates responsible. Interpreting this in light of formal personal *clientela* as practiced at Rome, he argued that provincial administration arose out of these client–patron relationships.[8] While more recent scholarship has demonstrated that Badian's model overemphasizes the importance and nature of *clientela* in the provinces, his

[4] Foucart 1903; Chapot 1904. E.g., Magie 1950; Mitchell 1993; Daubner 2006^2, 191–261; Marek 2010.

[5] Elites: Kirbihler 2016; Ventroux 2017. Citizenship: Heller & Pont 2012. Property: Lerouxel & Pont 2016. Civic Honours: see the volume by Heller & van Nijf 2017.

[6] Vitale 2012; Frija 2012; Edelmann-Singer 2015; Kolb & Vitale 2016.

[7] *I.Metropolis* 1A with comments of Dreyer & Engelmann 2003; Jones 2004.

[8] Badian 1958, 1–13. Cf. von Premerstein 1937, 13–15.

identification of the importance of informal networks as opposed to military conquest was farsighted.[9]

Harris provided an alternative, influential schema which focused on the internal drivers of Roman conquest. Responding to the 'defensive imperialism' thesis which, reflecting the rhetoric of late Republican authors, saw the expansion of Roman hegemony as prompted by the threats and bad faith of their imperial rivals, Harris argued that an aristocratic ethos of competition for military glory, an expansionist ideology, and, crucially, desire for economic spoils led to the systemic pursuit of an aggressive agenda. As a corollary to this, the Senate and *populus* sought to assume and maintain control over neighbouring territories and resources, shifting from a largely indirect to a more direct model over time.[10]

Pushing back against Harris' picture of consistent Roman aggression, Gruen concentrated on the external pressures on Roman foreign policy. His major contribution was to emphasize the extent to which Roman action responded to and engaged with existing Hellenistic norms and processes, while acknowledging that this was not always in good faith. He asserted that Rome did not seek to conquer territory for its own sake, suggesting that the Republic had no consistent policy towards defeated polities but responded on a case-by-case basis.[11] He also comprehensively rejected the *clientela* model as applying to Roman relationships with actors in the eastern Mediterranean, arguing convincingly that Roman action in the Greek East is best understood within a pre-existing Hellenistic framework.[12] Building on this work, a consensus has arisen that the languages of friendship and kinship, rather than *clientela*, were employed on a consistent basis, which nevertheless afforded the Romans broad latitude in dealing with individual communities and larger kingdoms.[13]

More recently, the view that the Romans did not seek or acquire a territorial empire in the Greek East until the first century BCE has attracted some support. In this respect, ancient historians have found Doyle's categorization of different modes of rule a useful heuristic tool. For Doyle, 'empire' exists only where one polity exercises effective control over internal policies and external relationships of another; if the nature of that control, whether formal or informal, extends only to foreign policy, then it should be defined as a different mode of dominance, what he terms 'hegemony'.[14] For instance, Kallet-Marx emphasized the importance of this distinction for understanding Roman expansion in the eastern Mediterranean, arguing that local interest in leveraging Roman power played a

[9] See also: Bowersock 1965. Critiques: Jehne & Pina Polo (eds.) 2015, esp. Pina Polo 2015, 19–22.
[10] Harris 1979, 133–62. [11] Gruen 1984, 273–87.
[12] Gruen 1984, 158–200, esp. 191–200. [13] E.g., Gruen 1984; Burton 2011.
[14] Doyle 1986, 30–45. This definition of the terms 'empire' and 'hegemony' is typical in neo-realist international relations studies (e.g., Donnelly 2006, 157–9) and is widely cited by ancient historians, including Kallet-Marx (1995, 3); Champion (2007, 256); Mattingly (2011, 5, 15–16); and Davies (2019, 10).

key role in the development of empire. He argued that the administration depicted in the late Republican sources for Asia—an extractive regime, aimed at securing substantial public and private revenue flows to the imperial centre, aided and abetted by governors using their judicial powers to interfere in local affairs—was largely a result of the First Mithridatic War. He claimed that the commitment of major military forces under L. Cornelius Sulla proved the catalyst for a new emphasis on the profits of empire, while highlighting the previously ad hoc arrangements for Roman *provinciae*.[15] This position has not achieved broad acceptance in current literature, which continues to emphasize the role of sweeping measures, implemented by magistrates serving the interests of the state, in shaping the administration of *provincia Asia*. For example Mitchell, in an influential article analysing the Roman administration of Asia, argued that from the earliest days of the *provincia* the Roman state imposed new organizational structures such as the *conventus iuridici* (assize districts) and the road network. For him, such decisions were deliberate, abrupt, and were swiftly decided upon by the proconsul M'. Aquillius and a senatorial commission despatched to establish a territorial province in the early 120s.[16]

However, recent scholarship has contested the view that *provinciae* assigned to magistrates during the late second and early first centuries were vehicles for Roman administration. Gargola has established that *provincia Africa* existed only in an abstract sense between the destruction of Carthage in 146 and the outbreak of the Jugurthine War in 112, perhaps even into the 70s.[17] Recent studies highlighting the relative disinterest of Romans in expanding state revenues complement these findings.[18] It has been long recognized that the Roman provincial administration depended on incorporating regional elites and offering significant autonomy. This was partially dictated by practicality. The tyranny of distance, prior to the development of modern communications, required that most decisions were taken and implemented at the local level, if within a framework authorized by the ruling power.[19] Here, the question arises as to whether this narrow definition of 'hegemony' is especially useful? While certainly describing a unique phenomenon, I argue that the concept as employed by Antonio Gramsci has greater value in a provincial context. Though never explicitly defined in his work, Gramsci uses the term 'hegemony' to describe a cultural phenomenon whereby political rule is based on the consent of the populace, secured through the internalization and popularization of the worldview of the rulers.[20] 'Hegemony' is a dialectical relationship between the political leadership and the population at

[15] Kallet-Marx 1995. [16] Mitchell 1999; cf. Ando 2010, 31–40; Kantor 2014, 254–9.

[17] Gargola 2017. See Richardson 2008, 17, 25, 43–9, 54–62. [18] Tan 2017.

[19] Generally, Runciman 2011, 103; Crooks & Parsons 2016, 18–27. For the ancient context: e.g., Jones 1940, 11; Brunt 1990 [1976], 270–2; Ma 2009, 125–7; Ando 2021. Compare the situation in the Spanish Americas in the sixteenth century CE (Storrs 2016, 296–305).

[20] Gramsci Q10ii§44; Q12§1. Bates 1975, 351–3, 359–60; Thomas 2009, 161–7.

large, neither imposed by the former on the latter, nor immanent and systemic. Instead, it is a lived system, responding to the interests, ideologies, and actions of all participants in society and politics.[21] In the context of the establishment of provincial institutions over a long first century BCE, this definition encapsulates a distinctive and intriguing dimension of the establishment and the extension of Roman power. Consequently, this study questions the implications of this framework for understanding how Roman administrative institutions emerged in Asia from the late second century onwards.

States, Institutions, and Hegemony

My work concentrates on the establishment of Roman power in a provincial context. This raises questions of: (i) how to describe the decision-making bodies of the Roman polity as a collective; and (ii) how to define 'power'. In the first instance, recent studies have emphasized that the term 'state' is historically contingent, conjuring notions of early modern European and modern 'nation states'.[22] Analysing the use of 'state' in modern historiography, Lundgreen argues that mostly authors fail to define the parameters of the term, even where it is crucial to understanding their methodology.[23] He engages explicitly with political theorists, especially Genschel and Zangl. These authors, analysing the modern political landscape, emphasize the extent to which nation states exercise 'power' (*Herrschaft*)—made up of three elements, 'decision-making authority' (*Entscheidungskompetenz*), 'organizational capacity' (*Organisationsmacht*), and 'ability to legitimize' (*Legitimationsfähigkeit*)—through managing and engaging with other 'governance actors', such as global organizations, major businesses, and non-government organizations.[24] When applied to the ancient world, where polities possessed far lower organizational or infrastructural capacity, this model sees the relative power of alternative 'governance actors' increase dramatically. Lundgreen concludes that the term 'state' is unhelpful as an analytical category. In his words 'statehood' (his English translation for *Staatlichkeit* and *statualità*) is not a 'state of affairs' (*Zustand*) but an evolving process and, moreover, a process to be framed in terms of intensity and penetrability, rather than of development.[25] In this sense he judiciously critiques the work of Scheidel, Morris, and Bang, among others, for taking an unduly teleological view of 'state formation'.[26]

As an analytical approach to the operation and evolution of ancient polities, Lundgreen's method has much to recommend it. In practice, the aggregate of

[21] Hall, Lumley, & McLennan 2007 [1978], 281–2; Thomas 2009, 194–5; Paterson 2021, 256–9.
[22] Winterling 2014; Davies 2019, 11.
[23] Lundgreen 2014, 18–28, citing as examples: Eich & Eich 2005; Eckstein 2006.
[24] Lundgreen 2014, 28–34; 2019, 100–5, with Genschel & Zangl 2008.
[25] Lundgreen 2014, 34.
[26] Lundgreen 2014, 21–2; *pace* Morris & Scheidel 2009; Bang & Scheidel 2013.

Roman political organizations was forced to engage with a multiplicity of actors in the provinces who exercised some governance functions, including, to name two obvious examples, the *societates publicanorum* and local civic assemblies. Moreover, the interplay between these organizations, despite their being embedded in a common framework of norms and customs, was in constant flux. This inquiry explores the implications of this observation for understanding how Roman administration and governance came to be established during the period of study. That said, a shorthand to refer to the collective of central decision-making institutions of the *res publica* is necessary. In this specific and limited sense, I use the 'Roman state' throughout to describe the collective of Senate, *populus*, and elected magistrates. From a practical perspective, 'government' and 'administration' both stand in this book exclusively for 'the process of organizing or controlling territories or people' to avoid any analogy with modern bureaucracies.

Though scholarly consensus regards 'power' as a social relationship, its precise nature is also contested. W.G. Runciman defines it as the 'capacity to influence actions, thoughts and feelings, through inducements and sanctions, derived through institutional means'.[27] This characterization functions for individuals or groups as both powerholders and subjects. My discussion focuses explicitly on 'state power', that exercised through the institutions and representatives of the (Roman) state.[28] This has three dimensions: political, economic, and ideological.[29] The political dimension represents the capacity of the state to organize a territory through institutionalized rules; the economic is located in the ability to extract and mobilize resources; and the ideological surrounds the ability of the state to shape norms and create consensus.[30] Given that power is a relationship, its extent is always contested, varying from moment to moment and responsive both to external circumstances and the choices of relevant actors.

The question of how Roman provincial government emerged in Asia can be framed in terms of design, development, and operation of institutions and their elements. In the 1950s and 1960s, social scientists viewed 'institutions' as monolithic, persistent entities structuring political and social interaction. In recent decades, however, more nuanced approaches, stressing their malleability over time, have become standard. These 'New Institutionalisms' offer insights into the complex interactions between structuring forces and human agency.[31] There are two common definitions of an 'institution': first, as a 'concrete organizational form', frequently though not always implicated in state administration.[32] Second, and more important for this enquiry, 'institutions' are 'rules' imposed and acknowledged as legitimate by a community which regulate social behaviour. These can

[27] Runciman 1989, 1–2. Cf. Foucault 2000 [1979], 324–5.

[28] I.e., the German *Herrschaft* rather than *Macht*. Weber 1978, 53–4; Mann 1984, 1986, 6–7; Foucault 2000a [1978], 219–22. In a Roman context see Harris 2017, 1.

[29] Runciman 1989, 61–4; *pace* Mann 1986, 10–11, 22–32.

[30] Discussion at Mann 1986, 22–8.

[31] Hall & Taylor 1996; Fioretos, Falleti, & Sheingate 2016, 3–10.

[32] Skoda 2012, 44–5.

be formal—such as laws or regulations—or informal.[33] Critically, institutions are dynamic and socially embedded. They evolve in response to changing circumstances and are shaped by the norms and behaviours of their social community. That is, embeddedness works two ways: as institutions guide social behaviour, so social behaviour affects the future evolution of institutions.[34]

One particularly useful theoretical tradition for analysing institutional change is historical institutionalism, described by Pierson as 'historical because it recognizes that political development must be understood as process that unfolds over time, . . . institutionalist because it stresses that many of the contemporary implications of these temporal processes are embedded in institutions'.[35] Broadly speaking, its exponents, while rejecting functionalist and neo-functionalist interpretations, emphasize the importance of timing and sequence in explaining both institutional design and change. New institutions can be introduced for non-instrumental reasons, be subject to changing policy preferences, and have consequences unintended by their designers.[36] That said, institutional change, though persistent, is incremental, since, in most cases, rapid evolution would harm powerful interest groups. Social costs act as a brake on the pace of changes. Evolution is largely 'path-dependent'; framed by historical context, even where agents propose specific changes. Crucially, as Levi shows, 'once a country or region has started down a track, the costs of reversal are very high'. Cognitive elements also hinder the creation of truly novel alternatives.[37] However, during moments of political or social crisis, when existing institutions break down completely, there is greater scope for agents to innovate.[38] In such 'critical junctures', the relative cost of inaction climbs substantially, and the inadequacies of the existing system offer a menu of potential improvements. If actors with sufficient power and political capital hold particular views on the role of institutions then significant change can occur swiftly, though not without cost.[39] Individual polities tend to be constituted by mosaics of institutions created at different times and for divergent purposes, each responding to their own internal logic, adding a further level of complexity to the state structure.[40] Although this theoretical framework prioritizes the role of structural elements in shaping political developments in a given context, it simultaneously facilitates analysis of personal and group agency.[41]

[33] North 1995, 15–16; Greif 2006, 14, 30–2; Mackil 2013, 13.

[34] Orren & Skowronek 1994, 325–6; Wendt 1999, 184–9; Greif 2006, 187–208.

[35] Pierson 1996, 126.

[36] Pierson 2004, 103–32.

[37] Levi 1997, 28–9; Pierson 2004, 22–48; Greif 2006, 189–208.

[38] Capoccia & Kelemen 2007, 348; Capoccia 2016, 91–2, drawing on Berlin 1974, 176. The criticism of Peters, Pierre, & King (2005, 1287–90) that such approaches require a model of 'punctuated equilibria' mischaracterizes the bulk of recent scholarship which emphasizes gradual changes (e.g., Pierson 2004, 50–3, 153–7; Fioretos, Falleti, & Sheingate 2016, 12).

[39] Capoccia 2016, 96–8.

[40] Orren & Skowronek 1994, 320–30, 2004, 108–18.

[41] Katznelson 1997, 104–5.

As such, similar approaches are increasingly recognized as offering heuristic value for explaining institutional change in the ancient world. The firm grounding of development and change in specific historicized and local contexts and the emphasis on how different factors intersected, reinforced, and hindered one another allows for more nuanced and suggestive accounts. For example, Mackil's recent investigation of *koinon* formation in Classical and Hellenistic Greece applied these ideas in a constructive way, showing how the development of common norms through religious and economic interaction facilitated the creation of formal political institutions, albeit in highly variable ways in different locations.[42] Likewise, Mack has profitably employed this lens to highlight the complex processes which led to the rise—and ultimate decline—of the inter-*polis* custom of *proxenia* across the Greek-speaking world during the fifth to first centuries.[43] By contrast, I apply these ideas to an imperial context, with structural power imbalances and several overlapping cultural and political contexts. Evaluating the evidence in this way helps to elucidate the relative significance of institutional inertia and human agency in the Roman imperial project.

'Speech-acts', Hegemony, and Roman Empire

Ideology, channelled through institutions, played a critical role in the establishment of Roman administration. Several important studies have analysed official documents issued to peripheral regions as a manifestation of power in ancient states; most obviously, Millar's scholarship on the governance of the Roman Principate, which posited that government primarily reacted to petitions from individuals and communities to the Emperor and his representatives, without having wider administrative ambitions.[44] More recent studies by Ma and Ando—addressing Antiochus III's relationships with cities in Asia Minor and the provinces of the Roman Principate respectively—draw heavily on sociological perspectives, especially 'speech-act' theory as formulated by Austin. Some communicative acts convey more than information, pursuing an objective which will not occur without the success of the communicative act itself. This 'purposive object' could be the affirmation of a shared understanding, the prohibition of an activity or an exhortation. The fact of the communication allows the recipient to perform or refuse to perform the required act based on three distinct criteria: both the authority and the sincerity of the original communicator, and the

[42] Mackil 2013, *passim*. Her preliminary treatment of Boiotia (15–17) is instructive.

[43] Mack 2015.

[44] For the 'petition-and-response model', Millar 2002 [1966] and 2004 [1967] are crucial, supplemented by 2004a [1998] and 2004b [1983], 342–50. Note the critique of Ando (forthcoming, cf. Edmondson 2014, 127–55), who proposes a parallel 'order-and-obey' model.

existential pre-conditions of the communication.[45] Official utterances by an imperial power to subordinate communities rarely contain only information: more often they contain instruction, whether specific or general regarding 'right action'. Should the power be regarded as legitimate, then even where communiqués do not contain explicit instructions, their origin imbues their content with a normative force allowing us to define them as 'speech-acts' with purposive objects of defining a shared understanding.

It is worth considering here how 'speech-act' theory intersects with the Gramscian concept of 'hegemony'. Ando drew explicitly and extensively on Jürgen Habermas' employment of speech-act theory, wherein meaning is constructed in a dynamic and sincere dialogue aimed at producing a rational outcome.[46] By contrast, Gramsci (and later neo-Gramscian theorists) saw meaning as emerging in the contest to establish a hegemonic narrative, in the conflicting attempts of parties to achieve and sustain control over the common discourse.[47] As Worth, inter alios, has argued from modern examples, this Gramscian schema can be usefully applied to an international system to analyse how dominant polities are configured and how they construct institutions to create transnational consent for the ruling parties' ideology and preferences.[48] While Gramsci was responding explicitly to the failure of orthodox Marxism to explain his contemporary political landscape, his concept emphasizes a crucial point, corroborated by later sociologists. That is to say, that societies integrate individual members to the extent that their experiences are based around shared convictions regarded as unproblematic. These principles form the basis of societal *mores*, which develop constantly in a dynamic and incremental fashion.[49] This is a useful hermeneutic precisely because it describes a process of generating a common understanding. While not denying the importance of non-linguistic elements, the content and framing of official communication provides one of the most direct ways for a government to affect the attitudes of local political actors: the utterances of legitimate wielders of authority constitute a means by which to generate and reinforce an official worldview.[50]

Within this framework then, successful speech-acts, affirming a shared world-view, push individuals into a common society. The greater the extent to which individuals regard the views of the political elite as normative, legitimate,

[45] Austin 1975, esp. 14–16; Millar 1992, 637. Cf. Bertrand 1990.

[46] Ando 2000, 21–3, referring to Habermas 1979, 65–94, 1984, 69–74, 1987, 119–52.

[47] Martin 2002; Ish-Shalom 2010.

[48] Worth 2011, esp. 373–9, 381–6. See also Cox 1996; Robinson 2001.

[49] Hall 1988, 144, 150–8.

[50] This raises the problem of audience for normative and instructional documents. Ando (2000, 101–5) constructs a plausible model for achieving widespread familiarity with normative documents among provincial communities in the imperial period and sees a strong motive for central government to consciously encourage this. However, in my view, he moves beyond the available evidence. Compare Meyer (2004, 184–7), who rightly emphasizes local imitation and Roman standards as explaining the process of centralization.

and unproblematic, the more integrated that society. In turn, having strong group identity engenders relative social stability.[51] Common understanding of the 'rules of engagement', 'political grammar', and 'syntax' limits the realm of acceptable dialogue and provides a framework within which negotiation can safely take place.[52] Regular repetition is crucial; encouraging individuals to reaffirm their commitment to shared values and norms. While these norms are never static, they are socially embedded and evolve incrementally.[53] Imperial examples are a notable exception: even where, as in the early years of Roman Asia, no military conquest has taken place, a cultural distance can exist between the imperial and subject communities. Both Ma and Ando highlight the role of consistency in language and format in facilitating engagement between local communities and the imperial elite. Similarly, Pocock has stressed the role of common adoption of concepts and terms in creating a common discourse.[54] Correspondingly, I propose that where a gap in understanding existed, such as that between Roman elites and the communities of Asia in 133, uniformity, regularity, and reproducibility of communicative formats and language would more efficiently generate and maintain the common ground necessary to engage with imperial administrative discourses and facilitate Roman hegemony in a Gramscian sense.

Moreover, the realities of a large, heterogenous, and culturally differentiated audience could create issues of meaning. Considering the divergent context, knowledge, and assumptions they held, individuals and communities, as audiences for Roman power, could challenge, reject, or reframe the norms, language, or content of official discursive acts.[55] Attempts by a central figure or institution, in our context the Senate or Princeps, to communicate directly with inhabitants on the periphery of the empire would suffer from problems of interpretation, beyond the immense practical challenges. The social, hierarchical, spatial, and cultural distance between the author(s) of such a message and its recipients was vast.[56] The conventions of different communicative media further hindered

[51] Note the critique of Scott (1990, 70–86, esp. 77–81), who argues reasonably that the reproduction of a hegemonic 'transcript' does not necessarily require its acceptance as legitimate. Nevertheless, the existence of resistance or countervailing readings does not invalidate the broader model.

[52] Bourdieu 1977, 187–9; Foucault 1980, 93–6; Habermas 1984, 70–1; Pocock 1987, 20–7. Cf. Ma (1999, 191–4) and Ando (2000, 20–1, 28–9) for applications to the ancient world.

[53] Cf. Mackil 2013, 11.

[54] Which he terms 'a language': Pocock 1987, 29–36. Cf. Chaniotis 2015, 88–9.

[55] Hall (1980, 128–38), drawing on Gramsci (Q12§1), argues that, in instances of mass communication, messages alter at several stages: first, the conventions of the communicative medium and language limit the creator; second, a mass audience, by definition heterogenous, holds differing knowledge and assumptions from the creator and one another, changing the context within which the message is interpreted; finally, those who disseminate the message also engage in an interpretative dialectic with the creator. For an application of this approach in Roman history, see Lenski's (2017, 8–12) recent discussion of the role of the Christogram and Staurogram on Constantinian coinage.

[56] The paradigm for Rome and the Hellenistic East is the encounter between the Aetolians and M'. Acilius in 191 (Polyb. 20.9.10–12; Liv. 36.27–29). A vast bibliography exists, see esp. Eckstein 1995, 271–88 contra Gruen 1982, 50–68; Burton 2009, 237–52.

attempts to convey a unified official discourse.[57] When issued to hundreds of communities scattered across the culturally fragmented landscape of western Asia Minor, this gap in context between the ruler and each recipient left room for myriad divergent local readings. Notwithstanding the complexity of this situation, following Hall, potential responses can be grouped into three broad categories: 'hegemonic', broadly accepting the dominant discourse; 'negotiated', allowing some premises of the author but challenging or ignoring others; and 'oppositional', interpreting the missive in a separate, more favourable social framework.[58] In simple terms, though administrative structures can appear rigidly hierarchical, political communicators, even more than in the modern world, lost control of their message the moment it was issued. More importantly, a context wherein communities had the capacity to make public pronouncements afforded the opportunity to negotiate or creatively interpret imperial documents. The constant change in language and channels of Roman official pronouncements during this period, along with the reframing required by changes in political context created conditions encouraging divergent readings. I argue here that generally the communities of Asia sought to engage constructively with Rome to create and constitute a new shared 'language' of empire and interaction. However, where expedient, some actors explored the utility of negotiated or oppositional readings of Roman discourse. Both approaches irrevocably altered the path of Roman administrative arrangements in the *provincia*.

Overview

This study commences with the death of Attalus III of Pergamum in 133 and closes with that of Augustus in 14 CE. This work is concerned with structural elements (of state power, institutions, and ideologies) which do not neatly map onto political narratives. The succession of Tiberius to the Principate marks a moment of seismic political importance, actualizing the monopoly of power by the Julio-Claudian dynasty and transforming it from a political position to a permanent institution.[59] The beginning of Tiberius' reign is also marked by subtle changes in the exercise of centralized power which, though moulded by the Augustan political project, laid the foundations for the future developments and, therefore, his accession marks an appropriate end for this study.

This study focuses on local communities as single units, and thereby on 'political elites' in a loose sense. This is not to deny the importance of sub-elite

[57] Jauss & Benziger 1970, 8; Iser 1972, 279; Pocock 1989 [1971], 21–2; Brems & Ramos Pinto 2013, 142–4.

[58] For this formulation: Hall 1980, 134–8. Hall's engagement with Gramscian hegemony is most visible in his work on Thatcherism in Britain, e.g., Hall 1988.

[59] Cooley 2019. See Maier 2000, 807; Flower 2009, 12–19.

groups to civic policy-making or suggest that decision-making bodies within the *poleis* of western Asia Minor were homogenous or monolithic. The boundary between political, economic, and cultural elites in late- or sub-Hellenistic *poleis* was often blurred, while the well-attested persistence of local democratic institutions well into the imperial period demonstrates the continued diffusion of civic political power.[60] That said, as a hermeneutic, the concept of a constantly evolving but culturally and politically coherent audience of local powerbrokers within each community has significant utility in exploring how attitudes and approaches towards Roman rule evolved across the period.

This study consists of eight chapters, divided into two parts. Part 1 ('The Institutions of Roman Government') focuses on the extent of Roman administrative ambitions through a close study of the evidence of the introduction and evolution of formal provincial institutions. Chapter 1 ('From the Attalids to Proconsular Administration, 133–88 BCE') begins with the historical context of Rome's decision to take responsibility for the former Attalid kingdom and a concise overview of the kingdom's organization. It scrutinizes the initial steps to arrange the province taken by M'. Aquillius, arguing that specific interventions beyond ensuring the freedom of the cities—however contested by Roman actors—were limited. Finally, it explores the impact of Roman hegemony on taxation, jurisdiction, and coinage within the former Attalid kingdom.

Chapter 2 ('The Government of Asia during the Late Republic, 81–49 BCE') analyses the reorganization of the province of Asia by L. Cornelius Sulla in 85/84, describing the decisions taken, before exploring the consequences. It argues that Sulla's decisions were largely structured by his immediate political and military needs rather than by longer-term administrative concerns. Subsequently, it examines the longer-term implications for the experience of Roman rule, focusing on three crucial issues: the establishment of the *conventus iuridici* (locations for the exercise of Roman jurisdiction, which developed a wider administrative significance); the emergence of the *koinon* of Asia (the so-called provincial assembly); and the impact of these changes on civic autonomy within the region. It proposes that Sulla's decisions, though not intended to reshape provincial government in Asia permanently, radically altered the paradigm of state involvement in the province.

Chapter 3 ('Change in a Time of Civil War, 49–30 BCE') analyses the instability brought about by the civil wars, arguing that this period represents a 'critical juncture' for institutional development. While this allowed newly powerful decision-makers including C. Iulius Caesar and the triumvirs to innovate rapidly, the new forms remained malleable.

Chapter 4 ('*Provincia* Asia and the Advent of the Principate, 30 BCE–14 CE') investigates three major institutional changes which took place during the

[60] E.g., Fernoux 2011; Zuiderhoek 2017, 122–30.

Principate of Augustus. First, it will analyse the evidence for the role of procurators in Asia during Augustus' lifetime, arguing that the early holders of this position likely did not possess clearly defined powers but helped shape new norms of imperial governance. Second, it will examine the evolution of the *koinon* of Asia into a body associated with the provincial imperial cult after 29. Finally, it will investigate the institutionalization of the Princeps' direct interventions in provincial administration, emphasizing the ongoing tension between central institutions of the Roman state and Augustus' practical authority.

Part 1 closes with a short summary of the argument so far: namely, that the Roman state had limited administrative ambitions vis-à-vis Asia until after Sulla's settlement in 85; that said 'settlement', the civil wars between 49–31, and the rise of Augustus represented 'critical junctures' which facilitated rapid institutional changes on the ground; and that the concentration of state power in the hands of ever fewer persons at Rome increasingly motivated the state to rationalize the institutional landscape of Roman governance in Asia.

Part 2 ('Roman Hegemony, Power, and Local Agency') investigates the discursive power of official utterances of the Roman state when placed alongside the limited formal institutional framework of provincial government. Chapter 5 ('Hegemony and the Discourse(s) of Power in Roman Asia') emphasizes the disjunction between existing frameworks through which cities negotiated their status with their hegemons and Roman institutional practices, before moving to consider the evidence for official communication in the early period of Roman hegemony. It argues that a new framework was needed to mediate between the Republic and individual communities, but that existing institutions hindered their establishment. It traces the evolution of official communication through the civil war and Augustan periods, arguing that an increasing emphasis on the personal benefactions granted to communities by powerful Romans, including Caesar, Octavian, and M. Antonius, emerges during the civil war period, even in documents issued by public institutions. Finally, it focuses on the presence of the Princeps in documents issued by other officials and bodies, such as the Senate and governors, arguing that Augustus' pre-eminent position catalysed the development of new discursive framework of Roman governance.

The final three chapters respond to this Roman perspective by concentrating on the responses and agency of inhabitants of the province. Chapter 6 ('The "Politics of Honour": Learning a New Set of Rules') investigates the role played by civic decrees in negotiating a relationship between individual communities and the Roman state. It begins by analysing how honorific decrees for individual magistrates intersected with divergent Greek and Roman praxes of honour, arguing that they continued to play a vital role in mediating the relationship between *poleis* and their hegemon. It then moves to the few examples of civic decrees which were not honorific in nature and dealt with Roman actors, arguing that public representations of loyalty to Rome in non-honorific contexts were primarily motivated by local concerns.

Chapter 7 ('Speaking to Roman Power: Diplomacy and Civic Privilege') concentrates on the attempts of individual communities to establish new norms of behaviour and interaction with the Roman state through diplomatic contact. It argues that embassies in the period concerned were proactive, strategic, and targeted; almost exclusively undertaken by individual cities, not on a collective basis. It then shifts the perspective to the increasingly prevalent phenomenon of unofficial contacts between individual provincials and Romans, which undermined existing institutional vectors, arguing that as power was progressively monopolized at Rome, personal contacts came to play an ever-more important role in the grant of privileges to provincial communities and they responded by relying on private relationships over public ones.

Chapter 8 ('Local Displays of Imperial Documents') analyses the display of Roman official documents in civic contexts, arguing that the most plausible explanation of this phenomenon during the period of study is that local agents inscribed these documents for their own reasons: for example, to protect privileges granted by Roman actors, to demonstrate their loyalty to a Roman magistrate or the Roman state, or to honour individual locals for their service as connections to Rome.

Finally, a brief Conclusion collates the previous analysis and explores the wider implications for the study of Roman imperialism, provincial administration, and local agency during the late Republic and early Principate. It summarizes the broader argument that Roman hegemony was established incrementally, in a responsive fashion, and in continuous dialogue with local agents over the course of a long first century (133 BCE–14 CE).

PART ONE

THE INSTITUTIONS OF ROMAN GOVERNMENT

1
From the Attalids to Proconsular Administration, 133–88 BCE

Before *provincia Asia*: The Kingdom of Attalus

In spring 133, Eudemus of Pergamum arrived in Rome and informed the Senate that Attalus III had died unexpectedly. Under the terms of the *basileus*' will, the *populus Romanus* would be his heir.[1] The specifics of this arrangement are unclear, but subsequent events show this entailed receipt of his property and kingdom.[2] This royal act, and its acceptance by the Senate and People, brought the Roman Republic permanently into western Asia Minor. Though magistrates had been active in the region since the early second century, the state retained no territory as a result of its victory over the Seleucid ruler Antiochus III in 188. The Romans sought hegemony not empire. Attalus' sudden passing fundamentally altered this situation and, despite violent disagreement at Rome over the disposition of the will's contents, the sources make clear that its acceptance was never in doubt.[3] As a direct consequence, for the first time a Roman magistrate was regularly sent out with *imperium* over and responsibility for much of western Asia.

The Attalid kingdom bequeathed to Rome in 133 emerged from the loose Seleucid control of western Asia Minor in the late third century. In 238, Attalus I, hereditary dynast of Pergamum, declared himself *basileus* after defeating the Galatians in a major battle at the Caïcus river.[4] Even following this success, his 'kingdom' consisted only of the *polis* itself and its immediate surroundings. The decision of Attalus, and his successor Eumenes II, to vigorously pursue a Roman alliance led to a swift upsurge in their fortunes after Antiochus III's defeat. Under the terms of the peace of Apamea in 188, the Romans awarded the majority of Seleucid territory north and west of the Taurus to the Attalids, increasing the size of the kingdom nearly tenfold.[5] The boundaries of the kingdom remained undefined, with the single exception of the southern border: the river Maeander marked the beginning of Rhodian

[1] Plut. *Ti. Gracch.* 14.1; Livy, *Per.* 58.3; Flor. 1.35.2. On the will: Liebmann-Frankfort 1966, 80–90; Braund 1983, 21–3.

[2] Braund 1983, 16–30, 44–53.

[3] Jones 2004, 483–5, with references contra Gruen 1984, 599–602; Kallet-Marx 1995, 104–5.

[4] Polyb. 18.41; Strabo 13.2.4. Allen 1983, 302.

[5] Polyb. 21.22.13. Allen 1983, 66–8, 76–80; Thonemann 2013, 1–3.

Imperial Power, Provincial Government, and the Emergence of Roman Asia, 133 BCE–14 CE. Bradley Jordan, Oxford University Press. © Bradley Jordan 2023. DOI: 10.1093/oso/9780198887065.003.0002

hegemony.[6] Even so, the degree of control exerted by the Attalid *basileis* over their newly acquired territory seems limited by design. Polybius notes that *poleis* not previously subject to Attalus were not required to pay tribute to Eumenes, provided they had sided with the Romans against Antiochus.[7] Consequently, the territorial extent of Attalid authority was a patchwork of free, independent cities, others—including Ephesus, Tralles, and Teos—subject to direct taxation and official oversight, and extra-civic territories, which endured more direct interference.[8]

The relative weakness of Attalid claims of legitimacy vis-à-vis their royal competitors explains their different practices of power and administration. Unable to credibly justify their rule through military prowess, they turned to civic benefaction within and beyond their kingdom to establish their influence.[9] Structurally, their administration was more localized and direct than that of their Seleucid predecessors. The Attalid state had a flatter hierarchy: centrally appointed officials, with responsibility for relatively small areas, maintained direct access to the monarch.[10] Meanwhile, less urbanized areas were subjected to semi-hereditary officials with greater autonomy, though the limits of their powers remain unclear.[11] In the absence of pre-existing bonds between local elites and Attalid rulers, Thonemann's characterization of this arrangement as an 'exercise in power-sharing' is apt. When tied to evidence linking wealthy, localized landowners to political positions, it reveals a devolved but intensive administrative system.[12] Attalid taxation reinforces this view: the kingdom operated a complex and extensive fiscal system. A 'tithe' on produce (δεκατή), a customs tax, poll-taxes, and a fixed tribute from communities are all attested.[13] Collection, in keeping with political arrangements, was devolved to civic communities, explaining the Attalid emphasis on community-foundation in marginal areas.[14] These numerous revenue-streams contributed to the Attalid rulers' proverbial wealth and supported their attempts to maintain panhellenic levels of euergetism and benefactions, upon which their rule depended.

Outside of the civic communities, βασιλικὴ χώρα (or γή, 'royal land') further framed the Attalid state's organization. Attested across the major Hellenistic kingdoms, Bikerman held that the βασιλικὴ χώρα was akin to the monarch's private property, on the twin grounds that no other ownership rights were upheld

[6] Polyb. 21.43.1–46.11; Livy 38.38.1–39.16. Allen 1983, 86–7; Dreyer 2007, 347–62.

[7] Polyb. 21.24.4–8; 45.3. Kay 2014, 126.

[8] Allen 1983, 85–111; Kaye 2022, 188–233.

[9] Dreyer 2009, 35–6; Thonemann 2013, 31–44.

[10] Allen 1983, 100–9.

[11] *SEG* 44.1108; 46.1434; 57.1109.

[12] Thonemann 2013, 12–17.

[13] See now Kaye 2022, esp. 8–14. E.g., *RC* 54.7–8; *SEG* 39.1180.36, 68 (Roman *lex portorii* referring to Attalid practice); *Griechische Mauerbauinschriften* 1.76.10–14, with (Ashton 1994, 57–60, poll-tax at Telmessos). Note that the δεκατή, despite its name, could be higher than 10 per cent in practice (Aperghis 2004, 122–3; Monson 2015, 190 with *SEG* 47.1745.43–47).

[14] As at Toriaion (*I.Sultan Daği* 1.393). Thonemann 2013, 18–20. Compare, later, Cn. Pompeius Magnus' policy in Pontus-Bithynia: Højte 2006, 15–17, 2009, 95–7; Madsen 2014, 75–6, 80–1.

within the 'royal land' and that land granted to beneficiaries first had to be attached to the territory of a *polis*.[15] More recent scholarship softens this position to view the *βασιλικὴ χώρα* as land subordinate to decisions of the *basileus* and administratively separate from other private or public forms of land, which the *communis opinio* sees as defined negatively, as land that did not fall within a city territory.[16] However, this does not mean that *βασιλικὴ χώρα* was sparsely inhabited or economically marginal. Outside of the cities, the Seleucids and Attalids established numerous *κατοικία* ('settlements'), while non-urbanized groups continued to interact sporadically with royal officials.[17] In such areas, where royal authority was strong and the settlements more readily legible by state institutions, claims on revenue could be far more extensive than on cities. For example, one fragmentary royal document from near Magnesia-under-Sipylos refers to taxes on orchards, beehives, and hunted animals, while at the settlement of Apollinoucharax inhabitants were subject to a poll-tax.[18] Royal property within *polis* territories—such as estates, city properties, economic assets (e.g., mines, forests), and other natural resources (e.g., salt-works)—was also classified *βασιλικὴ χώρα*.[19] Overall, royal territory under the Attalid kingdom was extensive, non-contiguous, and economically significant.

Beyond this, the Attalid kingdom and its cities produced several coinages in parallel. Most prominent are the silver *cistophori*, named for the standard obverse type tetradrachm, containing a *cista mystica*—a chest with a lid partially ajar—from which a snake emerges. Generally, the reverse shows two coiled snakes, with heads facing inwards and, between them, a bow-case with a strung bow.[20] Smaller denominations also shared distinctive types: the didrachms and drachms both display a club with a lion-skin on the obverse, with grapes and a vine leaf on the reverse, combining Heraclean and Dionysian imagery associated with the Attalid dynasts.[21] Crucially, cistophoric tetradrachms were underweight compared to the regionally dominant Attic standard by approximately 25 per cent, affording the authorities the capacity to make a substantial profit through the exchange of Attic-weight coins for *cistophori*.[22] Hoard evidence for the second and early first centuries shows that these coins were frequently deposited unmixed, implying their circulation within a 'closed-currency system'.[23] Profit through exchange was

[15] Bikerman 1938, 180–4; Aperghis 2004, 101–7. E.g., *I.Ilion* 33.18–25, 44–6, 70–2.

[16] E.g., Rostovtzeff 1941, 814–16; Aperghis 2004, 87–9; Capdetrey 2007, 136–44; Mileta 2008, 63–78. E.g., Mileta (2008, 41–52), deduces a triple meaning: 'Reichsgebiet', 'untertäniges Binnenland', and 'königliches Gebiet'.

[17] E.g., Sotas, *philos* of Attalus, who became a royal official by virtue of his background as local warlord: Thonemann 2013, 13–16; Kaye 2022, 193–203.

[18] *SEG* 33.1304 (Magnesia-under-Sipylos); *SEG* 61.982*a*.22–24 (Apollinoucharax); see Segre 1938, #190.1–4, 10–12. Aperghis 2004, 146–7; Kaye 2022, 77–88.

[19] E.g., *SEG* 39.1283, 1285; Livy 37.56.1; Strabo 14.1.26. On this phenomenon: Ma 1999, 130–1; Aperghis 2004, 152–7; Kaye 2022, 92–5, 117–22.

[20] Kleiner & Noe 1977, 21; Le Rider 1990, 683–5.

[21] Szaivert 2008; Kaye 2022, 134–7.

[22] Mørkholm 1982, 301; Butcher & Ponting 2014, 465.

[23] Carbone 2020, 2–3, 193–4, 222–6.

likely not the only motive for their creation. Given its light weight, it was undesirable as a medium of international exchange, ensuring by design that it would not flow beyond the core territories of the kingdom, reducing the need to strike replacement coins.[24]

This coinage was first produced during the reign of Eumenes II (*c.*197–158), though a more precise date remains controversial.[25] *Cistophori* were issued in the name of individual mint authorities, including major centres with a history of striking coins (Pergamum, Ephesus, Tralles, Sardis, Apamea, and Laodicea) as well as some smaller centres without a minting tradition.[26] Since Kleiner and Noe, in light of die-links between mints and the apparent specialization of Tralles in minting lower denominations, it has often been claimed that the production of *cistophori* was highly centralized.[27] However, Kaye has strongly argued against this position on two grounds. First, the number of confirmed die-links is minimal: one example between Pergamum and the minor mints at Dionysopolis and Blaundus, and five between Pergamum and Apamea. Given that the latter links seem to coincide with increased demand, it is likely that this die-sharing does mark a co-ordinated response. However, as Kaye points out, die-sharing in such cases is well attested across the Hellenistic world.[28] Moreover, he convincingly relates Tralles' minting of cistophoric fractions to the community's position in a transitional zone between cistophoric and Rhodian (and pseudo-Rhodian) plinthophoric monetary standards, another relatively closed system. Given traffic between the two zones, a capacity to exchange one currency for another was essential and may also have influenced minting choices at nearby communities outside of the Attalid kingdom.[29] While the co-ordination was certainly provided by the dynasts, the appearance and presentation of the *cistophori* has more in common with federal or civic issues than traditional royal ones. This was an epichoric coinage, aimed at a specific local audience.[30]

Early *cistophori* were issued alongside more traditionally royal silver coinage, the so-called *Philetairoi*, named for the portrait of the dynastic founder which

[24] Meadows 2013, 194–205.

[25] The debate lies beyond the scope of this study. Ashton (2013, 245–50) synthesizes earlier arguments in favour of a date in the 190s. More plausibly, Meadows (2013, 175–81) suggests a later date in the 160s.

[26] Kleiner & Noe 1977 on the major centres. Smaller authorities include: Blaundus, Dionysopolis, Lysias, either Diospolis or Dioskome (Le Rider 1990, 695–700; Drew-Bear & Le Rider 1991), and Kormasa (Thonemann 2008).

[27] Kleiner & Noe 1977, 120–5. Followed by, e.g., Crawford 1985, 159; Ashton & Kinns 2004, 103–4; Aperghis 2010.

[28] Kaye 2022, 149–52.

[29] Such as the similarly interchangeable fractions at Alabanda, Stratonicea, Oinoanda, and Cibyra: *BMC* Alabanda 10; Meadows 2002, Group 1, 98–9; Kaye 2022, 152–63.

[30] Thonemann 2013, 31–4; Meadows 2013, 202; Kaye 2022, 169–73. Note, the broader trend in the mid-late second century towards production of local epichoric types in Aegean, Asia Minor, and Levant: Meadows 2018.

appears on the obverse. Moreover, the introduction of the new series seems to have been co-extensive with decisions by autonomous cities to switch from minting posthumous Alexander-types to the Attic-weight 'wreathed tetradrachms'. Though it is frequently argued that this (collectively large) coinage was prompted by Attalid interests and produced for export, the switch in iconography reflects an Aegean-wide trend towards epichoric imagery. As Meadows argues, these issues were aimed at both an internal and external audience.[31] Even communities nominally subject to the Attalid dynasts, including Ephesus and Tralles, appear to have minted their own precious metal coinages in the form of gold staters, while civic bronzes continued uninterrupted at Adramyttium, Ephesus, and Apamea.[32] Indeed, the multiplicity of coinages seem to have been targeted at different localities for different purposes. Early *cistophori* are rarely found outside the Attalid kingdom, whereas 'wreathed tetradrachms' appear to have circulated widely across Asia Minor and the Near East.[33] This, together with the former's comparatively low weight, suggests strongly that the coinage was designed to function as only one part, albeit crucial, of an assemblage of coinages within the kingdom.

Upon the death of Attalus III, the territory he ruled over, though diverse, had a coherent administration, highly developed fiscal structure, and complex monetary system. In the space of five decades, a uniquely structured and intricate, though functional and wealthy, state had emerged centred on the Attalid monarchy. This set the initial conditions facing the Roman Republic in western Asia Minor. The question confronting the Roman state was if, how, and to what degree this system should be adjusted to achieve their own ambitions.

The Organization of a Roman Province

The arrival of Eudemus in Rome with news of the bequest was ill-timed: tension between the tribune of the *plebs*, Ti. Sempronius Gracchus, and his opponents had made the city a tinderbox. Gracchus threatened separately to use the *concilium plebis* to (1) appropriate the private fortune of the *basileus*; and (2) settle the affairs of the *poleis* within the kingdom in a way designed to maximize public profit, which could fund his expansive agrarian legislation.[34] In the event, his murder by his opponents, including P. Cornelius Scipio Nasica, brought an end to debate. The Senate took charge, despatching a commission of five senatorial *legati*—led by

[31] Meadows 2018, 307–11. *Pace* Crawford 1985, 156; Kinns 1987, 105–7; Le Rider 1999, 39–40, 47–50.
[32] Jenkins 1978; Le Rider 1989, 173–4, 185–9; Stauber 1996, 196–206; Marcellesi 2010, 198–200.
[33] Kinns 1987, 107; de Callataÿ 2013, 35.
[34] Plut. *Ti. Gracch.* 14.1–2; Livy, *Per.* 58.2. Badian 1972, 712–13.

Nasica—to Pergamum, where they had arrived by early 132 and set about negotiating with local powerbrokers.[35]

Events in Asia had overtaken them, however. *Cistophori* minted at Ephesus show that the city had already struck coins with a new civic era in late 134/133. While earlier commentators presumed that this new era on Ephesian coins was a 'provincial' phenomenon, though unrecorded elsewhere, Rigsby conclusively argued that this was a local Ephesian era inaugurated to reflect the city's new freedom under the terms of Attalus' will.[36] In turn, this demonstrates the incontrovertibly civic aspect of the coinage, produced by local magistrates, advertising the *polis*' status, and now, seemingly, minted for civic purposes. Though this action could indicate that Attalus pre-emptively freed the *polis*, more likely it was a unilateral action after his death in spring 133, before the Romans could have acted.[37]

A Pergamene civic decree also explicitly states that Attalus' will guaranteed the city's freedom, before the Romans had intervened:

> [ἐπε]ὶ βασιλεὺς Ἄτταλος | Φιλομήτωρ καὶ Εὐεργέτη[ς μεθισ]τάμενος ἐξ ἀν|θρώπων ἀπολέλοιπεν τὴμ̣ [πατρ]ίδα ἡμῶν ἐλευθέραν, | προσορίσας αὐτῆι καὶ πολε[ιτικήγ] χώραν, ἣν ἔκριν[εν], | δεῖ δὲ ἐπικυρωθῆναι τὴν διαθήκ̣[η]ν̣ ὑπὸ Ῥωμαίων…('since the *basileus*, Attalus Philometor and Euergetes, passing from the world of men, left our city free, having added to it the civic territory, as he adjudged it, and it is necessary for his will to be confirmed by the Romans…').[38]

The object of this political act, however, was the general safety of the community: it went on to grant citizenship rights to loyal members of the πάροικοι, the κάτοικοι, and mercenary forces serving the city, as well as groups called Macedonians, Mysians, and Masdynians.[39] These grants indicate rising social tensions within the *polis* and the will was contested immediately by Aristonicus, the illegitimate son of Eumenes II, whose coinage indicates that he claimed the Pergamene throne as Eumenes III.[40] While lacking support in the major cities of the kingdom—that is, those declared 'free' by the will of Attalus—he experienced initial successes at Phocaea and Myndos before a defeat inflicted by an Ephesian

[35] *IGR* 4.1681; Plut. *Ti. Gracch.* 21.4; Val. Max. 5.3.2e; *de vir. ill.* 64.9. Schleussner 1976, 103–12; Rigsby 1979, 39–40; Wörrle 2000, 566; Jones 2004, 484. On the dispatch of *legati* to settle disputes or organize *provinciae*: Schleussner 1978, 9–100; Yarrow 2012, 168–83.

[36] Rigsby 1979 contra Kleiner & Noe 1977, 53–4.

[37] Rigsby 1979, 39–40; Adams 1980, 313–14; Leschhorn 1993, 204–8; Kirbihler 2016, 22–3 n.8.

[38] *OGIS* 338.3–7. Gauthier (*BÉ* 1989, #279, with references) refutes Rigsby's assertion (1988, 130–7) that the dating of the decree by eponymous *hiereus* should mean the decree is not Pergamene.

[39] *OGIS* 338.10–19.

[40] For a full account of Aristonicus' revolt: Daubner 2006^2, 53–190. On the chronology: Jones 2004, 469–85; Coarelli 2005, 211–31, esp. 212–14; Hochard 2021. The royal name: Eutropius 4.18, 20; Robinson 1954, 2–4 with references.

fleet forced him into the interior. Nevertheless, he and his supporters minted *cistophori* with the legend *BA*(σιλεὺς) *EY*(μένης) in at least three communities, each without a prior history of minting (Thyatira, Apollonis, and Stratonicea-on-the-Caïcus), for five regnal years from 134/133 (*A*) to 130/129 (*E*).[41] The inclusion of Aristonicus' regnal name represents a significant innovation from standard issues, highlighting his dynastic claim and legitimacy to the kingdom. As Carbone notes, making these three cities cistophoric mints, even if from circumstance, extended traditional royal practices to new beneficiaries and provided a pointed riposte to Ephesus' retention of the denomination as a civic coinage.[42]

Aristonicus succeeded in killing the first Roman commander sent against him, P. Licinius Crassus Dives (*cos.* 132), before being defeated and captured by his successor M. Perperna (*cos.* 131) at Stratonicea-on-the-Caïcus in winter 130/129.[43] Epigraphic evidence from Caria implies fighting continued into the following year.[44] A growing corpus of inscriptions demonstrates the prolonged presence of Roman commanders in the region, as well as the direct involvement of several *poleis* and allied rulers in Pontus, Bithynia, Paphlagonia, and Cappadocia, underscoring the significance of the conflict.[45] Claims that Aristonicus had substantial support within Attalid cities go beyond the evidence but this was undoubtedly more than a 'slave revolt'.[46] Aristonicus' attempt to continue the Attalid line was a major threat to both Roman hegemony and local claims to freedom, and subsequent developments must be placed firmly in this context.

Meanwhile, in Rome, the Senate passed a resolution responding to the situation: the so-called *senatus consultum Popillianum*. Wörrle's autopsy of the stone has confirmed the presiding magistrate as [Πό]π̣λιος Ποπίλλιος Γαίου υἱός (P. Popillius, C.f., [Laenas]), firmly dating the text to late in his consulship in 132.[47] The text issued ἐντολαί ('instructions') [τοῖς εἰς | Ἀ]σίαν πορευομένοις στρατηγοῖς ('for the praetors crossing over into Asia'), which Kallet-Marx persuasively suggests included all future commanders in Asia. Specifically, it enjoined commanders to respect [δι]ωρθώθη ἐδωρήθη ἀφέθη ἐζημιώ[θη] ('items amended, given, taken away; penalties imposed') by Attalus III until one day prior to his death.[48] It did not, *pace* Kay, 'refuse the commissioners the right to change these arrangements'.[49] The extant document is concerned only with ensuring the legal validity of Attalus' acts

[41] Robinson 1954; Kleiner & Noé 1977, 103–6; Collins 1981, 39–43; Hochard 2021, 50–1.

[42] Carbone 2020, 12.

[43] Strabo 14.1.38. Daubner 2006², 119–31, with references.

[44] Collected by Briant, Brun, & Varınlıoğlu 2001, 252–9.

[45] Brun 2004, 44–52, for references; Jones 2004, 483–5; Daubner 2006², 103–7. See already Broughton 1938, 505–7.

[46] Delplace 1978, 37–53; Kirbihler 2016, 21–5; *pace* Mileta 1998, 52–64.

[47] Wörrle 2000, 567. Early editors dated it to 133, after news of Attalus' testament but before Aristonicus' revolt, as a necessary procedural step in creating a new province (e.g., Foucart 1904, 313; Sherk 1969, 61–2). Magie proposed 129 (Magie 1950, 1033–4; followed by Gruen 1984, 603–4); Wörrle's reading is now decisive.

[48] *RDGE* 11.5–10, with Wörrle 2000, 543. Compare Famerie 2021, 182–3.

[49] Kay 2014, 62.

vis-à-vis Roman justice.[50] The decisions of *legati* or commanders, past, present, or future, were not constrained by this ordinance. Nevertheless, the document's display was likely intended to bolster the community's claim to benefits granted under the terms of Attalus' testament, including its ἐλευθερία.[51] The *senatus consultum Popillianum* was not prescriptive legislation but an unprecedented starting point for a future relationship between Rome and the cities of Asia.[52]

An honorific inscription from Pergamum for one Menodorus highlights the complex transition of the city from royal seat to Roman ally in this period:

> *μεταπεσόντων τε τῶν πραγμάτων εἰς δημοκρατίαν* | [*κα*]*ὶ τοῦ δῆμου συνέδρους χειροτονήσαντος τῶν ἀρίστων ἀνδρῶν κατεσ*|[*τ*]*άθ*[*η*] *καὶ Μηνόδωρος καὶ μετὰ ταῦτα ἐν τῶι κατὰ τὴν Ῥωμαικὴν νομοθεσίαν βουλευ*|*τηρίωι γενόμενος διὰ τὴν πρὸς τὴν πατρίδα εὔνοιαν πολλὰ τῶν συμφερόντων* | *συνήργεσεν ἀεὶ ὑγιῆ καὶ καθαρὰν ἐκτιθέμενος κρίσιν*...*χειροτονηθεὶς* | [*δ*]*ẹ̀ κ̣α̣ὶ̣ στρατηγός τῆς πόλεως ὄντος ἐν τῆι Ἀσίαι Μανίου τε Ἀκ̣υλλίου σ̣τ̣ρ̣α̣τ̣*[*η*|*γοῦ*] *ὑ̣πάτου Ῥωμαίων καὶ τῶν δέκα πρεσβευτῶν τούτοις τε προσηνέχθη* | [*ὑπὲρ*] *τῆς πόλεως μετὰ παρρησίας δικαίως τὸν ὑπὲρ τῆς πατρίδος* [*προ*]*σ*|[*αγόμε*]*νος λόγον καὶ ἐν τοῖς κατὰ τὴν ἀρχὴν ἐ̣*[*πιμ*]*ε̣λ̣ῶ̣*[*ς καὶ μισο*]|*πονήρος ἀνεστράφη* ('Since further, when the state (*πραγμάτων*) changed to a democracy, and the people chose a committee (*συνέδρους*) of the best men, he, Menodorus, was chosen, and becoming a member of the council (*βουλευτηρίωι*) in accordance with the Roman legislation (*νομοθέσίαν*), through his goodwill he brought about many useful things for the Fatherland, always exercising reason and good sense... and then, chosen *strategos* of the city, when M.' Aquillius, consul of the Romans and the ten *legati* were in Asia, he negotiated with appropriate outspokenness (*παρρησίας*) on behalf of the city, putting forward arguments in favour of his homeland, and in these ways conducted the duties of his magistracy diligently and tirelessly').[53]

[50] Restorations of ll.19–20 to read that *στρατηγοί* were not 'to disturb the testament' or 'disturb anything to no good purpose' (e.g., Dittenberger (at *OGIS* 445) and Sherk (1969, 60)) are unconvincing. In this sense, it is not unlike the 'European Union (Withdrawal) Act 2018' passed by the United Kingdom. This confirmed existing European statutes and regulations as having standing in British law but did not preclude subsequent alterations or repeal.

[51] Drew-Bear 1972, 77.

[52] Compare Livy's explanation of the despatch of *legati* to Macedonia in 167: *ceterum quamquam tales uiri mitterentur, quorum de consilio sperari posset imperatores nihil indignum nec dementia nec gravitate populi Romani decreturos esse, tamen in senatu quoque agitata sunt summa consiliorum, ut inchoata omnia legati ab domo ferre ad imperatores possent* ('Moreover, although the men sent were so distinguished that it was to be trusted that the *imperatores* would enact nothing by their consul unworthy or foolish or disagreeable to the Roman *populus*, nevertheless, the most important points were deliberated also in the Senate, so that the *legati* were able to bring to the *imperatores* from home an outline of everything'). Livy then outlines five principles, starting with the abolition of the monarchy and tax-farming, before noting *cetera ipsis imperatoribus legatisque relicta, in quibus praesens tractatio rerum certiora subiectura erat consilia* ('the rest was left to the *imperatores* and the *legati* themselves, among whom the present discussion of the issue would be subject to more specific advice'). Liv. 45.17.7–18.8.

[53] *SEG* 50.1211.11–15, 17–22.

The city honours Menodorus for three distinct acts involving the Romans, which form the decree's core narrative. First, he acted as a συνέδρος for the city after its structural transition from a royal seat to a free city.[54] Other συνέδρια existed in Asia at this time, offering models for the *polis* in its transition from royal capital to free community. The appearance of homonymous bodies in Greece—aristocratic councils with oversight of proposals put to the *demos*—is strongly associated with Roman interventions after the Third Macedonian and Achaean Wars, which may suggest interference by the *legati* in the internal affairs of the *polis*.[55] However, Chankowski demonstrated that magistrates named στρατηγοί already carried out this oversight role at Pergamum under the Attalids and continued to do so until the 60s.[56] The role of the συνέδριον, consequently, cannot be reconstructed: in the absence of further comparanda, a plausible though speculative suggestion is that it served as an interim aristocratic body to propose changes to the Pergamene constitution. Though the *polis* placed great emphasis on its newfound freedom, this does not imply that existing civic elites were not keen to control the transition process.

Second, Menodorus served as a member of a βουλευτήριον in accordance with τὴν Ῥωμαικὴν νομοθεσίαν, an unparalleled phrase. Given that the decree places this before his activity as στρατηγὸς τῆς πόλεως which coincided with Aquillius' command (129–126), it must relate to the commission of Scipio Nasica, present in Pergamum from mid-132. Wörrle characterizes the νομοθεσία as 'die grundlegende römische Rechtsordnung für das Attalidenreich': a *lex provinciae*. However, the commission could not have issued a binding pronouncement in the absence of a serving magistrate *cum imperio*.[57] The prevailing view presents the βουλευτήριον as an assembly of delegates from the *poleis* of the former kingdom and some view it as a nascent provincial assembly, though this is highly speculative.[58] The possibility that this refers to a reformed, local institution should be considered. The text does not suggest that Menodorus left Pergamum, which would normally be mentioned to indicate service in an ambassadorial role. More significantly, the term βουλευτήριον does not describe comparable assemblies in Macedonia or Achaea. Consequently, if the συνέδριον were a temporary expedient, set up to

[54] 'Democracy' here stands for the absence of royal (or Roman) rule, i.e., as a synonym for ἐλευθερία (freedom), rather than implying anything about the form of constitution. Wörrle 2000, 564–5; Lehmann 2000, 228–30; Ferrary 2017, 48–9; Ventroux 2017, 36–7 n.44. Compare: *OGIS* 449.

[55] E.g., Thessaly in 197 (Livy 34.51.6), Macedonia in 167 (Polyb. 31.2.12; Livy 45.32.2), then the Achaian *koinon* in 146 (Paus. 7.16.9; Piérart 2013, 27). Gruen 1984, 523–5; Ferrary 1988, 206–10.

[56] Chankowski 1998, 180–90; Ventroux 2017, 86–7. Compare Ephesus, where the στρατηγοί, γραμματεύς τῆς βουλῆς, and προέδροι introduce decrees to the ἐκκλησία together (*I.Eph.* 8.17–22. Rhodes and Lewis 1997, 357–67; Kirbihler 2016, 114–16).

[57] *Pace* Wörrle 2000, 568, evoking *SEG* 38.1462.111 (with Wörrle 1988, 77–100, which cited this, hitherto unpublished, inscription to support that interpretation). More cautiously: Kirbihler 2016, 26–7; Ventroux 2017, 38.

[58] By analogy with Macedonia in 167: Livy 45.29.1, 32.1–7, with Papazoglu 1988, 58–64. E.g., Wörrle 2000, 569–70; Daubner 2006², 98–103; Edelmann-Singer 2011, 89–95; Ventroux 2017, 37–8.

reconstitute the *polis*' political organs, the *βουλευτήριον* may plausibly have been a permanent aristocratic council, selected in line with the wishes of the Roman *legati*. Both actions would establish the former royal capital as a Roman-aligned, functionally independent *polis*.

Third, the decree highlights Menodorus' service as *στρατηγὸς τῆς πόλεως*, during which he negotiated directly with Aquillius and the commission. The decree emphasizes Menodorus' *παρρησία* ('outspokenness') on behalf of the *polis*. This word rarely appears in the epigraphic record and, though details are lacking, should imply, at least, a robust exchange of views.[59] Its employment stresses both the importance of persuasion and the licence with which local powerbrokers felt able to approach their Roman hegemons. Given the limited intervention of Aquillius and his commission in civic affairs, Wörrle's suggestion connecting this discussion with the events culminating in the *senatus consultum de agro Pergameno* seems reasonable.[60] As presented by the Pergamenes in the Menodorus decree, Roman actions in the aftermath of Attalus' death established the city as an independent entity, though one firmly under Roman hegemony.

Another honorific decree from May 132, for Apollonius of Metropolis, who had perished fighting against Aristonicus, summarizes the background to the ongoing conflict in terms which relate explicitly to civic freedom:[61]

> *νῦν τε τοῦ μὲν Φιλομήτορος βασιλέως μεταλλάξαντος Ῥω|μαίων δὲ τῶν κοινῶν εὐεργετῶν τε καὶ σωτήρων* ***ἀποδόντων***, *καθάπερ* ***ἐδογμάτισαν***, *τὴν ἐ|λευθερίαν πᾶσιν τοῖς πρότερον τασσομένοις ὑπὸ τὴν Ἀττάλου βασιλείαν, Ἀριστονίκου δὲ παρα|γεγονότος καὶ βουλομένου παραιρεῖσθαι τὴν* ***ἀποδεδομένην*** *ἡμῖν ἐλευθερίαν ὑπὸ τῆς συγκλή|του*... ('Now, when King Philometor had died, and the Romans, common saviours and benefactors, had *restored*, as they had *decreed*, freedom to all those formerly making up the kingdom of Attalus, since Aristonicus arrived and wished to take away again our *ἐλευθερία*, *restored* by the Senate...').[62]

The text stresses through repetition that *ἐλευθερία* had been granted (*ἀποδόντων*; *ἀποδεδομένην*) and that a *senatus consultum* had been passed to that effect (*ἐδογμάτισαν*; *ὑπὸ τῆς συγκλήτου*).[63] The unusual qualification that the freedom extended to *πᾶσιν τοῖς πρότερον τασσομένοις ὑπὸ τὴν Ἀττάλου βασιλείαν* ('all those formerly making up the kingdom of Attalus') demonstrates that this was perceived as a universal grant.[64] Metropolis, a minor *polis* previously directly subject

[59] Parallels: *IG* 2³.1.1147 (Athens, 3rd century BCE); *Opramoas* (Rhodiapolis, 2nd century CE); *IG* 5.1.547 (Sparta, 3rd century CE).

[60] *SEG* 50.1211.18–22; compare esp. *SEG* 39.1243–1244. Wörrle 2000, 571–3.

[61] Date: Jones 2004, 478–82; Eilers 2005, 253–4 contra Dreyer & Engelmann 2003, 66–79.

[62] *I.Metropolis* 1A.13–17.

[63] Chaniotis 2014, 151. See Snowdon (2008, 378–91) on the sense of 'freedom' as innate to civic identity, even where the community may not have previously possessed it.

[64] Dreyer 2005, 59–62; Vitale 2012, 44; already Broughton 1938, 509.

to Attalus, had therefore already received ἐλευθερία *ex senatus consulto* by mid-132. Preserving that freedom provided a powerful motivation for co-operating with Rome against the uprising: self-interest was a major factor in generating a coalition of *poleis* to resist the pretender. A victory for Aristonicus would mean a return to the *status quo ante bellum*, where active support for Rome would lead to civic freedom. Moreover, the narrative implies that the news had arrived even before Aristonicus' revolt had commenced.[65] Consequently, one of the first administrative decisions taken by the Roman Senate was to grant ἐλευθερία en masse to the *poleis* formerly subject to, and taxed by, the Attalid monarchs, which should be taken to include the dependent *poleis* within the earlier kingdom.[66] The grant likely did not include military colonies or other sub-*polis* communities within the βασιλικὴ χώρα.[67] Nevertheless, those urban centres which had achieved recognition under the Attalids as political communities in their own right, were granted autonomy with the Roman inheritance of the Attalid kingdom.

The Limits of Civic Freedom

The meaning of ἐλευθερία in this context is especially complex. A.H.M. Jones argued that Rome, embodied by the Senate and its magistrates, appropriated the Hellenistic concept of ἐλευθερία ('freedom') in full: this was granted unilaterally and consisted of several elements—including, but not limited to, αὐτονομία (the community's right to use its own laws and customs), ἀφορολογησία (freedom from taxation), and being ἀφρούρητος (free from garrisons)—any number of which might be granted individually to create a complex and individualized hierarchy of freedoms.[68] By contrast, Bernhardt asserted that all grants of unqualified ἐλευθερία by the Roman state entailed exemption from regular Roman taxation (Lat. *immunitas*; Gr. ἀτέλεια) from the Republic through to Late Antiquity. Examples in which free cities clearly made financial contributions to the Roman state, he explained as irregular demands and posited a higher status of immunity (known in Greek as ἀλειτουργησία) which further exempted recipients from all financial imposts including the provision of supplies and billeting from Roman troops.

Buraselis, in an extensive critique, cited two passages of Appian describing Roman commanders exacting money from free cities as counter-examples, arguing that ἐλευθερία did not automatically imply freedom from taxation. However, both Sulla in the aftermath of the First Mithridatic War in 85 and M. Antonius

[65] Rigsby 1979, 46–7; *pace* Jones 2004. The memory of Apamea, where Roman allies were given freedom and enemies were subjected to Eumenes II or Rhodes, probably also contributed to enthusiasm for the Roman cause (Polyb. 21.45.1–11; Livy 38.39.7–17).

[66] Dreyer & Engelmann 2003, 30; Marek 2010, 321; Walser 2021, 165.

[67] Mileta 2002, 161–3; Ma 2013, 66–71. Cf. Ando 2021, 71–82.

[68] Jones 1939, 103–17. Earlier, Mommsen 1887[3] 3.683.

after Philippi in 41 had immediate and pressing fiscal and military needs.[69] Their actions should not be taken as indicative of normal practice during the late Republic. Buraselis' claim that, in the Augustan period, ἀτέλεια could be celebrated by cities on autonomous coinage which already possessed freedom does have weight, however, while observable differences in Cicero and Pliny's use of the term *immunitas* reinforce his point that in the imperial period things changed.[70] Moreover, we have clear evidence of tribute-paying *civitates liberae* during the Principate.[71] Given that institutions are not static, it is reasonable to question when Roman conceptions of *libertas* ceased to entail *immunitas*.

Dmitriev has argued strongly that the Roman conception of freedom, expressed through *libertas* and its cognates, had key differences from the Hellenistic model and required a period of adjustment. In non-Greek contexts, community statuses imposed by Rome were restricted to *libera* ('free'), *foederata* ('secured by treaty'), or *stipendiaria* ('tribute-paying'), implying by omission that the other categories entailed *immunitas*. Dmitriev concludes that the complicating factor in the Greek East is the employment of this framework in parallel and in interaction with existing Hellenistic models without consistency over an extended period.[72] Unqualified ἐλευθερία should originally have corresponded with *libertas*, and therefore the complete set of Hellenistic freedoms.[73] While Livy does describe the tribute-paying *poleis* of Macedonia as *liberae* in the aftermath of L. Aemilius Paullus' settlement in 167, these polities had been defeated enemies, where the communities of Asia had formed part of an allied kingdom with no record of transgression against Rome.[74] In this sense they were more akin to the cities of Lycia, freed from Rhodian rule in 167, who did not pay tribute to Rome.[75] As such, ἐλευθερία, in the Apollonius decree, should correspond to a grant of (Latin) *libertas* and implicitly include *immunitas* from Roman taxation. If so, the initial decision of the Roman Senate to free the cities of Attalus' kingdom *ipso facto* brought an end to the existing tax regime.

General Principles: The *lex provinciae* and *formula provinciae*

Central to most accounts of the organization of *provincia Asia* is the concept of the *lex provinciae*, supposedly passed by Aquillius after the conclusion of the

[69] App. *BCiv.* 1.102, 5.6.

[70] Buraselis 2000, 136–7 n.75, drawing on Jones 1939, 103–17; Ferrary 1988, 7–9.

[71] Jones (1971², 60) cites Ilium in 89, but see Bernhardt (1980, 198); Wallace (2014, 56–7). Otherwise, the earliest strong evidence is for Cos in the Augustan period (Strabo 14.2.19, with Buraselis 2000, 134–5 on freedom).

[72] Dmitriev 2017, 203–7.

[73] Note Piérart's similar argument (2013, 28–31) for the correspondences between συνέδριον and *senatus* in Greece.

[74] Liv. 45.29.4; Diod. 31.8.1. Bernhardt 1999, 58–61.

[75] Polyb. 30.5.12–16; Liv. 45.25.6. Dahlheim 1977, 255–77; Bernhardt 1980, 190–207, 1999, 55–68; Ferrary 1999, 71 n.8.

Aristonican War, before his return to Rome in late 126.[76] This is understood as an early task of the first Roman magistrate in a new province, laying down the basic framework for administration. Often, but not always, the formulation of this act would be facilitated by the presence of several *legati*, normally ten.[77] Where evidence exists for *leges provinciae*, their contents include various topics, including the framework for judicial actions between the inhabitants of diverse provincial communities, the organization of the grain supply (Sicily), and the constitutions of local civic communities (Pontus-Bithynia). However, they did not interfere with local legal practice.[78] Critically, the *lex provinciae*, for all the emphasis it receives in modern scholarship, was no more than a local regulation issued by a magistrate as a *lex data* or an *edictum*. It was not, strictly, binding on his successors, even where convention and the *auctoritas* of the *legati*, where present, strongly encouraged compliance.[79] Hoyos suggests employing the term as a convenient shorthand for the general organization imposed by Rome on a new territory. However, as Lintott stresses, no substantial difference existed between the establishment of a new *provincia* and a post-*bellum* settlement, which did not create a permanent province.[80] Given the apparently minimalist Roman approaches to governance in Africa, Achaia, Cilicia, and Cyrenaica, it begs the question to assume that a single detailed ordinance was routinely passed.[81]

Indeed, evidence for such a document in Asia is minimal. Strabo provides the clearest indication, stating that: *Μάνιος δ' Ἀκύλλιος ἐπελθὼν ὕπατος μετὰ δέκα πρεσβευτῶν διέταξε τὴν ἐπαρχίαν εἰς τὸ νῦν ἔτι συμμένον* ***τῆς πολιτείας σχῆμα*** ('Manius Aquillius, as consul, arriving with ten *legati*, organized the province to *the form of government* which even now endures').[82] However, ambiguity abounds. The phrase *τῆς πολιτείας σχῆμα* alone is insufficient to show that Aquillius established institutions such as the *conventus iuridici* or provincial *koinon*, first attested much later.[83] Given the numerous territorial and administrative changes within the *provincia* in the first century of its existence, the term presents, at best, a convenient shorthand. What Strabo may refer to here, rather is a *formula provinciae*. This document seems to have been a simple text, preserving the names of communities, grouped geographically, in list form, and their privileges vis-à-vis Rome. On most readings—and from the available evidence—it

[76] *MRR* 1.509. [77] E.g., Marquardt 1881, 1.500–501; Mommsen 1887³, 2.685, 692.

[78] Sicily: Cic. *Verr.* 2.2.15–16, 90, 3.92. Pontus-Bithynia: Strabo 12.3.1; Plin. *Ep.* 10.79, 112, 114; CD. 37.20.3. Marshall 1968, 104–6; Hoyos 1973, 49–50; Coudry & Kirbihler 2010, 133–8.

[79] Badian 1956, 116 n.4; Hoyos 1973, 50–3; Lintott 1993, 28–32; Yarrow 2012, 177–83. On the differences between these two categories, Lanfranchi (2019, esp. 77) has recently put forward the reasonable argument that the former was a type of *decretum*, originally a collective act, and the latter depended only on the issuing magistrate.

[80] Lintott 1981, 58–61; Freeman 1986, 254–7; *pace* Hoyos 1973, 53.

[81] Africa: Gargola 2017, 331–44; Achaia: Hurlet & Müller 2020; Cilicia: Freeman 1986, 253–8; Cyrenaica: Badian 1965, 119–20; Rafferty 2019, 214–16.

[82] Strabo 14.1.38.

[83] E.g., Mommsen 1906 [1899], 68 n.1; Magie 1950, 171–3; Mitchell 1999, 22–6; Dreyer 2015, 208.

contained no detailed information regarding civic boundaries on the ground.[84] At least one city, Aphrodisias, was not included in the *formula* during the imperial period; however, this appears to have been a specific privilege distinct from 'freedom'. Consequently, Dalla Rosa's claim that inclusion within the *formula* subjected communities to the *imperium* and *iurisdictio* of the governor should not hold, at least for the Republican period.[85] Instead the *formula* presented a list of legal statuses of communities within the territory nominally assigned to a governor, ordered by their local *conventus* centre. Richardson argued that *formulae provinciarum*, as conceived by modern scholars, are an imperial innovation, though Shaw has demonstrated the existence of an African *formula*, or similar document, in the 40s.[86] Some form of administrative organization, dividing the *provincia* into groups of communities, is also attested in the *lex de provinciis praetoriis* in 100. This statute, in allocating *provincia Cilicia* to a praetor, reaffirmed that the *ἐπαρχεία Λυκαονία* (sc. 'Lycaonian district') remained subject to the governor of Asia.[87] This district seems to correspond to the later *conventus* region centred on Philomelium. A regional structure based on groups of communities provided a basis for more complex administration, even if limited to organizing assizes for Romans conducting business in the *provincia* or deciding which geographic regions should be assigned to which commanders. The framework it provided, however, was critical to implementing all later changes. The most plausible interpretation takes *τῆς πολιτείας σχῆμα* literally as the 'form of government', that is, the regular, though not necessarily permanent, presence of a Roman magistrate, rather than encompassing specific acts of Aquillius.[88]

The Ambitions of M'. Aquillius

Ando has argued that the *lex de provinciis praetoriis* demonstrates a high level of administrative ambition by the Roman state. Not only did it establish the make-up of different *provinciae* in the eastern Mediterranean, but also extended administration and taxation to conquered regions north of Macedonia and crafted a policy against piracy in the region.[89] Although an astute observation regarding this statute, the document is exceptional. The text, which included several overt

[84] E.g., Shaw 1981 on Africa and Christol 1994 on Gallia Narbonensis. On the spatial indeterminacy of Roman *provinciae*: Gargola 2017a, 78–82.

[85] *IAph2007* 8.33.2–3; 34.13–14. *Pace* Dalla Rosa 2014, 31–3. Compare Cottier et al. 2008 *ad* l.89, referring to communities *ἔξο διοικήσεως* (*extra (formulam?) conventus*), and *SEG* 39.1243.2.48–53, implying that Colophon was outside the *provincia*.

[86] Shaw 1981; *pace* Richardson 2011, 2–3; Gargola 2017a, 69–70.

[87] *RS* 12. Cnidus.3.22–7.

[88] Compare metonymic references to annual magistrates for Roman hegemony or the use of the phrase *in formam provinciae redactam* as shorthand to describe the complex process of provincialization under the early Principate. Mitchell 1993, 63, with references at n.20; Gargola 2017, 335–42; 2017a, 69–78.

[89] Ando 2000, 80–2.

restrictions on gubernatorial action and required senators to take an oath to uphold its provisions seems strongly associated with the controversial tribune L. Appuleius Saturninus, and Ferrary's dating of the statute to February 100 is convincing.[90] That the law contains several unrelated measures *per saturam* and shows concern with the efficient imposition of taxation on newly subjugated regions should be linked to his contentious agenda and specifically his need to increase state income to fund his expensive agrarian and grain measures.[91] This statute ran counter to the senatorial consensus, indicates the increasing conflict at Rome over fiscal policy in this period, and, consequently, cannot be taken as straightforward evidence of typical Roman practice.

The evidence for the commission's decisions in 129–126 stresses the definition of territorial borders. Concerns over the extent of the new *provincia* predominate in the sources, though internal boundaries between civic territories and the former *βασιλικὴ χώρα* had more relevance from an administrative perspective. A significant portion of the Attalid kingdom was pared away, granted to allied rulers who helped defeat Aristonicus. The sons of Ariarathes V of Cappadocia received Lycaonia and Pisidia; Mithridates V of Pontos, 'Greater Phrygia'.[92] However, these arrangements did not last. On Aquillius' return he was arraigned for extortion, prosecutors alleging he had accepted bribes in return for favourable arrangements. Despite his acquittal, the commission's decisions were steadily reversed. Phrygia was brought into Asia sometime after the death of Mithridates V in 123, while the *lex de provinciis praetoriis* clearly refers to Lycaonia as a constituent element of the *provincia*.[93] Altogether, this shows both the wide scope afforded to the proconsul and the commission of ten *legati* from 129 and the flexibility for the Senate to alter elements of the settlement which it deemed imprudent.

A corpus of eleven milestones bearing Aquillius' name reveals another early concern of the first Roman governor. These fall into a series of distinct groups: four clustered between Ephesus and Tralles, two near Pergamum, four in southern Phrygia, near modern Yeşilova, and one 5 km west of Side in Pamphylia.[94] Based on distances recorded on the stones, French and Mitchell deduced that Aquillius marked several roads from two *capita viae* during his command: Ephesus, for roads towards Pergamum, Sardis, and Laodicea-on-the-Lycus (via Tralles); and

[90] Ferrary 1977, 627–8; cf. Hassall, Crawford, & Reynolds 1974, 218–20; Lintott 1976, 66–9 contra Giovannini & Grzybek 1978, 33–47; Giovannini 2008, 96. See, already, Colin (1924, 58–96) for Saturninus' involvement.

[91] Compare Tan 2017, 152–70.

[92] Nicomedes of Bithynia may have been rewarded but is seen contesting Mithridates' Phrygian possessions in 124 (Gell. *NA* 11.10). App. *Mith.* 57; Just. *Epit.* 37.1.2. Strabo 14.1.38; Eutrop. 4.20.

[93] Phrygia: App. *Mith.* 11–12, 15; Just. *Epit.* 38.5.3; *OGIS* 436. Lycaonia: *RS* 12.Cnidus.3.22–41. On the date of Mithridates V's death, Ramsay 1999, 236–42. Cf. Drew-Bear (1972, 82–3); McGing (1980, 35–42) and Sherwin-White (1984, 96), prefer later dates.

[94] *RRMAM* 3.1–10. Compare Thonemann (2003, 95–6), who discusses an earlier Attalid distance marker (*I.Eph.* 7.2.3601) from the Cayster valley.

Pergamum, for the main road running east to Side, via Sardis and Laodicea.[95] Mitchell asserts that this reveals 'the geo-political thinking which lay behind the creation of the new province'. However, this should be framed as 'Roman presence' rather than 'province' per se. These milestones almost certainly did not line new routes. Instead, they rebranded existing routes, serving the additional purpose of signifying Roman hegemony.[96] Some Attalid geographical divisions continued to be employed within the new *provincia*, giving further evidence of the limited nature of active Roman changes.[97]

Aquillius and the commission left a *provincia* encompassing the western littoral of Asia Minor, stretching from the southern border of Bithynia, near Cyzicus, to the northern bank of the Maeander, and reaching inland only to the fringes of the Anatolian plateau. Given the enthusiastic participation of Carian cities in the war against Aristonicus, the region south of the Maeander, which had never been subject to the Attalid *basileis*, likely remained outside the *provincia* at this time.[98] This is equally true of cities in the northern Troad, including Cyzicus and Lampsacus, which were also independent of the Attalid kingdom.[99] Aquillius' *provincia* covered a restricted geographic area and his reported activities do not suggest deep and intrusive intervention.

The Aims and Ambitions of Roman Administration

The frequency of Roman magistrates assigned to *provincia Asia* in the early period carries important implications for understanding the impact of Roman rule on the local communities. The text of *I.Priene*² 75 preserves the names of four Roman magistrates in Asia, who were visited by a Prienean ambassador between 126 and approximately 95, the praetors C. Atinius Labeo (*pr.* 122?), L. Calpurnius Piso (*pr.* 115?), M. Plautius Hypsaeus (*pr.* 100?), and a *quaestor*, L. Licinius(?) Murena.[100] *Cistophori* were also minted at Ephesus under the authority of Atinius, uniquely in this period, though his role is unclear.[101] Several other magistrates are attested in inscriptions from the Aegean islands, who have traditionally been ascribed to *provincia Asia*, including Cn. Papirius Carbo (*I.Délos* 1550.4–6; *pr.* 116?); Ser. Cornelius Lentulus (*I.Délos* 1845.1–5; *pr.* 110);

95 Mitchell 1999, 19–20, 24; Campanile 2003, 281–4; French 2012, 9–11; *pace* Rigsby 1988, 137–41.

96 French 1997, 179–87. There is no evidence of paved roads until the construction of the *via Sebaste* from Perge to Lystra, after 6 CE.

97 Mileta 1990, 438–44; Dreyer 2015, 208–10; *pace* Mitchell 1999, 24–5. Cf. Hatzopoulos' argument (1996, 248–60) that Paullus' division of Macedonia into four states was based on an Antigonid model.

98 Baronowski 1996, 241–8; Dmitriev 2005, 110–15.

99 Jones 1971², 53; Dmitriev 2005, 81–2 contra Campanile 2003, 274. See Thornton (1999, 497–508) on Cyzicus.

100 Eilers 1996, 175–82, with earlier literature; accepted by *I.Priene*² 75.

101 Stumpf 1991, #1; discussion, 6–13. See 'Republican *cistophori* in Post-Attalid Asia'.

Cn. Aufidius (*IG* 12.5.722.5–7; *pr.* 108?); C. Billienus (*I.Délos* 1854; *pr.* 107?); C. Rabirius (*I.Délos* 1859; *pr.* 106); and C. Cluvius (*I.Délos* 1679). Finally, Q. Mucius Scaevola Augur was hosted by Menippus of Colophon on multiple occasions in 120/119.[102] This list, though difficult to arrange into a narrative, provides a crowded *fasti* for the period from 122 onwards, highlighting the consistent appointment of commanders to the region.[103] However, this presence seems unrelated to any military commitment. The Romans relied heavily on allied contingents in the Aristonicus incident, while resistance to Mithridates VI of Pontus in 88 was led by *poleis*, if co-ordinated by Roman magistrates.[104] Commanders were accompanied by small units, but it appears that the Senate trusted the system of alliances cultivated with local rulers. There is limited evidence for Italian troops deployed before the First Mithridatic War, which may imply that the regular commanders in Asia relied more on persuasion than military force in their administration.[105] The physical footprint of the Roman state in *provincia Asia* seems limited, even after Aquillius' organization.

The *lex Sempronia de provincia Asia* and Roman Taxation

Most scholars suggest that after consolidating control in the 120s, Rome took advantage of existing Attalid taxation arrangements to increase its own state revenues. Indubitably, Roman *publicani* were active in the region soon after news of Attalus' death reached Rome. Lucilius, in a passage traditionally dated to 131, envisaged economic opportunities within the new *provincia*: *publicanus vero ut Asiae fiam, ut scripturarius | pro Lucilio, id ego nolo et uno hoc non muto omnia* ('I do not wish, in truth, to become a *publicanus* in Asia, as a collector of *scriptura*, instead of Lucilius; I am not exchanging everything for this single thing').[106] Additionally, the *senatus consultum de agro Pergameno*, usually dated to 129, refers to a dispute between the *polis* and *publicani* over civic boundaries.[107] Velleius Paterculus, writing under Tiberius, in a passage introducing the campaigns of Pompeius, further states that Perperna, in 130, *Asiam ... capto Aristonico, fecit tributariam* ('after capturing Aristonicus, made Asia tributary'). However, the imperial author's stated aim for the excursus is to explain

[102] *SEG* 39.1244.2.43–44. Cf. Cic. *de Orat.* 2.269; Brennan 2000, 742. On the date see 'Informal Contacts: Diplomacy Through Personal Contacts'.

[103] *I.Priene*² 75. Ferrary 2000, 162–93.

[104] E.g., *IAph2007* 8.2, 3.

[105] E.g., Glew 1977.

[106] Lucil. 650–1 (Warmington). Tibiletti 1957, 137. Kay (2014, 62–5) goes too far in labelling it a late insertion.

[107] *RDGE* 12. The name of one consul, M.' Aquillius, is preserved, offering potential dates of 129 or 101. A later fragmentary reference to another magistrate [———]νιος has been identified as C. Sempronius (*cos.* 129), though this is rejected by Magie (1950, 1055–6) and Mattingly (1972, 412–23). On the balance of probabilities, an earlier date seems more likely. Rostovtzeff 1941, 811–13; Sherk 1969, 71–2; Dmitriev 2005, 75–7; Tan 2017, 158, n.61, with literature.

cuiusque ductu gens ac natio reducta in formulam provinciam stipendaria facta sit ('under whose leadership peoples and nations were reduced to the form of a province and made tributary').[108] As Gargola has emphasized, throughout his digression Velleius conflates the defeat of the major power in a region with the imposition of tribute, even where this produces misleading outcomes. For example, he implies that L. Aemilius Paullus established a tributary *provincia Macedonia* two decades before the despatch of regular Roman governors, and, indeed, that Perperna, not Aquillius, established a territorial *provincia Asia.* Imperial narratives routinely assumed that conquest was accompanied with the establishment of a permanent province and tributary system; however, this is anachronistic when compared to third- and second-century practices.[109]

Other evidence speaks against immediate large-scale exploitation of the region's economic resources. The unique status of *provincia Asia* in the late second century, a region primarily constituted of staunchly allied communities with no record of transgression against Rome, often passes without comment.[110] However, as noted, the universal *ἐλευθερία* of the Metropolis inscription should correspond to Roman conceptions of *libertas* and include immunity from Roman forms of taxation for civic communities. Appian bolsters this claim having M. Antonius state to the assembled representatives of Asia in 41:

> *ὑμᾶς ἡμῖν, ὦ ἄνδρες Ἕλληνες, Ἄτταλος ὁ βασιλεὺς ὑμῶν ἐν διαθήκαις ἀπέλιπε, καὶ εὐθὺς ἀμείνονες ὑμῖν ἦμεν Ἀττάλου· οὓς γὰρ ἐτελεῖτε φόρους Ἀττάλῳ, μεθήκαμεν ὑμῖν, μέχρι, δημοκόπων ἀνδρῶν καὶ παρ' ἡμῖν γενομένων, ἐδέησε φόρων* ('Hellenes, Attalus, your king, left you to us in his will, and immediately we were better to you than Attalus was. For those taxes (*φόρος*), for which you were assessed by Attalus, we released you from, until demagogues arose among us and made taxes necessary').[111]

In Appian's reconstruction, Antonius claimed that among the first choices of the Roman administration of Asia was to end the complex Attalid taxation regime. Were revenue extraction their goal, the Romans could have maintained existing structures, as they did in Sicily, following the annexation of Syracuse, and Macedonia, albeit at a reduced rate.[112] The imposition of a new harsher system of taxation would not only cut against the accepted practice that *libertas* entailed *immunitas*, but the perception of just treatment for provincials. In a critical passage attacking Verres' regime in Sicily, Cicero draws a distinction between the taxes levied on communities peacefully incorporated into Roman *provinciae* and those collected from regions absorbed through conquest:

[108] Vell. 2.38.1, 5. [109] Gargola 2017, 341–4, compare 335–41 on Appian's similar practice.
[110] E.g., Sherwin-White 1984, 93–4; Santangelo 2007, 108–11. Compare Eckstein 2018, 237–8.
[111] App. *BCiv.* 5.4. [112] On Macedonia: Livy, 45.29.5. Prag 2014.

inter Siciliam ceterasque provincias, iudices, in agrorum vectigalium ratione hoc interest, quod ceteris aut impositum vectigal est certum, quod stipendiarium dicitur, ut Hispanis et plerisque Poenorum, quasi victoriae praemium ac poena belli, aut censoria locatio constituta est, ut Asiae lege Sempronia: Siciliae civitates sic in amicitiam fidemque accepimus ut eodem iure essent quo fuissent, eadem condicione populo Romano parerent qua suis antea paruissent. Perpaucae Siciliae civitates sunt bello a maioribus nostris subactae...praeterea omnis ager Siciliae civitatum decumanus est, itemque ante imperium populi Romani ipsorum Siculorum voluntate et institutis fuit...non modo eorum agris vectigal novum nullum imponeret, sed ne legem quidem venditionis decumarum neve vendundi aut tempus aut locum commutarent, ut certo tempore anni ut ibidem in Sicilia, denique ut lege Hieronica venderent ('Between Sicily and the other provinces, judges, there is a difference in this matter of the agricultural revenue; since in some, either the imposed tribute, which is called stipendiary, is fixed, as in the Hispaniae or many of the Carthaginian regions, just as if a prize of victory or punishment for war; or it is decided through the *locatio* of the censors, as for Asia under the *lex Sempronia*. But the communities of Sicily we received into friendship and alliance so that they were under the same laws as they were before, being subject to the Roman people in the same way which they were subject to those before. Very few of the Sicilian communities were subdued by our ancestors in war...Moreover, all the land of the Sicilian communities is subject to the *decuma*, as again it was by the will and decisions of the Sicilians themselves before the *imperium* of the Roman people...not only, did they [the Roman *populus*] impose no new tribute on their lands, but did not even alter the law regulating the selling of the contracts for the *decuma*, nor that regulating the time or place for the sale, so that they are sold still at a fixed time of year, in Sicily, in short, just as under the *lex Hieronica*'.)[113]

The attitudes evinced by Cicero are enlightening. He states that, since most Sicilian communities were absorbed into the Roman *provincia* as free allies, they retained their privileges vis-à-vis their former rulers, the Hieronids of Syracuse. As the Sicilians already paid a tithe on agricultural produce, they retained their own system of collection.[114] Crucially, Cicero contrasts this right with the levy of *vectigal stipendiarium* on Africa and Spain, described *quasi victoriae praemium ac poena belli* ('as if a prize of victory or punishment for war').[115] Cicero's distinction between peaceful incorporation into empire and conquest implies that popular elite opinion would recognize the application of correspondingly

[113] Cic. *Verr.* 2.3.12–14.

[114] Dubouloz & Pittia 2009, 101–7; Prag 2014, 168–73; Corvino 2016, 156–9.

[115] On the term *stipendiarius*: Soraci 2010, 43–80, esp. 72–80; Ñaco del Hoyo 2019, 70–87. France's suggestion (2007, 176–82) that this discussion refers to all Sicilian taxes is unconvincing.

lighter or heavier tax burdens as manifestly just.[116] Even in Spain, during this period, such 'prizes' or 'punishments' tended to be ad hoc, situational, and not centrally directed.[117] However, the explicit contrast drawn by Cicero between these territories, Sicily, and Asia is in the method of assessment and collection. In Asia, the *decuma*: *censoria locatio constituta est* . . . *lege Sempronia* ('was established by a *locatio* of the censors . . . under the *lex Sempronia*').[118]

This legislation must form part of C. Gracchus' programme in 123/122, although the precise scope of the statute remains unclear. In light of Appian's argument, voiced by Antonius, that the activities of 'demagogues' made taxes necessary, several scholars have argued that this was the moment that Roman taxation was extended to the cities of the province.[119] However, the principle that territories of free cities were, in some way, separate from the *provincia* and the authority of the Roman governor is well established even in the 120s.[120] Cicero's purpose here is to draw a distinction between the provinces only based on the methods of assessment and collection. Indeed, the possibility that Gracchus' intent may have been to enshrine in law a precise method of collection, rather than (re)introduce a different tax, is worth exploring. As noted, the βασιλικὴ χώρα was separate from the civic territory, even where the former contained buildings and other economic assets located within and encircled by the latter. In at least one case, this situation was further complicated by the decision of a Roman magistrate to return some formerly 'royal' land at Selinousia to the custody of the temple of Artemis.[121] In most cases, where Hellenistic kingdoms were taken into Roman hands, these royal lands were incorporated into the *ager publicus*, whose rents were farmed by *publicani*.[122] In light of the controversy ascribed to Ti. Gracchus' proposals to tax the cities in 133, which does not seem to have attached itself to this legislation, and Cicero's emphasis on its content, it seems most plausible that the *lex Sempronia* initially regulated the collection of the *decuma* from the former βασιλικὴ χώρα, the non-civic land within the *provincia* which had unambiguously fallen into the purview of the Roman state.[123]

The classification of some land as *ager privatus vectigalisque* in the *lex agraria* of 111 offers a further attractive possibility. According to Roselaar, this statute rendered *ager publicus* in Africa private property, thereby alienating it from

[116] Cic. *Verr.* 2.3.12. Yakobson 2009, 61–6; Kay 2014, 64. Compare the fragmentary speech *de rege Alexandrino* and *de lege agraria* (2.43–25) and *de imperio Gnaei Pompei passim*.

[117] Ñaco del Hoyo 2007, 228–30 contra France 2007, 182.

[118] Cic. *Verr.* 2.3.12.

[119] Broughton 1938, 511–12; Magie 1950, 1005–6; Mattingly 1972, 412–23; Daubner 2006², 227–9; Kay 2014, 59–83.

[120] E.g., *SEG* 39.1244.2.1–7, with Ferrary 2017a [1991], 177–9. See discussion in section 'Gubernatorial Jurisdiction and the Free Cities'.

[121] Strabo 14.1.28.

[122] Cic. *Leg. agr.* 2.50. Rostovtzeff 1910, 283–5; Magie 1950, 1047–8; Merola 2001, 183–6 contra Frank (1927, 148–9) and Broughton (1934, 207–8), who draw a contrast between the treatment of royal estates and 'crown-lands' which is not borne out by the evidence.

[123] App. *BCiv.* 1.7. Roselaar 2010, 90–3.

state control, while retaining for the state the former income as an annual rent, potentially a tithe.[124] The consequence of this were twofold: to guarantee annual revenue from these lands in the longer term, allowing it to offset ongoing spending measures, such as those in Gracchus' substantial programme; and to theoretically prevent—and certainly complicate efforts by—the state from repossessing the land or reassessing the *vectigal*, thereby de-funding these measures. Accordingly, I suggest that the *lex Sempronia* may have given the *ager publicus* in Asia this status, assigning it to existing inhabitants as private property, complicating future attempts to appropriate this land for other uses which could deprive the state of the necessary revenues to support Gracchus' programme.

This argument would explain the apparent absence of *ager publicus* in Asia in 63, when the tribune P. Servilius Rullus attempted to appropriate large swathes of public land in the Roman East for his *lex agraria*. Cicero lists the lands Rullus sought to seize, including the *regii agri* (i.e., the *βασιλικὴ χώρα*) of the Macedonian kings Philip V and Perseus, the Bithynian rulers, Mithridates VI of Pontus, and Ptolemy Apion in Cyrenaica. The only Attalid lands mentioned are those in the (Thracian) Chersonesus, outside of *provincia Asia*.[125] Given the exhaustive scope of Rullus' appropriation of available land, it is implausible to suggest that he would have passed over the former Attalid possessions in Asia: consequently, their absence must be accounted for.[126] One solution would be that they were alienated from the *ager publicus* in less advantageous circumstances, but few plausible candidates for effecting this exist: tribunes of the *plebs* tended to focus on lands in Italy to settle colonists, while the mass alienation of the only state revenue-producing lands in Asia cuts against the interests of a typical tribune. Aquillius is the most likely alternative, considering the ongoing contest over the fiscal policy at Rome in this period. Plausibly, some former royal land was allocated to communities as a reward, as the case of the lakes at Selinousia indicates, but the large-scale divestment of all royal property would be unprecedented and radical.[127]

Viewed through this lens, the legislation's core function was to regulate the means by which the *vectigal*—the *decuma* from *provincia Asia*—was to be collected: that is, by a single *societas publicanorum*.[128] The fragmented nature of the territory to be regulated lent itself to exploitation by tax-farmers.[129] By insisting on the method of *censoria locatio*, C. Gracchus benefitted from immediate payment

[124] *RS* 2.48–49, 63–6; Festus 516.14–16L. Rathbone 2003, 152–4; Roselaar 2010, 233–6. On the concept generally: Mommsen 1905 [1862], 127–8; De Martino 1956, 557–79; Lintott 1992, 257; de Ligt 2007, 89–94.

[125] Cic. *Leg. agr.* 2.50–51. Compare 1.5–6.

[126] Contra Magie 1950, 1047–8.

[127] Strabo 14.1.26.

[128] Later comparative evidence demonstrates that taxes were auctioned as single concerns within specific *provinciae*: compare the situation in Sicily in the 70s (Cic. *Verr.* 2.2.171); Asia and Bithynia in the 50s (Cic. *Fam.* 13.9, 65, with Cotton 1986; *Att.* 11.10.1). Broughton 1938, 511; Badian 1972a, 106–7; Cotton 1986, 367–73; Nicolet 2000 [1979], 301–3; Daubner 2006^2, 226–7; Poitras & Geranio 2016, 103–4.

[129] Tan 2017, 42–4.

of a proportion of the contracted amount, allowing immediate return to the treasury and ensuring the swifter realization of his policy goals.[130] The *lex Sempronia*, while reorganizing the collection of the *decuma* in Asia to favour C. Gracchus' goals, did not impose new and unprecedented dues upon the free cities of Asia. This less extreme interpretation of what remained radical legislation, then, shifts the emphasis to the alienation of public lands and the method of collection, rather than imputing a wanton disregard for purportedly free allies.

The general flexibility of Republican legislation regulating taxation is crucial to explaining the evolution of this statute: for example, the *lex portorii Asiae* has repeated recourse to indefinite pronouns with verbs of obligation (e.g., *ἐν οἷς τόποις κατὰ δόγμα συγκλήτου ἢ κατὰ νόμον | [ἢ κατὰ δήμου κύρωσιν δεῖ τειμευτὴν ἢ ὕπ]ατον [τ]ελωνείαν ἐκμισθῶσαι* 'in whatever places by decree of the Senate or *lex* or *plebiscitum*, it is necessary for the censor or consul to lease out the *portorium*'). This, alongside copious reference to current *leges locationis*, left the annual or quinquennial administration of the legislation overwhelmingly to the magistrates in office.[131] The most likely formulation of the *lex Sempronia* laid out the basic conditions and geographic applicability of the law, before leaving its specific administration to each iteration of magistrates. Consequently, as discussed in Chapter 2, the subject-status of many cities in Asia after 85 would make it 'appropriate' for the *decuma*, and likely the *scriptura*, of their territories to be included by administering magistrates in the text of the *locatio*. This is critical as changes in administrative status of civic land and the decisions of magistrates on the ground could have a significant impact even in the absence of legislative change. Taken together, the evidence would suggest that the initial organization of *provincia Asia* was unconcerned with the extraction of public profits from the cities of Asia, although the exploitation of public property—formerly belonging to Attalus—was the subject of political dissension at Rome.

Gubernatorial Jurisdiction and the Free Cities

Beyond his *imperium*, a Roman magistrate also possessed *iurisdictio*, the right to oversee judicial proceedings involving Roman citizens or subjects.[132] Indeed, writing in the late 60s, Cicero noted that, in his opinion: *non sane magna varietas esse negotiorum in administranda Asia, sed ea tota iuris dictione maxime sustineri*

[130] *ILLRP* 518; Cic. *Planc.* 136; *Att.* 1.17.9. Badian 1972a, 75–8; Kay 2014, 77–82. Given the complex eco-system of finance and exchange around public contracts, up-front payment through loans would not have been difficult to achieve and would broaden the appeal of this legislation to the elite writ large. See Polyb. 6.17. Nicolet 1966, 326–39.

[131] E.g., Cottier et al. 2008 ll.9–11, 28–9, 32–4. Cf. the *lex agraria* of 111 (*RS* 2.85–90), with Lintott 1992, 272–5. Spagnuolo Vigorita 1997, 157–8.

[132] Summaries at Mommsen 1887^3, 1.116–161; Lintott 1993, 54–9, 65–9.

('there is not really a great variety of business in the governing of Asia, but this whole province rests mainly on the administration of justice').[133] In the earliest days of the Roman *provincia*, however, the exercise of this power was limited by the general prevalence of civic *ἐλευθερία*. Two honorific decrees from Claros, published in 1989, overturned the consensus on Roman practices of power by providing unequivocal evidence for extensive privileges granted to the *polis* of Colophon. The texts, for Polemaeus and Menippus, emphasize the complexity of local realities and their impact on Roman judicial practice. Both men undertook multiple embassies to Rome and Roman officials in the course of lengthy careers, spanning the latter half of the second century, that is, the transitional period from Attalid possession to Roman protectorate.[134]

Polemaeus made two attested visits to Roman magistrates in Asia. First, when a Colophonian citizen had been condemned *Ῥωμ(α)ϊκῷ κριτηρίωι ἐν τῆι ἐ|παρχείᾳ* ('by a Roman judgement in the *provincia*'), he succeeded in overturning the decision. The text uses stark rhetoric to diminish the agency of the magistrate, claiming that the ambassador *τὸ<ν> γένομενον ἄκυ|ρον ἐποίησεν* ('made him [sc. the commander] powerless').[135] Though, in practice, this need not mean more than reminding him of the community's free status, it is tempting to see a parallel with Menodorus of Pergamum's earlier *παρρήσια* ('outspokenness') in his negotiations with Aquillius and the senatorial commission. Later, Polemaeus persuaded a Roman commander against issuing a *πρόσταγμα* (sc. *edictum*) which would have compromised Colophon's legal autonomy: *πάλιν | τε προστάγματος ἐνεχθέντος | ἐναντίου τοῖς νόμοις κατά τι|νων, ἐπελθὼν ἔπεισε τοὺς | ἡγουμένους ὡς δεῖ τὰ κριτήρια* [———?] ('once again, when an edict was issued against certain men [sc. Colophonian citizens], contrary to our laws, he journeyed and persuaded the hegemons that it was necessary to [reverse?] the decisions').[136] In any case, these examples highlight the extent to which local elites were prepared to challenge robustly Roman decision-making during this formative period, both verbally and in official pronouncements aimed at a Greek audience.

The career of Polemaeus' fellow-citizen, Menippus, underscores the tension between Roman and local jurisdiction. He embarked on five embassies to Rome, of which the final two hold particular significance. The fourth dealt with governors taking on cases which pertained to local issues and demanding surety from Colophonian citizens; the fifth with an accusation levelled against the city before the consuls, and the arraignment of a Colophonian on

[133] Cic. *QFr.* 1.1.20.

[134] *SEG* 39.1243–1244. Robert & Robert 1989, 17–18; Rigsby 2005, 112–15. Given that Menippus was active in the Aristonicus War (*SEG* 39.1244.2.7–8, 33), his embassies date to the late second century; consequently, the Q. Mucius Scaevola named in the text (2.42–46) is likely 'the Augur', governing *c.*120/119. Robert & Robert 1989, 98–9; Ferrary 2017a [1991], 161–2; Lehmann 2000, 223–4 contra Canali De Rossi 1991, 646–8; Eilers 2002, 127.

[135] *SEG* 39.1243.2.51–58.

[136] *SEG* 39.1243.2.58–62. Compare *SEG* 50.1211.20.

a capital charge in Rome.[137] As his honorific inscription makes clear, his diplomatic skill had extensive repercussions:

> *τοὺς δὲ κατοι|κοῦντας τὴν πόλιν ἠλευθέρωσε κατεγγυήσεων | καὶ στρατηγικῆς ἐξουσίας, τῆς ἐπαρχείας ἀπὸ τῆς | αὐτονομίας χωρισθείσης· κυρίους δὲ τοὺς νόμους | τετήρηκεν ἐπὶ παντὸς ἐγκλήματος καὶ πρὸς αὐτοὺς | Ῥωμαίους, τῆς συγκλήτου δεδογματικείας καὶ τὸν | ἀδικοῦντα καὶ τὸν ἐνκαλοῦντά τινι τῶν ἡμε|τέρων πολιτῶν Ῥωμαῖον κρίνεσθαι παρ' ἡμῖν, τόν | τε κατητιαμένον πολίτην ἐπὶ Ῥωμαϊκῶι θανάτωι | καὶ μετάπεμπτον γενόμενον πρὸς ἔγκλημα κεφαλι|κὸν καὶ κριτηρίωι παραδιδόμενον ἅμα τῆι πόλει μετὰ | τῶν νόμων ἀνασέσωκεν* ('He freed the inhabitants of the city from judicial summons and the power of the commander; when the province had been separated from the *autonomia* [sc. the city]. He protected the authority of the laws over all accusations, and even those against Romans themselves, since the Senate decreed that a Roman, whether committing a crime or bringing an accusation against one of our citizens should be judged among us, and he saved that citizen, who was accused of a crime with punishment in the Roman style and summoned on a capital charge and handed over for judgement, preserving at the same time the city and its laws').[138]

These events suggest that Roman magistrates lacked detailed knowledge of or wilfully ignored the rights of free *poleis* in Asia. Given the Apollonius decree implies that the initial senatorial grant referred only to *ἐλευθερία* without further definition, this is understandable.[139] In this case, the city had already received clarification on its local juridical primacy. Yet still Menippus' fifth embassy was necessary. Crucially, the rights of Colophon secured by their ambassador, as viewed by the community, 'freed the residents of the city' from the power of the governor and provincial courts including in cases when Romans were the plaintiff or defendant. This extends far beyond the rights enjoyed by contemporary Sicilian communities.[140] More strikingly, when, it seems, a governor had been asked by the Metropolitans to intervene in a dispute with Colophon, Menippus travelled to Rome and returned with a *senatus consultum* stating in no uncertain terms that: *διότι* ***τῆς ἐπαρχείας ἐκτὸς*** *οὔτε κρίνειν οὔτε πολυπραγμονεῖν τῶι στρατηγῶι καθήκει* ('it is not appropriate for the governor to judge or to interfere *outside of*

[137] *SEG* 39.1244.1.23–31. The clause *ἐπὶ Ῥωμαϊκῶι θανάτωι* historically provoked much controversy. The Roberts (1989, 87) saw this straightforwardly as referring to the murder of a Roman citizen, but Ferrary (2017a [1991], 171–2) objected that the previous embassy established the primacy of local law in all cases. An increasingly popular explanation, first proposed by Lehmann (1998, 162–8, 2000, 234–8; accepted by Sánchez (2010, 41–60), Hamon (2011, *BÉ* #509); Laffi (2010, 15–18) and Ferrary (2017a [1991], 180)), is that this refers to 'punishment in the Roman style' (i.e., flogging and decapitation). In either case, a discrepancy existed between Roman and Colophonian expectations of the legal process.

[138] *SEG* 39.1244.1.37–48.

[139] Kallet-Marx 1995, 115–17; Boffo 2003, 231–5; Fournier 2010, 431.

[140] Kantor 2010, 194–9.

the province').[141] This statement reasserts the basic principle that the city of Colophon, on account of its free status, lay outside the purview of Roman magistrates in *provincia Asia*.

The point at issue is the propensity of Roman commanders to exercise their own *iurisdictio* and disregard local laws. The decision of the Roman Senate to confirm the right of residents to a trial at Colophon under local law in cases involving Roman citizens is critical here. This corresponds to rights agreed through treaties between *poleis* in Asia Minor, including that between Sardis and Ephesus, brokered by Q. Mucius Scaevola.[142] Moreover, the text states that the Romans affirmed a principle that the *polis* was distinct from and external to the *provincia*.[143] This reinforces the view that the Senate initially respected the independence and territorial integrity of local communities in Asia. In this context specifically, however, the judicial ramifications of this decision become clear. If communities stood outside of the purview of the Roman administration, then, Roman magistrates held no legitimate jurisdiction over their citizens in intra-civic disputes.[144] *Pace* Fournier, who argues that these privileges were exceptional to Colophon, this was the logical consequence of Roman respect for the ἐλευθερία confirmed by the Senate after 133: a free city stood beyond the *imperium* and *iurisdictio* of a Roman commander.[145] However, the potential benefits of imposing Roman jurisdiction offered clear incentives to challenge this status. The collection of *vadimonia* (Gr. ἐγγύας, 'bond' or 'security' in the event of non-appearance at tribunal) from individuals could be lucrative and effective means for locals to hold magistrates to account were lacking.[146] Powerful incentives also existed for Roman citizens at law to encourage gubernatorial intervention or at least the application of Roman law in their cases. Similarly, the *publicani* had the direct motivation of greater profits encouraging them to roll back or ignore the boundaries of the civic territories.[147] While most *poleis* would already *stricto sensu* have possessed the right to use their own laws, the epigraphic evidence highlights the contested nature of that judicial autonomy.

Scaevola's governorship in the early 90s offers another view of this exchange. The sources uniformly present him as a unique *exemplum* of virtuous government. Two especially praiseworthy qualities were his non-interference in the judicial affairs of the *poleis* and his defence of the populace of Asia against abuses

141 *SEG* 39.1244.2.5.

142 Ager 1996, 501–2; Laffi 2010, 19–24.

143 *SEG* 39.1244.1.38–39.

144 Compare the clause from a *senatus consultum* of 60, later included in the *lex Iulia de repetundis*, explicitly forbidding governors from exercising their *iurisdictio* in matters of debts contracted by free cities to Roman moneylenders (Cic. *Prov. cons.* 6–7, 57; *Att.* 1.19.9, 2.1.10. Morrell 2017, 148–51). These empire-wide acts established the principle for communities, e.g., in Sicily, beyond those which already enjoyed the use of their own law in disputes with Romans.

145 *Pace* Fournier 2010, 429–30. Laffi 2010, 31–2; Boffo 2003, 238–47; Dmitriev 2017, 203–6; contra Guerber (2009, 451–3) who believes a specific treaty was necessary to clarify the rights of each free community.

146 Ferrary 1999, 78–82. On *vadimonia*: Metzger 2005.

147 Czajkowski 2019, 121–2.

perpetrated by the *publicani*.[148] The most complete source is Diodorus Siculus, who may have drawn on the work of Posidonius of Apamea, a contemporary resident of nearby Rhodes.[149] He emphasizes that Scaevola's conduct was notable for its strict application of the law: he dismissed false accusations, appointed honest judges, and both issued and exacted the correct penalty, even in capital cases. He also ensured that the rights of *poleis* to use their own laws were respected, a trait echoed by Cicero in 51/50, if with a degree of scorn.[150] In this, Scaevola appears exceptional, as his reception by later authors demonstrates.[151]

The internal dynamics of Roman elite society further drove this conflict: though the power of an individual commander within his *provincia* was substantial choosing to oppose wealthy and influential *negotiatores* or *publicani* could bring dire consequences.[152] Famously, Scaevola and his staff faced bitter recriminations on their return to Rome, with his *legatus*, P. Rutilius Rufus charged with extortion and sent into exile.[153] The concern for balancing justice for the inhabitants of the province and self-preservation was a live issue throughout the period. The Senate as a collective body was less subject to the pressures than individual commanders: as an institution representing the collective will of the former magistrates, its utterances demanded respect. It is, in this sense, unsurprising that so many commanders took refuge in referring cases of allied discontent back to the Senate.

Even so, commanders on the ground could act on their own initiative. Five fragments, discovered at Pergamum, produced two near-identical letters from Scaevola himself, described as ἀνθύπατος Ῥωμαίων, to two cities, and a treaty between the cities of Ephesus and Sardis.[154] The letters focused on a dispute between the two *poleis* which had disrupted the planned institution of new penteteric games in the governor's honour.[155] Scaevola writes that he had been told that both Ephesus and Sardis had withdrawn from the planned celebration as a result.[156] The commander sent an *amicus*, an Athenian, to persuade the two cities to come to an agreement, and the treaty appears to have been the result of mediation by Pergamum. It is noteworthy that Scaevola chose to send a Greek representative to persuade the two disputants to submit to arbitration. However,

[148] Scaevola: Diod. Sic. 37.6; Cic. *Planc.* 33; *Att.* 5.17.5; 6.1.15; *Fam.* 1.9.26; Livy, *Per.* 70.8; Val. Max. 8.15.6. Badian 1972a, 89–92; Ferriès & Delrieux 2011, 207–30; Ferrary 2018, 11–21. On the date of Scaevola's command: Ferrary 2012, 157–79 with full literature nn.1–8; Rafferty 2019, 210–13 contra Badian 1956, 104–25.

[149] Kallet-Marx 1995, 143.

[150] Cic. *Att.* 6.1.15.

[151] Ferriès & Delrieux, 2011, 218–19.

[152] Meier 1966, 82–6; Davenport 2019, 84–93.

[153] Badian 1972a, 90–2, with references. Kallet-Marx (1990, 123–6) highlights the prominence of Rutilius himself in crafting this tradition and the close ties between Cicero, a major source, and Scaevola. The role of the *publicani* in orchestrating the trial is incontestable, however. On the courts: Sherwin-White 1982, 18–31; Davenport 2019, 75–93.

[154] Laffi 2010a, for previous editions, 15; Ferriès & Delrieux 2011, 218–19 contra Rigsby 1988, 141–2.

[155] For the *Soteria kai Moukieia*, see Rigsby 1988, 145–9; Thériault 2011, 377–80.

[156] Laffi 2010a 2.A+B.1–8.

we may see this as a sign of respect for the autonomy of Ephesus and Sardis or a sign that they were more suited to the task than a member of the gubernatorial *consilium*.[157] The clauses regulating judicial relations between the two cities are significant insofar as they underscore the point that Roman (pro)magistrates would not normally be expected to intervene in cases of a local character. This further highlights Kantor's point that, in this period, inter-community lawsuits were governed by existing inter-civic agreements, rather than mediated through Roman courts.[158] Instead, the treaty between Sardis and Ephesus should be taken as evidence for the continued vibrancy of inter-civic judicial relations, even if with the mediation of Roman officials.[159]

A final example emerges from Cicero's prosecution of Verres, in which he recounts an incident involving the *quaestor* M. Aurelius Scaurus and the city of Ephesus, most likely in the mid-90s:[160]

> *nuper M. Aurelio Scauro postulante, quod is Ephesi se quaestorem vi prohibitum esse dicebat quo minus e fano Dianae servum suum, qui in illud asylum confugisset, abduceret, Pericles Ephesius, homo nobilissimus, Romam evocatus est, quod auctor illius iniuriae fuisse arguebatur.* ('Recently, when M. Aurelius Scaurus demanded it, because he said that as *quaestor* at Ephesus he was prevented by force from retrieving his slave from the temple of Artemis, where he had fled for asylum, Pericles of Ephesus, a most noble man was summoned to Rome, since he was accused of being the author of that injury').[161]

Crucially, Cicero here contrasts the 'appropriate' severity of Scaurus in defending the dignity of his magistracy with Verres' failure to prosecute the ringleaders of a riot in Lampsacus.[162] Pericles may even have been charged formally, before Ephesus became officially subject to the *iurisdictio* of the commander; while the Colophon inscriptions demonstrate the willingness of the Senate to intervene, they show that magistrates had fewer qualms. Cicero does not adduce any punishment for Pericles, however, and a diplomatic intervention, like that of Menippus, may have saved him from further consequences.[163]

The Roberts correctly emphasized the critical role of persuasion in both Colophonian cases, however, it does not follow that the Roman state had

[157] Laffi 2010a 2.C.1–14. *Pace* Rigsby 1988, 143. [158] Kantor 2010, 195–6.

[159] Scaevola possibly had input, but the treaty was likely mediated by Pergamum without significant interference. The outcome, not the process, held primary importance to Roman administrators (*pace* Laffi 2010a, 113–14).

[160] Sumner 1973, 79–82; Badian 1984, 298–301 (cf. 1964, 86–7).

[161] Cic. *Verr.* 2.1.85. [162] Cic. *Verr.* 2.1.63–85. Steel 2004, 233–51.

[163] Ferrary's characterization 2017 [1991], 176) of this incident as evidence of 'un net déclin de l'autonomie des cités libres' is uncertain; compare Laffi 2010, 36–40. Compare Timotheus of Dyme: *SEG* 45.417.24–27. Kallet-Marx 1995a, 140.

uniformly and firmly asserted its authority over local jurisdiction in *poleis*.[164] Although our evidence may be tilted in favour of successful claims, the regularity with which the two Colophonians achieved success suggests that the norm was for general respect towards civic autonomy. The shift in significance between embassies to commanders, undertaken by Polemaeus, and embassies to the Senate, as pursued regularly by Menippus, points towards a burgeoning understanding of the Roman institutional hierarchy and its limiting factors. While an individual commander might agree to respect Colophon's freedoms, his successor could, through ignorance or self-interest, choose not to.[165] In turn, this forced cities to more regularly find citizens to undertake expensive—and dangerous—embassies to Rome to defend their interests. While not a deliberate strategy by the state, the actions of Roman citizens and magistrates undeniably had a significant impact on provincial life.

Republican *cistophori* in Post-Attalid Asia

Under Roman hegemony, the production of Attalid *cistophori* continued at Ephesus and Pergamum without interruption or changes in imagery. As Carbone has shown, average annual output increased during the first five decades of Roman governorship, largely due to a major increase in production in *c.*105/104. Although no catalyst is obvious in the sources, production at both centres went from *c.*3 observed obverse dies p.a. in the previous two decades to *c.*20 for that year. Both mints continued to produce at an increased rate (*c.*9.3 observed obverse dies p.a.) until 99/98, before tailing off.[166] In the same period, other cistophoric mints, which had not produced coinage since the Attalid period once again began to strike in this period. Hoard evidence for Trallian issues suggest that these recommenced only shortly before 105/104.[167] Mints at Laodicea-on-the-Lycus and Apamea appear to have begun production in the 90s, while Nysa's series can now be re-dated to the late 90s.[168] Meanwhile Smyrna, which, though a significant city, had never previously struck *cistophori* began a series at around the turn of the century.[169] Kinns argued that Smyrna was asked to mint *cistophori* by the Roman authorities for a specific purpose—notwithstanding the epichoric character of their imagery and legends—and it seems plausible that the Romans were involved in supporting the minting of

[164] Robert & Robert 1989, 39. Compare *I.Priene*^{2} 67.117, 139–42.

[165] The interests of *publicani* and the Roman diaspora provided a pull factor. Lintott 1993, 44–5; Kallet-Marx 1995, 115–17; Boffo 2003, 231–5 contra Corvino 2016, 161–3. Rigsby's solution (2005, 112–15) is unnecessarily elaborate.

[166] Kinns 1987, 109; Carbone 2020, 83–8, 117–21. For the methodology employed to estimate production from observed dies, see Esty 2006.

[167] Carbone 2020, 151–6.

[168] Carbone 2020, 161–2, 167–72, 183–5; *pace* Metcalf 2015.

[169] Carbone 2020, 187–90.

coins at these revived centres, leaving the cities themselves responsible for the actual production.[170]

This gradual and co-ordinated reintroduction of Attalid mints into Roman monetary supply elucidates two points. First, that there was a perceived need for higher production of coins at the provincial level. Though we know of no particular crisis in Asia from *c.*105–95, Carbone has highlighted the reduced supply of coinage from other sources, such as royal and autonomous civic issues in the post-Attalid period.[171] It is likely that Roman administrators recognized a problem in the monetary supply and sought to rectify this through the authorization of new, though largely historic Attalid, mints. That said, clear elements of local agency persisted: Ephesus' use of their own civic era appears to have been matched by Smyrna and Nysa, while, by the late 90s, Pergamum seems to have included the names of civic *prytaneis* on their issues.[172] Tralles' particular focus on producing cistophoric fractions carried over from its earlier issues. As noted, these fractions integrated well with Carian coinages on the plinthophoric standard, while as Meadows highlights the cistophoric *diobol* also had near-equivalence with the Roman *sestertius*. If we accept Kaye's argument that the specialization of Tralles was linked to the particular monetary needs of the region, this provides further confirmation for local decision-making in minting.[173]

Second, this gradual process of reviving Attalid mints and adding a new participant in Smyrna suggests a link between Attalid mints, the road system of Aquillius, and the *conventus*. Certainly, Aquillius' milestones asserted Roman authority through reorientating Attalid space into provincial framework. However, as French emphasized, the proconsul's work was almost certainly restricted to refurbishing existing Attalid routes.[174] The nodal points along this network were already major centres within the Attalid administration and largely existing mints. Consequently, they were prime candidates for organically developing a *conventus* to serve the needs of the Roman inhabitants. Roman cistophoric mints were continuations of Attalid mints, rather than specifically chosen Roman administrative centres as Carbone, for example, contends.[175] The singular exception of Smyrna can be explained through its significance within the region. Roman ambitions extended to ensuring a functional monetary supply within the province but not to determining its nature. This followed the path of least resistance in light of Ephesus' decision in 134/133 to continue minting civic style *cistophori*, possibly already followed by Pergamum. Moreover, this choice on the part of Roman authorities to take a hands-off approach to minting within the region fits

[170] Kinns 1987, 108. [171] Carbone 2020, 226–32. Cf. Kinns 1987, 109; Burnett 2022, 21–5.

[172] Smyrna/Nysa: Carbone 2020, 185 n.8, 188 n.4. Pergamum: Kleiner 1978, 79, 103–4.

[173] Kleiner 1972, 30–2; Carbone 2020, 148–51; Kaye 2022, 152–63. On this denomination: Ashton, Kinns, & Meadows 2014, 17–19.

[174] French 1997, 179–87.

[175] *Pace* Carbone 2020, 14–33; see discussion at 'The Emergence of the *conventus iuridici*'.

with the general attitude shown by Aquillius towards the freedom of formerly Attalid cities.

Finally, the evidence of die-studies shows that a major spike in production occurred in 90/89, coinciding with the outbreak of the First Mithridatic War. The mints at Pergamum (9 observed tetradrachm equiv. dies), Ephesus (11), and Tralles (9) suddenly produce coins at much higher rates. For Ephesus, this represents a fourfold increase; for Tralles, nearly tenfold.[176] Meanwhile, the evidence of the 90/89 hoard has redated the commencement of Nysa's cistophoric sequence to this year, possibly under the authority of Pythion, son of Chaeremon, a noted Roman sympathizer.[177] This clearly coincides with increased need by Roman authorities for coin to meet military expenses and demonstrates a high degree of co-ordination between the mints and Roman authorities. This fits with the general pattern of Romans commandeering and using local currencies to pay military expenses, but does not necessarily indicate any long-term articulation of fiscal policy.[178]

There are earlier indications of overt Roman involvement in the production and supply of coinage. An unparalleled issue of *cistophori* from Ephesus, dated to year 13 (= 122/121) bears the reverse legend C. AT(monogram)I|N. C. F.[179] The same inscription appears on an Ephesian gold stater, which should also be dated to this year.[180] In both cases, the text is in Latin and omits any title, though as Stumpf notes, the signer must have been a governor and is best identified with the plebeian tribune of 131/130: C. Atinius Labeo Macerio.[181] The reasons for his association with the coinage cannot be reconstructed. The historiographical and epigraphic sources provide no hints, while production rates seem to have been stable in this period. Aside from the inclusion of Atinius' name, the types are entirely standard.[182] The most that can be said is that Atinius was involved in the process, whether, for example, through requesting the issue of coinage or, more practically, in supplying the bullion. Carian Stratonicea also issued drachms bearing the Roman name *ΓΑΙΟΣ* (i.e., Gaius), apparently as a mint magistrate, possibly during the First Mithridatic War.[183] While Carbone suggests that this indicates Roman 'interference' in local minting practice, the context of the military emergency and the absence of a meaningful number of Roman troops in the region may indicate that this 'Gaius' was in fact a long-term resident embedded

[176] Carbone 2020, 120–1, 158–9. [177] Carbone 2020, 183–5 contra Metcalf 2015, 315–17.

[178] Giovannini 1978; de Callataÿ 2016; critiqued astutely by Burnett 2022.

[179] Stumpf 1985, 187–8; 1991, 6–12. De Callataÿ (2011, 61) notes that unsigned *cistophori* from this year also exist and seem to have been struck after the Atinius issue.

[180] French 1991.

[181] Stumpf 1985, 187–8. On Atinius: Cic. *dom.* 123; Liv. *Per.* 59; Plin. *N.H.* 7.143; *I.Priene*² 75.

[182] French 1991, 202–3.

[183] Meadows 2002, 91, 122–3 (group 3, #3, 4); 2022, 160–1 acknowledges the potential for a date in the 40s. Another issue, perhaps from Adramytteum, bearing the legend *ΑΣΙΝΙΟΥ ΑΝΘΥΠΑΤΟΥ ΡΩΜΑΙΩΝ* is also of uncertain date, though most likely the 30s (Grant 1946, 394–6; Kinns 1987, 118, n. 57).

within the community.[184] As Meadows notes, the personal risk in including personal names on coinage in the context of resistance to Mithridates suggests a performative display of loyalty by pro-Roman elements, within which the inclusion of a locally respected Roman would make sense. This should not be seen as deliberate interference, but rather an indication of the increasing interpenetration of Roman and local governance.[185]

The end of the Attalid dynasty had an impact on bronze coinage issues at Pergamum. Prior to 133, the royal treasury issued bronze in various types with the legend *ΦΙΛΕΤΑΙΡΟΥ*, referring to the dynastic founder.[186] However, after the death of Attalus III, these cease and three new types appear, bearing on their obverse *ΑΣΚΛΗΠΙΟΥ ΣΟΤΗΡΟΣ*, *ΑΘΗΝΑ ΝΙΚΕΦΟΡΟΥ*, or *ΠΕΡΓΑΜΗΝΩΝ*. Chameroy has plausibly argued that these types were issued by the temples of Asclepius and Athena, or the civic authorities respectively, likely in parallel, to meet their particular expenses.[187] More broadly, civic bronze issues were unaffected by the advent of Roman hegemony. As Galani's recent survey has shown, iconography, the use of ethnics, and legends continued to follow traditional patterns throughout the first century. The administrative organization of the province through the *conventus* has no visible impact on the minting practices of communities.[188] That said, the emergence of bronze coinage in Phrygia after the First Mithridatic War seems to be connected to the increasing presence of the Roman diaspora in the region.[189] However, throughout the period, notwithstanding patterns of devaluation in times of crisis, bronze issues were largely unaffected.[190]

This, in turn, highlights how, in addition to *cistophori*, autonomous, and civic coinages were long-standing traditions within the region. Despite largely corresponding to a few inter-*polis* weight standards, these types were generally intended to fulfil a primarily local need and circulate locally. Notably, prior to the establishment of Roman hegemony, the juridical status of communities seems not to have determined their capacity to mint autonomous coinages, as the example of Attalid Ephesus, which minted 'bee' and 'stag'-type coinages, demonstrates.[191] Though Carbone notes a decline in the number of cities issuing civic types in the aftermath of the war with Aristonicus, most had already ceased to mint in the 140s. Those which continued to mint were unevenly distributed, with numerous Carian communities joined by five in the Troad.[192]

[184] *Pace* Carbone 2014, 16–18.

[185] Meadows 2002, 123. Compare also *ΚΟΙΝΤΟΣ* (Quintus) at Athens in 89/8 and 86/85: de Callataÿ 2011, 64.

[186] Chameroy 2012, 140–7.

[187] Chameroy 2012, 147–54; 2013, 714–18 contra Marcellesi 2012, 86, 114, 167.

[188] Galani 2022, 114–15, 118–20.

[189] Thonemann 2013a, 28–31.

[190] Harl 1996, 109–10; Bransbourg 2021, 116.

[191] Ephesus: Kinns 1999. Carbone 2014, 14–16.

[192] For a full list, Carbone 2014, 19 n.84.

In summary, the initial Roman approach to the coinage of Asia matches their limited ambitions in administration during the late second century. *Cistophori* continued to be issued and came to act as a de facto provincial coinage. Local mints seem to have had greater autonomy to experiment with iconography and ethnics, while Roman officials intervened where necessary to support the monetary system. We may, for example, see the increased production and re-opening of Attalid mints as the result of a perceived need by Roman governors for greater monetary supply. Nevertheless, the overall policy was entirely conservative.

Summary

The Attalid kingdom, upon the death of its last independent ruler in 134/133, was a relatively cohesive entity with substantially effective administrative institutions. The unique circumstances surrounding extension of Roman hegemony over the region—one populated with Roman allies and annexed without a war of conquest—explains the apparent absence of overt gubernatorial interference in the period which followed. Based on the available evidence, Roman administration between 133 and 88 was neither wide-ranging nor intensive. Most civic communities were freed from taxation, although the former *βασιλικὴ χώρα* continued to be exploited through agents of the state. Though the *publicani* routinely attempted to rezone parts of civic territory and assets for their own private profit, the Senate seems to have taken complaints seriously. From a judicial perspective, similar principles applied. Civic jurisdiction over cases involving local citizens, as asserted by Menippus of Colophon, could be contested by individual Romans and governors alike. However, our evidence suggests that, when consulted, the Senate generally respected local claims. The grant of freedom to the communities of the former Attalid kingdom had significance both for its recipients and for Roman actors but created an unusual and conflicting socio-legal environment for governors to negotiate. Without claiming that the advent of Roman hegemony had a negligible impact on the agency of the inhabitants of Asia, the ambitions of the state remained limited in the initial post-Attalid period.

2

The Government of Asia during the Late Republic, 81–49 BCE

In 89 the Roman presence in western Asia was abruptly challenged. Goaded by the collusion of Roman officials with his enemy, Nicomedes III of Bithynia, Mithridates VI Eupator invaded the province in force.[1] Brushing aside poorly organized resistance, Mithridates drove Roman officials out of Asia entirely. In the absence of a Roman military presence, most *poleis* co-operated with his demands. Shortly afterwards, Mithridates ordered the massacre of Romans and Italians remaining in western Asia Minor. Again, many communities followed this command, allegedly resulting in 80,000 deaths.[2] Traditionally, scholars have explained this collaboration as reprisals for Roman brutality.[3] However, abuses at the hands of the *publicani*, facilitated by governors, though real, fell disproportionately outside the *poleis* in the period before the so-called 'Asian Vespers'. Without minimizing the trauma experienced by individuals and communities, Bernhardt rightly emphasizes the importance of the immediate circumstances to the cities' decisions. One decree passed at Ephesus in late 86 or early 85, in a bold attempt to rewrite recent history, claimed that Mithridates *ἐκράτησεν* ('conquered') the city, *[τῶι] τε πλήθει τῶν δυνάμεων καὶ τῶι ἀπροδοκήτωι τῆς ἐπιβολῆς* ('through the vastness of his [Mithridates'] forces and the suddenness of his attack').[4] Even within Mithridatizing communities, significant pockets of opposition existed. Several cities would revolt against the Pontic king swiftly, when the opportunity arose.[5] However, given the swift evaporation of Roman-led resistance in 89, the overwhelming force of Mithridates, and the difficulties faced by Rome in the Social War with its Italian neighbours, it was far from clear that Roman hegemony would be re-established in *provincia Asia*.

[1] Sherwin-White 1984, 112–20, with references.

[2] Cic. *Imp. Pomp.* 7; App. *Mith.* 21–22; Memnon *FGrH* 434 F22.9; Vell. Pat. 2.18.2; Plut. *Sull.* 24.4; Val. Max. 9.2.ext.3.

[3] Magie 1950, 176; Amiotti 1980, 132–9; Thornton 1998, 271–90.

[4] *I.Eph.* 8.7–8. Bernhardt 1985, 33–64; Kallet-Marx 1995, 153–8, 284–5; Buraselis 2000, 122–3.

[5] McGing 1986, 108–18; Marek 1988, 294–302; Campanile 1996, 146–73; Niebergall 2011, 7–20; 2011a, 67–70. Note the presence of pro-Roman individuals and groups within Asia from 88–85, including Chaeremon of Nysa (*RDGE* 48; *RC* 73b–74) and Pyrrha[kos] of Alabanda (*SEG* 60.1073). Niebergall (2011, 7–8) provides a full list of cities which continued to resist after the defeat of the Roman commanders.

Imperial Power, Provincial Government, and the Emergence of Roman Asia, 133 BCE–14 CE. Bradley Jordan, Oxford University Press. © Bradley Jordan 2023. DOI: 10.1093/oso/9780198887065.003.0003

Despite the pressures in Italy and ructions over the command against Mithridates—resulting in civil war and two separate mutually hostile armies, under L. Cornelius Sulla and C. Flavius Fimbria respectively, being despatched to Asia—after four years of conflict, Sulla achieved strategic success. Eager to return to Italy and confront his antagonists, he concluded an agreement with Mithridates at Dardanus in 85, returning the geopolitical situation to the *status quo ante bellum* in exchange for the payment of an indemnity and the loan of a fleet. This restored Macedonia, Greece, and Asia to Roman hegemony and re-established the allied rulers of Bithynia and Cappadocia whom Mithridates had deposed. Plutarch emphasizes the restiveness of Sulla's troops, partly due to Mithridates' lenient treatment, partly the Pontic ruler's retention of the spoils of Asia. The sources stress that Sulla's compact with Mithridates aimed at acquiring resources for his return to Italy.[6] Irrespective of whether either party viewed the arrangement as temporary, it offered Sulla, in the short term, space to organize his Italian campaign.[7]

Sulla and the Settlement of Asia

After Dardanus, Sulla, though still beset by civil war, had the opportunity to reinvent the administration of Roman Asia. The initial collaboration of most cities with Mithridates made the recovery of the region by Roman arms almost a conquest and afforded the proconsul a free hand in dealing with many individual communities. Late that year, Sulla summoned civic representatives to Ephesus and took three major decisions, one political and two financial. First, some named *poleis* were to be 'free': the logical corollary, most cities were not.[8] This had an immediate symbolic effect and encapsulated the shift in power dynamics: Sulla could not allow the *poleis* to go unpunished, irrespective of his own fragile position, with a chastened but undefeated Mithridates on the horizon, a disaffected army, and opponents in Rome mobilizing forces against him. The

[6] Memnon *FGrH* 424 25.2–26.4; App. *Mith.* 56–58; Vell. Pat. 2.23.6; Plut. *Sull.* 22.1–24.4; Gran. Lic. 70. Cf. Livy, *Per.* 83.7; Strabo 13.1.28. The agreement was never ratified by the Senate: Glew 1981, 109–30.

[7] E.g., Kallet-Marx (1995, 262–5) infers that Sulla did not insist on Mithridates' compliance with all aspects of the agreement.

[8] Appian (*Mith.* 61) names Rhodes and Lycia (both outside the province), Chios, Ilium, and 'Magnesia', adding 'some others'; epigraphic evidence confirms Carian Stratonicea, Tabae, Alabanda, Aphrodisias, and Astypalaea; Cicero's *Verrines* implies strongly that Lampsacus was free (*Verr.* 2.1.81). Santangelo (2006, 133–4) and Kinns (2006, 41–8) both identify Appian's Magnesia as Magnesia-under-Sipylos (Livy, *Per.* 81.2). Strabo may imply Cyzicus retained its freedom even before its heroics during the Third Mithridatic War (12.8.11, with Heller 2006, 71–6). Santangelo discusses Byzantium, Sardis, Halicarnassus, Apollonis, and Smyrna as possibilities, while Buraselis (2000, 17–20 with *I.Cos* 229.7–9) adds Cos. Finally, Guerber (1995, 409 n.60) suggests that *I.Eph.* 1201–1202 could indicate that it retained its freedom or, more likely, had it restored before the end of the first century BCE. See Jones (1971², 62–4), and table of Santangelo (2007, 122–3) with references.

incorporation of southern Caria and the Troad into *provincia Asia* should be dated to this period, after some *poleis*, notably Caunus, sided with Mithridates.[9] Second, he imposed an extraordinary exaction, which Plutarch calculates at 20,000 talents, equivalent to five years of tribute and his war expenses on the subject cities.[10] Finally, he despatched troops to the cities to collect the money, with instructions that they should be billeted at local expense and paid a hefty allowance of 4 tetradrachms *per diem* and other benefits; *tribuni militum* received 50 drachms.[11] The outrageous allowance served twin purposes of assuaging his troops' desire for plunder while incentivizing swift collection on the part of the *poleis*.[12] Both the fine and the soldiers' allowance were tied to his immediate military needs and were an ad hoc response to his particular circumstances. After three years of warfare with no support from Rome and about to embark on a potentially protracted civil war, Sulla needed both his troops' loyalty and a war-chest, especially given his reluctance to forage in Italy.[13] With the absence of earlier systemic exploitation, the explanation that Sulla sought to re-establish Rome's revenues holds little water.[14] While his opponents held Rome, the orderly extraction of taxes was irrelevant to his goals: he needed cash on hand. State-level fiscal considerations were almost certainly not germane to his decisions, and political and military exigencies explain Sulla's attested policies perfectly well.

Some evidence does hint at a Sullan project to streamline government in Asia. Though Giovannini has disproved persistent suggestions that Sulla, as dictator, promulgated a *lex Cornelia de provinciis* aimed at reforming provincial government across the empire, references to *leges Corneliae* in Asia continue to be linked to his actions.[15] Specifically, Santangelo suggests they derive from a *lex* or *leges datae* issued at, or shortly after, the settlement at Ephesus. The *lex Valeria* of 82, retroactively recognizing the validity of Sulla's *acta*, placed these decisions on a firmer footing.[16] Three references may pertain to Sullan provincial legislation. In 9/8, when the provincial calendar was reorientated around Augustus' birthday, the *koinon* of Asia decreed that local elections should continue to take place within the

[9] Marek 1988, 302–8; Dmitriev 2005, 103–6; Vitale 2012, 84–5.

[10] Plut. *Sull.* 25.2; *Luc.* 4.1; App. *Mith.* 62. Böttcher 1915, 56–62; Broughton 1938, 561; Santangelo 2007, 114. It should be noted here that there is no necessary requirement that the 'tribute' pre-dated this period, especially considering the new *discriptio* upon which this was based (Cassiod. *Chron.* p. 130 (Mommsen); Cic. *Flacc.* 32, *QFr.* 1.1.33. Merola 2001, 108–9, 177–9).

[11] Plut. *Sull.* 25.2. Magie (1950, 1115) and Kallet-Marx (1995, 266–7) highlight that the demands were unusually high. Sallust's claim that Sulla's troops were corrupted by the wealth of Asia, though often interpreted as referring general booty, may also allude to this incident (*Hist.* 1.13; *Cat.* 11.5–6). Cf. Mastrocinque 1999, 91; Santangelo 2007, 108, 113.

[12] Keaveney 2005, 297–8.

[13] Plut. *Sull.* 27.3. Zoumbaki 2018, 354–7.

[14] E.g., Santangelo 2007, 112; Dreyer 2015, 209–10.

[15] Giovannini 1983, 75–101, with reference to Mommsen 1887^3, 94–7. More recent discussion: Santangelo 2007, 117–18, with nn.42–45; Coudry & Kirbihler 2010, 138–69.

[16] Frederiksen 1965, 189; Santangelo 2007, 120.

first ten days of the tenth month, under the terms of a *lex Cornelia*.[17] However, a concern with standardizing local political calendars fits more neatly into an Augustan context. This rule could easily be ascribed to other Cornelii who governed Asia, and P. Cornelius Scipio, governor in *c*.12–10, is a potential author.[18] At Thyatira, a document cites a *lex Cornelia* regulating a διάταξις, though the fragmentary nature of the text leaves the precise meaning unclear.[19] Finally, Cicero, while governor in Cilicia, reminded communities in Phrygia Epictetus to respect a *lex Cornelia* which limited expenditure on embassies. Santangelo suggests that Cicero consciously drew on provincial legislation for Asia due to its effectiveness. However, the location of this community in Phrygia may be significant. Certainly, it formed part of *provincia Asia* before 56.[20] Suggestions that the passage cited by Cicero formed part of a comitial law *de repetundis* or *de maiestate* are also plausible.[21] These examples neatly show the range of potential legislation which could have been introduced by Sulla during his command, which directly regulated local political and fiscal action, though, significantly, not legal practice.[22] Evidence linking these examples specifically to Sulla is limited; though collectively they demonstrate the capacity for late Republican governors to affect local institutions.

Fear and Loathing in Late Republican Asia: The Long Shadow of Sulla

Roman Taxation after Sulla's Settlement

In funding his own military activities through the co-ordinated extraction of communities' wealth across the province, Sulla was engaging in something new. Typically, at the conclusion of a military campaign, a defeated opponent would agree to an indemnity as the price of peace; as Mithridates appears to have done after Dardanus.[23] However, in imposing a collective penalty on the inhabitants of the *provincia*, which had, by-and-large, abandoned Mithridates, and collecting it systematically through his troops, Sulla inaugurated a new era of Roman rapacity

[17] *RDGE* 65.d.82–84. Leschhorn (1993, 216–21, followed by Santangelo 2007, 121 n.59 contra Coudry & Kirbihler 2010, 163–4) argues prudently that the adoption of the Sullan era was a spontaneous local development rather than imposed by Sulla.

[18] Date: Eilers 2001, 201–5.

[19] *IGR* 4.1188; though, given the references elsewhere in the document to fiscal issues, it should pertain to local finances (Coudry & Kirbihler 2010, 143–6). Compare the letter at Thyatira dealing with financial acts (*RDGE* 66.4–8), ascribed to the aforementioned P. Cornelius Scipio, another candidate for issuing this *lex data*.

[20] Cic. *Fam.* 3.10.6. Morrell (2017, 240 n.16) notes that Cicero did not insist that the communities follow the *lex*; *pace* Santangelo 2007, 119–20.

[21] Ridley 1975, 100; Campanile 2001, 254.

[22] Hoyos 1973, 49–50.

[23] For indemnities as a proportion of state income in the second century: Frank 1933, 127–38.

towards allied communities. His lead was subsequently followed by a succession of commanders engaged or successful in civil wars, needing coin to pay troops across the first century.[24] At this juncture, our sources state that some cities paid to be granted *immunitas*, which was later revoked by the Senate.[25] Sulla's response to the specific set of circumstances facing him, namely provincial communities which had aided (or failed to robustly resist) an enemy of Rome, restive troops, and further conflict on the horizon, led him to rigorously seize resources from the cities of Asia, and laid down a blueprint for his emulators in the following generation.

When Sulla addressed the assembled representatives of Asia at Ephesus, no framework to collect such large sums of cash existed and, in any case, the existing network of *publicani* had been disrupted by the 'Asian Vespers'.[26] A notice in Cassiodorus' *Chronicon*, from the fifth century CE, sheds light on his solution. Under the year 84, Cassiodorus states: *his cons(ulibu)s Asiam in XLIIII regiones Sylla distribuit* ('under these consuls, Sulla divided Asia into 44 *regiones*').[27] This is insufficient to represent the number of *poleis* within Asia, while the earliest evidence for the *conventus* implies that there were twelve districts, which precludes an easy identification with this organizing principle.[28] Given that these later districts necessarily contained varying numbers of *poleis* of differing prosperity, this Sullan *discriptio* may well reflect a more efficient or negotiated means of dividing the penalty. Although the formula was employed by later commanders, notably Cn. Pompeius Magnus and L. Valerius Flaccus, it also does not relate obviously to the routine collection of provincial taxes.[29] Accordingly, the forty-four *regiones* should represent another ad hoc measure designed for efficiency, which, together with the heavy *per diem* allowances for the troops exacting the money incentivized cities to pay swiftly.[30] This reflects Sulla's unprecedented position and need for haste. His exactions from Asia were not regular contributions to the state, but an irregular and spontaneous levy to satisfy his military needs.

Nevertheless, the concurrent decision to strip most *poleis* in *provincia Asia* of their freedom, and subject them to direct Roman rule for the first time, was far reaching. It exposed their citizens and territories to regular Roman taxation, already exacted on non-civic territories in the province in the form of the *decuma*

[24] Pompeians: Caes. *BC.* 3.31–33, 105; Caesar: Caes. *BCiv.* 3.105; App. *BCiv.* 2.92; CD. 42.491–50.5; Brutus and Cassius: App. *BCiv.* 4.63–82; CD. 47.31.1–4, 33.1–34.6; Plut. *Brut.* 30.1–32.4; Val. Max. 1.5.8; Vell. Pat. 2.69.6; Antonius: App. *BCiv.* 5.4–6; Plut. *Ant.* 23.1–24.5; Joseph. *BJ* 1.242.

[25] Cic. *Off.* 3.87. Mastrocinque 1999, 92. Cf. Sall. *Hist.* 1.77.20; *RDGE* 23.41–42.

[26] Brunt 1990a [1956], 1–8 contra Delplace 1977, 246–7.

[27] Cassiod. *Chron.* 1.483–484.

[28] Broughton 1938, 518–19; Magie 1950, 1116; Merola 2001, 177–9; *pace* Gray 1978, 971–4; Mitchell 1999, 29–30; Kantor 2014, 256–7.

[29] Cic. *Flacc.* 32–33. Marshall 1966, 234 n.12; Bertrand 1978, 803–4; Merola 2001, 64–5; Le Teuff 2010, 208; *pace* Santangelo 2007, 116–17.

[30] Cassiod. *Chron.* 670 p. 132 (Mommsen). Fröhlich (*RE s.v.* Cornelius 392); Magie 1950, 1117–18, with criticism of earlier literature.

and *scriptura*, for the first time.[31] By the late 80s, in stark contrast to the situation at the death of Attalus, Rome's state finances were in parlous shape, partially due to a decade of civil strife and the devastation caused by Mithridates. Critically, as argued above, the *lex Sempronia* already regulated the *decuma* in Asia, mandating the auction of this tax as a single concern to *publicani* by the censors at Rome, and continued to do so until at least 61.[32] However, the aforementioned flexibility of Roman legislation ensured that the vast increase in communities affected did not materially undermine its application. Given that the *lex Sempronia* most likely restricted itself to outlining the basic scope of the tax's collection, before leaving its specific administration to each iteration of magistrates, the new 'subjection' of many cities in Asia made it appropriate for the *decuma* of their territories to be included by magistrates in the text of the *lex locationis*.

This explanation accounts for the unusual and ongoing employment of *publicani* to collect taxes which were directly gathered by *poleis*, unprecedented before this period. It was not Sulla's intended outcome but arose from the interaction of his decisions with existing legislation as enforced by later magistrates. Not only was this system inefficient, limiting the amount of revenue which accrued to the state in favour of increasing the profits of the tax-farmers, but it also provoked widespread discontent among the peoples of Asia.[33] Caesar's later reduction of Asian tax rates by one-third in 48, which coincided with the removal of the *publicani* from their privileged position in Asia and the reintroduction of local collection, demonstrates the inefficiency of this arrangement. As Tan has argued, the one-third figure should represent, at minimum, the publican profit margin and expenses of the city-based system which replaced it.[34] Were boosting state revenue in the long term Sulla's goal, a more efficient and less punitive means of taxing Asia existed: the *discriptio* introduced by the proconsul himself to collect the indemnity levied in 85.

After the *societates publicanorum* had acquired this position, normalized after Sulla's retirement from public life, structural factors made it immensely difficult to change. The *publicani* and other *equites* held a critical position not only as regards returning magistrates—note here their key role as jurors in the *quaestio de repetundis* from 123–81 and again, though less pronounced, from 70—but also in facilitating an individual's rise to office in the first place.[35] Such changes

[31] App. *Mith.* 118. Kallet-Marx 1995, 265–6.

[32] Cic. *Verr.* 2.3.13. Frank 1933, 345–6, with references.

[33] Inefficiencies: Kiser & Kane 2007; Tan 2017, 40–67; unpopularity: e.g., Cic. *QFr.* 1.1.33; *Flac.* 19–20; *Att.* 5.16.2.

[34] App. *BCiv.* 5.4; CD. 42.6.3; Plut. *Caes.* 48. Brunt 1990b, 380–1; Tan 2017, 55 contra Badian 1972a, 116–17.

[35] Davenport 2019, 75–84. Cf. Cicero's argument in *Imp. Pomp.* 14–17, grounded in the physical and financial interests of the *equites*.

contrary to the interests of entrenched actors tend to self-reinforce and are difficult to revoke.[36] Even after the restoration of the tribunate later that decade, it would be a brave consul or tribune of the *plebs* who sought to reverse this arrangement.[37] The new province-wide tax farm was the worst of all possible worlds. If its introduction resulted from an ad hoc process based on Sulla's personal motives then the anomaly is explained, with the further implication that the state itself did not seek to maximize short-term resource extraction to its own detriment at the expense of the provinces.

Sulla's settlement in Asia resulted in a major shift in the dynamics of Roman imperialism and the economic networks within the Mediterranean, albeit not by design. Previously, the Roman state placed limited emphasis on increasing its own state revenues. A province-wide tax-farm for the *decuma* of civic communities, let at Rome, had no precedent at this time. Given that most *poleis* had previously not paid direct taxes to Rome and the underlying (agricultural) wealth of the region, irrespective of the cut taken by the *publicani*, we can surmise a significant increase in public revenue deriving from the Sullan settlement and a corresponding growth in the importance of Asia to the Roman economy.

Indeed, in 66, arguing in favour of Cn. Pompeius Magnus' appointment to the command against Mithridates, Cicero sought to stress the importance of the revenues of *provincia Asia* to the *res publica*.

> *nam ceterarum provinciarum vectigalia, Quirites, tanta sunt ut eis ad ipsas provincias tuendas vix contenti esse possimus, Asia vero tam opima est ac fertilis ut et ubertate agrorum et varietate fructuum et magnitudine pastionis et multitudine earum rerum quae exportentur facile omnibus terris antecellat... nam cum hostium copiae non longe absunt, etiam si inruptio nulla facta est, tamen pecua relinquuntur, agri cultura deseritur, mercatorum navigatio conquiescit. ita neque ex portu neque ex decumis neque ex scriptura vectigal conservari potest...* ('For the revenues of the other provinces, Romans, are such that we can scarcely derive enough from them for the protection of the provinces themselves. But Asia is so rich and so productive, that in the fertility of its soil, the variety of its fruits, the vastness of its pasture lands, and in the multitude of all those things which are exported, it is greatly superior to all other lands... For when the troops of the enemy are not far off, even though no actual invasion takes place, still the flocks are abandoned, agriculture is relinquished, the sailing of merchants is at an

[36] North 1995, 15–20; Pierson 2004, 20–1.

[37] Compare Tan's recent assessment (2017, 149–56) of the violent resistance to the Gracchi, emphasizing the threat to vested interests both of the reforms themselves and the framework they provided to delegitimize the status quo. More generally, on escalating factors of political violence: Tilly 2003, esp. 75–7. See also, the famous cases of P. Rutilius Rufus and L. Licinius Lucullus, discussed elsewhere, who also opposed the interests of the *publicani* and *equites*.

end. And accordingly, neither from customs dues (*portoria*), nor from tithes (*decuma*), nor from the tax on pasture lands (*scriptura*), can any revenue be maintained...').[38]

Cicero describes three pillars of the Asian revenues: the *decuma*, the *scriptura*, and the *portoria*.[39] One important element of the *decuma*'s administration—as regulated by the *lex Sempronia*—and possibly the *scriptura*, was the *pactio*, an agreement between *publicani* and taxpayers on the amount to be paid. This was a legally binding contract, negotiated ahead of the harvest, possibly in five-year blocks to coincide with censorial *lustra*. In Asia, these contracts came to be concluded by communities. This denied *publicani* opportunities to employ violence and intimidation at the individual level, while allowing *poleis* more leverage with the governor.[40] Some factors, especially evidence for the large-scale transportation of grain by the *publicani*, suggest that they collected the *decuma* in kind. Indeed, Carbone has recently demonstrated that during the late Republic, the average annual production of coinage across the *provincia* would be grossly insufficient to pay the standard Roman demands in cash alone, leaving aside extraordinary exactions, such as those made by Sulla, Pompeius, and Flaccus.[41] However, the well-attested practice of *poleis* paying multiple years' taxes at once demonstrates that at least some payments were made in cash. The apparently widespread issue of civic debt further supports this view.[42] It seems likely, in practice, that both systems operated in parallel: while the entrepôts of the western littoral would have little difficulty in converting grain to cash, smaller, agrarian settlements, such as those in the former βασιλικὴ χώρα, would have struggled. It behoved the *publicani* to operate flexibly, as this created more opportunities for profit. Cicero shows that governors were intimately involved in the process. On his departure for Cilicia in 51/50, he evinced relief that the *pactiones* for the *provincia* had already been concluded.[43] Similarly, in providing unsolicited advice to his brother, during the latter's Asian command, he emphasized the governor's role in ensuring both sides adhere to the contract. Less equitably, he stressed to Quintus the utmost importance of maintaining good relations with *publicani* and suggested that he persuade

[38] Cic. *Imp. Pomp.* 14–15.

[39] The same formulation at Cic. *Flacc.* 19. *Scriptura* were fees collected from individuals grazing animals on *ager publicus*. Plaut. *Truc.* 141–151. Rathbone 2003, 167–70; Roselaar 2010, 92; Kay 2014, 163.

[40] Unlike in Sicily (Cic. *Verr.* 2.3.112). The precise date at which communities came to take responsibility for *pactiones* remains unclear, though firmly attested during the Augustan period (Strabo 10.5.3; 14.2.19, later *AA* (1942), 176 #9). Cicero (*QFr.* 1.1.34) implies that, even in 59, the bargaining was done at the civic level. Rostovtzeff 1902, 357–8; Broughton 1938, 536–7; Brunt 1981, 161, 169; Merola 2001, 102 n.2; de Ligt 2002, 57. Five-year contracts: see discussion at Tan 2017, 53 n.71.

[41] Carbone 2020, 232–5, drawing on Kirbihler's estimate (2013, 354–9) for the annual tax burden of 3,000–4,000 talents p.a.

[42] Grain: Cottier et al. 2008 l.75, with Nicolet 1994, 224–6; taxes and debt: Cic. *Att.* 6.2.5. Tan 2017, 53, with nn.71–2. Merola 2001, 105; de Ligt 2002, 55–7.

[43] Cic. *Att.* 5.13.1, 14.1.

the locals not to push for the *lex locationis* to be respected.[44] This dichotomy between an insistence on good faith in negotiated agreements and a flexibility in interpreting central regulations, further underscores the imbrication of the governor in the process. Overall, administration of the *decuma*, after the institution of a major tax-farm in the early 70s, increasingly impinged upon the attention of Roman magistrates in Asia.

The most important evidence for taxation in late Republican Asia is the *lex portorii Asiae*. This document dates to 9 July 62 CE, when records from the Basilica Iulia in Rome were copied for translation and eventual inscription at Ephesus.[45] The text outlines the regulations for the collection of customs dues on imports and exports from Asia by land and by sea and incorporated earlier legislation.[46] A reference to a *lex locationis* issued by the consuls of 75, L. Octavius and C. Aurelius Cotta, the earliest date in the document, led the original editors to date the *lex* to this year, or shortly afterwards.[47] Subsequently, every addition to the statute is introduced with the names of the year's consuls and the aorist προσέθηκαν 'they added'.[48] However, Mitchell has argued that the original legislation, which he considers to be clauses 1 to 30 (ll. 7–72), dates to the earliest period of the post-Attalid settlement adducing three pieces of evidence. First, he notes four occasions on which this section authorizes *publicani* to use Attalid-era buildings, or refers to Attalid administration, asserting that this should allow only a brief gap in their use. Second, he highlights the inclusion of four Pamphylian ports among the customs stations of Asia, noting that, from 102 onwards, commanders responsible for the *provincia Cilicia* were regularly present in Pamphylia.[49] Consequently, he asserts that the statute must pre-date the establishment of a *provincia Cilicia*. Finally, he states that the inclusion of Byzantium and Calchedon within the Asian customs zone requires that it pre-date the organization of the province of Bithynia in 74.[50] Accepting this argument, Kay strongly proposed 123 and associated the *lex* with the programme of C. Gracchus.[51]

However, each of these assertions is vulnerable to challenge. First, the survival of buildings over a sixty-year period is not unreasonable in the ancient world. These customs-posts appear to have been located within civic territories and it is likely that they were reused during the intervening period. An additional

[44] Cic. *QFr.* 1.1.35. Badian 1972a, 80–1.

[45] Corbier 2008, 212–16. On the ambitions of central government in publishing this statute: Rowe 2008, 243–8.

[46] Nicolet (2000a [1991], 353–7) refutes the suggestion of the original editors (*ad* ll. 71–74) that the text also regulated the *decuma* or *scriptura*.

[47] Cottier et al. 2008, ll.73, 75; 36, 68 (buildings); 27, 69 (royal land and subjects). Engelmann & Knibbe 1989, 160–2. Cf. Merola 1996, 281.

[48] Spagnuolo Vigorita 1997, 133–4.

[49] Ferrary 2000, 167–70; Mitchell 2008, 188–90; Migeotte 2014, 417 contra Merola 1996, 294–6.

[50] Mitchell 2008, 198–200, ruling out Nicolet's (b [1993], 383–4) suggestion that lines 72–74 refer to the *lex Terentia-Cassia* of 73.

[51] Vell. Pat. 2.6.3. Kay 2014, 73–5; already, Frank 1933, 255.

clause requiring *publicani* to use these buildings where they existed reinforces this point.[52] References to former 'royal land' and 'cities and tribes not subject to Attalus' are descriptive and had not lost relevance across this period. In fact, the integration of non-Attalid subjects into the provincial tax regime implies a date after the Sullan settlement.[53] The inclusion of Pamphylian and Bosporan ports with those of Asia in a single customs-zone does not pose an insurmountable problem.[54] The definition of the law's extent, in Mitchell's reconstruction, as the boundaries of Asia with Cappadocia, Galatia, and Bithynia would accurately describe the situation before the death of Nicomedes III in 74. The inclusion of Byzantium and Calchedon implies that they had lost their free status, placing the law after 85.[55] While this *lex* demonstrably defines territorial limits for tax purposes, it does not follow that these affected commanders on the ground. The fact that Cilician governors were routinely active outside of Pamphylia, for example, in the coastal waters of Rough Cilicia, in Cappadocia, or in Isauria, and the continuity of non-territorial definitions of *provincia* into the first century further emphasizes the probability that Pamphylia remained in some way attached to *provincia Asia* in this transitional period.[56]

Instead, returning to Heil's suggestion, clauses 31 to 36 (ll. 73–84) should also be considered part of the original legislation, since the organic inclusion of later material is unlikely.[57] Clauses 35 and 36, providing exemptions for private use and by treaty, seem pertinent to the original function of the statute.[58] The first addition to the law occurred under the consuls of 72, providing a firm *terminus ante quem*. Heil's attempt to connect the *lex* with the regulation of Bithynia after the death of Nicomedes IV in 74 does not follow. Instead the inclusion of Byzantium and Calchedon, paired with the absence of other Bithynian harbours implies that the news of Nicomedes' death had not yet reached Rome.[59] Moreover, if we assume annual consular *leges locationum* in lieu of regular censorships, the reference to the consuls of 75 provides positive evidence for promulgation in that year.[60] This year also saw the first attempt to collect revenues from Cyrenaica, which Sallust links to problems with the grain supply, but may be linked to the fraught fiscal

[52] Cottier et al. 2008, ll.36–38. Spagnuolo Vigorita 1997, 160 n.135.

[53] Cottier et al. 2008, 126 (*ad* ll.67–72), defending an early date, suggest unconvincingly that these lines are a post-Sullan supplement.

[54] de Laet 1949, 273–7; accepted by Heil 1991, 11; *pace* Nicolet 2000b [1993], 377–82.

[55] Merola 1996, 285–90; Mitchell 2008, 170–2; *pace* Santangelo 2007, 123 n.72. See Merola 2001, 125 n.103 on Byzantium.

[56] E.g., M. Antonius in 102/101 (Magie 1950, 1161–3, with references); Sulla in the 90s (Livy, *Per.* 70; Plut. *Sull.* 5.3–4); and P. Servilius Isauricus from 78–74 (Sherwin-White 1984, 152–8; Dmitriev 2000, 350–2, with references), respectively.

[57] Heil 1991, 9–11; *pace* Cottier et al. 2008, 10.

[58] Mitchell 2008, 198–200.

[59] McGing 1995, 283–5; Merola 1996, 272–90; Mitchell 2008, 182 contra Heil 1991, 9–14; cf. Merkelbach 1990, 100.

[60] On the desuetude of the censorship under the Sullan constitution: Astin 1985, 182–4; Steel 2014, 335–6.

situation in this year.[61] In sum, this statute most likely dates to 75, after the Sullan settlement, but before the outbreak of the Third Mithridatic War.

The implications of the new *lex portorii* for inhabitants of Asia were less radical than the expansion of the *decuma*. As internal references make clear, the statute effectively reintroduced an Attalid tax and relied on existing infrastructure. However, the underlying landscape had fundamentally changed. Most obviously, the scope of the new law extended far beyond the former Attalid kingdom, into the northern Troad, southern Caria, and the Bosporus. The identity of the 'free cities', which lay outside of either the kingdom or the *provincia* and hence the customs zone, had radically changed both as a result of the original universal declaration of ἐλευθερία and Sulla's subsequent settlement.[62] No islands are included among the ports subject to the *lex*, which the original editors took as evidence that they were not considered part of the *provincia* at that time. Dreher emphasized the fact that most were explicitly free, and consequently immune from taxation. However, Mitchell highlights the high level of bureaucratic effort necessary to regulate a transmarine customs zone and convincingly proposes that the drafters were content to simply charge all traffic between the islands and mainland.[63]

From a local fiscal perspective, there were also radical changes. The lucrative Bosporan tolls, previously contested between local powers, were consolidated into a single charge at one nominated collection point, namely Calchedon.[64] From the perspective of traders, this simplified the process of navigating the straits, but significantly reduced the revenues of regional cities. Moreover, the explicit authorization granted to Termessus in Cilicia, on the restoration of its *libertas*, to collect its own *portoria*, provided Roman *publicani* were exempt, implies that subject cities were routinely denied this right.[65] In 59, Cicero remarks on the financial plight of subject Asian communities, which were struggling to pay Roman taxes. He notes that only two means of raising money existed: borrowing or exacting *tributum*, that is, local direct taxation.[66] The inability to levy customs dues on goods moving through territory removed a crucial lever from *poleis*' revenue-raising toolbox, limiting their reach to property and transactions within their territory.[67]

[61] Note the struggles to fund troops and supplies in Spain during 75/74: Sall. *Hist.* 2.82 (McGushin); Plut *Pomp.* 20.1. Cyrenaica: Sall. *Hist.* 2.43–44 (McGushin). Compare Cic. *Verr.* 2.3.18, noting a *senatus consultum* transferring the auction for Sicilian tithes on wine, oil, and fruits to Rome in the same year (Badian 1972a, 95; Brunt 1988, 167). Generally, Kay 2014, 245–58.

[62] For 'free cities' located outside of the custom's zone, Mitchell 2008, 186–7; Kaye 2013.

[63] Mitchell 2008, 192–3 contra Engelmann & Knibbe 1989, 62; Dreher 1996, 118–27.

[64] Cottier et al. 2008, *ad* ll.13–15. Merola 2001, 124–5; Mitchell 2008, 181–2.

[65] *RS* 19.2.31–36. Ferrary 1996, 340; Merola 2001, 139–41.

[66] Cic. *Flacc.* 20. On local taxes: Broughton 1936, 134–6 (referring to Cic. *Flacc.* 91 contra Rostovtzeff 1941, 41); Merola 2001, 116–21.

[67] Both wealthy locals and merchants had the opportunity to avoid these charges by relocating, potentially creating a 'race to the bottom' between *poleis*. Note the Aphrodisian citizens, Dionysus and Hierocles, Trallians by birth. *IAph2007* 2.503; compare Canali De Rossi 2005, 106 n.40; Kokkinia 2008, 56–7.

This newly circumscribed tax-base contributes a further explanation as why after Sulla's fine and the imposition of Roman taxation, many communities spiralled into debt.

According to Plutarch, due to the severity of this burgeoning debt crisis, on returning to Asia from Pontus in 71, Lucullus reduced interest rates to 12 per cent p.a., required that no interest be levied in excess of the principle, and that no lender appropriate more than 25 per cent of a debtor's income. These limitations on usury played a major role in reducing the debt burden within the province, especially in light of attested interest rates as high as 48 per cent compound. Plutarch emphasizes that these measures were so successful that the public debt of 120,000 talents incurred as a result of Sulla's indemnity was entirely eliminated within four years, that is, by 67. Lucullus' reforms were undeniably significant, and he seems to have been well regarded by provincials.[68] However, the specific measures taken seem only to have alleviated a private debt crisis for local elites resulting from their financing of original indemnity. Appian provides the further information that he levied a *decuma* of 25 per cent, as well as instituting house- and slave-taxes in this year.[69] Although the amount paid by elite provincials may have been reduced, the overall tax burden increased. It is also in precisely this period that the minting of *cistophori* begins to stall.[70] While, from a state perspective, Lucullus' intervention substantially affected the dynamics of local economies, it is likely that the macroeconomic impact was limited. Finally, his measures were limited by his tenure as governor. Indeed, his checking of the moneylenders, often Romans of consequence, resulted in a backlash at Rome and, ultimately, his removal from the Mithridatic command.[71]

Cities also now had to respect Roman grants of immunity to individuals. The so-called *senatus consultum de Asclepiade*, issued in 78, confirmed privileges for three Greek naval captains as a reward for service during the Social War. Two of these men, Asclepiades of Clazomenae and Meniscus of Miletus, were citizens of *poleis* within *provincia Asia*. Consequently, the document offers an insight into Roman governance soon after Sulla's changes. Significantly, they were to be ἀλειτούργητοι καὶ ἀνείσφοροι ἐν ταῖς ἑαυτῶν πατρίσιν, ('exempt from civic contributions or taxes within their own cities'). This does not include Roman taxes but does seem to imply immunity from contributions to the cities which could be used to pay them. Given Sulla's fine, this was an important concession.[72] By contrast, the document does grant exemption from directly levied Roman taxation elsewhere in the document. Here, however, the text is even more specific, ordering both: εἴ τινα χρήματα αἵ πόλεις αὐτῶν δημοσίαι ὀφείλωσιν, μή τι εἰς ταῦτα τὰ

[68] Plut. *Luc.* 20.1–4. Cf. Cic. *Acad.* 2.3; *SEG* 60.908; Ferrary 2000, #3. [69] App. *Mith.* 83.

[70] Carbone 2020, 221–36.

[71] Plut. *Luc.* 20.4. Cf. *Sull.* 25.2. On borrowing, including from locals: App. *Mith.* 63 with Migeotte 1984, 339–41; *I.Cos* 193 with Buraselis 2000, 127–8.

[72] *CIL* 6.40890.12. Raggi 2001, 89–90. Cf. Santangelo 2007, 56.

χρήματα δοῦναι ὀφείλωσιν | ἄρχοντες ἡμέτεροι, οἵτινες ἂν ποτε Ἀσίαν Εὔβοιαν μισθῶσιν ἢ προσόδους Ἀσίαι Εὐβοίαι ἐπιτιθῶσ<ι>ν, φύλαξωνται μὴ τι οὗτοι δοῦναι ὀφείλωσιν ('if their cities owe any public debt, they are not to be obliged to contribute towards these debts; our magistrates, any of those who let out or assign the revenues for Asia and Euboea, are to take care that these men are not obliged to give anything').[73] The injunction here is upon the magistrates letting out the contracts, rather than the commander in the field, who might logically be approached by the grantees in the event of a dispute. This could be taken as further evidence that the taxes for Asia and Greece were being collected via short-term measures—perhaps involving locals—in this period, rather than by Roman *publicani*.

The biggest winners from this arrangement were the *societates publicanorum*: little benefit accrued to the state. The profits flowed through to private (primarily non-senatorial) individuals, with some benefits for commanders willing to smooth their path. The direct corollary was the consistent maltreatment of provincials by Roman citizens: put another way, the intense unhappiness of the local population directly attributable to Rome and Romans.[74] When Cicero spoke in favour of the *lex Manilia* in 66, he dwelt on the private, as well as the public, impact of an invasion of Asia: the threat to property, wealth, and lives of Roman *negotiatores*, as well as *publicani*.[75] The revenues of Asia catalysed the formation of new interest groups among the *equites*. However, a distinct set of circumstances allowed them to acquire and entrench their power. When the kingdom of Attalus III was originally organized as a province, entrepreneurial groups could lobby for a favourable outcome, but their leverage over the Senate, or individual senators, was limited. The *lex Sempronia de provincia Asia* created an ongoing equestrian-managed concern and C. Gracchus' alterations to jury composition and the *lex repetundarum* gave the *publicani* and their backers institutional power vis-à-vis individual magistrates.[76] The archetypal example is the conviction of Rutilius Rufus. That said, the tendency of the Senate to support local communities in disputes with the *publicani* in this period highlights the limits of equestrian influence.[77] Their capacity to generate positive legislative change was also limited. However, after Sulla's decisions interacted with existing legislation, Asia's taxation was set up in a manner which favoured private interests. Institutional inertia and the power of established interest groups to resist change took over.[78] Despite growing concerns among the Senate over the exploitation of the provinces during 60s and 50s, the costs of an individual stance could be grave. For example, Lucullus' attempts to ameliorate the debt crisis gripping Asia resulted in his

[73] *CIL* 6.40890.22–23. [74] Tan 2017, 77–8.
[75] Kay 2014, 255–7; Eberle & Le Quéré 2017, 10–12. [76] Brunt 1988, 150–6.
[77] E.g., *RDGE* 12; *I.Priene*² 67; Strabo 14.1.26. Tan 2017, 45–54. Cf. Wallace 2014, 50–62.
[78] Levi 1988, 85–93.

removal from the Mithridatic command. Similarly, A. Gabinius' resistance to *publicani* in Syria, condemned by Cicero, may have contributed to his conviction in the *repetundae* court.[79]

Even governors who avoided legal action walked a fine line when mediating between *publicani* and provincials. Cicero privately praised P. Cornelius Lentulus Spinther for his conduct in Cilicia from 56–54. However, he expressed his dismay that the latter had not managed to accommodate the interests of the *publicani*, who were now attacking his decisions publicly.[80] Similarly, in his correspondence with Quintus, Cicero repeatedly emphasized the importance of cultivating positive relationships with *publicani*, even where this existed in tension with his injunction to treat locals fairly.[81] For example, he anticipates visits from delegates sent by various *poleis* in response to a disagreement about *portoria*, which Quintus had referred to the Senate against his advice.[82] It seems *publicani* were charging *portoria* twice on goods which had been brought into one port and then moved to another, in contravention of a clause in the *lex portorii Asiae*.[83] Indeed, Cicero also berated his brother at length for forcing him to put out numerous political fires at Rome and insisted that he pay more attention to requests made of him by Roman actors.[84]

During his own tenure as provincial governor, in Cilicia in 51/50, Cicero did try to strike a balance. As he reported proudly, he managed to secure full repayment of tax arrears by some *poleis* by offering them an opportunity to repay at 12 per cent p.a. interest, rather than the agreed rate, if they paid immediately. This equitable policy, he crowed, endeared him to provincials and *publicani* alike.[85] However, the orator did not completely avoid this tension. The most significant example involves a debt contracted by the city of Salamis on Cyprus in 56. A consortium involving the influential M. Iunius Brutus offered a loan with 48 per cent compound interest p.a. and secured two *senatus consulta* exempting this arrangement from an existing *lex Gabinia*.[86] Ap. Claudius Pulcher, Cicero's predecessor and Brutus' father-in-law, had granted one M. Scaptius a position as *praefectus* and troops to exact repayment. After he had besieged the Salaminian council house and caused five deaths, Cicero arrived in the *provincia* and revoked

[79] Generally, Badian 1972a, 59–66, 85–109; Brunt 1988, 152–3. On Lucullus: Plut. *Luc.* 20.5, 24.3; Keaveney 1992, 114–15; more cautiously, Tröster 2008, 86 n.42. On Gabinius: Cic. *Prov. cons.* 10; *Pis.* 41, 48; Val. Max. 4.2.4; App. *BCiv.* 2.24; CD. 39.55.4–56.6. Braund 1983a, 241–3.

[80] Cic. *Fam.* 1.9.26. [81] Cic. *QFr.* 1.1. [82] Cic. *Att.* 2.16.4.

[83] Cottier et al. 2008, ll.16–20.

[84] Cic. *QFr.* 1.2. Cotton (2013, 43–6) argues that letters of recommendation played an essential role in the conduct of administration during the late Republic, and highlights that their typical language allowed governors to refuse politely. However, this underplays the extent of political and social pressures exerted on individuals to favour their acquaintances.

[85] Cic. *Att.* 5.21.7, 6.1.6–7, 16. Cf. Badian 1972a, 114–15.

[86] Cic. *Att.* 5.21.10–11. On Salamis: Magie 1950, 394–5; Lintott 2008, 263–5, with references. Compare *IG* 5.1.1146 at Gytheum for the same interest rate, with Santangelo 2009a, 363; Girdvainyte 2019, 149–50.

his position.[87] Seeking to mediate between the parties in February 50, he proposed his standard compromise, allowing the Salaminians to pay back the loan immediately at 12 per cent p.a. However, under pressure from Scaptius over Brutus' involvement, Cicero chose not to make a ruling, despite admitting privately that his successor would favour Brutus.[88] Throughout these exchanges, Cicero sought to rationalize his decisions within the framework of his relationships with other members of the political class. He justified his decision not to accord Scaptius a *praefectura* on the grounds that he has denied several other requests from eminent *amici*. Despite his intent to govern justly by the inhabitants of the province, Cicero's frame of reference for conflict resolution was based the reception of his conduct at Rome.[89] Ultimately, the goodwill and esteem of the Salaminians held less weight than those of Brutus. During the Late Republic, provincial elites lacked the leverage to consistently ensure positive outcomes in marginal cases.

Beyond the mismanagement of financial matters, direct gubernatorial action could have an equally large impact. The favouring of Romans in legal disputes which came before the governor and his representatives, as in the Salamis affair, could have dire consequences for locals. Giving moneylenders and their agents official status and troops to collect added an element of violence to the economic hardship already inflicted.[90] Another common practice involved making extortionate demands on communities for the upkeep of the proconsul and his staff, something theoretically limited by the *lex Iulia de repetundis* in 59. Cicero also praises his brother for ending the practice of requiring Asian *poleis* to contribute funds for aedilician games, noting the resistance this had generated in some quarters.[91] Finally, most egregiously, some larger *poleis* would pay bribes to avoid the possibility that soldiers would be billeted in their territory.[92]

From the 60s onwards growing evidence exists for concern among the elite for the protection of provincials from abuses. This appears prominently in the self-aggrandizing rhetoric of Cicero's Cilician correspondence, but similar themes appear in the early *de imperio Cn. Pompei*: Pompeius' moral character and its effect on local populations is emphasized more than his military qualities.[93] We have evidence from this period for the increasing prominence of the 'Stoic' rhetoric of just empire in public discourse. Most notably, Cicero and Cato present provincials as akin to citizens and worthy of protection, and their views seem to reflect a broader consensus.[94] This is also the period in which Caesar's *lex de repetundis*—imposing firm limits on requisitions made of provincials and strict

[87] Cic. *Att.* 6.1.5, 2.8–9. [88] Cic. *Att.* 5.21.12, 6.1.7.

[89] Rauh 1986, 21–30; Braund 1989, 143–8.

[90] Cicero eventually consented to Scaptius' request and sent him to bother Ariobarzanes of Cappadocia: Cic. *Att.* 6.1.4.

[91] Cic. *QFr.* 1.1.26. Cf. *Att.* 6.1.21. [92] Cic. *Att.* 5.21.7.

[93] Röthe 1978, 60–6; Tröster 2009, 25–7; Morrell 2017, 59–62, 71–2, 77–82. Cf. Gruber 1988, 243–58.

[94] Griffin 1989, 34–7; Asmis 2005, 407–12; Morrell 2017, 99–101.

reporting requirements—was passed, with widespread support.[95] However, above all, Cicero levels practical arguments in favour of just treatment in his public pronouncements. Restraint prevented rebellion and disaffection, as well as ensuring prompt payment for the *publicani* themselves. In this context, it is unsurprising that one of Caesar's first actions upon achieving military dominance was to unilaterally remove the tax-farm for the Asian *decuma*. Throughout its operation, this system had a significant impact on Roman fiscal and political development, greatly increasing public revenues and reorientating Rome's geopolitical focus towards the East.

A Coin for Asia?: The Decline and Revival of the *cistophorus*

After the First Mithridatic War, the production of *cistophori* in Asian cities becomes more sporadic, though in the late 70s and early 60s a surge of increased production corresponds with renewed conflict with the Pontic monarch.[96] However, the cistophoric coinage seems to end in the late 60s or early 50s. Earlier commentators, assuming co-ordination at a provincial level, dated this abruptly to 68/7, the last extant issue at Ephesus. However, dated issues at Nysa persisted for at least another year and Backendorf has convincingly argued that Pergamum continued to mint into the mid-60s. Moreover, Carbone has suggested that Trallian production actually climbed in the early 60s, in part to compensate for the cessation of minting elsewhere.[97] How, then, to explain this collapse? While regular Roman taxation cannot have been exacted entirely in coin, that the Sullan indemnity of 20,000 talents was to be paid in silver, at least in part, as can be inferred from Plutarch's description of Lucullus' re-coining the collected metal. This demand, even spread over multiple years through loans must have had a catastrophic impact on civic bullion reserves. As Carbone shows, the entire annual production of *cistophori* was orders of magnitude lower than this impost.[98] Later extraordinary demands, such as those by later governors, including Pompeius and L. Valerius Flaccus appear to have overwhelmed the provincial monetary supply. At Ephesus, paradoxically, production increased in the early 60s before abruptly ending, suggesting a sudden crisis. We may detect similar concerns behind Flaccus' attempt to restrict the export of gold from Asia in the

[95] Cic. *Rab. Post.* 8; *Pis.* 37, 90; *Vat.* 29; CD. 38.7.5–6; *Dig.* 48.11.6.2.

[96] Carbone 2020, 218–19.

[97] Backendorf 1999; Carbone 2020, 212–18, 222–6 contra e.g., Kinns (1987, 109–11) speaking of a 'province-wide monetary policy'. Though Backendorf's claim (1999. 197–9) that Nysa's coinage persisted until 61/0 cannot be sustained given Carbone's redating of the series to five years earlier (2020, 183–5), his broader argument is sound.

[98] Plut. *Luc.* 4.1. Carbone 2020, 232–5. This reconstruction also explains the dramatic halt to minting after a sustained increase to support fighting in the Third Mithridatic War: de Callataÿ 1997 176; 2011, 71–3; Burnett 2022, 23.

late 60s.[99] A possible explanation for Tralles' apparent robustness is its notable wealth in this period.[100] Essentially, the extraordinary exaction of coin and bullion by successive Roman governors in the context of Sulla's indemnity and the ongoing wars with Mithridates and Tigranes created a fiscal crisis in the early to mid-60s which overwhelmed the already teetering cistophoric system.

Cicero, writing to Atticus in April 59, notes that he has written to the urban quaestor on behalf of Quintus, then praetor *pro praetore* in Asia, asking that his brother be paid in *denarii* rather than in *cistophori Pompeiani*.[101] Shortly afterwards, he notes that the quaestor is vacillating over a decision, but that he would, from necessity, accept payment in *cistophori*.[102] These brief notes raise several questions: why did the *aerarium* have holdings in *cistophori*? What made these *cistophori* Pompeian? Why would Cicero (and Quintus) prefer payment in *denarii*? Carbone suggests that the coins referred to by Cicero were seized by Pompeius as spoils during his wide-ranging campaigns.[103] Given that circulation of *cistophori* was limited to the province of Asia and production was in what turned out to be terminal decline, it is more likely that Pompeius had requisitioned the coinage to pay for his campaigns.[104] In the event, the money was not disbursed and was brought back to Rome by Pompeius and entered into the treasury.

Carbone states that it was entirely appropriate for the governor of Asia to be paid in *cistophori* and, in light of the absence of Roman currency in circulation, that 'there was no alternative'.[105] However, Cicero's query and the quaestor's confusion make clear that this was an open question. One possible reason may be found in the fact that a physical transfer of coins from Rome to Asia was unlikely. Indeed, in 48, Cicero wrote to Atticus that he had 2,200,000 HS in *cistophori* on deposit, asking his friend to arrange a transfer of credit to Rome to address his growing debts.[106] Later he refers to a transaction, which Atticus is managing for him, with a steep exchange rate (*collybus*), likely this transfer of his proconsular stipend.[107] This suggests both that there was no fixed exchange rate for *cistophori* to *denarii* and that such transfers, presumably via communities of Roman *publicani* and *negotiatores*, were fairly common. Cicero's objection is grounded in the nature of the gubernatorial *ornatio*, which could be used at the

[99] Cic. *Flac.* 67–69. Broughton 1937, 249; Marshall 1975, 151–3. [100] Strabo 14.1.42.

[101] Cic. *Att.* 2.6.2: *sed ut ad rem: scripsi ad quaestores urbanos de Quinti fratris negotio. vide quid narrent, ecquae spes sit denarii an cistophoro Pompeiano iaceamus.*

[102] Cic. *Att.* 2.16.4: *quaestores autem quaeso num etiam de cistophoro dubitant? nam si aliud nihil erit, cum erimus omnia experti, ego ne illud quidem contemnam quod extremum est.*

[103] Carbone 2020, 221.

[104] Plut. *Pomp.* 25.3. Marshall 1975, 153. Cf. Cic. *Flac.* 27–31. De Callataÿ 2011.

[105] Carbone 2020, 221.

[106] Cic. *Att.* 11.1.2: *ego in cistophoro in Asia habeo ad sestertium bis et viciens. huius pecuniae permutatione fidem nostram facile tuebere.* Hollander 2007, 42.

[107] Cic. *Att.* 12.6.1: *de Caelio vide, quaeso, ne quae lacuna sit in auro. ego ista non novi. sed certe in collubo est detrementi satis.* Kay 2014, 98–9.

magistrate's discretion and even invested at Rome for private gain. Cicero explicitly condemns L. Calpurnius Piso and, in *de lege Manilia*, contrasts the virtuous Pompeius with unnamed individuals who have done so.[108] Quintus had already been in Asia for two years—any funds would not be transferred physically and, as *denarii*, could have been invested profitably. However, finding a Roman banker who would accept payment in *cistophori* may have proved a challenge. The overvaluation of *cistophori* must also have contributed to Cicero's attempts to avoid this arrangement.[109] Indeed, in June 58, writing from exile, Cicero apologizes to Quintus for using his *pecunia ex aerario* in an attempt to curry political favour, though he does note that he managed to pay off his brother's debts to M. Antonius and M. Iunius Brutus.[110] Consequently, this episode is grounded not so much in Roman snobbishness as in the practicalities of Roman administration and the continuation of a relatively closed currency system within Asia.

The Mithridatic Wars proved highly disruptive to autonomous minting, forcing cities to produce coinage intensively to support military action and higher expenses.[111] After Sulla's settlement, four autonomous mints (Cibyra, Cos, Ephesus, and Ilium) did not produce autonomous precious metal issues again. Though the consensus links this development to the reduction of most communities to subject status, this fails to explain every case. Indeed, Ilium was explicitly favoured by Sulla: its sack by Fimbria better accounts for the end of its mint. Meanwhile, Miletus, which was not a free city, continued to mint civic coinage throughout the period. Given the fiscal crisis provoked by Sulla's demand for an indemnity, we might theorize that the collapse of minting in this period was linked rather to problems with the supply of bullion. The end of autonomous silver across the Troad in the late 70s and early 60s, for example, seems to correspond well with the failure of cistophoric mints.[112] The civil war period saw another major reduction in the number of active autonomous mints, though, in light of the widespread upheaval and conflict, not to mention intense demand by roving armies for bullion and spoils, this is unsurprising. The consequence was that by the Augustan period only five autonomous mints were functioning in *provincia Asia*: Rhodes and Chios, minted on a cistophoric standard; while Stratonicea, Tabae, and Mylasa, minted on a *denarius*-standard.[113]

In 57/56, cistophoric coinage suddenly revived, albeit in a more co-ordinated and centralized fashion. This new 'Later Republican' coinage maintained the weight standard and imagery of the Attalid and post-Attalid coinage but

[108] E.g., Cicero's critiques of the practice (*Pis.* 86; *Man.* 37). On the *ornatio*: Rafferty 2019, 87–94.

[109] Walker 1976, 35–6. Note, his suggestion that *cistophori* in the 70s/60s are debased from *c.*95 per cent to 79.75 per cent (33–34). Butcher & Ponting (2014, 466) record three proconsular *cistophori* at just below 90 per cent and one of Augustus at 83 per cent but advise caution.

[110] Cic. *Q. fr.* 1.3.7.

[111] Meadows' Group 3 coinage (2002) at Stratonicea; Kinns 1987, 111.

[112] Ellis-Evans 2016, 2020, 99, 106–7.

[113] Carbone 2014, 24; cf. Meadows 2022; Delrieux 2022, 200–2.

incorporated three stylistic changes: (i) it included the name of the Roman governor with authority in the relevant *provincia* in Latin script; (ii) it contained an abbreviated name of the minting authority (as opposed to a monogram) in Greek script; and (iii) some issues included modifications to the *cista* reverse.[114] All of these issues included a Greek signer, which, at minimum, demonstrates continued local involvement in the practical aspects of minting.[115] This cistophoric revival is well dated on account of Ephesian issues and near-annual replacement of governors during this period. It was limited to five mints: Ephesus, Pergamum, and Tralles—the three major Roman cistophoric mints—as well as Apamea and Laodicea-on-the-Lycus, both of which were transferred to *provincia Cilicia* in 56. As Metcalf notes, this coinage was small scale and will have had a limited economic impact. He theorizes that it will have served only to replace coins dropping out of circulation.[116] It seems designed to meet a practical need within the region after the collapse of the only major circulating silver coinage. In this respect it may be similar to the production of a standard silver coinage at Antioch, which began under the governorship of A. Gabinius in 57, reprising the portrait of the late Seleucid monarch Philip II Philorhomaios but bearing monograms of Roman governors. This coinage continued until the Augustan period and seemed to serve economic needs in the region rather than Roman military costs.[117] Accordingly, we see here action of Roman administrators in response to a crisis provoked by the direct, if unintended, consequences of their own actions.

The production of *cistophori* continued until 49, shortly after the outbreak of civil war. A closely associated and extremely large issue is minted in the name of Q. Caecilius Metellus Pius Scipio, governor of Syria, which replaced the *cista mystica* with a legionary eagle. Metellus' sojourn in Asia is described by Caesar as being particularly brutal in seeking bullion to support the Pompeian war effort and, notwithstanding some licence taken, we should see this issue firmly within this context.[118] Another issue, containing a monogram, potentially resolved as ATRA(tinus) bears a Q on the reverse, suggesting a quaestor, rather than governor. This issue also likely belongs in the chaos of civil war, likely the mid-late 40s.[119] Again, the production of *cistophori*, a de facto provincial coinage, supported military action in a Roman civil war, just as previously, during the Mithridatic period. Throughout the post-Sullan period, provincial monetary production came under pressure from Roman demands in the form of the indemnity, the debt crisis, and warfare. The collapse of cistophoric production and decline in civic silver led to Roman intervention in the form of the revived 'proconsular' *cistophori*, though the minting communities appear to have largely

[114] Metcalf 2017, 65. [115] Metcalf 2017, 9. [116] Metcalf 2017, 67–8.
[117] E.g., *RPC* I.4124–4139. Burnett 2022, 23. [118] Caes. *BC* 3.32–33. Metcalf 2017, 7–8.
[119] Metcalf 2009, 2017, 66–7 contra Stumpf 1991, 13–17.

retained their role in the production of the coinage. Roman action was prompted by the consequences of earlier decisions and was limited in scope.

The Emergence of the *conventus iuridici*

Originally, the term *conventus civium Romanorum* stood for a collective of Roman citizens in a foreign community. Numerous inscriptions from second- and first-century Greece and the Aegean use the label in this sense to denote the source of honorific statues.[120] In an administrative context, however, it came to designate the group with access to gubernatorial jurisdiction, and swiftly came to mean the court assemblies held by a Roman magistrate. In time, the word *conventus* also acquired a geographic meaning, designating the region for which assizes were held in a specific community, that is, the administrative structure of the court. The prevailing view sees this structure as established in Asia by M'. Aquillius from 129–126, or shortly afterwards.[121] However, this geographic element translated into Greek as *διοίκησις*, a word with strong fiscal implications which has no easy Latin equivalent.[122] Consequently, some scholars have argued that the early Roman administration repurposed an underlying Attalid system.[123] The strong correlation between *conventus* centres and Attalid mint authorities reinforces this suggestion. The minting authorities which issued *cistophori* (Pergamum, Ephesus, Tralles, Sardis, Apamea, Laodicea, and (likely) Synnada) each eventually achieved this status.[124] These authorities are confirmed by a set of uniform countermarks on Pamphylian Attic-weight tetradrachms, along with others; namely, Adramyttium, Stratonicea-on-the-Caïcus, Sala, and Toriaion.[125] The last three do not appear as *conventus* centres and Kantor offers plausible explanations: the former

[120] Note the consistent employment of *conventus* by late Republican authors as shorthand for Roman communities in the provinces (e.g., Cic. *Lig.* 24; *Verr.* 2.2.32; 5.94; Caes. *BCiv.* 2.19; 3.9, 40; see Hatzfeld 1919, 261; Broughton 1938, 546–8). A link between *οἱ κατοικοῦντες/πραγματευόμενοι Ῥωμαῖοι vel sim.* (resident Romans/Roman *negotiatores*) and *conventus civium Romanorum* is attested in the Greek East (e.g., *SEG* 36.1200; Magie 1950, 1051–3; Delplace 1977, 240–1; Kirbihler 2007, 20 with fig. 2; Thonemann 2010, 169–70), though note Girdvainyte (2019, 151–7) highlighting the difference in these terms from the local perspective.

[121] E.g., Mitchell 1999, 20–2; Fournier 2010, 62–6; Vitale 2012, 43–5. Cautiously, Haensch 1997, 311–15; Campanile 2003, 277–84.

[122] Ameling 1988, 16: 'dort aber kein Äquivalent besitzt'; Mileta 1990, 443–4; Burton 1975, 92; Fournier 2010, 41–6.

[123] Wilamowitz *ap.* Schulten 1892, 12 n.2; Ameling 1988, 14–18; Mileta 1990, 427–44; Fournier 2010, 64.

[124] On Attalid mint authorities: Kleiner & Noé 1977, 120–2; Gray 1978, 975; Mitchell 1999, 24–5; Kantor 2014, 257–8. Thonemann (2008, 55–8) plausibly identifies the authority abbreviated as *KOP* as Cormasa.

[125] Bauslaugh (1990, 39–64) on countermarks; Thonemann (2008, 43–53) identifying Toriaion, noting a single specimen of an eleventh authority (*ΕΛΗΣ*), potentially the Hellespontine district (58–60).

punished for siding with Aristonicus, and the latter two losing significance prior to the establishment of the *provincia*.[126]

However, Strabo has often been held to complicate this picture. In characterizing the ethnic and social groups in the upper Maeander valley, he suggests that the Romans ignored earlier arrangements in their administrative choices:

> *εἰς δὲ τὴν σύγχυσιν ταύτην οὐ μικρὰ συλλαμβάνει τὸ τοὺς Ῥωμαίους μὴ κατὰ φῦλα διελεῖν αὐτούς, ἀλλὰ ἕτερον τρόπον διατάξαι τὰς διοικήσεις, ἐν αἷς τὰς ἀγοραίους ποιοῦνται καὶ τὰς δικαιοδοσίας* ('To this confusion, no little has been contributed by the fact that the Romans did not divide them according to *phyla* (tribe), but organized their *diokeseis* in a different way, within which they hold their assemblies and their courts').[127]

Ando argues that this passage reflects a deliberate Roman policy of disrupting pre-existing local networks through new administrative organization.[128] However, as Thonemann highlights, the geographer organized his work by culturally distinctive population groups (e.g., Lydians, Carians, Phrygians), which were already difficult to disentangle for this region.[129] Taken at face value, Strabo seems rather to be complaining that the Romans had chosen an alternative means of organization to his own preferred method. Moreover, despite Strabo's earlier claim to the finality of Aquillius' settlement, it is not clear that the situation described reflected the original organization of the *provincia*. During the late Republican and Augustan periods, several changes were made to the *conventus* organization, and these possibly went beyond the designation of different centres.[130]

The method by which the Roman *provincia* mapped onto underlying geographic assumptions also holds significance. Territorial limits in the ancient world were often contested, while natural features which to modern eyes seem boundaries, such as rivers and mountain ranges, often served as major routes

[126] Kantor 2014, 258.

[127] Strabo 13.4.12. Radt 2002–2011 *ad loc.* is unhelpful here; compare Syme 1995, 122–3.

[128] Syme 1979 [1939], 125; Ando 2010, 33–4. Cf. Mitchell 2000, 120–2.

[129] Thonemann 2011, 22–6.

[130] See Table 2.1, discussed *infra*. Gruen 1984, 604–5; Kallet-Marx 1995, 117. Debate over which *polis* should be considered the 'capital' of Asia is not meaningful: Haensch's concept (1997, 11–17) of a 'Provinzialhauptstadt' attains relevance only under the Principate. Governors throughout the period were mobile and divided their time between the major centres of the *provincia* including Ephesus and Pergamum. Evidence collected by Rigsby shows governors acting in both cities. Pergamum's association with Attalid power explains why, initially, Roman magistrates seem to have based themselves there (1979, 137–41, cf. *SEG* 64.1302, 1303, Augustan governors' letters from Pergamum and Ephesus respectively). However, the practical advantages of Ephesus' location, made it an attractive seat—by the 50s, it seems to have become the main centre of Roman rule (e.g., Cic. *Att.* 5.13.1, 20.10; *Fam.* 13.55.1, 57.2), and Sulla, Caesar, and Antonius all summoned civic representatives to meet there. Nevertheless, the institutionalization of this reality happened slowly.

or zones of local exchange.[131] Even so, Roman decision-makers, like their imperial forebears, did use natural features as convenient markers, where political and cultural considerations would seem point in a different direction.[132] Consequently, Roman modes of organization evolved to prioritize urban communities. Pliny the Elder's geographic account of the *poleis* of Africa seems to reproduce, for example, a version of the *formula provinciae*, that is, the list of communities comprising the province, previously considered Augustan but now firmly dated by Shaw to 46/45.[133] By analogy, this interpretation—and, without firm evidence, the Augustan date—has been extended to Pliny's list of Asian cities. Consequently, there is strong evidence to show that by the late first century BCE Asia was organized locally into *conventus* districts, as lists of communities administratively subordinated to the assize centre, and subsequently into larger units.[134]

Across the period the cities making up the *conventus* varied. As illustrated in Table 2.1, between the late 60s and the Flavian period, sixteen different cities are attested as *conventus* centres in *provincia Asia*, though never more than thirteen at one time. Without strong evidence, it is unclear which political body decided these issues during the Republican period. Linking decisions on constituent elements of provinces to the allocation of magistrates' *provinciae* seems most plausible, which would ordinarily give the Senate the central role. However, the *lex de provinciis praetoriis*, assigning Cilicia to a praetor in 100, states clearly that the *ἐπαρχεία Λυκαονία* should remain subject to the governor of Asia, demonstrating that comitial legislation could also affect the make-up of *provinciae*.[135] Accordingly, it is impossible to be specific in any given context. Cicero provides the earliest evidence for the provincial *conventus* organization, referring to several Asian *poleis*, which correspond to later assize centres, as the site of gubernatorial activity in his *pro Flacco*. Moreover, when seeking to emphasize the breadth of Rullus' agrarian proposal in 63, he refers to six cities as constituting *tota Asia*.[136] Together they provide a list of nine potential *conventus* centres for this period.

The earliest epigraphic evidence derives from two copies of a letter found at the *bouleuterion* in Miletus and near the *agora* in Priene. The first part of the text is

[131] Boundaries contested: Lintott 1981, 54–8; Mitchell 1993, 5–11; 1999, 32–3; Drogula 2015, 252. Natural features: Purcell 1990, 179–81; Horden & Purcell 2000, 80–2; Crawford 2003, 59–66.

[132] Thonemann (2011, 45–6) on the choice of the Maeander as a boundary between Attalid and Rhodian hegemony after 188.

[133] Plin. *HN*. 5.29–30. Shaw 1981, 424–56.

[134] Plin. *HN*. 5.105–106, 109, 111, 120, 122–3, 126. Marshall 1966, 234–6; Habicht 1975, 69; Ameling 1988, 16–17; Nicolet 1988, 201–6; Vitale 2012, 349–51; Dalla Rosa 2014, 31–3. Critique of the Augustan date: Shaw 1981: 424–30. Compare Dmitriev's observation (2000, 350) that individual geographic labels could be used in several different senses.

[135] *RS* 12.Cnidus.3.22–27.

[136] Cic. *Flacc.* 68; *Leg. agr.* 2.39. On Cyzicus, Cic. *Fam.* 13.53 with Campanile 2004, 140–2; Thonemann 2008, 59 contra Robert 1949, 231–2; Habicht 1975, 70–1. Ameling (1988 11–14) stresses that these locations held an administrative importance for inter-civic groups: Asian Jewish communities appear to have collected taxes bound for Jerusalem here without Roman prompting.

Table 2.1 Attested *conventus* centres by date

63/61 BCE Cicero, *Leg. agr.* Cicero, *Flacc.*	**29/28 BCE** *RDGE* 52	**17 BCE** Cottier et al. 2008	**Augustan (?)** Pliny *NH* 5	***c*.38/39 CE** *I.Didyma* 148	**Flavian** *I.Eph.* 13
Pergamum	Pergamum	Pergamum	Pergamum	Pergamum	Pergamum
Ephesus	Ephesus	Ephesus	Ephesus	Ephesus	–
Adramyttium	Adramyttium	Adramyttium	Adramyttium	Adramyttium	–
Smyrna	Smyrna	Smyrna	Smyrna	–	Smyrna
Miletus	Miletus	Miletus	–	Miletus	Miletus
Apamea	(Apamea)[137]	Apamea	Apamea	Apamea	Apamea
Laodicea[138]	(Laodicea)	Laodicea	Laodicea	Laodicea	–
–	(Synnada)	Synnada	Synnada	Synnada	–
–	Alabanda	–[139]	Alabanda	Alabanda	–
Tralles	Tralles	–	–	–	–
–	–	Sardis	Sardis	Sardis	Sardis
–	Mylasa	–	–	–	–
–	–	Halicarnassus	–	Halicarnassus	Halicarnassus
Cyzicus	–	Cyzicus[140]	–	Cyzicus	–
–	–	Cibyra	Cibyra	Cibyra	–
–	–	Philomelium[141]	Philomelium	Philomelium	–

extremely fragmentary, neither the author nor addressee survive, but the final twenty-three lines can be reconstructed with a high level of confidence. Crucially, it contains a list of recipients of the letters, which largely corresponds with Cicero's *conventus* centres.[142] This list omits three Phrygian communities—Apamea, Laodicea, and Synnada—which formed part of the *provincia Cilicia* between 56 and 50.[143] The *communis opinio* identifies the author as Q. Minucius Thermus, governor in Asia in 51, drawing support from the appearance of a Cicero, usually identified as the famous orator, in the text.[144] However, Bowersock offers a viable

[137] Parentheses indicate *dioceses* attached to the *provincia Cilicia* from 56–50 and likely part of Amyntas' Galatian kingdom from 41–25.

[138] Laodicea-on-the-Lycus.

[139] Likely missing through a mason's error. Haensch 1997, 308.

[140] Robert 1950, 229–31. In Cottier et al. 2008 Cyzicus is referred to *διοίκησις Ἑλλησποντία* and Philomelium as *διοίκησις Λυκαονική*. Campanile 2004, 132–42, argues that the Hellespontine district was formed in the 50s.

[141] From Cicero (*Fam.* 13.67.1) it appears Lycaonia was, in the 50s, considered a regular diocese of Cilicia. Syme 1979 [1939], 132–3; Mitchell 1999, 20–2; Kantor 2013, 154–5.

[142] *I.Priene*[2] 13 (incl. *Milet* 1.2.3).

[143] Cic. *Fam.* 13.67.1. Kantor 2013, 155.

[144] Sherk 1969, 275, with references; Merkelbach 1995, 73–6; Blümel & Merkelbach 2014, 34. Canali De Rossi (2000, 164–71, cf. Strabo 14.1.7), argues that the use of Magnesian ambassadors to carry the letter implies that the author was not present in the *provincia*: he proposes Cn. Pompeius Magnus as consul in 52. His explanation (2000, 166) that Cicero and his brother Quintus were involved as they served as *patroni* in some capacity is unconvincing, while his emendation of l. 37 to read: *Κοΐν[τ]ου Τ[ύλλιο]* creates an inconsistency in forms of address, with his brother referred to as: *[Μάρ|κω]ι Κικέρ[ων]ι* in ll. 38–39. Compare Oppius making use of Aphrodisian ambassadors at the conclusion of the First Mithridatic War (*IAph2007* 8.2.i.25–28), who was still within the *provincia*, on Cos, when he received the Aphrodisian delegation.

alternative. Suggesting the orator's son (*cos.* 30), the governor of Asia during the early 20s, as the named Cicero, he proposes that Octavian was the author.[145] He stresses that while the Phrygian dioceses were within *provincia Asia* in 44, their subsequent fate is unknown. Considering the large tracts of formerly provincial territory granted to local rulers by M. Antonius and dismemberment of *provincia Cilicia* during the 30s, the Phrygian dioceses were likely assigned to Amyntas of Galatia until that kingdom's dissolution in 25.[146] The appearance of Mylasa in the text presents an apparent problem for this interpretation, since the *communis opinio* links its disappearance from the record in favour of Halicarnassus, confirmed by 17, to its devastation by Q. Labienus and the Parthians in 40/39. However, the strength of this objection is limited. Even allowing a connection between the prosperity of a settlement and its suitability as a judicial centre in the eyes of Roman administrators, it does not follow that such a step was taken immediately.[147] Accepting Canali De Rossi's speculative reconstruction of a *formula valetudinis* in the early lines would further hint at a later date.[148] Overall, weight of evidence supports the dating of this document of the period after Actium but before the Octavian's settlement of the *res publica* in 27.

The *lex portorii Asiae* includes a list of the Asian διοικήσεις in the year 17. As noted, Halicarnassus replaces Mylasa and the three Phrygian dioceses are restored. The list also includes Sardis (presumably at the expense of the absent Tralles, devastated by an earthquake in 27/26), Philomelium, and Cyzicus.[149] The apparently near-contemporary list drawn from Pliny omits Miletus, Halicarnassus, and Cyzicus but is incomplete in any case.[150] Two epigraphic finds provide later evidence. An inscription from Didyma records the appointment of νεοποιοί (temple-works overseers) for the construction of a temple to Gaius (37–41 CE). The list of appointees apportions one νεοποιός per city, which Robert identified as representing a wider διοίκησις. These mostly come from the *conventus* centres, though Ephesus, Cibyra, and Synnada appear to have been represented by citizens of other *poleis* within their district.[151] Finally, a Flavian inscription lists a series

[145] Cicero's governorship is attested by coins of Magnesia-under-Sipylos (*RPC* 1.2448) and an anecdote recorded by the elder Seneca (Sen. *Suas.* 7.13). Atkinson's (1958, 303, 325) dating to 24/23 assumes a five-year gap between his consulship (30) and governorship which Eilers (2001) demonstrates was not uniformly applied even in the following decade.

[146] Bowersock 1970, 226–7; Syme 1979 [1939], 141–4. Cf. Magie 1950, 418, 1271–2; Täuber 1991, 207 contra Bikerman 1947, 354–9.

[147] Halicarnassus: *SEG* 39.1180.39. Bowersock 1970, 226–7; Habicht 1975, 69–72. Contrast Haensch (1997, 308–10) prioritizing administrative geography.

[148] Canali De Rossi 2000, 165. See Chapter 5, 'Caesar and Reconstruction'.

[149] Cottier et al. 2008, ll.88–91. Tralles: Strabo 12.8.18; CD. 54.31.3; Euseb. *Chron.* p. 164 (Helm); Agathias 2.17; *SEG* 49.1447 with Jones 2011, 107–15.

[150] Robert 1949, 224–7, with references.

[151] *I.Didyma* 148; cf. 107. Robert 1949, 223–6; Habicht 1975, 70; Herrmann 1989, 191–6.

of communities ordered by their διοίκησις, together with amounts of currency and rubrics.[152]

Across the period, the *conventus* appear in diverse administrative contexts. The earliest evidence prioritizes its judicial function. In the Republican period this did not equate to a fixed 'circuit'. Instead, the governor's preferences dictated which centres would be visited. For example, Cicero, during his Cilician command in 51/50, reports two rounds of assizes. First, en route to the eastern part of the province he stopped for a number of days at Laodicea-on-the-Lycus, Apamea, Synnada, and Philomelium for this purpose.[153] Second, on his return to Laodicea, he held assizes for all districts north and west of the Taurus between 13 February and 1 May 50.[154] Finally, he sent his *legatus*, Q. Volusius, to Cyprus to hold the assizes for that island, constrained by an earlier *lex data* which protected its inhabitants from judicial summons to the mainland.[155] The two-and-a-half months set aside for the assize at Laodicea has contributed to the impression of a heavy judicial workload for late Republican governors.[156] However, there are grounds to question this position. First, Cicero held a special interest in appearing a diligent governor and a prolonged *conventus* bolstered this impression. Second, an extended session allowed litigants from distant *dioceses* to make the journey with less fear of missing the governor due to unanticipated delays.[157] Finally, Laodicea, the venue chosen for this major session, had comparatively good communications with Rome and was close to hot springs at Hierapolis.[158] Cicero's arrangements demonstrate that, despite his complaints that his plans to conduct all judicial business in winter were overturned, there was no established circuit or calendar for the *conventus* of this province at this time.[159]

The appearance of διοικήσεις in the *lex portorii Asiae*, however, demonstrates their utility in non-judicial contexts. In this case, they are used to enumerate the constituent parts of *provincia Asia*.[160] An intriguing point here is provided by an apparent exception found in the clause immediately following this. The text on the stone reads: εἰ μὴ αὐταὶ ἀγοραὶ εἰσιν [sc. δικῶν], that is, 'unless they are *conventus* centres'. The editors of the comprehensive recent text are split on its interpretation: Crawford, Reynolds, and Ferrary see the inscription of μὴ as an error for <καὶ>, rendering the translation, 'and <also> if they are *conventus* centres'.

[152] Habicht 1975, 66. [153] Cic. *Fam.* 15.4.2.

[154] Cic. *Att.* 6.2.4. Haensch (1997, 705–7) gives a full list of attested *conventus* sessions.

[155] Cic. *Att.* 5.21.6. Given Cicero's later reference to a *lex P. Lentuli* relevant to Cyprus (*Fam.* 13.48), Badian thought that Lentulus Spinther issued this regulation when incorporating it into *provincia Cilicia* (1965, 113–18; cf. the treatment of the Caenice in *RS* 12.Cnidus.4.1–31) contra Zarecki 2012, 46, 48–9.

[156] E.g., Lintott 1993, 43–69. [157] Compare Cic. *Fam.* 3.8.4–5. [158] Lintott 2008, 262–3.

[159] Cic. *Att.* 5.14.1; 5.21.9, 6.2.4. Caesar indicates a similar flexibility: Caes. *BGall.* 1.54.3, 6.44.3, 7.1.1, 8.46.5. Burton 1975, 99; Fournier 2010, 56–8, 86–7; Kantor 2013, 155; *pace* Habicht 1975, 68.

[160] Showing continuity with the identification of second-century Colophon as 'outside the *provincia*'. See Chapter 1, 'Gubernatorial Jurisdiction and the Free Cities'. Cottier et al. 2008, *ad* l.89; Dalla Rosa 2014, 40–2.

Their colleagues, Cottier, Crowther, and Mitchell prefer to accept the reading on the stone.[161] Mitchell suggests that this restriction ensured that *conventus* centres which were not otherwise exempted could not claim to be outside of the *formula* of the other διοκήσεις, but this interpretation is difficult to accept. Even if the centres themselves stood at the head of the *formulae*, they were still included within it implicitly.[162] Either reading presents problems. The first implies that *conventus* centres, irrespective of their formal status, were now exempt from the *portorium*: that is, that they possessed a customs-free zone starting from eight *stades* within their own territory. This would indicate that the *res publica* was willing to forego the customs revenue from several major ports without tax-exempt status due to their importance from a judicial perspective. Mitchell's alternative, that this is a legal redundancy, is therefore preferable. Similarly, the Flavian fragment seems to refer to indirect taxes at the provincial level.[163] In turn, this shows that by 17, the *conventus* was used to organize fiscal as well as judicial administration.

Overall, the *conventus* in Asia seems to have developed gradually. Though the disjunction between the Latin and Greek terms implies either a basis in an original Attalid institution, a fiscal function, or both, I argue that the initial *conventus* served purely as a judicial structure, with relevance to Roman citizens only, emerging between 129 and 89 in major centres associated with the former Attalid administration due to convenience.[164] After the Sullan settlement and the practical subjection of most *poleis* to the governor's jurisdiction, the organization acquired more formality. It seems likely, on account of the Greek translation to διοίκησις, that an earlier form of organization, linked to Attalid taxation, was repurposed. However, particularly in regions which had not previously been subject to Attalid rule, the Sullan *discriptio* may have formed a basis for the districts, assigning different numbers of *regiones* to the new διοικήσεις. The Roman diaspora and *publicani* were active in the newly regulated region and had recourse to a familiar legal structure in disputes. Since the governor was the fundamental source of law in his *provincia*, by means of his *edictum* and *ius iurisdictionis*, the *conventus* structure appears to have been a formalization of the natural process by which disputes could be referred to him.[165] Certainly, throughout this period, the growing Roman presence in the region gave increasing importance to the regional *conventus*.[166] Once established, notwithstanding their

[161] Cottier et al. 2008, *ad* l.91.

[162] *Pace* Mitchell 2008, 197.

[163] *I.Eph.* 13. Most rubrics occur with amounts listed in *denarii* or without denomination, though a single appearance of τετραχαλκία highlights the continuing flexibility of Roman administration. Habicht 1975, 64; Burnett, Amandry, & Ripollès Alegre 1992, 370.

[164] Kallet-Marx 1995, 116, 135–7; *pace* Merola 2001, 172–81. See also: Ryan (2022, 74–9, 86–9) on the spatial implications: a *conventus* centre needed public spaces appropriate and large enough for litigants to gather.

[165] Including those between locals: e.g., Cic. *Att.* 6.1.15. Compare Bryan 2012, 775–85.

[166] Debord 1985, 351; Kallet-Marx 1995, 134–7; Merola 2001, 172–81; Marek 2010, 330–3.

potentially irregular employment by commanders, they proved a convenient means of co-ordinating other elements of provincial administration, including communication with individual *poleis* and arranging provincial taxation.

The Origins of the Provincial *koinon*

The *koinon* of Asia—an institution which, under the Principate, played a crucial role in co-ordinating the imperial cult and served as a mutual forum for the civic communities of *provincia Asia*—also had its roots in the Republican period. *Koina* were a well-worn solution in the Greek-speaking world to the problem of balancing poliadic autonomy against increasing economic, religious, and political co-ordination.[167] While often associated with the political coalitions of Hellenistic Greece—such as the Boiotian and Achaian *koina*—as Hallmannsecker has argued the Ionian *koinon* in Asia, attested from the Archaic period to the third century CE, served primarily as a means of expressing and reaffirming Ionian cultural identity through shared festivals, ritual gatherings, and euergetic practice.[168]

The name of the institution which became the *koinon* of Asia passed through several forms, starting with *οἱ δῆμοι οἱ ἐν τῆι Ἀσίαι καὶ τὰ ἔθνη* ('the cities and peoples in Asia'), attested from the early first century, to the *κοινὸν (ἐπὶ τῆς Ἀσίας) τῶν Ἑλλήνων* ('the community of the Greeks in Asia'), from the middle of the first century, through to the *κοινὸν τῆς Ἀσίας*, which appears from the Triumviral period onwards.[169] The earliest title appears once in a collective decree and five times in honorific contexts: once at Olympia—for Q. Mucius Scaevola—and four times in local contexts: twice at Ephesus, and once at Pergamum and Poimanenon. Each is dated to the first quarter of the first century based on the connection to Scaevola's governorship in the early 90s.[170] This raises the question who comprised the group which referred to itself as the *δῆμοι καὶ ἔθνη*. Laffi suggests it referred to the communities of Asia acting in concert, with *poleis* described as *δῆμοι* and less urbanized groups as *ἔθνη*.[171] The inclusion of 'free' cities in this group, on which Laffi is equivocal, must be possible, on the basis that the vast majority of *poleis* were free during this period. In honorific inscriptions, the *δῆμοι καὶ ἔθνη* were joined by other groups, as that for Herostratus of Poimanenon makes clear: *οἱ ἐν τῆι Ἀσίαι δῆμοι κα[ὶ τ]ὰ ἔθν[η] | καὶ οἱ κατ' ἄνδρα κεκριμένοι ἐν τῆι πρὸς | Ῥωμαίους φιλίαι καὶ τῶν ἄλλων οἱ εἰρη|μένοι μετέχειν τῶν Σωτηρίων καὶ | Μουκιείων* ('the cities and peoples in Asia and those judged, individually, to be in friendship with the Romans and the rest who are agreed to

[167] E.g., Mackil 2013. [168] Hallmannsecker 2022, esp. 60–83.
[169] Full discussion in Mellor 1975, 80–2; Laffi 2010a, 31–7 and *infra*.
[170] *OGIS* 439, 438; *I.Eph.* 615A, 205; *IGR* 4.921.
[171] Laffi 2010a, 35–7; Cf. Merola 2001, 186–91.

participate in the *Soteria* and *Moukieia*').[172] The intriguing formulation of οἱ κατ' ἄνδρα κεκριμένοι ἐν τῆι πρὸς Ῥωμαίους φιλίαι, which the *senatus consultum de Asclepiade* translates as *qui in amicorum formulam relati sunt* ('those included in the *formula amicorum*' [i.e., the list of individual Roman friends]), demonstrates that membership of the nascent organization was not limited to communities. In turn, this implies a degree of separation between the communities themselves and those on the *formula*.[173] Critically, this phrase implies an initial choice joining in the institution, outside of a core group, by participating in the penteteric festival decreed for Scaevola by the more precisely defined group [τῶν ἐν τῆ]ι φιλίαι κριθέν[των]| δήμων τε καὶ ἔ[θνων] ('the cities and peoples judged to be in friendship [sc. with the Romans]').[174] That said, the active involvement of the honorand in reconciling the contentious cities of Ephesus and Sardis indicates that pressure from individual magistrates may have played an important role in facilitating this novel religious movement.[175]

Both the δῆμοι καὶ ἔθνη and the later *koinon* had a significant religious dimension. The earliest evidence all pertains to honours based around the new festival, the *Moukieia*, which the assembled communities participated in. The body defined itself by reference to the festival. Beyond this, however, other early evidence points to a religious focus. Plutarch attests that, after Lucullus' reforms to alleviate the impact of Sulla's levies in 71/70, the *poleis* of Asia celebrated a festival, the *Leukolleia*, in his honour.[176] Moreover, Cicero, defending L. Valerius Flaccus, refers to a festival honouring his client's father, commander in Asia in the late 90s.[177] He asserts that the money for the festival had been assembled *a tota Asia* (from all Asia): strong evidence that one of Scaevola's immediate successors also received a common festival funded by *poleis* within the *provincia*.[178]

[172] *OGIS* 438.3–5. Parallels: *OGIS* 439; *IGR* 4.921. Laffi (2010a, 46 n.44) argues that the two names represented a single festival against suggestions that the new name *Moukieia* was attached to a pre-existing festival, the *Soteria* (Pfister *RE* s.v. Σωτήρια, 1228–9; Brennan 2000, 550; Thériault 2011, 379–80). Buraselis (2012, 247–58) on the broader phenomenon of double festivals in the Hellenistic period.

[173] Parallels at Laffi (2010a, 32–4). Raggi 2010, 148–50.

[174] Laffi 2010a, 38–44; Vitale 2012, 62–3.

[175] Honouring Roman magistrates with festivals is attested in Greece from the early second century (T. Quinctius Flamininus at Gytheum, *AÉ* 1929, #99). For a comprehensive list: Erkelenz 1999, 44–5 n.9; for Asia, with discussion: Thériault 2011, 377–84.

[176] Plut. *Luc.* 23.1; cf. App. *Mith.* 76. Mileta (2008a, 104–6) suggests this entails full cult honours, though compare Tröster's more reserved stance (2008, 38, 132–6). Thériault (2011, 381) theorizes a gap of some years between the establishment of a local festival at Cyzicus and the provincial festival.

[177] While other civic festivals are attested, these are the only 'provincial' examples. Rigsby's suggestion (1988, 148–9) that the provincial *Euergesia* celebrated at Pergamum was the same festival as the *Soteria kai Moukieia* and *Flakkeia* is unconvincing as Cicero (*Verr.* 2.2.51; cf. [Asc.] 202, 262 Stangl) explicitly attests the survival of the *Moukieia* through the Mithridatic Wars. The *Leukolleia* shows that other commanders received the named festivals and a 'generic' festival runs against such honours' purpose—to leverage favour with a specific commander. Erkelenz 1999, 49; Ferrary 1997, 217 n.46; Thériault 2011, 379.

[178] Cic. *Flacc.* 54–9. Maselli 2000, 176–8. On the financial implications of this passage: Erkelenz 1999, 51–7 contra Edelmann-Singer 2015, 67–8.

Unlike Scaevola or Lucullus, there is no evidence to suggest that Flaccus *père* was regarded as a paragon. Instead, this should imply that the honour of a provincial festival was not limited to exceptional individuals, but was, on that occasion, employed as a strategy by the provincial community to engage with the governor.[179] While, cautiously, such honours may have reflected an acceptable public acknowledgement of Roman hegemony, a 'public transcript' to use Scott's term, it is just possible that the *Flakkeia* was tied to a concrete action in defence of the province.[180] These examples emphasize the extent to which the earliest provincial organization of communities was concerned with the creation and administration of common religious events to celebrate Roman officials within a traditionally Greek context.[181]

Mackil argued that shared religious festivals allowed communities to create and articulate social bonds. Concentrating on pre-Roman Greece, she contended that regular rituals practiced together can forge a group identity.[182] Shared festivals generated networks of interaction across the involved communities and strengthened social contact between the participants.[183] Though this was unambiguously an elite phenomenon—the delegates from any given city probably had significant standing to be selected—these networks facilitated integration between the upper-social strata of diverse *poleis*, alongside other institutional links such as *proxenia* and *theorodokeia*.[184] Regular contact also allowed individuals to build influence among their peers and may have nurtured the slow growth of an inter-civic or provincial elite, encompassing men like Diodorus Zonas, and perhaps, Hierocles and Dionysus, dual-citizens of Tralles and Aphrodisias.[185] This group almost certainly shared priorities in navigating Roman governance, increasing the centripetal factors for participants. Economic issues appear to have been at the forefront, but retention of the local status quo must also have loomed large. The participation in communal rituals affirming a common relationship with Rome through physical acts and utterances could also instantiate a feeling of community.[186]

However, state formation, or the formation of inter-community institutions, requires a process of negotiation to 'balance and articulate unobjectionable power-relationships and legitimacy'. Since individual communities possess their own interests and agency, involvement in larger organizations, even if mutually beneficial involves trading away some autonomy over aims, strategy, and action.[187] The insistence of the earliest inscriptions on the constitutive framing of the institution

[179] Thériault 2011, 380; *pace* Frija 2012, 90–1. The only other evidence for his command is a single bland honorific inscription from Claros: Tuchelt 1979, 161, comments from Ferrary 2000a, 337–8.

[180] Scott 1990, esp. 17–44.

[181] Drew-Bear 1972, 461–2; Mileta 2008a, 109–11 (with caution); Laffi 2010a, 31–2.

[182] Mackil 2013, 183–91, 215. Anthropological studies: Geertz 1973, 87–125; 1983, 29–30, 124–5; note, the critique of Thompson 1990, 130–5.

[183] Mackil 2013, 242.

[184] Ando 2000, 336–42; van Nijf 2001, 306–18.

[185] Mileta 2008a, 112; Frija 2019. Cf. Jones (2012, 214–17) for imperial examples.

[186] Cf. Ando (2000, 199–205) on imperial acclamations.

[187] Mackil 2013, 216. Already, Price 1984, 62–5.

may indicate precisely this process of negotiation and balancing. Herostratus' inscription also mentions a *συνέδριον*, which may indicate the formation of broader institutions within the group.[188] The socialization and renewal of the ritual bonds brought about by the penteteric repetition of the new *Moukieia*, which persisted even through Mithridates' control of Asia, laid the foundations for later and more coherent action by the group.[189] The increasing propensity of the emerging group to honour individuals with inscriptions further supports this view.[190]

The most compelling evidence for the consolidation of this loose body from a collective focused on festivals to a more politically minded institution is a decree, issued by a body calling itself the *κοινὸν τῶν ἐπὶ τῆς Ἀσίας Ἑλλήνων* ('the *koinon* of the Greeks in Asia'). This document, as Drew-Bear demonstrated, must date to the Republican period: the content and specifically the reference to the 'utmost despair' wrought by *δημοσιῶναι* (sc. *publicani*) gives a likely date between the re-establishment of *provincia Asia* in the late 80s and Caesar's removal of Roman tax-farmers of the *decuma* in 48.[191] The decree honours two statesmen, Dionysius and Hierocles, citizens of both Tralles and Aphrodisias, who had undertaken an embassy to Rome *διὰ τὸ κοινῇ συμφέρον τῶν Ἑλλήνων* ('for the common good of the Greeks'). Following their success, the *koinon* voted them golden crowns and bronze statues.[192] This inscription raises several pertinent questions regarding the form, date, nature, and aims of the *koinon* as a body.

The issuing body names itself in several ways within the text. The full title appears once (ll.24-25), with an abbreviated version (*κοινὸν τῶν Ἑλλήνων*, ll.4, 21, 22) employed three times. However, twice—and crucially when laying out the text to be inscribed beneath the statues decreed for the honorands—the body refers to itself as *οἱ ἐν τῇ Ἀσίᾳ δῆμοι καὶ τὰ ἔθνη* ('the peoples and tribes in Asia', ll.23–24, 28). This echoes the titulature of the group which organized the *Soteria kai Moukieia*, demonstrating a link between the so-called peoples and tribes of Asia and the institutional form of the *koinon*.[193] This document presents a transition between the two modes of reference, and all other attestations of the title *κοινὸν τῶν Ἑλλήνων* date to the Augustan period or later.

The text demonstrates conclusively that representatives of this body could meet, and did so at Ephesus, though whether this was a regular or irregular occurrence the text leaves unclear. It resembles contemporary civic decrees, containing motivation clauses, a rationale, and culminating in a resolution clause. Self-evidently, the body had a reasonable expectation that its membership would

[188] Though this could post-date the Mithridatic Wars. Raggi 2010, 148. Cf. Kaufmann & Stauber 1992, 58–60.

[189] On the *Moukieia* under Mithridates: Cic. *Verr.* 2.2.51.; cf. [Asc.] 202, 262 Stangl. Mileta 2008a, 103–4.

[190] E.g., *OGIS* 438.

[191] Drew-Bear 1972, 469–71.

[192] *IAph2007* 2.503.

[193] Vitale 2012, 62–4.

respect its utterances: the bronze statues for the ambassadors, not insignificant honours, were to be erected παρ' ᾧ ἂν βούλωνται δήμῳ ἢ ἔθνει ('among whatsoever people or tribe [the honorands] wish').[194] Moreover, this decree is predicated on previous decisions taken by the group, namely to dispatch ambassadors on behalf of the collective group to the Senate in Rome, to give an account of the issue and beg for protection. The decree also refers to officials (πρόεδροι), tasked by the original meeting to send letters to Aphrodisias in order to locate Dionysus and Hierocles, and a γραμματεύς.[195]

Scholars have generally dated the decree to the 70s, before Lucullus' actions against the *publicani* in Asia.[196] This claim originates with Drew-Bear's treatment of the decree which, while showing due caution in noting the *termini ante* and *post quem*, then asserts without argument it should date 'probablement avant les réformes opérées par Lucullus en 71'.[197] This date is routinely reproduced without qualification and warrants scrutiny.[198] Drew-Bear's reasoning appears to be based on Lucullus' well-attested alleviation of the debt crisis gripping the *poleis* of Asia. Indeed, the fiscal situation of provincial communities remained stark across the period. Cicero, defending Flaccus in 59, implies a fierce resentment of Roman taxes. Similar sentiments appear in his correspondence with his brother.[199] His own later experience in Cilicia demonstrates the speed with which conditions could fluctuate. The power of the governor to set and enforce provincial rates of interest could have a major impact on the solvency of communities.[200] Despite Lentulus Spinther's resistance to the *publicani* before 54, on Cicero's arrival in the province in 51, civic finances were in a sorry state.[201]

Crucially, the proposed date does not leave much time for an appeal to Rome based on the activity of *publicani* specifically. Immediately after Sulla's reorganization, the *societates publicanorum* were not active in Asia, and the system of *censoria locatio* may not have been revived until 75. If so, one would expect (if the decree had been produced before Lucullus' arrival) emphasis to be laid on the suddenness or novelty of the crisis. Instead, the text underscores the longstanding nature of the problems facing the cities. Cn. Pompeius Magnus, who held the command against Mithridates from 66 to 62, likewise had crafted a reputation as a commander sensitive to the hardships of provincials and his command would seem an odd context for the *koinon*'s action.[202] Moreover, given that Lucullus' long service in Asia afforded him a pre-existing, and largely positive, reputation, it would be unusual to see a direct approach to the Senate preceding his actions

[194] *IAph2007* 2.503.27. [195] Vitale 2012, 62 contra Edelmann-Singer 2011, 89; 2015, 67–8.
[196] On these actions: Tröster 2008, 86, with references. [197] Drew-Bear 1972, 471.
[198] E.g., Ferrary 2001, 25 ('sans doute, des années 70'); Edelmann-Singer 2015, 64–7. More cautiously, Reynolds 1982, 26.
[199] Cic. *Flacc.* 19. Cf. Cic. *QFr.* 1.1.33–34; 1.2.6. [200] E.g., Cic. *Att.* 5.21, 6.1.
[201] Cic. *Fam.* 1.9.26; *Att.* 5.16.2–3. [202] Morrell 2017, 70–6.

which did not leverage his name and authority.[203] Instead, the situation described in the decree better suits the late 60s, under Flaccus, or, more likely, the 50s.[204]

The second 'Republican' attestation of the *koinon* often cited appears in the letter preserved at Miletus and Priene, which, I have already suggested above, dates rather to the post-Actian period. Here the *koinon* appears only as addressee, alongside the *conventus* centres of the *provincia*. Even so, this illustrates that the body was sufficiently well established to receive, and presumably act on, correspondence from Roman officials. It suggests a means of simplifying Roman administrative practice. As noted already, the distribution of significant correspondence through major centres to other communities reduced the demand on the system: it handballed responsibility for administrative communication to the communities themselves. Though speculative, it could be observed that this process fits well with the style of governance introduced by the triumvir M. Antonius, who was also the first attested magistrate to write to the *koinon*, no earlier than 41.[205] In a period where the institutional basis of collective government was dissolving, it would be plausible for Antonius to actively reduce the number of moving parts with which he had to communicate. However, though the advent of the *koinon* as a coherent mouthpiece of the assembled *provincia* presented a means for Roman officials to reduce their own responsibilities, this was an outcome, rather than carefully formed intention.

Exogenous factors also played their role in pushing the communities of Asia into ever-closer union. The shared trauma of the First Mithridatic War, whether experienced through devastation inflicted by either side or the decisions of Sulla, offered participants common ground over which to bond. The abuses of the *publicani* and other fiscal travails were mutual difficulties for most *poleis* in *provincia Asia* after Dardanus.[206] Unrestrained Roman acquisitiveness provided a real threat, encouraging communities to surrender more of their individual agency to ensure the leverage of the collective, and consequently their own advantage in the longer term. Both Campanile and Edelmann-Singer argued that a major factor in the *koinon*'s engagement with Roman administration was to provide a direct conduit for communal concerns to be communicated to the Senate in Rome. Rather than many *poleis* besieging the *curia* (or the governor) with complaints or a cacophony of discordant voices, the *koinon* provided a clear channel for the whole province to speak. This afforded the Senate the luxury of responding definitively to a single list of complaints at the cost of offering more

[203] Keaveney 1992, 29–30; Tröster 2008, 81–2.

[204] Cf. Canali De Rossi (2005, 101–8) contextualizing this decree in a slew of cases in the early 50s (Cic. *Flacc.* 52–53, 98).

[205] *RDGE* 57.

[206] This holds for even for free cities (e.g., *RDGE* 70). Even where the intentions of Sulla were clear, *publicani* could, and did, attempt to maximize their own return. This continues the trend from the early *provincia* where most *poleis* were unambiguously free, yet the *publicani* remained a significant nuisance.

leverage and gravitas to the ambassadors, as seems to have been the case in the imperial period.[207] However, the evidence is ambiguous for the Republican manifestation of the *koinon*. Beyond the decree for Hierocles and Dionysus, little evidence of province-wide co-ordination exists. Though Cicero states that the accusation levelled against Flaccus for illegally collecting money for a fleet was a *commune totius Asiae crimen*, in contrast to those brought by individual cities, this need not mean that it was brought by the *koinon*. The involvement of all, or even most, of the communities represented in the suit would adequately explain this remark.[208] Moreover, such a development was not obviously in the interests of the Senate. The staple Roman strategy of *divide et impera*, which Strabo notes as underpinning the basic organization of *provincia Asia*, cuts against a policy of giving a single voice to a diverse range of communities.[209] More tellingly, there is no evidence of another provincial *koinon* until the Augustan era.[210]

Furthermore, Ferrary highlights the increasing frequency over the course of the first century of collective phrases including οἱ Ἕλληνες to describe the benefactors of Roman magistrates in honorary contexts. Rejecting Raubitschek's suggestion that the rush of inscriptions honouring Caesar in collective terms derived from a decree of the Delphic Amphictiony, he links it explicitly to the emergence of the *koinon*.[211] Ferrary cites two crucial earlier examples; first, an inscription for Q. Cicero at Claros describing him as εὐεργέτην ὄντα | τῶν Ἑλλήνων καὶ | πάτρωνα τοῦ δή|μου ('benefactor of the Greeks and patron of the *demos*'), likely during his governorship (61–59).[212] As governor, he showed an interest in reducing financial hardship for local communities, eliminating the levies paid to

[207] Campanile 2007, 130–4; Edelmann-Singer 2015, 69–71.

[208] Cic. *Flacc.* 34. Note Cicero's attempts to dismiss this group here and elsewhere as unrepresentative of the province or individual civic bodies (Cic. *Flacc.* 18, 34, 42–3, 45, 52).

[209] Strabo 13.4.12. Knoepfler (2010, 700–5), notes the phenomenon of *koinon*-revivals on the Greek mainland during the late second and early first centuries. He adduces a decree of Chalcis celebrating a *Romaia* with the κοινὸν τῶν Εὐβοιῶν, dated by him to after 146, an honorary inscription from Olympia, which he dates to after 122, and the re-establishment of the *koinon* of the Boiotians, which he places soon after Sulla's reconquest of Greece in 86. None of these dates, however, are uncontroversial, and the traditional dates for the first two examples fall in the first half of the second century. Each institution already existed and had interacted with the Roman state in an earlier period. This distinguishes them from this example, the formation *ex novo* of a coalition of relatively significant cities into a single institutional entity. Cf. Mackil 2013, 139–43.

[210] Fernoux (2004, 180–3 contra Deininger 1965, 16–19; Marek 1993, 73–82) emphasizes that Augustus' concession of the right to erect a temple to Rome and himself at Nicomedia, as reported by CD. (51.20.6–7), does not itself demonstrate preceding existence of a κοινὸν τῶν ἐν Βιθυνίᾳ Ἑλλήνων ('*koinon* of the Greeks in Bithynia'). Instead, he draws on the evidence of *CIL* 6.1508, which he dates to 31–29 and attests the patronage over several Bithynian *poleis* by a certain 'Rufus', as counting against the existence of a *koinon*, while suggesting Augustus' reorganization of Asia and Bithynia in 20 may have included its establishment (cf. CD. 54.7.4–5). The broader argument holds even if accepting Eilers' earlier date of pre-44 (2002, 254–6; cf. Eck 1984, 209). The next attested provincial *koinon* is that of Galatia (cf. Mitchell 1993, 103–4; Vitale 2012, 117–18). The assumption of Burrell (2004, 166) that this was established in the 20s with the *provincia* itself is unsupported by the evidence.

[211] Ferrary 2001, 20–4 contra Raubitschek 1954, 74–5.

[212] *BÉ* (1958) #390. See now: *SEG* 49.1511. For Q. Cicero's governorship: *MRR* 2.181, 185, 191; Magie 1950, 381–3, 1244.

support a fleet based in the *provincia*, as well as contributions to aedilician games at Rome. These unparalleled inscriptions help to demonstrate the collective impact of his actions.[213] M. Cicero's semi-public and private injunctions to his brother treat the *publicani* with caution may indicate further sympathy for locals in exercising his juridical responsibilities.[214] A statue-base from Priene for M'. Aemilius Lepidus, *proquaestor*, is less overt. Most commentators identify this individual with the consul of 66, giving a date of 80/79 assuming his election *suo anno* to both magistracies.[215] The Prienean *demos* honours Lepidus ἀρετῆς ἕνεκεν καὶ εὐνοίας | καὶ εὐεργεσίας τῆς εἰς ἑαυτὸν | καὶ τοὺς ἄλλους Ἕλληνας ('for his excellence, goodwill and benefactions to them and the other Greeks').[216] This is the earliest appearance of this shorthand for a collective of Greek communities relating themselves to Roman magistrates and may indicate an increasing group identity as a result of the longer-term co-operation in organizing festivals or the more sudden collective imposition of direct and intrusive Roman rule. Similarly, in 39, M. Cocceius Nerva was honoured at Teos as τὸν κοινὸν | εὐεργέτην καὶ σωτῆρα τῆς ἐπαρχήας, | καὶ τῆς πόλεως πάτρωνα ('the common benefactor and saviour of the province, and the patron of the city').[217] This example, like the others contrasts the position of the honorand vis-à-vis the province as a whole and Teos specifically. Ferrary's argument, however, that these inscriptions depend in some way on a collective decision, or indeed, decree of the *koinon*, while not implausible, lacks positive evidence. In both cases the honouring city seems to act on its own initiative. Q. Cicero is explicitly highlighted as the civic patron of Colophon, while Lepidus is honoured by the Prieneans for services to their city first. These examples stand in contrast with documents of the δῆμοι καὶ ἔθνη which explicitly enumerate the collective membership of the group participating, eliding individual identities in favour of solidarity.[218]

In sum, the *koinon* originated as a collective assembly of local communities in *provincia Asia* based around the celebration of common religious festivals honouring individual Roman magistrates. First attested in the 90s, it slowly coalesced into a venue for collective action and began serving as a co-ordinating body for common complaints to Rome. However, when compared to Roman management of other provincial communities in the late second and early first centuries, the prevailing view that it emerged from imperial planning is unlikely. Though certainly acknowledged as a legitimate organization and later employed by Roman administrators to simplify communication with *poleis* and co-ordinate the

[213] Cic. *Flacc.* 33; *QFr.* 1.1.26. [214] Cic. *QFr.* 1.1.33–34, 2.6.

[215] Ferrary (2001, 24) adduces *I.Délos* 1659 and 1953, which honour Lepidus at Delos under the ἐπιμελητής Nicanor to further bolster this date, but note Mattingly's (1979, 166–7) suggestion of 65/64.

[216] *I.Priene*² 233.

[217] *Carie* 2.103. Cf. *I.Stratonikeia* 509. On Nerva: Delrieux & Ferriès 2011, 421–52.

[218] Vitale's insistence (2012, 32–3, 38–9; 2014, 287–308) that ἔθνος and *koinon* are two sides of the same two coins cuts against the deliberate framing of the nascent organization as δῆμοι καὶ ἔθνη.

provincial imperial cult, this evolution in form and responsibilities is more likely to have occurred during the chaos of the civil wars in the 40s and 30s. Instead, the *koinon* was a strong example of local agency: a self-managed collective organization to deal with Roman power.[219]

Civic Freedom in Republican *provincia Asia*

The position of the remaining free *poleis* presents a final, critical, element of late Republican Asia: the effects of the broader changes in civic status on the meaning of *ἐλευθερία* in *provincia Asia* were not insignificant. The *senatus consultum de Stratonicensibus* provides a key example. Passed in 81, it accorded eleven specific privileges to the city, mostly senatorial confirmations of Sulla's own decisions in the field. Most prominent were the renewal of *amicitia et societas* (l.69) and the guaranteed use of their own laws as before the war (*νόμοις ἐθισμοῖς τε ἰδίοις πρότερον*, l.91).[220] Crucial, however, was the assignment of several communities (*πολιτεῖαι*) and their revenues (*πρόσοδοι*) to the *polis*. These revenues recur three times in the extant text: first, Themessos, Keramos, and a third community are listed, together with their *χωρία [κώμας λιμένας προσόδους τε τῶν] πόλεων* ('lands, [villages, harbours, and revenues of the] *poleis*'), which Sulla had assigned them.[221] Later, they appear as *πολιτείας* ('communities').[222] Heller notes the novelty of this situation, wherein the communities themselves, though subordinate to Stratonicea, retained their own identities and *polis*-status.[223] Importantly, the *senatus consultum* also includes the clause that Sulla was to *ἐπιγνῶι διατάξῃ[ι ὅσας ἑκάστη] | προσόδους Στρατονικεῦσιν τελῆι* ('decide how much revenue each was to pay to Stratonicea'). Having done so Sulla was enjoined:

> *πρὸς ταύτας τὰς πολιτείας, ἃς Στρ[ατονικεῦσιν] | προσώρισεν, γράμματα ἀποστείλῃι, ἵνα τοσοῦτον τ[έλος] | Στρατονικεῦσιν τελῶσιν | [τ]οῦτό τε, οἵτινες ἄν ποτε ἀεὶ Ἀσίαν τήν τε Ἑλλάδα ἐ[παρχείας] | [δια]κατέχωσιν, φροντίζωσιν διδῶσιν τε ἐργασίαν, ἵν[α ταῦτα] | οὕτως γίν[ω]νται* ('to send letters to those communities which he assigned to the Stratoniceans, that each will pay such an amount to the Stratoniceans; and that those who, at any time, are in charge of the provinces of Asia or Greece shall consider and ensure that things are done in this way').[224]

219 Price 1984, 62–5. 220 Heller 2006, 65.
221 *RDGE* 18.55–58. See Ando (2021, 82–5) on the implications. 222 *RDGE* 18.106–108.
223 Heller 2006, 66–8. Kallet-Marx (1995, 276) takes it as a rule that the remaining free cities were assigned new territories. Santangelo's caution (2007, 123 n.71) seems justified. Keramos, at least, seems to have broken free swiftly (*I.Keramos* 18, 27, 31 with Gabrielsen 2000, 167–8).
224 *RDGE* 18.107–112.

This reveals the intimate personal involvement of the dictator in the decision-making process and the details of how, from the perspective of the communities, this new arrangement would operate. Rather than taking all the lands and revenues of a given city, which would be impractical to enforce without erasing the existing *polis*-community, Sulla would define a (presumably annual) 'contribution' due to the dominant *polis*, Stratonicea. The fragmentary *senatus consultum* for nearby Tabae bolsters this picture. The stone suffered substantial damage in key places at lines 7 and 10–11. However, Crawford and Reynolds plausibly restored it to simply confirm the grants of Sulla including the right to [ἀρίσ]τοις τοῖς νόμοις αἱρέσεσιν ('the best laws and conditions').[225] Together, the two documents emphasize that in the aftermath of the First Mithridatic War freedom was supplemented by the grant of lands and revenues from neighbouring, presumably less loyal communities.

An honorific decree from Alabanda further clarifies this period of transition. The text for Pyrrha[kos] refers to several embassies he undertook including to the Romans and an unnamed *basileus*. The date remains disputed: some scholars identify the king as Eumenes II, suggesting a date in first half of the second century.[226] However, a reference to fiscal immunity (ἀφορολογησία) decreed by the Senate suits the aftermath of the First Mithridatic War better.[227] Pyrrha[kos] engaged in at least two exchanges with representatives of the *res publica*. First, he is reported to have renewed οἰκ[ειό]|τητα καὶ φιλίαν ('kinship and friendship') and ποιήσασθαι συμμαχ[ίαν] ('made an alliance'), while assisting Roman forces in the region.[228] Afterwards, he went on an embassy to the Senate περὶ φόρων ('concerning the tribute') and returned with a decree of ἀφορολογησία ('*immunitas*/fiscal immunity').[229] Santangelo, persuasively, takes this as evidence for Alabanda's freedom, highlighting the extent to which, after the inclusion of southern Caria in *provincia Asia*, even free communities had to reassert their rights vis-à-vis the *publicani*.[230]

The *lex Antonia de Termessibus*, promulgated (on the most likely dating) in 68 BCE, provides the best evidence for the implications of *libertas* in Asia Minor in the post-Sullan era.[231] This statute granted several privileges to the inhabitants of Termessus Maior in Pisidia, including declaring them *leiberi amicei socieique populi Romani* ('free, friends and allies of the Roman People').[232] Though

[225] *RDGE* 17.10–11 with Crawford & Reynolds 1974, 289–93.

[226] *SEG* 60.1073. Cousin & Diehl 1886, 299–306; Canali De Rossi 1992/1993, 35–40; Errington 2010, 125–30.

[227] Willrich 1899, 305–11; Marek 1988, 294–302; Santangelo 2007, 54–5, 2009, 67.

[228] *SEG* 60.1073.11–15. [229] *SEG* 60.1073.25–34.

[230] Santangelo 2007, 123. Plin. *HN* 5.109 attests to Alabanda's freedom under Augustus.

[231] This statute was based on an earlier *senatus consultum*, probably passed, from internal evidence, in 72. *RS* 19.1.1–4. Griffin 1973, 210–11; Ferrary 1985, 439–42 contra Mattingly 1997, 68–78.

[232] *RS* 19.1.4–8.

Ferrary persuasively ascribes the *polis* to *provincia Cilicia*, the text nevertheless reveals broader trends in Roman attitudes towards freedom in the post-Sullan period.[233] The *communis opinio* sees Termessus as subjected to direct rule and having its territory confiscated in the aftermath of the First Mithridatic War and its freedom restored for resisting the invasion of the Pontic commander Eumachus in 73. However, this *libertas* was specifically defined. The legislation, though explicitly enrolling the Termessians as *amici et socii*, represents a simple grant of privileges which could be revoked unilaterally.[234] These privileges included protection from magistrates or *legati* from billeting troops, except at the discretion of the Senate, or requisitioning supplies except under the terms of the *lex Porcia*.[235] The *polis* was also authorized to collect local customs duties, the *portoria*, provided that they were not levied on Roman *publicani*.[236] The surviving text does not preserve any explicit reference to *immunitas*, though it is admittedly incomplete. The question of whether these rights were specific to Termessus, or a general package of rights which could be granted to any *polis* along with *libertas* remains unclear. References within the document to islands and maritime *portoria*, when Termessus' territory was almost certainly landlocked, prompted Magie to see this as a general formula.[237] However, while an existing formula may have offered a model, other elements, including references to the *lex locationis*, carried immediate and historically contingent implications.[238]

Important testimony for the continued variability of rights for free *poleis* during this period comes from a letter of an Augustan proconsul to Chios, which cites a *senatus consultum* from 80:

> *ἡ σύ̣γκ̣[λη]|τος εἰδικῶς ἐβεβαίωσεν ὅπως νόμοις τε καὶ ἔθεσιν καὶ δικαίοις χ[ρῶν]|ται ἃ ἔσχον ὅτε τῇ Ῥωμαίων φιλίᾳ προσῆλθον, ἵνα τε ὑπὸ μηθ' ῷ̣τινι[οῦν] | τύπ̣ῳ̣ ὦσιν ἀρχόντων ἢ ἀνταρχόντων· οἵ τε παρ' αὐτοῖς ὄντες Ῥωμ̣[αῖ]|οι τοῖς Χε̣ίων ὑπακούωσιν νόμοις* ('the Senate specifically confirmed that they might enjoy their laws and customs and rights which they had when they entered into the friendship with the Romans, so that they might be subject to no written

[233] *RS* 19.1.22. Ferrary 1996, 338.

[234] This fits the 'surrender and grant' model proposed by Bikerman (1932, 56–61, 1938, 14–17, 133–41, 1939, 344–5) to explain relationships between *poleis* and Hellenistic kingdoms. According to this view, at the moment of surrender, a *polis* formally ceased to exist as a political entity before being reconstituted by the grace of the ruler. Subsequently, any rights, up to and including full ἐλευθερία, flowed directly from the ruling power and could be revoked at any time (compare the archetypal example: *I.Priene*[2] 1). Ma 1999, 111–13; Kantor 2014, 249–51. Note the recent critique of Strootman 2020.

[235] *RS* 19.2.6–17. On requisitions, which could be heavy, even on free communities, compare *IG* 5.1.1146.32–40 with Santangelo 2009a, 361–6; *I.Sagalassos* 3; Linderski 2007 [1999], 309–18.

[236] *RS* 19.2.31–36.

[237] Magie 1950, 1176–7; Ferrary 1996, 338; Merola 2001, 118–19. Cf. Heberdey 1929, 5–15.

[238] E.g., *RS* 19.1.22 (restored as: *e*[*x*] *l*[*ege Ciliciae locandae dicta*]). Ferrary (1996, 338) notes that this clause of the statute deals with the restitution of confiscated property to the Termessians, including *ager publicus* which may have been contracted out in the *censoria locatio* of 70.

directive whatsoever of Roman magistrates or promagistrates; and that the Romans among them may be subject to the laws of the Chians').[239]

The reference to interstate 'friendship' appears to offer a terminal limit at which these privileges were fixed, and perhaps constrained future constitutional and judicial innovation. Two territorial disputes between Greek communities mediated by the Senate in the second century offer comparanda. During the first, involving Priene and Magnesia-on-the-Maeander, the Senate instructed the Mylasans, as arbitrators, to award the disputed lands to the community which possessed it *ὅτε εἰς τὴν φιλίαν τοὺ δήμου τοῦ Ῥωμαίων παραγένετο* ('when the city entered into the friendship of the Roman people').[240] Similarly, in *c.*140 representatives of two Thessalian *poleis*, Melitaia and Narthakion, sought to argue to the Senate that they possessed disputed territory at the time at which they acquired *amicitia* with Rome.[241] Most commentators assert that this represents the common practice of the Senate during this period, though Kallet-Marx cautions that these are the only two examples of this formula being employed in this context.[242] Critically, however, the date at which *amicitia* was established could be contested, the Mylasans avoided any reference to *amicitia* in their final decision.[243] Practicality suggests that Roman officials did not exercise oversight of Chian law-making on a regular basis. However, that does not preclude this clause serving as a potential justification for Roman interference in the case of regime change within Chios.

Beyond the typical privilege of using their own laws (*αὐτονομία*; *uti suis legibus*), the Chians received confirmation of an existing right to exercise local jurisdiction over resident Romans. Kantor convincingly classifies this as 'the use of Chian law in Chian courts' and raises the pertinent issue of whether this applied for citizens of the *polis* outside the island.[244] The surviving text would imply the negative, though the author's paraphrase likely only contained information relevant to the issue at hand: most likely a dispute between a Roman landowner/s and the *polis* in which his predecessor had interfered.[245] Notwithstanding the possibility that the original *senatus consultum* included more details, the fact remains that the rights and privileges of free cities during this period were variable and decided on a case-by-case basis.[246]

A stele containing two letters from Sulla regarding the privileges of the Ionian and Hellespontine guild of Dionsyian artists underscores the impact of the settlement on inter-polis institutions. The second letter, which seems to have

[239] *RDGE* 70.14–18. [240] *RDGE* 7.51–55. [241] *RDGE* 9.21–22, 46–8.

[242] Kallet-Marx 1995, 174; *pace* Marshall 1980, 648; Ager 1996, 27.

[243] Ager 1996, 327; Snowdon 2014, 428–9, 432–9. [244] Kantor 2010, 196–7.

[245] Marshall 1969, 262–9.

[246] Thornton (1999, 520–1) plausibly concludes that this decree belongs in the context of other *senatus consulta* confirming Sullan grants of privileges, e.g., to Stratonicea, Tabae, Thasos.

been written *c.*84, established privileges and honours including *ἀλειτουργησία* ('exemption from public services') which the Roman state had already bestowed upon the artists, before adding a tax-exemption (*μήτε τινὰ [εἰσφορὰν ἢ δαπά]|νας εἰσφέρητε*) and other privileges.[247] Its companion, written by Sulla in 81, sanctioned the right of the guild to erect a stele recording the privileges granted by the dictator himself, ratified *ex senatus consulto*.[248] This raises the interesting point that in referring back to earlier decisions of the Senate, Sulla verifies that that body and magistrates felt no qualms about interfering in the local administration of ostensibly free cities to exempt individuals and groups from local charges. In each case discussed, the involvement of the Senate in the final instance conferred a broader legitimacy to the provincial actors beyond the simple fact of the *acta* themselves. The specific grants here are largely concerned with the reward of cities which had supported Rome. The result defined privileges far more precisely than in previous eras, tightening the leeway afforded even to loyal allies.[249]

Summary

Within three-and-a-half decades of Sulla's reorganization of Asia, government in the region had been radically altered. The catalyst was the subjection of most *poleis* to the *imperium* and *iurisdictio* of the Roman governor after 85. Suddenly, communities were liable for Roman taxes, previously restricted to the former *βασιλικὴ χώρα*, and open to gubernatorial oversight of local legal cases. Pre-existing Roman institutions played an expanded role in the post-Sullan period. Since the establishment of a regular *provincia*, governors had always exercised *iurisdictio* over the *conventus civium Romanorum* in any given city and had the capacity to issue *leges datae* affecting provincial communities. However, with the addition of most *poleis* in Asia to the province, these institutions adapted to new circumstances. The primacy of Roman jurisdiction over local courts resulted in the formalization of regional courts, the outlining of a *conventus* structure. This likely followed an earlier Attalid form of organization, given the co-optation of the Greek term *διοίκησις*, but this does not rule out changes based on the *formula provinciae* at this time. Similarly, governor's decisions, whether expressed as *edicta*, *constitutiones*, or *leges datae* came to affect the inhabitants of most *poleis* in Asia for the first time, providing a new framework for Roman rule. While no

[247] *RDGE* 49.B.8–11. [248] *RDGE* 49.A.8–15.

[249] Cf. *RDGE* 44: letters to the Isthmian–Nemean guild, renewing privileges and exemptions from local liturgies, and, though extremely fragmentary, to the Ionian–Hellespontine guild. Sherwin-White (1978, 140) claims Sulla's 'language [is] of advice rather than command'. By contrast, Buraselis (2000, 128–9) sees Sulla's intervention as decisive and intrusive.

major increase in the number of Roman troops in the *provincia* occurred, magistrates and their associates could deploy their small entourages as leverage on communities.[250] Consequently, the Roman state, after Sulla, effectively extended the coercive and fiscal elements of its power in Asia in a novel and unique form, with existing institutions evolving to support the new situation.

[250] Cic. *Imp. Pomp.* 66.

3
Change in a Time of Civil War, 49–30 BCE

The collapse of republican government in early 49 as civil war broke out between C. Iulius Caesar and Cn. Pompeius Magnus provoked another round of intensive institutional change for the inhabitants of *provincia Asia*. Most notably, despite widespread support for the Pompeian cause by communities and allies in the East, tales of exploitation by commanders in this period abound.[1] While a rump Senate persisted with a semblance of government as normal, their defeat at Pharsalus heralded the demise of traditional processes of decision-making at Rome. Caesar's assassination within four years triggered further rounds of blood-letting and institutional innovation, while *provincia Asia* was devastated by a Parthian invasion led jointly by Q. Labienus and Pacorus in 40/39.[2] Though the division of the Roman world between the *tresviri rei publicae constituendae* provided short-term stability, with Asia beneath the remit of M. Antonius, the difficult relationship between the wielders of the *summum imperium*—culminating in the Actium campaign—required major adjustments to the Roman administrative system. For nearly two decades the imperial centre and its officials were in a state of flux: this central instability prompted an environment in which sudden changes in allegiance, process, and policy could be expected, though from the local perspective their direction was unpredictable.

Caesar, Civil War, and Critical Junctures

After Pharsalus, with his authority unchallenged, Caesar fundamentally changed the fiscal administration of *provincia Asia*. The sources agree that after arriving in Asia in pursuit of the defeated Pompeius, Caesar abolished the tax-farm for the Asian *decuma* and reduced tax-rates by one-third.[3] Merola suggested that the tithe was abolished and replaced with a fixed annual tribute. Though appealing, prima facie, the strongly positive view of variable rates offered by Appian's Antonius

[1] E.g., Marek 2010, 375. [2] App. *BCiv.* 5.10; CD. 48.24.3–26.1. Sherwin-White 1984, 298–304.
[3] App. *BCiv.* 5.4; CD. 42.6.3; Plut. *Caes.* 48. Whether this decision took effect in 48 by virtue of Caesar's personal authority or only after legislated in Rome in 47/46 is an open question (Morrell 2017, 149).

Imperial Power, Provincial Government, and the Emergence of Roman Asia, 133 BCE–14 CE. Bradley Jordan, Oxford University Press. © Bradley Jordan 2023. DOI: 10.1093/oso/9780198887065.003.0004

counts against this position.[4] Regardless, these related decisions demonstrate the fundamental inequity and inefficiencies of collection by the *publicani*. The new reality of Caesar's unhindered power allowed him to remake the fiscal system from the ground up, and his personal interests pushed him further in this direction. Like Sulla, Caesar needed coin immediately, to reward his troops, facilitate his pursuit of Pompeius, and win the loyalty of his erstwhile enemies. While Dio states that Caesar exacted an immediate contribution from the *poleis*, the permanent reduction of tax rates allowed him to present a strong contrast with Sulla and his contemporary opponents, allowing him to 'win hearts and minds'.[5]

The civil war and its consequences present a 'critical juncture' in the history of the *res publica*. Contemporary institutions had proven unable to contain the ambitions of its leading figures and had broken down. The concentration of authority in the person of Caesar and the manifest inadequacy of the existing system afforded him, like Sulla a generation earlier, an opportunity to remodel the state in his preferred image. Unlike his predecessor as dictator, Caesar's programme remained incomplete at his death, however. Accordingly, it is critical to recognize that structural factors, particularly the collapse of central authority, catalysed the profound institutional changes in the relationship between the communities of Asia and the Roman state. Caesar's decision to remove responsibility for collecting the *decuma* from the *publicani* provides an excellent example. His victory and the authority it granted allowed him to bypass the vested interests of the *publicani*, as well as the *equites* and senatorial class more generally, and act, as he saw it, in the interests of the state. His position minimized factors leading to institutional inertia and afforded him the space to implement bold proposals.[6] Certainly, these reforms improved the lot of the Asian cities and their taxpayers; possibly even the state treasury.[7] This change to the collection of the *decuma* in Asia highlights how dangerous inefficiencies, baked into state structures, could be solved by the confluence of events and interests which resulted from Caesar's victory.

During his short period of dominance, between campaigns undertaken across the Mediterranean, Caesar altered the relationship between Rome and the *poleis* in several other ways. Significantly, he granted freedom to several communities, and the sources underscore the role of Greek agents in encouraging these decisions.[8] Certainly these grants had been made by August 47, when the author of the *Bellum*

[4] Corbier *AÉ* 2001, #1863; Tan 2017, 56; *pace* Merola 2001a, 461–72.

[5] CD. 42.6.1. Contrast [Caes.] *BAfr*. 90, 97, where his exactions targeted Roman citizens.

[6] Compare Capoccia 2016, 96–8.

[7] Brunt (1990b, 380–1), followed by Tan (2017, 55), deems it implausible Caesar intentionally reduced state revenue given his fiscal needs, though his immediate concerns likely took priority over broader fiscal planning. He may also have barred the *publicani* from Judaea and other provinces (Joseph. *AJ*. 14.202–210. Rostovtzeff 1941, 1000–1; Braund 1983a, 243–4). However, *publicani* were retained for indirect taxes, such as the *portoria*.

[8] See further Chapter 7, 'Informal Contacts: Diplomacy through Personal Relationships'.

Alexandrinum records: *in Asiam iter facit omniumque earum provinciarum de controversiis cognoscit et statuit; iura in tetrarchas, reges, civitates distribuit* ('[Caesar], making the journey into Asia, became acquainted with and ruled on disputes of all of those provinces; he assigned rights to the tetrarchs, kings and cities').[9] Pergamum benefitted from the close association of a leading citizen with the dominant power in the Roman world. Mithridates, who had been involved in the trial of Flaccus in 59, subsequently led reinforcements to Caesar in Alexandria, before being sent by the dictator to take control of the allied kingdom on the Crimean Bosporus.[10] An inscription dated to Caesar's second dictatorship praised him for restoring *τοῖς θεοῖς τὴν πόλιν καὶ τὴν χώραν* ('the city and its territory to the gods'), which could stand for the city's freedom but more likely *ἀσυλία*.[11] Given that honorific inscriptions for Mithridates use the same phrase and that he was subsequently honoured at Pergamum as *Φιλέταιρον νέον κτίστην* ('the founder, new Philetaerus'), Robert argued that he personally persuaded the dictator to act.[12]

Moreover, from 46–44, P. Servilius Vatia Isauricus held the command in Asia. Servilius, epigraphically, is the best-attested Republican governor, due to the high number of honours accorded to him by a wide range of cities.[13] At Pergamum, he was honoured as *σωτὴρ καὶ εὐεργέτης* ('saviour and benefactor') for his actions towards the *polis*, specifically: *ἀποδεδωκότα τῇ | πόλει τοὺς πατρίους νόμους καὶ τὴν δημοκ[ρα]|τίαν ἀδούλωτον* ('he restored to the city the ancestral laws and unenslaved democracy').[14] For Magie and Bernhardt, this proves that Servilius was responsible for implementing the grant of *ἐλευθερία*, though there is no barrier to seeing the honours for Mithridates as also arising in this context.[15]

Servilius proved a popular governor among the communities of Asia. He served as the relevant authority in cases of dispute between *poleis* and Roman citizens and the evidence shows his propensity to intervene on the side of the former. As early as 60, he had been involved in attempts to protect provincials from extortionate demands by Romans.[16] One document preserved at Pergamum, described as an *ἐπίκριμα* (*edictum*), dealt with a dispute between a Roman citizen and the community over the *ἀσυλία* of the Asclepeum, the inscription of which implies local success.[17] The heading of another letter survives at the end of the *senatus consultum Popillianum* and hints at a wider dossier of correspondence displayed at Pergamum which has been lost.[18] Several conferrals of religious privileges are also attested across the *provincia*.[19] His protection of local interests was recognized

[9] [Caes.] *BAlex*. 78.

[10] Strabo 13.4.3; [Caes.] *BAlex* 26–8, 78; CD. 42.42. Heller 2011, 239–42; Ventroux 2017, 57–61.

[11] *IGR* 4.1677, 4.1682.

[12] *RDGE* 54. Robert 1937, 227–30; Sherk 1969, 283.

[13] Dates: Cic. *Fam*. 13.68.1 (Sept. 46, in Asia), 12.2.1 (Sept. 44, at Rome). Inscriptions collated at Kirbihler 2011, 255–6, based on Robert 1948, 38–42.

[14] *OGIS* 449.

[15] Contra Magie 1950, 405–6.

[16] Cic. *Att*. 1.19.9, 20.4, 2.1.10. Morrell 2017, 149.

[17] *RDGE* 55.

[18] *RDGE* 11, 20–1. Drew-Bear 1972, 76; Haensch 2009, 185.

[19] Robert 1948, 38–9, with references; Kirbihler 2012, 128–9.

by Roman observers: Cicero, writing in 45, expresses his happiness that Servilius has been sent *istam partem rei p(ublicae) male adfectam tueri* ('to protect that part of the *res publica* which has been badly treated'), implying a concern with recovery of a devastated region.[20] Moreover, a letter from Caesar to Servilius has recently come to light in an inscription at Aezani. This text, discussed in more detail in Chapter 5, provides direct instructions from the dictator to the governor, providing a sharp contrast with surviving material regarding Sulla's decisions. Instead of the careful employment of senatorial authority to bolster the unambiguous supreme *imperium* of the dictator, here we see the dictator's authority enhancing the provincial commander's actions on the ground. Caesar acted through Servilius, as the Senate and People would ordinarily act through magistrates on the ground. Despite this, on a local level, Servilius' personal services were significant enough to merit cult honours at Ephesus, which persisted into the first century CE.[21] Despite the close collaboration between Caesar and the governor, communities were nevertheless motivated to publicly honour Servilius, emphasizing the extent to which the local implementation of policy was crucial to the experience of Roman government.

Evidence from Mytilene demonstrates Caesar's declared respect for the rights of the free cities, even those closely associated with his opponents. As Kirbihler notes, no evidence exists for Caesar stripping an Asian *polis* of its freedom[22] In late 48, the newly appointed dictator responded to an embassy by reassuring them of his benevolent intentions. Another letter, from 46, introduced a *senatus consultum* confirming the privileges conceded to the *polis*.[23] This document also reaffirmed a principle that individuals should not receive grants from Roman magistrates of immunity from civic taxes: Caesar responded that, cognisant of this, he intended not to grant this privilege to anyone.[24] This statement reveals that, despite their existing status as free allies, granted by Pompeius as a favour to his associate Theophanes in 62, the decisions of Roman magistrates continued to constrain local government. Though these arrangements possibly pre-dated the restoration of their freedom, Caesar's undertaking to refrain from making new grants would be odd in this context. As already noted, Sulla had no qualms about instructing the Coans to respect the privileges of the guild of Dionysiac artists. In sum, this reveals the growing impact of Roman decisions on free cities.

A series of honorific statues erected for Caesar in cities of Asia in late 48 after Pharsalus, some of which obliquely reference the *koinon*, seem to show the organization responding to the seismic shift in imperial power collectively. A dedication to Caesar on Samos, which emphasized his qualities *καὶ κοινῶς πρὸς πάντας τοὺς Ἕλληνας καὶ κατ' ἰδίαν εἰς ἑαυτῶν* ('both in common to all the Greeks and in a private capacity to our own [city]').[25] At Pergamum, a statue base

[20] Cic. *Fam.* 13.68.2.
[21] Friesen 1993, 9–10, esp. n.11, with references; Ferrary 1997, 207.
[22] Kirbihler 2012, 135.
[23] *RDGE* 26.a–b.
[24] *RDGE* 26.b.27–34.
[25] *IGR* 4.970.

regards Caesar as σώτηρ τῶν Ἑλλήνων ἁπάντων ('saviour of all the Greeks'), while Raubitschek identified three pairs of statues at Kartheia, Pergamum, and Chios, in which the local aspect as 'saviour' of the city was paralleled by a global aspect, as σώτηρ τῆς οἰκουμένης ('saviour of the inhabited world') in the first instance, and by the κοινὸν τῶν Ἑλλήνων ('*koinon* of the Greeks') in the latter two.[26] Further example can be adduced at added examples from Delos, Phocaea, and Samos.[27] The connection to the *koinon* as a supra-civic body would offer a strong explanation for this explosion of global references.[28] The interesting question arises from this discussion as to who comprised the *koinon* in practice. When Caesar was victorious, how practical was it to assemble delegates and vote through a decree of this nature? Pharsalus took place on 9 August, and Caesar arrived in Alexandria on 2 October, which leaves a short window for a decision of the *koinon* to have been agreed by all constituent members, passed, and presented to the dictator during his flying visit to the province.[29] While the titulature requires that they fall within the Roman year 48, it seems more likely that delegates met and decided on collective action without reference back to civic assemblies. Intriguingly, no similar examples appear in the final three years of Caesar's life. This, more than any other detail, points to a supra-civic decision to honour Caesar as a collective and highlights local innovation and centralization in response to the global crisis of imperial civil war.

Treaties: A Caesarian Innovation?

The series of treaties concluded between Caesar's Rome and communities in and around *provincia Asia* show another innovation.[30] From the third century onwards, treaties, though far from universal, were an element of Rome's relationships with polities in the eastern Mediterranean.[31] Currently published epigraphic texts preserve elements of eleven *foedera* prior to 14 CE, of which four pertain to *poleis* in Asia and two to the Lycian *koinon*. Another six unambiguous attestations

[26] *IG* 12.5.556–557 (Kartheia); *IGR* 4.303, 307 (Pergamum); *IGR* 4.928–929 (Chios). Raubitschek 1954, 74.

[27] *SEG* 14.502 (Delos); 15.748 (Phocaea); 14.557 (Samos). Dobesch 1996, 61; Kirbihler 2012, 141–2.

[28] Compare Mileta 2008a, 107.

[29] Rawson 1994, 433, with references.

[30] Latin *foedera* or *iusiuranda*; Greek συνθῆκαι or ὁρκωμόσια. Mitchell 2005, 178.

[31] The prevailing view emphasizes the role of informal *amicitia* in Roman imperialism within the Greek East (Eckstein 1999, 2006; Kallet-Marx 1995, 184–97; Burton 2011 contra Derow 1991), disassociating *foedera* from friendship and suggesting that they were not a necessary condition of 'alliance' with Rome (Heuss 1933, 53–9; Gruen 1984, 47–55; Ferrary 1990, 217–24; Rich 2008, esp. 58–65 contra Zack 2001). That said, the existence of standard formulae for treaties implies a regular phenomenon (Schuler 2007, 64–6). While not excising Roman motivations and agency completely, the view that the small communities which most extant texts relate to benefitted more from direct association with Rome than vice versa has weight. Most examples from the early period of Roman involvement in Asia should derive from local agency (Kallet-Marx 1995, 184–93; *pace* Gruen 1984, 49–50).

of treaties exist, of which three involved Asian communities.[32] The corpus shows remarkable consistency, first emphasized by Täubler, who identified four common elements: a general statement of alliance involving perpetual friendship between the two parties; a neutrality clause whereby neither party should assist actively or passively the enemies of the other; a defensive alliance clause, mandating that each party help the other against attack, if requested; and a final clause laying out the circumstances in which the treaty may be altered, namely if both parties agreed.[33]

These clauses served as the basis of formal Roman relationships with allied communities, though extant *foedera*, particularly during this transitional period, do vary. The agreement with the Lycian *koinon* in 46, for example, includes several more precise clauses regulating the movement of goods from Roman to Lycian customs zones (ll.26–32), the trying of capital (ll.32–38) and private cases (ll.38–43) involving citizens from both states, and arrangements for pledges, return of captives, and restitution of goods (ll.43–52).[34] Finally, the treaty explicitly confirms the territory to be possessed by the Lycian *koinon*, a grant paralleled in the early Augustan treaty with Mytilene, which recognizes the territorial claims of the *polis* both on Lesbos and the mainland.[35]

The designation of some *foedera* as *aequa* ('equal, equitable') reveals a contemporary view that such agreements could be inequitable. Proculus, during the mid-first century CE, articulates a distinction between *foedera aequa* and those including a so-called '*maiestas*-clause', which, crucially, had no bearing on the free status of a community.[36] Such injunctions are known from both treaties imposed on defeated enemies, notably the Aetolian League in 189, and agreed with allies, such as Gades in 78.[37] In the latter case, Cicero notes the clause *maiestatem populi Romani comiter conservanto* ('let them maintain the *maiestas* of the Roman People in solidarity').[38] Proculus indicates that, by the imperial period, there was an observable hierarchical difference between those polities explicitly required to uphold the *maiestas* of the Roman people and their counterparts.[39] The Lycian treaty of 46 features just such a clause unambiguously requiring the signatories to uphold the authority of Rome:

[32] Mitchell (2005, 173–5) and Schuler (2007, 67–74) for references.

[33] Täubler 1913, 47–62, discussed at Mitchell 2005, 185–7. Note de Libero's claim (1997, 304–5) that the standard clause, *ut eosdem quos populus Romanus amicos atque hostes habeant*/τοὺς αὐτοὺς ἐχθροὺς καὶ φίλους νομίζειν ('that they regard as friends and enemies those who the Romans do'), represented a unilateral assertion of 'hegemony'.

[34] For a detailed discussion of these clauses: Mitchell 2005, 195–209 (with comments of Ferrary & Rousset, *BE* 2006, 143); Sánchez 2007, 365–80; Schuler 2007, 74–8; Rousset 2010, 135–41; Raggi 2010a, 45–67; Fournier 2010, 447–56; Kantor 2013a, 219–24.

[35] *SEG* 55.1452.52–64. Mytilene: *RDGE* 26.d.18–27. Ellis-Evans 2019, 252–8.

[36] *Dig.* 49.15.7.1.

[37] Polyb. 21.32.2 = Liv. 38.11.10. Kallet-Marx 1995, 26–9; Baronowski 1990, 347–50, 368–9.

[38] Cic. *Balb.* 35–7.

[39] Baronowski 1990, 346–52.

> *τήν τε ἐξουσίαν καὶ ὑπεροχὴν τὴν Ῥωμαίων | [βεβαί]ạς καθὼς πρέπον ἐστιν διατηρείτωνσαν Λύκιοι διὰ παντὸς ἀξίως ἑαυτῶν τε [καὶ τ]οῦ δήμου τοῦ Ῥωμαίων* ('let the Lycians observe the power and pre-eminence of the Romans [firmly], as is proper, in all circumstances in a manner worthy of themselves and of the Roman people').[40]

Its insertion into an agreement with a notionally free ally and partner appears dissonant. Other examples can be restored in the Cnidus and Mytilene treaties of the mid-40s, both of which had *ἐλευθερία* restored prior to the conclusion of the *foedera*.[41] Ferrary viewed the inclusion of a *maiestas*-clause in treaties of this period as reflecting a change in Roman practice, incorporating elements from a unilateral grant of privileges to a subordinate or defeated power into a bilateral agreement. This, he argued, had the effect of situating communities more firmly within Rome's geopolitical grasp.[42] While Mytilene, for example, retained its freedom, it was constrained by mutual agreement to recognize the power of Rome and respect its decisions. As per the definition offered by Doyle, *maiestas*-clauses definitively established Rome's hegemony over its partners. The Lycian treaty from Tyberissos, likely dating to the 80s, which Schuler has shown cannot contain a *maiestas*-clause, confirms Ferrary's view that this was a phenomenon of the civil war period.[43]

The older treaties in the epigraphic corpus, those not including *maiestas*-clauses, tend to be generic and constrained their signatories in ways which did not *ipso facto* establish Roman hegemony. The reciprocal defence, neutrality, and alliance clauses were mutually binding, even if the power distribution was asymmetric.[44] By contrast, later treaties were indubitably more specific, delineating rights and obligations of signatories which had previously been unexpressed, ad hoc, or contested. The Lycian treaty of 46 provides an archetype; the second fragment of the Cnidus text of 45 alludes to questions of law; and Sánchez plausibly argues that the Mytilene treaty contained clauses regulating judicial practice between the signatories. The length of this document is at least the same as the Lycian example, and therefore much longer than the earlier texts such as the Lycian treaty from Tyberissos, dated to the 80s.[45] Specific clauses and language naturally constrained the action of the signatories, including the Romans

[40] *SEG* 55.1452.9–10.

[41] E.g., Täubler's ambitious restoration of *I.Knidos* 33.11–13 (1913, 450); Famerie 2009, 273–7. On Mytilene Ferrary 1990, 232 contra Sherk 1969, 157.

[42] Ferrary 1990, 226–35, esp. 233–4: 'un mélange d'un traité bilatéral de neutralité et d'alliance défensive, et de décision unilatérale garantissant aux Mytiléniens un certain nombre de privilèges, mais fixant par cela même leur statut l'intérieur de l'empire romain'.

[43] Schuler 2007, 66. Mitchell (2005, 189) is correct to point out that the Lycians were not 'within the Roman empire', but this does not invalidate Schuler's broader point. Cf. Doyle 1986, 40.

[44] Gruen 1984, 46–53; Schuler 2007, 65–7.

[45] *I.Knidos* 33b.4–6 with Famerie 2009, 279–80; *RDGE* 26.d with Sánchez 2007, 380–1. Tyberissos: *SEG* 57.1664, with Schuler 2007, 59–60.

themselves. In the Lycian case, the legal clauses were reciprocal, and accorded the citizens of each group proportionate rights.[46] This is not to say that the agreement applied equal burdens, though. Roman citizens accused in capital cases were to be tried before the *praetor peregrinus* in Rome rather than before a proconsul, placing a much higher burden on Lycian plaintiffs.[47] This echoes, in a more restricted fashion, the situation at Colophon in the early second century, guaranteeing the use of their home courts to both Roman and Lycian citizens, though not defining the situation for the non-citizen inhabitants of either polity. Unlike the earlier case, however, these guarantees are enshrined in a bilateral document.[48] Generally, despite the bold assertion of Roman hegemony embodied in the *maiestas* clauses, treaties from the period of Caesar's dominance onwards appear to have routinely defined the rights of local communities vis-à-vis Rome.[49] Given the uniqueness of this example, caution is necessary. However, it seems that Caesarian and Augustan *foedera* were intended to protect the rights of the cities through explicit definition, rather than constrain their action. Since both Caesar and Augustus presented themselves as concerned for provincial well-being, it would be unsurprising were *foedera* to move into a more explicit preventative role.[50]

This is not to claim that treaties were always respected: as Yarrow has noted, from the provincial perspective, Roman magistrates on the ground disregarded agreements made with the state or other representatives on a regular basis.[51] The tradition that Sulla had agreed at Dardanus to respect the freedom of the Asian *poleis*, deriving from Memnon, runs counter to Roman self-presentation.[52] Meanwhile, L. Licinius Murena's argument that Mithridates' agreement with Sulla did not bind him was tendentious, even allowing that it had not been ratified by the *populus Romanus*.[53] Memnon's admittedly parochial construction of the relationship between Heraclea Pontica and Rome highlights the extent to which the limits of treaties and agreements were contested, though in the 80s the city was able to cite conflicting obligations to refuse aid to Rome without suffering consequences in the aftermath of that war.[54]

Foedera, then, were a tool which could be employed by communities to attempt to formalize a relationship with Rome.[55] While not necessary to enjoy 'friendship and alliance', a *foedus* entailed a more formal element which offered a mote of

[46] *SEG* 55.1452.11–14 and 17–22. The Lycians appear to have obligations to Rome's allies which are not reciprocated to Lycia's allies, but later clauses do refer to Lycian allies: Mitchell 2005, 190.

[47] Raggi 2010, 45–7, 58–67.

[48] *SEG* 39.1244.1.37–39. For further examples: Kantor 2010, 194–9.

[49] Schuler 2007, 64–7; Fournier 2010, 446–59.

[50] E.g., Tan 2017, 55–8.

[51] Yarrow 2006, 250–4. Compare treaties in the Hellenistic East more generally at Eckstein 2006, 101–2.

[52] Memnon *FGrH* 434 F25.2. Magie 1950, 229, 240 contra Sherwin-White 1984, 143 n.48.

[53] App. *Mith.* 64. *Pace* Kallet-Marx 1995, 263.

[54] Memnon *FGrH* 434 F27.5. Kallet-Marx 1995, 196.

[55] See Buis' useful discussion (2014, 151–85) highlighting the Greek antecedents and the impact of the obvious power imbalance between Rome and local partners.

security to the relationship between a 'free' *polis* and Rome. The evidence, though lacunose, implies that the junior partners, the communities of the east, were the driving force behind most treaties. The existence of a standard format until the early first century indicates that this was not a rare occurrence: well-worn modes of discourse already existed. However, the corpus hints at a shift, at least by the early 40s, whereby *foedera* became more specific. Given the absence of evidence, concrete conclusions are impossible, though the concern of Caesar and Augustus with presenting their treatment of provincials and allies as just and equitable may provide a measure of explanation.

Sardis and the Last Days of Caesar

The last of Caesar's decisions epigraphically attested, an *edictum* dated securely to 4 March 44, underscores the centralization of power under the dictatorship. This text granted ἀσυλία to several Sardian shrines, modelled on that of the Ephesian Artemision. Unlike Hellenistic grants, Caesar's, following his Roman predecessors, clearly applied only to the temples themselves, not the whole civic territory.[56] Consequently, references to tax-farmers (δημοσιῶναι)—possibly local—and freedom from the *fasces* (ῥάδων) should be correspondingly limited.[57] Crucially, however, Caesar explicitly links the grant of these privileges, through his dictatorial *imperium*, to the Sardians' consistent loyalty to the Roman state. He adduces Sardis' friendship (φιλία) towards Rome through all time (διὰ πάντος) and their consistent loyalty (πίστις) to the Senate and *populus*. By eliding the civil war period and stressing the city's actions towards the state as a whole, Caesar constructs a new basis for the relationship between himself, as benefactor on behalf of the Roman state, and the city. While it should be noted that active supporters of Pompeius' forces, such as Deiotarus of Galatia and the city of Massalia in Gaul, were less fortunate, Caesar's generosity to the civic communities seems to have generated considerable goodwill.[58] Mitchell emphasizes Caesar's skill in aggrandizing a position as the legitimate representative of the Roman People. By rewarding erstwhile opponents through guaranteeing their status, eventually through treaty, he created new allies directly beholden to him.[59] In turn, the dictator in his final days continued to build a personal basis for government at the provincial level, reprising in some ways the position of Hellenistic monarch.

[56] *SEG* 39.1290.45–59. Rigsby 1996, 21–2. Lines 11–30, erased, seem to be a letter from M. Antonius introducing the *edictum*, perhaps through his possession of Caesar's papers after the latter's assassination. On this issue: Jordan 2017, 177–8, with references.

[57] *SEG* 39.1290.62–69. This latter clause should describe freedom from gubernatorial *iurisdictio* and *imperium* rather than prevent governors from entering this territory. Cf. Herrmann 1989a, 149–53.

[58] On friendship discourse and the treatment of allies in civil war: Jordan (forthcoming a).

[59] Mitchell 2005, 235.

The Triumviral Period: A New Model of Provincial Government

The renewed outbreak of hostilities after Caesar's assassination in 44 created significant new problems for communities in the Greek East. His sudden murder negated any ambitions he may have had to reform the imperial structure in a more holistic fashion and ushered in a new wave of conflict and attendant extortion.[60] While Sulla's swift retribution after Dardanus had pushed *poleis* to remain loyal to Rome in subsequent conflicts with Mithridates, no framework existed for dealing with two Roman factions, each claiming to wield the legitimate authority of the Senate and *populus*. While Caesar's defeat of Pompeius was fait accompli before his arrival in the region, the self-styled 'Liberators', having overwhelming military superiority in the region by mid-43, sought to extract funds and support from the cities. As in 88, the fraught political situation generated intra-civic conflict, as elements of the political elite championed the benefits of supporting the Liberators or the divided political heirs of their benefactor. All choices carried a high-level of risk: Lycia and Rhodes, after seeking to remain neutral, were confronted by the troops of Brutus and Cassius respectively, sparking internal dissension over the best course of action.[61] Later, the contest between Antonius and Octavian generated similar dynamics, best attested at Tarsus.[62] These examples demonstrate that the violent convulsions seizing the central organs of the *res publica* had a significant impact on the internal dynamics of communities in the Greek East, which must have affected the exercise of Roman power during this period.

Nevertheless, the establishment of *tresviri rei publicae constituendae* on 27 November 43 provided a new framework for administrative practice across the empire. On his arrival in Asia, Antonius, like Sulla before him, summoned the representatives of the cities to Ephesus and insisted that they pay him ten years taxes, within twelve months, in lieu of further punishment. According to Appian, after the representatives complained of their inability to meet this demand, highlighting the exactions by Brutus and Cassius in the previous year, this was reduced to nine years' worth payable in two years.[63] This should be the context for Plutarch's anecdote that Hybreas of Mylasa persuaded Antonius not to exact a second tax in a single year, and it emphasizes how communities could negotiate directly with Roman powerbrokers.[64] We also learn that Anaxenor of Magnesia, a citharoede, was appointed by Antonius as a φορόλογος ('collector of tribute') for four cities. This should not mean a typical collector of Roman taxes. Instead, like Sulla's own makeshift arrangements in 85, Antonius implemented ad hoc

[60] On Caesar's institutional ambitions: Jehne 1987, 372–422; Welch 1990, 53–69.

[61] App. *BCiv.* 4.65–73; CD. 47.33.1–4; Plut. *Brut.* 30.3–32.4; Val. Max. 1.5.8; Vell. Pat. 2.69.6. Börm 2016, 101–20, on Rhodes specifically, 106–12.

[62] Strabo 14.5.14. [63] App. *BCiv.* 5.4–5; CD. 48.2.2, 30.2. [64] Strabo 14.2.24.

measures, employing local actors, albeit supported by Roman troops.[65] Drawing on previous practices of both Sulla and Caesar, Antonius forged his own path in dealing with the post-war landscape.

Cities, the Senate, and the *tresviri*

One revealing document about the triumviral approach to *provincia Asia* appears in a papyrus fragment from Alexandria. The leaf preserves a letter of M. Antonius to the *koinon* of Asia regarding privileges for the association of wreath-bearers for the sacred games. The text, dated to 41, records that, while at Ephesus, the *triumvir* was visited by M. Antonius Artemidorus, his friend and 'trainer', and the eponymous priest of the association. The two requested confirmation of the association's former privileges, in addition to freedom from military service, immunity from liturgies, freedom from billeting, the rights of ἀσυλία and to wear the 'purple stripe', and truces during games. They also asked Antonius to write to the *koinon* and, separately, to be allowed to dedicate a bronze tablet.[66] The text highlights the personal nature of government in this period. Neither the Senate nor other magistrates are referred to. In this respect, it provides a stark contrast with other grants of privileges to associations, which derive from commanders in *provinciae*.[67]

The decision to address the *koinon* may be linked to the religious topic of the letter. Nevertheless, the crucial implication of this document, which does not require its own publicization or dissemination, is that the petitioners viewed the *koinon* as the peak, or indeed only, body to guarantee their privileges. In turn, this implies a broad oversight of common festivals within Asia, rather than specifically those celebrating Romans: a stark contrast with the earliest honorific documents, which stress their connection with the *Moukieia*. Similar grants to the guild of Dionysiac artists by Sulla in the 80s had been sent directly to cities.[68] This letter illustrates neatly that while the *koinon*'s focus remained collective, religious, and honorific, its role in organizing the communities of Asia was becoming more pronounced throughout the late Republic.

However, that the privileges involved affected the communities of Asia generally implies that in the aftermath of two quickfire civil wars the *koinon* had become the most efficient means through which to disseminate information to

[65] Strabo 14.1.41; Plut. *Ant.* 24.2; *Syll.*[3] 766. Gray 1978, 973; Syme 1979a [1963], 571; Buraselis 2000, 131.

[66] *RDGE* 57. The text may be abbreviated. A very fragmentary inscription from Tralles seems to reproduce the first lines of this text but adds the προέδροι to the addressees. Keil 1911, 123–7; see Sherk 1969, 292; Kirbihler 2016, 96–7.

[67] E.g., Sulla, in two letters confirming privileges for the Dionysiac artists (*RDGE* 49), explicitly refers to decisions of the Senate, earlier magistrates, and his own *consilium*.

[68] *RDGE* 18.2–4.

the *poleis* of the *provincia*. This has two further implications. First, that the *koinon* now consisted of all the major civic communities in Asia: disseminating such a command to only a limited number of cities would not achieve Antonius' goal in delineating the privileges of the association. Second, it raises questions about the practical engagement between Rome and the *koinon*: how did the organization process correspondence and did it operate from a fixed location? During the early Principate, when the organization became tied to the imperial cult, the Temple of Augustus and Rome was based in Pergamum, though the leadership positions rotated through the cities. Suggestions that the well-attested irregular summons of civic representatives to Ephesus by Roman commanders indicates the location of the *koinon*'s headquarters in this period are not persuasive.[69] It seems more credible that the necessity of intense contact between participants in different cities had resulted in the slow development of established lines of communication, similar to the letter-carriers of the *publicani* for Roman travellers.[70] In either case, Antonius' decision was based on a principle of economy of effort, rather than implying a fundamental and deliberate change in the structure of the institution.

Most surviving documentary evidence for the triumviral period refers to the invasion of Labienus and the Parthians in 40/39. With Antonius distracted by the aftermath of the Perusine War in Italy, most of Caria was overrun.[71] During this invasion, the *polis* of Mylasa suffered particularly: having initially accepted a garrison from Labienus, the orator Hybreas roused the populace to resist with the result that the city was sacked.[72] A fragmentary letter of an unknown magistrate, dated to the 30s, discusses the economic crisis which the city had fallen into after the sack. Among other hardships, the city had been forced to use loans from private citizens to pay their taxes, alongside selling the rights to collect them.[73] While these tax-farmers and usurers appear to have been locals, rather than Romans, the potential for debts and obligations to spiral out of control persisted.[74] Indeed, prevailing opinion holds that the damage and subsequent failure to recover from Labienus' activities led directly to Mylasa's loss of status as a *conventus* centre.[75] Evidence from Stratonicea and Miletus indicates that these cities had their freedom restored in 39, which likely refers in the latter case to liberation from Labienus rather than juridical status.[76] Nevertheless, in these grants of civic privileges they explicitly solicited senatorial involvement.

[69] E.g., Kirbihler 2016, 67–8. [70] Cf. Broughton 1938, 539, with references.

[71] Magie 1950, 430–2.

[72] Strabo 14.2.24; CD. 48.26.4. Curran 2007, 47–8 for details. On Hybreas, *I.Mylasa* 534–6; Noé 1996; Delrieux & Ferriès 2004, 51–68.

[73] *RDGE* 59. Sherk 1969, 309. Canali De Rossi (2000, 178–81) speculates that Antonius was the author.

[74] Cic. *QFr.* 1.1.31. Magie 1950, 442.

[75] See Chapter 2, 'The Emergence of the *conventus iuridici*'.

[76] Stratonicea: *ILS* 8780 with *RDGE* 27; Miletus: *Milet.* 1.3.126, (cf. *OGIS* 193).

The best documented *polis* during the triumvirate is that of Plarasa-Aphrodisias, which, in the third century CE, inscribed several documents relating to this period on an 'archive wall' documenting their relationship with Rome.[77] A letter of Octavian dated to 39/38 provides context for the wider dossier of triumviral documents, commending the community's ambassador, Solon, and referring to the latter's happiness with οἰκονόμημα which have been made. Robert takes this term as meaning judicial decisions, but Reynolds persuasively assigns it the broader meaning referring to the series of official acts outlining the privileges of the city which had been given to Solon: an *edictum*, *senatus consultum*, *foedus*, and *lex*.[78] The *edictum* and *senatus consultum* both survive largely intact. The former was issued only by Octavian and Antonius, without their colleague Lepidus, and seems to have concerned relief for cities effected by the pre-Philippi manoeuvres of Brutus and Cassius. The text is fragmentary, but the document confers privileges on the Rhodes, Lycia, Tarsus, Syrian Laodicea, and Aphrodisias.[79] Appian describes these communities, excluding Aphrodisias, as receiving tax relief and territory in 41, which raises the question of the date. Since the letter of 39/8 must post-date the *edictum*, there is no need to suppose with Reynolds that Octavian lobbied for the inclusion of Aphrodisias after the fact of Antonius' decision. Instead, it is probable that the city was one of the original recipients.[80]

The *senatus consultum de Aphrodisiensibus* can be dated from the consuls' names to October 39. The document shows that the consuls proposed a motion renewing *amicitia* and alliance with the community and granting it freedom and *immunitas*, in addition to bestowing a number of specific privileges: exemption from levies, freedom from billeting or provision of supplies, ἀσυλία for the temple of Aphrodite, freedom from liturgies, and the right *suis legibus uti*.[81] Despite the Republican appearance of these proceedings, however, the document also emphasizes the presence of both Octavian and Antonius, who explicitly spoke in favour of the motion.[82] Moreover, the Senate unambiguously pre-authorized any other privileges already granted or to be granted in the future by the two named *tresviri*, which Appian extends to a general right.[83] The accent here is on Republican form operating alongside and in addition to the innovative magistracy designed to preserve peace in that time.

[77] Kokkinia 2015–16. [78] Robert 1969, 269–70; Reynolds, 1982, 45. Cf. *LSJ* s.v. οἰκονομήμα.

[79] Mitchell (1984, 295; *pace* Reynolds 1982, 51) argues that Syrian Laodicea is more likely than Laodicea-on-the-Lycus, as it fits the pattern of communities mistreated by Brutus and Cassius (App. *BCiv.* 4.62).

[80] App. *BCiv.* 5.29–30. The relative unimportance of Aphrodisias may account for Strabo's failure to mention the city, though Appian's omission may not require an elaborate explanation. Reynolds 1982, 51; Jones 2017, 355.

[81] *IAph2007* 8.27.32–51, 58–62. [82] *IAph2007* 8.27.26–27. Raggi & Buongiorno 2020, 109–11.

[83] *IAph2007* 8.27.48–51; App. *BCiv.* 5.75; CD. 48.34.1. Raggi & Buongiorno 2020, 77.

Ultimately, the triumvirate was unstable and experimental. Its sudden genesis and short duration meant that norms in the process of being established never solidified fully. The treatment of individual cases by a *triumvir*, each with diverse preferences, could result in very different outcomes, as the comment of Octavian to Stephanus, that in Aphrodisias *μίαν πόλιν ταύτην | ἐξ ὅλης τῆς Ἀσίας ἐμαυτῷ εἴληπφα* ('this one city out of all Asia have I taken as my own'), reveals.[84] Nevertheless, it seems clear that, generally, the *tresviri* built on the autocratic regime of Caesar in dealing with matters of provincial administration. The capacity for *poleis* to deal with one or two individuals created opportunities to advance their positions within the provincial hierarchy at a stroke. These new prospects, however, bore new risks: siding with one powerful magistrate against another could have catastrophic ramifications.

The Coinage of *provincia Asia* during the Civil Wars

The civil war period contained a number of developments in coinage, not least the first minting of Roman denominations in Asia, if in exceptional circumstances. A *denarius* with the head of Jupiter on the obverse, opposite a standing Artemis in the Ephesian style bears the Latin legend: L. LENTVLVS MAR(cellus) CO(n)S (ules). The reference to the consuls of 49 and allusion to Artemis suggest strongly that these were minted at Ephesus during Lentulus' sojourn in Asia, recruiting troops for the Pompeian forces.[85] Consequently, these were almost certainly minted to pay citizen recruits. Moreover, in the context of other coins minted in Illyria bearing the consular signatures alongside a Q, indicating quaestorian involvement, we may imagine that the Pompeians had brought die-making equipment and specialists with him during his flight from Rome.[86] As such, the minting of *denarii* in Asia may also be taken as an assertion of the capacity to carry out functions of Republican government in exile rather than relating to provincial government per se. Subsequent examples also seem to follow this pattern of emergency pay for Roman troops. Several issues of *denarii* and *aurei* were struck for Cassius and Brutus in 43 and 42 at unidentifiable Asian mints, undoubtedly from bullion extorted and plundered from Asian and Lycian *poleis*.[87] Antonius, too, issued *denarii* and *aurei* after Philippi, as did Q. Labienus in 41/40, emphasizing the military connection.[88] The early minting of Roman denominations by magistrates was not intended to disrupt the circulation of *cistophori*—the coins were intended for different recipients—but nevertheless, the consumption of

[84] *IAph2007* 8.29.3–4.
[85] *RRC* 445/3a, 3b. Caes. *BC* 3.4.1; Jos. *AJ.* 14.228–240. Woytek 2016, 177–80, 200–1, with references.
[86] *RRC* 445/1, 2. Woytek 2016, 175–6.
[87] *RRC* 498–501, 505–8.
[88] *RRC* 517, 520–2 (Antonius); 524 (Q. Labienus). Kinns 1987: 112–13.

bullion and extractive demands of repeated Roman armies must have taken its toll on the monetary supply of the *provincia*.[89]

However, during Antonius' triumvirate in the eastern Mediterranean, two highly innovative issues of *cistophori* were briefly minted, possibly at Ephesus in *c*.39. The first (*RPC* 1.2201) displays a head of the *triumvir* himself, wreathed in ivy, surrounded by the Latin legend: M. ANTONIVS IMP(erator) CO(n)S(ul) DESIG(inatus) ITER ET TERT(ius). The reverse includes his title IIIVIR | R(ei) P(ublicae) C(onstituendae) either side of the traditional *cista mystica*, crowned with a bust of his wife Octavia. The second (*RPC* 1.2202), bearing the same titulature, shows the heads of Antonius and Octavia on the obverse, with a standing Dionysus atop a *cista* on the reverse. Both coins display overtly Antonian political messaging, which, as Rowan stresses, was a revolutionary step for the post-Attalid coinage.[90] Meanwhile, the inclusion of Octavia, sister to his rival and co-magistrate, emphasizes the fragile unity of the two men in the fraught aftermath of the Perusine War. Finally, Antonius' ivy wreath and the inclusion of Dionysus echoes his deliberate cultivation of an image as a new Dionysus, as in his triumphal entry into Ephesus in 41.[91] Each of these changes is strongly linked to Antonius' preferred self-presentation towards both Roman audiences, in the case of Octavia, and local audiences, in the case of Dionysus. Given that these were the only cistophoric issues during the 30s, it seems probable that Antonius or someone familiar with his intentions was involved in selecting this imagery.

A contemporary civic series in bronze from Ephesus similarly blends Roman and local concerns in its imagery.[92] These appear to be based on a long series of Ephesian bronzes which displayed a bust of Artemis on the obverse, with the cult statue on the reverse.[93] In this series, however, the obverse is replaced with heads of all three *tresviri rei publicae constituendae*. This is the first representation of the triumvirate as a single unit on non-Roman currency and seems designed to celebrate the unity of the three men and, subsequently, the Roman world. However, a smaller denomination depicts Octavia alone opposite the traditionally Ephesian symbol of a bee.[94] Neither the *tresviri* nor Octavia are identified by legends, which refer to the city and the responsible magistrates, presenting this issue as an unambiguously civic coinage. However, alongside a rotating cast of mint magistrates, the *archiereus* and *grammateus* Glaucon is named on each type.[95] It is possible that this local magistrate had a supervisory role and sought to massage the coinage's messaging in an Antonius-friendly direction,

[89] *Pace* Bransbourg 2021, 112.

[90] Rowan 2019, 83–4. Cf. *IG* 2^2 1043.22–24 (Athens); CD. 48.39.2, associating Antonius with Dionysus.

[91] Plut. *Ant.* 24.3. Compare: Plut. *Ant.* 26.5, 60.5; CD. 48.39.2; *IG* II^2 1043.22–23. Pelling 1988, 179–80; Carbone 2020a, 43, 47–8.

[92] *RPC* 1.2569–2573. [93] Carbone 2020a, 46. [94] *RPC* 1.2574.

[95] Compare Asklas, *archiereus* under Augustus (*RPC* 1.2585–2592), and Alexander, *archiereus* and *grammateus* under Tiberius (*RPC* 1.2613–2618).

rather than having instructions directly from the *triumvir*. Carbone, connecting the Octavia coin to an issue at Eumeneia depicting Antonius' earlier wife, Fulvia—for whom the city was briefly named—suggests that cities were tapping into existing repertoires of honouring Hellenistic dynasts together with their queens.[96] Although the wives and daughters of magistrates had been persistently honoured in statuary across the period this does present a major change in Roman-era coinage. Overall, the coinage during this period trended towards centralization. While local mints largely continued to produce coins, the urgency of civil war led to increasing recourse by Roman commanders to emergency production of imperial denominations. Similarly, even coins for local circulation, including *cistophori* and local bronzes, increasingly contained Roman political imagery suggesting growing links between the producers and the Roman authorities.

Summary

The civil wars were characterized by the relative weakness of central administrative institutions vis-à-vis powerful individuals, first Caesar and Pompeius, then the *tresviri rei publicae constituendae*. In conjunction with the frequent changes in political alignment and military success, the period consisted of a series of critical junctures, affording leaders the capacity to effect radical institutional change swiftly on an empire-wide level. This had correspondingly major consequences for the inhabitants of the provinces, including Asia. The evidence from Caesar's brief dictatorship emphasizes, perhaps unrealistically, his concern for the prosperity of the cities of Asia. The ending of the province-wide tax-farm, while popular locally, clearly improved state revenue in the long term. Caesar's unprecedented position allowed him to bypass the entrenched interests of the *publicani* to the benefit of the state, his policies, and provincial inhabitants. Similarly, the evidence suggests an increasing trend towards the use of treaties to manage the relationship between Rome and the cities of the empire. These offered, at the most basic level, written confirmation of the rights of communities vis-à-vis the Republic and its representatives, though the circumstances of civil strife rendered them precarious.

Local strategies and demands also played a key role in facilitating the changes during this period. We see Caesar responding to a Mytilenean request that Roman magistrates not grant local citizens immunity from taxation, while the same city later requested a renewal of the Caesarian treaty from Augustus. In a similar vein, the stark movement towards a more individualized mode of government, with requests made of and granted by powerful figures without initial reference to the

[96] *RPC* 1.3139. Carbone 2020a, 44–9.

Senate emerged from the recognition of local agents of the reality of the situation. In the aftermath of Pharsalus, Philippi, and Actium, a direct approach to the victor(s) was likely to be more efficacious than reference to their governor or Senate. The concentration of power within the Roman state continued spasmodically to evolve incrementally, notwithstanding the turmoil of the late Republican civil wars, which had a commensurate effect on the institutions and practical government of the province of Asia.

4
Provincia Asia and the Advent of the Principate, 30 BCE–14 CE

The defeat of Antonius at Actium left Octavian with the power to reshape the institutions of the Roman state and its empire. Over the remainder of his life, he carved out a pre-eminent position for himself alongside a semblance of the traditional Republican structure. Through a series of incremental 'settlements', in 27, 23, and 19, Augustus acquired a constitutional basis to exercise his supreme power at Rome.[1] Crucially, from 27, the existing provinces were divided between *provinciae publicae*, to be administered by proconsuls, chosen by lot from eligible ex-magistrates, and *provinciae Caesaris*, governed by *legati pro praetore* chosen personally by Augustus. The overwhelming majority of the legions were concentrated in the latter, granting the Princeps, ultimately, their command.[2] Asia, unthreatened by war, was to be a *provincia publica* and, in the new schema devised by Augustus, to be governed by a consular at least five years after the expiration of his magistracy.[3] These substantive changes to the organization of the state had a commensurate impact on the institutions through which the empire was governed. The evolution of Augustus' powers and the ways in which they were exercised during his rule created ambiguities and prompted a period of adaptation by both magistrates and provincials. Consequently, the extent of Augustus' authority and its limits were an important factor in how the inhabitants of Asia experienced Roman hegemony in this transformational period.

Augustus as Princeps: The Cyme Dossier

The accumulating powers and unparalleled *auctoritas* of Augustus allowed him to act even within ostensibly public *provinciae*, as the example of two documents from Cyme illustrates. These were found on a single stone and show the growing

[1] The bibliography for the Augustan settlements is vast. Recent works include Ferrary 2001a, 101–54; Cotton & Yakobson 2002, 193–209; Rich 2012, 37–121; Dalla Rosa 2014, esp. 269–310; Vervaet 2014, 253–75.

[2] Ferrary 2001a, 108–15; Vervaet 2014, 254–5. Hurlet 2006, 147–58 on the continued military capacity of proconsuls.

[3] CD. 53.12.4, 14.2.

Imperial Power, Provincial Government, and the Emergence of Roman Asia, 133 BCE–14 CE. Bradley Jordan, Oxford University Press. © Bradley Jordan 2023. DOI: 10.1093/oso/9780198887065.003.0005

influence of Augustus' pronouncements over proconsuls shortly after Actium.[4] The first, a Greek text, issued by Augustus with his consular colleague M. Vipsanius Agrippa, escapes easy categorization. It specifies that public and sacred property should not be alienated from public ownership, and where this has happened, it should be restored. The second is a proconsular letter from P. Vinicius to the city, in Latin and in Greek translation, responding to a request by the *thiasoi* of Dionysus that their shrine be restored *iussu Augusti* ('by the order of Augustus'). Vinicius issued specific instructions to the archons of Cyme to investigate whether the shrine had become the property of one Lysias. If so, they should ensure that Lysias accepted the offered compensation and restored it to public ownership. Moreover, they should inscribe upon the shrine: *Imp. Caesar Deivi f. Augustu[s] re[stituit]* ('Imperator Caesar, son of the god, Augustus restored [sc. this shrine]').[5] Finally, in the event Lysias refused to comply, he should pay a *vadimonium* (a bond) and Vinicius would decide the case.

The two texts were intended to advertise the success of the petitioners, the *thiasoi* of Dionysus, though they had wildly different scopes.[6] The opening lines of the first text pose problems for interpreting the date and nature of the document: [*Α*]*ὐτοκράτωρ Καῖσαρ θεοῦ υἱὸς Σεβαστὸ*[*ς vac*?) | *Μ*]*ᾶρκος Ἀγρίπας Λευκίου υἱὸς ὕπατοι vac ἐ*[*—c.* 7—] ('Imperator Caesar, *divi filius*, Augustus, M. Agrippa, son of Lucius, consuls…').[7] The title of Augustus seems to date this document to 27, though the possibility of stonecutters updating the text to match contemporary reality cannot be excluded.[8] The text is likely a consular edict, though the erosion of the final word creates doubt. For an *edictum* one would expect *λεγοῦσιν*, which is definitively ruled out. The *editio princeps*' *ἐ*[*κέλευσαν*] ('commanded') preserves this sense, though Crook's *ἐ*[*πέκριναν*] ('decided') seems most plausible.[9] The inclusion of the edict on the stone strongly suggests that this should be identified as the *iussum Augusti* of Vinicius' letter and this likely reflects a local interpretation of the document. As Dalla Rosa remarks, the omission of Agrippa from this characterization 'non modifica nulla della natura dell'ordinanza'.[10] The simplest explanation is the ongoing shift in the local perception of Roman political hierarchies. While the process of administration resembled that under the Republic—with general instructions issued by the Senate, and local implementation left to the commander on the ground—new expectations and norms were emerging. The litigants' assumption that the *iussum Augusti* would solve their problem, and

[4] Crook (1962) offers the best text. Compare: *SEG* 18.555; *BÉ* 1961, #97; *RDGE* 61; *I.Kyme* 17.

[5] Crook 1962, ll.19–20. [6] Dignas 2002, 124 n.71. [7] Crook 1962, ll. 1–2.

[8] Compare, e.g., *IAph2007* 8.26.1, 32.1. Crook 1962, 24.

[9] Dalla Rosa 2014, 121–3. Earlier, Crook 1962, 24–5; Bowman 1993, 406–7; Giovannini 1999, 104–6; Ferrary 2001a, 134; Hurlet 2006, 204–8. Alternatives include a *lex* (Kunkel 1962, 595; Oliver 1963, 121–2); and a consular letter (Atkinson 1960, 237–44; Arangio-Ruiz 1961, 326–32, 338; Charbonnel 1979, 212–25). Alternatively, Engelmann 1976 restores *ἐ*[*νέχυρα*] and integrates it into the main text, followed by Dignas 2002.

[10] Dalla Rosa 2014, 124–9. See already Sherk 1969, 315–16.

Vinicius' apparently unprompted decision to stress the agency of Augustus, point to a fundamental shift in the practical government of *provincia Asia.*[11]

Another issue emerges from the potential breadth of the *edictum*. The ruling refers ambiguously to sacred lands *πόλεως ἑκάστης ἐπαρχείας*. Natural word order would imply an *edictum* with force in every *provincia*; but this creates problems vis-à-vis the extent of Augustus' power, post-settlement of 27.[12] The alternative reading, that the document pertains to 'each city of the province (sc. Asia)', also raises issues regarding Augustus' propensity to interfere *in alienis provinciis.*[13] However, three reasons suggest this instruction was particular to Asia. First, Crook notes that the use of the singular *πόλεως* implies it agrees with *ἑκάστης*. This remains true with any of the restorations proposed for the end of line 3—the omission of *τῆς* before *ἐπαρχείας* through haplography seems more likely than an error of number.[14] Second, the Cyrene edicts provide a parallel for Augustus issuing administrative rulings in public provinces.[15] Though, in 27, he was yet to acquire his full suite of powers, he retained the consulship with its *summum imperium auspiciumque*, and hence the capacity to issue binding *edicta* with relevance across the empire. Augustus was at perfect liberty to rule on the subject of sacred land in Asia, even if the exercise of this power to bind promagistrates *cum imperio* was unusual.[16] Finally, Augustus' own *Res Gestae* refer to a similar initiative, undertaken after Actium: *in templis omnium civitatium provinciae Asiae victor ornamenta reposui, quae spoliatis templis is cum quo bellum gesseram privatim possederat* ('as victor, I restored to the temples in all the cities of *provincia Asia* the ornaments which my opponent in the war, when he had despoiled the temples, appropriated for private use'). That, in his own aggrandizing account, the Princeps focused attention on a single *provincia* is suggestive.[17] The date of the *edictum*, a mere four years after Actium, and the legal struggle described by Vinicius, fits the context well.

Finally, the fragmentary text at the end of Vinicius' letter presents difficulties in restoration. Following Crook, this sentence should not undermine the decision already reached, namely, that Lysias should restore the shrine to the *thiasoi* on the payment of the inscribed price. Consequently, the lacunose sections should read:

[11] E.g., Ferrary 2001a, 134–5.

[12] Ando (forthcoming), following Oliver (1972) and Culley (1975), argues that *IG*² 1035, an Athenian decree, relates to the same edict: however, the parallels are restored in the Athenian example, and it is unclear why a Roman edict, uncited in this text, was necessary for the *demos* to act on the matter.

[13] I reject the suggestions of Arangio-Ruiz (1961, 330–2), Oliver (1963, 113–15), and Bertrand (1991, 127–35) that *ἐπαρχεία* could mean 'district' or 'prefecture' rather than '*provincia*' in this context. Stasse 2009, 165–8.

[14] Crook 1962, 25 n.1; Bowersock 1970, 227; Dalla Rosa 2014, 123–4.

[15] *RDGE* 31.

[16] Ferrary 2001a, 134–8; *pace* Vervaet 2014, 275–6 n.192. On consular *edicta* under the Republic, Pina Polo 2011, 84–7, 277, 280–1.

[17] *RGDA* 24.1. Stasse 2009, 167–8 contra Atkinson 1960, 232; Charbonnel 1979, 199–201; Giovannini 1999, 103–4.

[*sei*] *autem Lusia contradeicit quae Apollonides po*[*su*]|[*it et vadi*]*monium ei satisdato ubi ego ero Lusiam prom*[*it*]|[*tere volti*]*s probo* ('but if Lysias disputes what Apollonides demands and if you wish Lysias to give security to appear where I shall be, I approve').[18] This would mean that Vinicius, while delegating the role of enforcing his decision to the archons of Cyme, allowed them the option of referring the matter back to his authority, should Lysias prove reluctant.[19] Consequently, we witness the proconsul making an initial ruling, though remaining sensitive to the possibility that, by employing civic officials to enforce its strictures, the aggrieved party may contest it. Overall, this case-study reinforces the changed reality of government in *provincia Asia* under the Principate. Not only could local litigants use an edict of Augustus, framed as a command, to persuade the governor to rule in their favour, but the governor himself, taking the edict as a cue, went beyond its limits to emphasize the agency of the Princeps.

Augustus and the Province of Asia

Augustan *procuratores*

The powers and prominence of Augustus were not the only new challenge for governors to negotiate in the early Principate: this period also saw the emergence of imperial *procuratores*. This office never became a recognized *honos* and, crucially, at the beginning of the period, it possessed no formal powers beyond acting as the representative of the Princeps.[20] Consequently, notwithstanding Augustus' immense prestige, governors in Asia ought not to have had their range of activity unduly constrained. It has often been asserted that procurators in public provinces were restricted to administering imperial property, rather than public funds as attested elsewhere.[21] However, Wörrle's recent reading of a proconsular letter from Aezani, dating to the penultimate decade of the first century, emphasizes the influence that early imperial procurators did have.[22]

[18] Crook 1962, ll.20–22.

[19] Contra Atkinson 1960, 251–52, followed by Oliver 1963, 119. Compare now *SEG* 64.492 with Kantor 2017: 68–9. L. Aemilius Paullus' letters to Gonnoi, ordering the civic authorities to enforce a decision by ten *legati* in the aftermath of the Third Macedonian War to grant confiscated land to Demophilos of Doliche, are extremely blunt. The key point is that civic authorities were held responsible for enforcing Roman dictates on behalf of non-citizens and risked the commander's ire by delaying.

[20] Taking on the role of Republican *procuratores*, 'whom a Roman empowers to administer his property or act in court' (Brunt 1983, 52). Aubert 1994, 106–10; Eich 2005, 86–9; Dalla Rosa 2018, 499–501.

[21] Sherwin-White 1939, 14–15; Pflaum 1957 *RE* s.v. *procurator*; Jones 1960, 123; Eich 2005, 104–5. See Brunt (1983, 69) for an indicative list of attested imperial *procuratores*. On the development of imperial estates in Asia: Dalla Rosa 2017, 110–14.

[22] Wörrle 2011, 357; Dalla Rosa 2018, 508. A date of 18–16 seems most likely: Atkinson 1958, 321–2; Wörrle 2011 362 n.22 contra Smallwood 1970, 309–10.

The proconsul of Asia, C. Norbanus Flaccus, recounted that the community's representatives had presented him with a letter from Augustus, in which the Princeps confirmed that: *συνκεχωρηκέναι ὑμ̣ῖν ἐκκ̣λησίαν|συνάγε̣ι̣ν̣ Ὀφίλι̣[ο]ν̣ Ὀρ̣ν̣ᾶτ̣ον ἐπίτροπ̣ο̣ν̣ [π]ε̣ρ̣ὶ̣ [ἀ]τ̣ε[λ]εί̣α̣ς̣ τ̣ῶ̣ι̣ [ἱε]|ρεῖ θ̣υ̣σ̣ι̣ῶ̣ν̣ ἕ̣νεκα, μὴ̣ συνχωρήσειν δ' ἄλ̣λ̣α̣ σ̣υ̣ντ̣ε̣λ̣ε̣ῖ̣ν̣ τ̣ὴ̣ν̣ | πόλιν* ('Ofilius Ornatus, procurator, had allowed your assembly to come together concerning the *ateleia* of the priest in charge of the sacrifices, but will not allow that the city offer anything further').[23] Norbanus goes on to state that he accepts the decision of Augustus before the text breaks off. This letter stresses both the degree to which multiple sources of authority existed in late first-century Asia, and the ambiguity of the procurator's role. It appears that the Aezanetans had consulted Ofilius before granting *ἀτέλεια* to a local priest, which Dalla Rosa plausibly associated with the cult of Augustus.[24] Crucially, it represents the accommodation of an innovation in the structure of the state, based around Augustus' unparalleled and unprecedented position: this marks the beginning of the institutionalization of a formerly private position. The tension between Ofilius as *procurator Augusti* and Norbanus as governor is a prime example of the phenomenon of intercurrence—whereby institutions formed at different times operate at cross-purposes due to their own internal logic.[25] Post-Actium, Augustus had the means and motivation to reinvent state structures to bolster his own position. However, in Asia, Republican magistracies continued to operate and the relationship between new and old institutions was yet to be fully established.

P. Vedius Pollio may provide the earliest example of a procurator acting as an agent of Augustus within Asia. Vedius is a well-attested equestrian figure, the son of a freedman, famed in antiquity for his appearance in an anecdote illustrating his cruelty, and the Princeps' corresponding mildness.[26] Amphora stamps from Chios and Cos, bearing his name, together with his personal exemption from the Asian *portoria*—granted *ex s.c.* and restricted to the value of 10,000 *denarii* in the *lex portorii Asiae* in 17—demonstrate his extensive financial interests, and likely property ownership in the *provincia*.[27] The evidence for Pollio's procuratorship derives from three sources. First, while reorganizing the finances of the Artemision at Ephesus, the Claudian proconsul Paullus Fabius Persicus refers on three occasions to *constitutiones* ('decisions') of Vedius as precedents.[28] Second, his portrait appears on two coin issues of Tralles, identified by the legends *ΟΥΗΙΔΙΟΣ* and *ΠΩΛΛΙΩΝ* respectively. These issues share a mint magistrate

[23] *SEG* 61.1134, updating *MAMA* 9.13. See now Dalla Rosa (2018, 509) identifying Ofilius' cognomen as Verus.

[24] Dalla Rosa 2018, 510–11.

[25] Orren & Skowronek 1994, 108.

[26] CD. 54.23.1–6; Sen. *Clem.* 1.18.2; *Ir.* 3.40; Plin. *NH.* 9.39.

[27] Eberle & Le Quèrè 2017, 44–5 with references; see Syme's (1961, 28) suggestion that the later senatorial Vedii from Ephesus were his descendants.

[28] *I.Eph.* 17–19. For detailed discussion of Persicus' actions: Dignas 2002, 151–6. Earlier: Atkinson 1962. On Vedius himself: Syme 1961, 23–30; Kirbihler 2017, 129–52.

and, in one case, a reverse type with contemporary issues bearing Augustus' portrait.[29] Since the civic ethnic is Caesarea, this should be dated to after the earthquake of 27 and may be associated with the imperial funds disbursed to support the rebuilding. Dalla Rosa's suggestion that Vedius' interests in the region made him an ideal representative through which to transfer and disburse imperial funds is correspondingly convincing.[30] Finally, two honorific inscriptions, without titles, commemorate his relationship with Ilium and Miletus.[31]

Given his equestrian status, he cannot have served as a formal magistrate and scholars are divided between two possibilities: that he served either in an extraordinary capacity as interim governor, entitled as *praefectus* between 31 and 27; or as a procurator after the first settlement in 27.[32] The former position cannot be excluded, especially in light of parallel examples from the 40s and 30s.[33] However, Norbanus' letter renders Dio's claim that procurators were employed by Augustus from 27 onwards plausible.[34] While probably not fulfilling the role played by later patrimonial procurators, the institutional malleability of the post-civil war period encouraged experimentation by Augustus and his representatives on the ground.[35] It is unnecessary to assume that Vedius or Ofilius possessed precisely defined authority. Instead, testing the limits of their position as the Princeps' representatives vis-à-vis magistrates, they shaped a new set of norms; a new institutional reality. The fact that *procuratores Augusti* from the same formative period in the West were engaged in a wider range of state fiscal activities, including tax collection in Gaul and supplying troops in Spain, supports this claim.[36] While Augustus' constitutional position was evolving rapidly, wider state structures including those central to provincial governance were adapted over a lengthier period.

The Imperial *koinon* of Asia

The *koinon* of Asia, during Augustus' lifetime, came to play a prominent role mediating between the imperial centre and individual communities: the orientation

[29] *RPC* 1.2634–5. The Augustus issues: *RPC* 1.2633, 2636, 2637–8. Discussion at Kirbihler 2017, 135–44.

[30] On the earthquake: Strabo 12.8.18; Jer. *Chron.* ad Ol. 188.2. Jones 2015; Kirbihler 2017, 138–40.

[31] *I.Ilion* 101; *I.Didyma* 146.

[32] *Praefectus*: Kreiler 2006, 200–2; Erkelenz 2003, 255; procurator, or personal representative: Skramkiewicz 1976, 2.138–139; Wörrle 2011, 370. See now: Kirbihler (2017, 133–52), attempting to reconcile the contradictory evidence.

[33] E.g., Q. Caecilius Atticus: *AÉ* 1991, 1503 (with Jones 1999, 90); C. Proculeius *RPC* 1.1359–1362. Compare Pomponius Macer at Priene (*I.Priene*² 244) and C. Iulius Demetrius at Cyprus (CD 48.40.6).

[34] CD. 53.15.3. Note earlier scholars' judicious scepticism: e.g., Pflaum 1968, 386; Eck 1995–1998, 1.43–46.

[35] Dalla Rosa 2018, 506–7.

[36] E.g., Licinus in Gaul before 15 (CD. 54.21.3–8); Strabo (3.4.20) refers to *procuratores* in Spain supplying troops. More generally, CD. 53.15.3–4. Eich 2005, 106–9, 111; Dalla Rosa 2017, 108.

and purpose of the institution were radically altered after the establishment of the imperial cult at Pergamum in 29. Tacitus and Dio both stress the collective action of the province in dedicating a temple to Augustus and Rome.[37] This community coalesced around a single festival based at the temple in Pergamum, though eventually this honour was accorded to other *poleis*.[38] Discussions of *koina* in the Imperial period focus on the role they played in perpetuating the imperial cult, though crucially they performed important administrative functions.[39] That said, the leading officials of the *koinon* in the early Principate are ἀρχιερεῖς θεᾶς Ῥώμης καὶ Αὐτοκράτορος Καίσαρος θεοῦ υἱοῦ Σεβαστοῦ ('high-priests of Roma and Imperator Caesar *divi f.* Augustus').[40] This close connection between the institution, its titulature, and worship of the Princeps emphasizes the extent to which religious considerations framed the *koinon*'s functions. However, some evidence shows it acting as a conduit between the central state and its constituent communities.[41]

The *koinon*'s internal organization in this period remains opaque. Deininger argued the title of ἀρχιερεύς (high-priest) denoted the annually elected leader of the institution from the beginning of the imperial period and was synonymous with that of ἀσιάρχης.[42] Despite persistent critiques, new evidence from Phrygian Hierapolis seems to confirm that by the mid-second century CE ἀρχιερεῖς were elected from the ranks of the ἀσιάρχεις, the heads of neocorate temples in Asia.[43] However, this new insight sheds little light on the Augustan period. Moreover, Strabo seems to demonstrate that during the first century BCE ἀσιάρχης was a title which stood outside the *koinon*'s purview and the date at which it was co-opted cannot be reconstructed.[44]

However, a large monument from Sardis for Menogenes preserves some crucial evidence for the organization of the *koinon* during the Augustan period. The stone, a single stele found near the temple of Artemis, contains eleven documents

[37] Tac. *Ann.* 4.37; CD. 51.20.6–7. Compare Suet. *Aug.* 52; Nic. Dam. *FGrH* 90 F125. Deininger 1965, 16–19; Price 1984, 66–7; Madsen 2016, 24–34. Kirbihler (2016, 359–81) argues that the *tresviri* adopted a conscious policy of promoting Caesar's cult in Asia from the late 40s, but Frija (2012, 32–4) notes the significant conceptual distance between this and the imperial cult. See also Prignitz (2011, 210–12), plausibly redating *SEG* 58.578, which refers to a local priesthood of Roma and Augustus in Macedonia, from 88/89 CE (Actian era) to 28/27 (Macedonian era).

[38] See *I.Eph.* 7.2.3801. Price 1984, 104–7. For the subsequent development of the cult and its infrastructure: Burrell 2004, esp. 346–7.

[39] E.g., Guerber (2009, 81) sees its purpose as 'pour encourager les Grecs à jouer un rôle dans l'administration de leur province'. Compare Deininger 1965, 156–69; more cautiously, Burrell 2004, 2; Vitale 2012, 31–2.

[40] *Sardis* 7.1.8.75, 83, 99. See Campanile 1994, #4, 3 and 1 respectively; other early examples #2 and 5–7.

[41] E.g., Burrell 2004, 2–3; Guerber 2009, 80–2; Frija 2016, 161–4. Note the swift expansion of local civic cults: Frija 2012, esp. 34–41; Ventroux 2017, 120–3 at Pergamum.

[42] Deininger 1965, 41–50, followed by Campanile 1994, 18–22; Carter 2004, 41–68; Vitale 2014, 287–94. Criticized by Kearsley 1986, 183–92; 1989, 57–65; Friesen 1999, 275–90.

[43] Ritti's plausible restoration (2017, 463–71 (texts and commentary at 372–5, 437–48), see Jones 2018, 924) of the two preambles identifies one Ti. Claudius Miletus as both ἀσιάρχης and ἀρχιερεὺς τῆς Ἀσίας ναοῦ τοῦ ἐν Ζμύρνῃ. Given both decrees involve a single ἀρχιερεύς and three ἀσιάρχαι, Ritti returns to Magie's earlier suggestion (1950, 1298).

[44] E.g., Strabo 14.1.42, 14.2.24; cf. *Acts* 19:31.

dating between 5 and 2. The preface to the inscription accentuates how the extensive contents emerge from *koinon*, the *demos*, and the *gerousia* of Sardis.[45] Of the relevant documents, two letters from different ἀρχιερεῖς occur first, followed immediately by two decrees of the *koinon*. The first letter is sent by the ἀρχιερεύς Charinus:

> *Χαρῖνος Χαρίνου Περγαμηνὸς, ὁ ἀρχιερεὺς θεᾶς Ῥώμης καὶ Αὐτοκράτορος Καίσαρος θεοῦ υἱοῦ Σεβαστο[ῦ, Σαρδιανῶν] | ἄρχουσι βουλῇ δήμῳ χαίρειν· ἐ<κ>κλησίας, ἀρχαιρετικῆς συναχθείσης καὶ συνελθόντων τῶν ἀπὸ τῶν [πόλεων ἑ]|κατὸν κ(αὶ) ν' ἀνδρῶν τιμᾶν ἐπηνέχθησαν ἄθροοι τὸν καθ' ἔτος ἔκδικον τοῦ κοινοῦ τῶν ἐπὶ τῆς Ἀσί[ας Ἑλ]|λήνων Μηνογένην Ἰσιδώρου τοῦ Μηνογένους τὸν πολείτην <ὑ>μῶν, διὰ τὴν ἐξ αὐτοῦ ἰς τὴν Ἀσίαν [εὔδη]|λον εὔνοιαν καὶ διὰ τὸ τὴν ἀρχὴν αὐτὸν τετελεκέναι καθαρῶς καὶ συνφερόντως, ἰκόνι γραπτῇ ἐνόπλῳ <ἐ>πιχρ[ύσῳ] | ἣν καὶ ἀνατεθῆναι ἐν ᾗ ἂν βούληται πόλει τῆς Ἀσίας, ἐφ' ἧς καὶ ἐπιγραφῆναι· οἱ ἐπὶ τῆς Ἀσίας Ἕλ<λ>ηνες ἐτίμησ[αν] | Μηνογένην Ἰσιδώρου τοῦ Μηνογένους Σαρδιανόν, ἔκδικον, τελέσαντα τὴν ἀρχὴν κα<θ>αρῶς καὶ σ[υν]|φερόντως τῇ Ἀσίᾳ· δι' ὃ καὶ γεγράφαμεν ὑμεῖν περὶ τῶν τιμῶν αὐτοῦ ἵνα ἰδῆτε* ('Charinus, son of Charinus, of Pergamum, High-priest of the goddess Roma and of Imperator Caesar, *divi f.*, Augustus, to the archons, *boule*, and *demos* of the Sardians, greetings. An assembly for the selection of officials being held, and the 150 men from the cities meeting, they were moved to honour, unanimously, Menogenes, son of Isidorus, grandson of Menogenes, this year *ekdikos* for the *koinon* of the Greeks in Asia, your citizen, on account of his conspicuous goodwill towards Asia and his completion of this office with integrity and for the public good, with a gilded equestrian statue, to be set up in whichever city of Asia he wishes, on which should be inscribed: "the Greeks of Asia honoured Menogenes, son of Isidorus, grandson of Menogenes, of Sardis, *ekdikos*, who completed this office with integrity and for the public good of Asia." For this reason, we have written to you about his honours, for your information.')[46]

Several elements, echoed in the other documents, command attention. Most significant is Menogenes' position as ἔκδικος for the *koinon*, reprised for a second and third time in the two decrees. During the Hellenistic and late Republican periods, this term seems to have generally indicated a public advocate, though its employment is haphazard. In 51/50, Cicero suggests that ἔκδικοι were officials legally authorized by *poleis* to conduct negotiations with creditors; by contrast, typical ambassadors, termed *legati* or πρεσβευταί, were restricted to petitioning governors.[47] Fournier argues convincingly that ἔκδικοι in the Hellenistic period

[45] Buckler & Robinson 1914, 337–9. On the chronology, see now Chin (2022, 424–34).
[46] *Sardis* 7.1.8.75–82.
[47] Cic. *Fam.* 13.56.1–2.

were akin to *σύνδικοι*, irregular officials elected to represent a city's interests in legal cases involving external powers.[48] However, the Menogenes dossier makes clear that this was an annual office; his remit appeared to extend to representing the interests of the *koinon* at Rome, though in a more general fashion than Cicero would recognize.[49] It is significant that under Augustus the inhabitants of the province felt it expedient to regularly elect magistrates on behalf of the whole *koinon* whose role, historically, was to represent communities in legal and financial disputes. It underscores that, while the abolition of the *decuma* tax farm in Asia brought down gross taxation rates, it did not eradicate corruption and abuse of provincials and provincial communities.[50] As Fournier highlights, the scope of this office far exceeded the role of representative: in one *koinon* decree associated with Paullus Fabius Maximus' dossier, *ἔκδικοι* of the organization are enjoined to ensure the display of the proconsul's *edictum* (*δελτογράφημα*) together with the *ψήφισμα* itself.[51]

Furthermore, Menogenes' honorary decree demonstrates that by the mid-Augustan period established practices provided for regular annual election to several positions. The letter of Charinus mentions an *ἐ<κ>κλησίας ἀρχαιρετικῆς συναχθείσης καὶ συνελθόντων τῶν ἀπὸ τῶν [πόλεων ἑ]|κατὸν κ(αὶ) ν' ἀνδρῶν* ('assembly for the selection of magistrates and meeting of the 150 men from the cities').[52] The following letter of Demetrios simplifies this to *ἀρχαιρέσια* ('election').[53] Aside from the interesting point that the letters show lexical variation—the language of the institution had not become static and over-ritualized—this illustrates that a meeting of a set number of representatives, 150, took place at regular intervals, annually in early August.[54] This raises the question of how the representatives were allocated among the communities of the *provincia*. The neatness of the number 150 makes it unlikely that it corresponded to the number of *poleis* which made up the *koinon*; nor is the total easily divisible by the number of *conventus* districts (13) or the number of Sullan *regiones* (44). Consequently, a more imaginative method to arrive at this number of delegates was necessary. The example of Lycia and the division of representatives based on the size and significance of the community on a scale from three to one offers a simple explanation.[55] The appearance of four different

[48] Fournier 2007, 26. On *σύνδικοι*: 9–17. Prior to the creation of the Roman *provincia*, these mediated with other *poleis* but with increasing Roman control their focus shifted to questions arising from imperial administration. For the imperial period: Dmitriev 2005a, 213–16.

[49] Fournier 2007, 25–6. Earlier: Magie 1950, 648; Dmitriev 2005a, 214.

[50] Brunt 1961, 189–223.

[51] *RDGE* 65.d.64. Fournier 2007, 27. See, by contrast, the well-attested *ἔκδικοι* of civic *gerousiai* in the Imperial period (e.g., *I.Eph.* 26.21). Robert 1958, 28–9.

[52] *Sardis* 7.1.8.76–77. [53] *Sardis* 7.1.8.85. [54] *I.Priene*² 14.82–84. Chin 2022, 426.

[55] Strabo 14.3.3. The ratio of *poleis* to representatives in Asia would be far lower than in Lycia—perhaps not every *polis* had the right to participate. The *Album Canusinum* (223 CE) provides another potential comparandum. Given the tidy number of 100 representatives, Salway (2000, 126–33) proposes that additional members were adlected to the *ordo decurionum* on an ad hoc basis to fill gaps.

ἀρχιερεῖς over four years from different *poleis* strongly suggests that this position was one of those elected by the representatives, and hints that some principle of rotation operated within the minds of the delegates, though this is, admittedly, speculative.[56] The use of χειροτονηθείς to describe Menogenes' appointment to his second term implies that this was also a regularly elected office. The shorthand employed by Demetrios implies a familiar process and prioritizes the electoral aspect of the meeting, where Charinus' language could imply a wider forum for discussion.[57] This text shows a comprehensive, functional regional structure within which communities had traded agency for co-operation and stability.

The honours, voted in four consecutive years, exceed those offered to his forebears Hierocles and Dionysus. On each occasion he was granted the right to a gilded equestrian statue (ἰκὼν ἐνόπλον ἐπιχρύσον); significantly more extensive than the bronze statues (ἰκόνας χαλκᾶς) accorded to his predecessors.[58] Menogenes continued to have the choice of *polis* in which his honours were to be erected and, in the final case, this was extended explicitly to sacred precincts. The militaristic connotations of an equestrian statue seem at odds with an ambassadorial role. In earlier periods, equestrian statues were reserved for Hellenistic *basileis* and Roman commanders, though they are included among the gaudy honours of Diodoros Pasparos at Pergamum.[59] Inflation of honours in Asia over the course of the first century, for local magnates and Romans, may explain this difference in scale.[60] Nevertheless, that Menogenes, unlike Diodorus, was repeatedly honoured for apparently regular missions in his institutionalized role as an advocate for the *provincia* is striking. One plausible reason for this development would see civic and, later, provincial elites as valuing the role of ἔκδικος as a protector of the *provincia* and its constituent communities on a scale commensurate with earlier royal or Roman actors. This final *koinon* decree added the right to display Menogenes' honours on marble stele, presumably the surviving monument. It also affords Isidorus, Menogenes' son, the right to his own gilded statue. Isidorus is presented not as a citizen of Sardis, but as an Ἀσιανός ('citizen of Asia'), further pointing to the strengthening group identity of the elites of the *provincia*. Menogenes retained control of the placement of his son's honorific monument, and this could present evidence of increasing heritability of honour and office.[61] The number of honours granted to Menogenes also gave him options in terms of display. He could choose to concentrate them in one *polis* or spread them across several increasingly interconnected provincial hubs. His apparently exceptional

[56] Campanile 1994, 17. [57] Compare Strabo 14.3.3.

[58] On portraits, see Ng 2016, 235–60. On the types of honorific inscriptions: Ma 2013a, 24–39.

[59] *Sardis* 7.1.8.118–119. Cf. *OGIS* 764, A.21–33 (Diodorus Pasparos). Generally, Gauthier 1985; Ma 2013b, 139–40, 167–9.

[60] Heller & van Nijf 2017, 10–15.

[61] Chin 2022, 447–9. Compare: *I.Knidos* 51–61, with Thériault 2003, 240–2; *SEG* 46.1709, with Hall, Milner, & Coulton 1996, 121–43.

success requires that caution be applied in using him as an exemplum. However, this dossier offers some insight into how a provincial elite began to coalesce through progressively stronger regional institutions and connectivity.[62]

The development of the *koinon* of Asia in the Augustan period demonstrates an increasing institutionalization of the existing organization. While the establishment of the imperial cult at Pergamum pushed the body into a role co-ordinating religious activity in honour of the Princeps, this did not involve a change in purpose, only in intensity. While the temple of Roma and Augustus at Pergamum offered the novelty of a single physical focal point for the *koinon*, its magistracies continued to rotate through a range of civic communities. By the turn of the first century CE, the organization possessed several officials, both religious and administrative, together with a complex annual electoral process and an assembly with the authority and legitimacy to issue honorific decrees with broad relevance across the *provincia*.

The Coinage of Asia under Augustus

Under Augustus, the hitherto emergency measure of minting Roman denominations began to change: an issue of *denarii* and *aurei*, originally attributed to the mint at Ephesus, have been convincingly related by Sutherland to the major issue of *cistophori* at Pergamum in 19/18. While the reverses of each issue are distinctive, the style of carving and subject—the return of Parthian standards and victory in Armenia—are similar.[63] A comparison of known specimens and dies emphasizes the fact that the cistophoric issue was substantially larger (in the order of three times so) than the *denarius* and *aureus* issues.[64] Sutherland argued these Roman denominations were intended for military pay and not for circulation within Asia on account of the difficulties integrating the *denarius* and cistophoric standards.[65] However, it is in the Augustan period that we see an increase in epigraphic attestation of Roman denominations in Asia and, potentially, if originating from Verrius Flaccus, the well-known equation of a *cistophorus* with three *denarii*, a calculation which continued to undervalue the currency.[66] Sutherland is likely correct that this issue was minted for use outside of the *provincia*, but the increasing integration of the Aegean region into an imperial

[62] Compare Chin (2022, 440–54), who plausibly sees in this monument an attempt to assert Sardian primacy and identity within the framework of the *koinon*. Inter-*polis* and inter-regional competition was a crucial dynamic of Imperial Asia Minor, however, the crucial point here is that this contest was framed by the burgeoning provincial elite and mediated within the *koinon*. Cf. Heller 2006, 85–120; Hallmannsecker 2020, 4–22.

[63] Sutherland 1973, 139–40 contra Mattingly 1923, cxviii–cxix, cxxv.

[64] Sutherland 1973, 140–2; Carbone 2022, 254–5.

[65] Sutherland 1973, 142, 150.

[66] Carbone 2022, 264–84.

monetary system in precisely this period saw a further loosening of the closed-currency area under the early Principate.

Another well-known *aureus*, now in the British Museum, highlights the increasing interconnectedness with provincial denominations. The obverse shows a laureate head of Octavian with the legend 'IMP CAESAR – DIVI F COS VI' and the reverse a togate Octavian seated on a *sella curulis* holding a scroll with the suggestive text 'LEGES ET IVRA P R RESTITVIT'. The consulship dates this issue to 28. Rich and Williams provide a survey of gold and silver coinage issued by Octavian in the period 34–27, which includes issues from Asia which seem closely related.[67] Notable is a *cistophorus* which shows a laurelled head of Octavian on the obverse, with the legend IMP CAESAR DIVI F COS VI LIBERTATIS P R VINDEX, and the personification of Pax, identified by a legend, on the reverse.[68] This issue, containing the extraordinary label of 'champion of the liberty of the *populus Romanus*' seems to directly respond to the Antonian cistophoric issues. The obverse legend wraps around the coin as did Antonius' titulature; Pax replaces the Antonian exemplar Dionysus; and the traditional ivy wreathes are replaced by laurel signifying Octavian's success. The recurrence of motifs such as the overt political slogans and stylistic features lead Rich and Williams to identify the new *aureus* as originating at the same Asian mint as the *cistophorus*.[69] Consequently, they link the assertion of the title *vindex libertatis* not only to the defeat of Antonius and Cleopatra, but also to the political settlement at Rome, which began in 28.[70] Rich and Williams emphasize that while it is possible that local mint-magistrates designed the imagery and slogans, it is more likely that for this coinage the title had been officially conferred and suggest that both legends were inspired by a single *senatus consultum*.[71] Indeed, Cornwell argues convincingly that this coin deftly combined distinctive repertoires to speak to Roman citizen and provincial audiences and emphasize the return of peace.[72]

After Actium, Octavian revived *cistophori* within Asia, seemingly responding directly to Antonius' issues from a decade earlier. Sutherland, in his 1970 study of Augustan *cistophori*, established seven groups minted between 28 and 18. The earliest group, already discussed above, is firmly dated to 28 and retains the *cista mystica*; however, it includes Augustus' portrait, *pax* and Latin legends aimed at a Roman audience.[73] The second to sixth groups represent a further and

[67] Rich & Williams 1999: 171. The coin in question is described at p. 169, picture at plate 20, #1.

[68] *RPC* I.2203.

[69] Rich & Williams 1999, 173–5. Compare Antonian issues of *denarii* and *aurei* from Ephesus (Sutherland 1970: 88–9; Mannsperger 1973) and joint issues in 19 BCE (Sutherland 1973).

[70] Rich & Williams 1999, 183–6. Compare *RG* 1.1 (*rem publicam a dominatione factionis oppressam in libertatem vindicavi*), itself already drawing on Caesar (*BC* 1.22.5) and Cicero (*Phil.* 3.4, 14).

[71] Rich & Williams 1999, 186–7. They also link this to his *edictum* annulling his own illegal acts in the civil war and triumviral period (Tac. *Ann.* 3.28.1–2; CD. 53.2.5. Rich & Williams 1999, 191–8; Mantovani 2008; Dalla Rosa 2015, 178–83).

[72] Cornwell 2017, 116.

[73] Sutherland 1970, 12–14.

fundamental shift in iconography. Though the weight standard remained unchanged, there was no longer a *cista* on the coins. Instead, there were a variety of reverse types paired with the head of Augustus, identified through the legend IMP CAESAR AVGVSTVS, starting with a sphinx and capricorn. Both images are intimately tied to Augustus, suggesting imperial involvement in suggesting types.[74] The largest issues (Sutherland's groups five and six) include a reverse type depicting an altar with two hinds, clear allusion to Ephesus.[75] The final issue represents a further innovation. The obverse legend—IMP IX TR POT IV (and later V)—dates the coinage firmly to between 20 and 18. Three reverse types exist. The first depicts an arch topped with eagles with the legend SPQR SIGNIS RECEPTIS, alluding to the return of Roman standards by the Parthians and Augustus' subsequent ovation in 20. The second depicts a domed temple with the legend MARS VLTO(r), vowed by Octavian in 44 and completed in 20, which also housed the returned standards.[76] The final type depicts a hexastyle temple with the twin legends ROM(a) ET AVG(ustus) and COM(mune) ASIAE, referring to the dedication of the imperial cult at Pergamum.[77] This final group, bearing legends and symbols personal to the achievements of Augustus bears no similarity to the original *cistophori* beyond the weight standard and mints. Indeed, the first two types reflect contemporary issues of coin types, both precious metal and bronze, from Spain.[78] While some local variation seems to have been retained in the coins of Ephesus and Pergamum, this was now a demonstrably imperial coinage. This was the last cistophoric issue under Augustus, but subsequent emperors including Claudius, the Flavians, and the Antonines continued to strike in Asia on this standard.[79]

One final enigma is presented by a bronze series bearing Augustus' portrait, identified by a legend, on the obverse and the legend C. A. within a wreath on the reverse. It is obverse die-linked to issues of a similar design with AVGVSTVS on the reverse.[80] This was struck in several Roman denominations and has been widely found within Asia, but also distributed across Syria, Aegean, and Danube.[81] They likely date to *c.*27–23, though a few issues with the additional legend TRIB (unicia) POT(estas) must post-date 23.[82] The meaning of C. A. remains unclear: Grant's assertion that it stood for *Caesaris auctoritate* has been rightly rejected as an anachronistic and unusual formulation; Mattingly suggested *Caesar Augustus*, which jars with the reverse legend; and Burnett asserted that it stands for *commune Asiae* as a mint authority.[83] In light of the apparently wide distribution of

[74] Suet. *Aug.* 94.12. Price 1979, 277–8 (with references); 1984, 173–4. Note, however, Metcalf's caution (2007, 152–3) in ascribing this imperial control of imagery beyond precious metal coinage.

[75] Sutherland 1970, 99–102. [76] *RIC* 1².508–510. [77] Sutherland 1970, Group 7, 33–7.

[78] *RIC* 1².132–137. Rose 2005, 23–5; Cornwell 2017, 132–3.

[79] Claudius: *RPC* 1.221–2225; Flavians: *RPC* 2.859–875; Antonines: *RPC* 3.1298–1320.

[80] *RPC* 1.2227–2235. [81] Howgego 1982, 4.

[82] Howgego 1982, 6–7, followed by *RPC* p. 380.

[83] Grant 1946, 108; Mattingly 1951, 141 (followed by Woytek 2019, 396); Burnett 1977, 46–7.

this coinage, the latter has further argued that the coinage was in part an abortive attempt to establish a new imperial bronze standard. As Dio had Maecenas argue anachronistically to Augustus, for Burnett the imposition of a standard imperial coinage could have been intended to reduce local civic expenses.[84] Nevertheless, while his critique of the dominant narrative that military activity was the primary driver of coin production is well judged, the evidence is extremely limited. Consequently Howgego's aporia, with the acknowledgement that some proposed military expenditure may have lain in the background like other Roman denominational issues in the Augustan period, seems most convincing.[85]

Under Augustus we witness the unusual phenomenon of governors appearing on local bronze issues. The earliest example occurs at Magnesia-under-Sipylos in the early 20s, portraying the head of M. Tullius Cicero the younger, identified by a Greek legend opposite a hand holding a wreath, two ears of corn, and a vine branch, together with a civic ethnic.[86] The city had minted coinage under the Attalids, but not during the Republic, and never with this imagery. Soon afterwards, between 26 and 24, Aezani struck coins with the portrait of Potitus Valerius Messalla, again identified in Greek, opposite a scale and the civic ethnic. This is associated (through the local magistrate's monogram) with an issue showing Augustus unlabelled, opposite Zeus, who is bearing an eagle and sceptre.[87] Approximately a generation later Pitane minted a series displaying Augustus on the obverse and P. Cornelius Scipio on the reverse.[88] This coin has often been interpreted in the context of a broader set of coins containing gubernatorial portraits from the last decade of the first century from Asia and Africa. Grant, arguing from the evidence available to him, noted that all were related to Augustus by marriage or particularly close *amici*. Earlier consensus held that this was a particularly short-lived phenomenon.[89] However, subsequent finds have rendered this commonplace untenable.[90] Again, this issue appears to have been struck in conjunction with another pairing Gaius and Lucius Caesar, the adoptive sons of Augustus.[91] The clearest example emerges at Hierapolis with a series of parallel issues of coins bearing either the portrait of Augustus or that of Paullus Fabius Maximus in 9/8. Intriguingly, Augustus is portrayed opposite a lyre on a single occasion, then Apollo Citharoedus, whereas Paullus is presented opposite a double axe, perhaps hinting at the *fasces*, then plain text acknowledging the local magistrate.[92] In 6/5, Temnus issued bronze bearing the portrait of C. Asinius Gallus opposite the head of Dionysus, again in conjunction with a series of coins showing Augustus, here portrayed opposite

[84] Burnett 2022, 30–1. [85] Howgego 1982, esp. 18–19 contra Burnett 1977, 47–8.
[86] *RPC* 1.2448. [87] *RPC* 1.3067 (Augustus); 3068 (Messalla).
[88] *RPC* 1.2392. [89] Grant 1946, 229; Syme 1956, 265.
[90] On the date, most likely 11/10, Eilers 2001. See appendix for an updated list of gubernatorial portraits on coins, with Burnett 2011.
[91] *RPC* 1.2393. [92] *RPC* 1.2390–2942.

Athena Nikephoros.[93] Finally, Pergamum minted a series in 4/5 CE showing M. Plautius Silvanus, togate, carrying patera, and being crowned by a figure in cuirass. The reverse, bearing the legend *ΣΕΒΑΣΤΟΣ*, depicts the cult statue of Augustus in the temple of Rome and Augustus at Pergamum. Again, this was struck in conjunction with an issue displaying the heads of Gaius and Lucius Caesar.[94]

While this was never a common phenomenon, after Silvanus' coins there are no further extant examples within Asia.[95] In the context of Roman officials increasingly performing *recusatio* when offered honours this development is unsurprising. Taken as a group however, these issues have striking similarities which shed light on this crucial transitional period. First, each of these examples contains a Greek legend identifying the Roman magistrate, and a means of identifying the responsible local official. These bronze coins were for local use and consequently designed with a local audience in mind. Consequently, the choice of the Aezanetans to not label Augustus' portrait in the mid-20s suggests broad familiarity with the imperial image even at this early stage. Moreover, these issues are likely to have been issued and designed on local initiative, even where the imagery suggests some form of input from sources familiar with Roman ideology. Second, with the exception of the earliest example, for Cicero each of these issues was struck in conjunction with another celebrating Augustus, or Gaius and Lucius Caesar. Each of these Augustan issues featured imagery distinct from that of the parallel gubernatorial issue, which was more appropriate for the Princeps. By contrast, the governors were largely shown with practical imagery invoking prosperity in the case of Cicero, or order in the cases of Messalla and Paullus. The exception here is Silvanus, depicted in an overtly honorific fashion. While Atkinson speculates that this issue parallels the crowning of Paullus Fabius Maximus in 9/8 for his suggestion to honour Augustus, the precise context must remain unclear.[96] A variant on this trend emerges at Tralles. A large bronze issue, in multiple variants and denominations, was struck under the authority of Menander, son of Parrhesius. While two examples reflect longstanding Trallian obverse types (humped bull; laureate Apollo), the remainder display the head of either Augustus without an identifying legend (three types) or P. Vedius Pollio (two types) identified in Greek.[97] As noted previously, Vedius acted as an early iteration of an imperial *procurator*, representing the Princeps on the ground in Asia in the early 20s. Though it is possible that he held no official position at this

[93] *RPC* 1.2446 (Augustus); 2447 (Gallus). Heller and Suspène (2019) note the unusual honorific ἁγνος ('pure', 'holy') ascribed to Asinius and tentatively suggest his involvement in dialogue with the city over the coinage.

[94] *RPC* 1.2364 (Silvanus); 2365 (Gaius and Lucius Caesar).

[95] Though Eilers (2001, 205) includes three Cibyran issues under Tiberius, Claudius, and Nero, Burnett (2011, 22) is rightly sceptical as to whether these depict Roman governors.

[96] Atkinson 1958, 328–9.

[97] Typical types: *RPC* 1.2636, 2639; Augustus: *RPC* 1.2633, 2637–8; Pollio: *RPC* 1.2634–2635.

time, Dalla Rosa's suggestion that he played a role in distributing imperial funds after the earthquake in 26/25 is attractive. His euergetic role and association with Augustus may have led to the community's decision to honour him on their coinage. A later issue from Priene bearing the name and perhaps the portrait of Pompeius Macer, another *procurator* in Asia for Augustus, may be viewed in a similar light.[98]

Overall, the coinages of Asia under Augustus continue to develop in a consistent, incremental fashion. The cistophoric standard remained dominant and local issues in bronze remained robust and responsive to local concerns. That said, *aurei* and *denarii* were minted more frequently and became more visible in the region. Moreover, the iconography of Augustan *cistophori* not only reflected that of Roman denominations but explicitly reproduced Augustan messaging: the *cistophori* became an unambiguously imperial coinage. Finally, the experimentation with honouring Roman magistrates and other non-imperial figures on local bronze issues swiftly ends, in line with broader trends in honorific practice. Via a lengthy, largely unplanned process, *provincia Asia* acquired a functional imperial monetary system.

Augustus, Jurisdiction, and Government

After wintering in Samos in 21/20, Augustus travelled through the eastern provinces, including Asia, personally interfering in some aspects of their administration. Cyzicus presents the most obvious example: Augustus stripped the *polis* of its ἐλευθερία due to its role in flogging and killing some Roman citizens during a period of internal unrest.[99] The Princeps' decision highlights the detachment of status from loyalty in military contexts, which had been the norm in earlier periods. Instead, failure to observe the special status of Roman citizens resulted in the unilateral revocation of privileges.[100] Dio's account possibly implies that the Cyzicenes, as a community, executed these Romans in a judicial context.[101] If so, this could explain the swift and summary outcome, while also elucidating the limits of civic freedom under the new regime.

[98] *RPC* 2687. On Macer: Str. 13.2.3.

[99] CD. 54.7.6; Euseb. *Chron.* p. 165 Helm. Dio adds that Tyre and Sidon, in Syria, a *provincia Augusti*, were similarly punished, though without any suggestion of Romans coming to harm. Possibly alluded to by Suetonius (*Aug.* 47.1). Jones 1971², 86–7; Fournier 2010, 492–4. Cf. Tiberius' relationship with Cyzicus (Tac. *Ann.* 4.36.2–3; Suet. *Tib.* 37.7; CD. 57.24.6. Edmondson 2014, 142) and CD. 60.17.3, with Suet. *Claud.* 25.3; *SEG* 44.1205.a.11–27 on Lycian *stasis* and political turmoil leading to provincialization under Claudius.

[100] Guerber 2009, 73–4.

[101] CD. 54.7.6. Ferrary 2017a [1991], 172–3; Thornton 1999, 509–16 contra Magie 1950, 1052; Marshall 1969, 261 n.23.

The well-known letter of Augustus to the free city of Cnidus reveals significant changes in hierarchies of jurisdiction. In the second half of 6, an embassy arrived in Rome and presented Augustus, then consul designate, with a decree. Notably, the Senate is not mentioned here, perhaps intimating that this embassy was directed to the Princeps personally. If so, this further demonstrates the evolution of central institutions during Augustus' lifetime.[102] The ambassadors accused two Cnidian residents, Euboulus, son of Anaxandrides, and his wife, Tryphera, of murdering Euboulus, son of Chrysippus, during an armed dispute. The couple fled to Rome rather than face local judgement and in the interim the husband died.[103] It seems clear that no trial process had preceded the defendants' escape. On receiving the embassy Augustus recounts that he deputed an *amicus*, Asinius Gallus, to investigate by torturing the household's slaves.[104] Subsequently, having formed his own opinion, Augustus gives a reconstruction of the events, asserting his belief that the murder was committed in self-defence and castigating the Cnidians for pursuing, as he saw it, the wrong party.[105] He ends his missive with a strong statement that Tryphera and her husband committed no crime at all (*ἠδικηκότων δὲ οὐδ' ἔστ[ιν ὅ τι]*) and requiring that the city adjust their public records (*τὰ ἐν τοῖς δημ[οσίοις] | ὑμῶν ὁμολογεῖν γράμματα*) to reflect his decision.[106]

This cannot have been an instance of *appellatio* (appeal) in a formal sense, both as no trial had taken place to be appealed and no participant appears to have held Roman citizenship.[107] Instead, this seems to be an ad hoc process instituted in response to an impasse reached by the defendants' flight. The Cnidians, here a group of local powerbrokers, unable to assert jurisdiction outside their territory, sought the Princeps' assistance in achieving 'justice'. In the absence of established mechanisms for dealing with conflicting jurisdictional principles, the Princeps, on the participants' invitation, involved himself. The Cnidian gamble backfired, and the document's appearance at Astypalaea suggests that Tryphera did not return to the city.[108] The involvement of the Princeps bears some resemblance to the role of the Senate in mediating territorial disputes during the second century. As a powerful player and source of extra-civic authority, communities and individuals were tempted to involve them for their own purposes.[109] Over time, through increasing use, this process became institutionalized, fundamentally

[102] *RDGE* 67.5–6. Cnidus' freedom granted by Caesar (Plut. *Caes.* 48.1; Strabo 14.2.15); maintained in Augustan period: Plin. *HN.* 5.104.

[103] *RDGE* 67.8–10. Oliver 37; Sherk 1969, 344.

[104] On the torture of slaves in Roman law: Watson 1983, 56–9. Compare Athens: Hunter 1994, 91–5.

[105] *RDGE* 67.13–36.

[106] *RDGE* 67.36–39.

[107] Viereck 1888, 10 contra Wankerl 2009, 11–12, citing *Dig.* 49.15.7.2. Compare Jones 1960a, 53–5; Millar 1992 [1977], 443, 509–10.

[108] Viereck 1888, 10; Wilamowitz-Moellendorf 1902, 257–8.

[109] Millar 1992 [1977], 473–7; Kallet-Marx 1995, 161–77; see now Czajkowski (2016, 483–6) on Herod's employment of Roman agents to bolster his own decision-making. Note her judicious caution over use of the word 'trial' in these contexts.

altering the balance of jurisdictional power between Princeps and communities in the Greek East, irrespective of their status.

Further evidence emerges from the famous dossier of Paullus Fabius Maximus, which consists of six documents: an *edictum* of the proconsul in Latin, with an appendix; Greek translations of both; and two decrees of the *koinon* of Asia. The edict contains a long justification of Paullus' proposal that the whole *provincia* reform its calendar so that the year commence on Augustus' birthday.[110] The text also notes that a ψήφισμα of the *koinon* was required to execute this plan. That is, Paullus deemed the written decision of representatives of the provincial community necessary before implementing his idea.[111] The first *koinon* decree echoes the proconsul's praise of Augustus before organizing the standardized calendar for the provincial communities. This moved beyond Paullus' original suggestion, hinting at the representatives' zeal to be seen as honouring the Princeps. The intent of the reform was to publicly exhibit collective loyalty to Augustus. In the second decree, the *koinon* reiterated that the changes to the calendar were not to contravene the existing *lex Cornelia*.[112] In both instances, the *koinon* appropriated decision-making authority over *provincia Asia* as a whole. Notwithstanding its patchy adoption, the calendar continued in use until at least the fifth century CE.[113] Paullus' recommendation and the *koinon*'s decision to fundamentally change the calendar of the whole region must be read in the context of the development of new institutional norms. The overwhelming influence of Augustus, whether directly exercised, mediated through the Senate, or in case of provincials, the governor, dictated that he be honoured to maximize the potential privileges. Even so, in this case the exercise of Roman governance was at a distance: the calendrical reform within *provincia Asia*, a major undertaking, resulted from and was driven by a local organization.

A proconsular letter to Chios provides another insight into the shifting administrative landscape for free cities in this period. Though the author is unknown, a reference to his predecessor, Antistius Vetus, allows a secure date of *c.*5 CE.[114] From the surviving text it appears that a land dispute between resident Romans on the island and the *polis* had been referred on at least three occasions to the governor. Bitner contextualizes these exchanges within the framework of the assize court and uses the document to investigate procedural elements of the

[110] *RDGE* 65, with *SEG* 56.1233. On the new calendar, Stern 2012, 276–9; Thonemann 2015, 123–5.

[111] *RDGE* 65.A.21–23, 26–8. Heller (2014, 222–3) argues that Augustus himself may have prompted this innovation; more cautiously, Stern 2012, 278.

[112] *RDGE* 65.D.79–84. Santangelo 2007, 118. See Chapter 2, 'Sulla and the Settlement of Asia'.

[113] As Thonemann notes (2015, 125), Καῖσαρ did not generally displace the Seleucid-Macedonian name of the opening month, Δίος, and (129–131) calendrical variation certainly continued in parts of Asia. Testimonia for the use of Paullus' calendar collected at (126–129), advancing Laffi 1967, 75–81.

[114] *RDGE* 70, with *AÉ* 2014, #1254 correcting l.11. For the date, Marshall (1969, 255 n.2, followed by Atkinson 1958, 328; Badian 1969, 200–4; Bitner 2014, 648–50) against Forrest, arguing for 64/65 CE (*SEG* 22.507).

gubernatorial *conventus*. However, this is not uncontroversial—the Chians, we learn from this document, were from the time of Sulla not subject to the *τύποι* ('written directives') of Roman magistrates. They enjoyed their own laws and customs, which applied even to resident Romans.[115] Accordingly, the elements of the process initiated by the Chians should have initially stood outside any legal process, instead forming a standard diplomatic approach to the governor.[116] However, it is possible that the original decision of Antistius did take place in a legal context: the complex and varying realities of each community's privileges make gubernatorial 'misunderstandings', wilful or otherwise, comprehensible.[117]

This document reveals three important elements of governance during the Augustan period. First, the author seems to have rejected the initial request of the Chians on the grounds that his predecessor had already done so. This reflected the general practice of the late Republic that magistrates would respect existing decisions.[118] It also emphasizes that a written version of this decision was available to the new governor, highlighting the role of archives, or its provision to the parties involved in the original dispute.[119] Second, the author makes clear that he has settled upon his own procedure for judging disputes, stressing that his decision to respect Vetus' ruling is *κατακλουθῶν τῇ καθολικῇ μου* ('following my general procedure'), while a request of both parties for further documentation is *κατὰ τὴν ἐμὴν συνήθειαν* ('in accordance with my customary procedure').[120] Placing this strong emphasis on his personal practice underscores the agency which governors continued to hold in this period. Despite the increasing centralization of the levers of empire, proconsuls retained the capacity to personally decide judicial and diplomatic matters in the field. Indeed, their consular rank in Asia divorced provincial government from the politics of entrenched vested interests.[121] Finally, based on the text's publication that the author, disregarding his own preliminary decision, eventually overturned Vetus' judgement when confronted with documentary evidence. This reinforces the impression that the

[115] Bitner 2014, 647–8. *Pace* Marshall (1969, 257–9), whose rendering 'written documents used in a legal procedure' begs the question. *IAph2007* 8.33.3 and 11.412.23 show *τύπος* could be employed in the phrase *τύπος τῆς ἐπαρχείας* to mean *formula provinciae*, although the context makes this meaning unlikely here (Bitner 2014, 662 n.84; *pace* Thornton 1999, 522).

[116] Cotton (2013, 45–6) on legal disputes not necessarily leading to court action. On the analogy of Roman administration as diplomacy: Eck 2009, 193–207. Compare Cicero's emphasis on governor's availability outside of formal court proceedings (e.g., *QFr.* 1.1.7–9; *Att.* 5.13.1; 6.2.5. Bérenger 2011, 176–9).

[117] Sherk 1969, 353 n.2.

[118] *RDGE* 70.1–7. Bitner 2014, 651 n. 49 (drawing on Lewis 1999, 47). Cf. Haensch 1992, 232 n.60; Lintott 1993, 65–6; Meyer-Zwiffelhoffer 2002, 268–77.

[119] Bitner 2014, 652, 655–6, though note Plin. *Ep.* 10.58–60, 65–6; Burton 1975, 103; Eck 1995–1998, 64.

[120] *RDGE* 70.4,

[121] Consular commanders no longer relied on equestrian support in elections. By the end of the first century innovations in the *repetundae* court had also strengthened the hand of governors (*RDGE* 31).

proconsuls of Asia in the Augustan period continued to hold a wide discretion on their conduct of affairs.

This text demonstrates that in 26 Augustus had reconfirmed by letter that the *polis* retained its ἐλευθερία, almost certainly on the same terms as the earlier *senatus consultum*.[122] That Augustus' correspondence is cited here, and not a ratifying senatorial decree, marks another change from the post-Mithridatic period.[123] It is possible that in view of the Princeps' position his *ipsissima verba* were considered by the Chians to hold more weight.[124] In any case, the use of the letter in this context, a mere two decades into the Principate, reiterates the striking extent to which administrative practice and the relations of communities to the empire at large hinged on Augustus' pronouncements and decisions.

A final document neatly capturing the dynamics of this period is a response from Augustus to a Samian request to be granted ἐλευθερία. Like the Cnidian letter, this text is unusual in preserving the denial of a civic request and appears to have been adduced by Aphrodisias to demonstrate their strong relationship with the Princeps.[125] The actual decision must pre-date the winter of 20/19, when Augustus did grant the island its freedom. Reynolds' suggestion that the war in which Aphrodisias was captured was that against Labienus, rather than the prelude to Actium, has much to recommend it. However, this does not exclude that the initial request was made after Antonius' defeat, even if Bowersock's suggestion dating the document to the late 20s is implausible.[126]

This text reveals two crucial points. First, that civic freedom now lay in the imperial gift. The intercession of Livia in the Samians' favour emphasizes the personal element to the decision and the use of the first person throughout elides any role for the institutions of the *res publica*.[127] This does not mean that a grant would not be confirmed by a later *senatus consultum*, but rather that the pretence that the decision of the Senate could overrule or contradict that of Augustus disappears. Second, the Princeps explicitly links freedom to immunity from Roman taxation, stating, for the record, that fiscal considerations did not affect his decision. Instead, he asserts a principle of reciprocity guiding his choices—as yet, the Samians had not performed actions worthy of reward with τὸ πάντων μέγιστον φιλάνθρωπον ('greatest privilege of all').[128] This demonstrates that Augustus, at least, saw the privilege of freedom in its complete sense as including

[122] *RDGE* 70.18–20.

[123] The corpus of documents attesting Sulla's grants to communities in Asia Minor consists exclusively of *senatus consulta*, even where covering letters are included (*RDGE* 18, 19, 20).

[124] E.g., *IAph2007* 8.25 implies that Aphrodisias did not have copies of the documents provided to its ambassador Solon.

[125] *IAph2007* 8.32.

[126] Reynolds 1982, 105; Jehne 2015, 308; Kokkinia 2015–16, 30; *pace* Bowersock 1984, 52; Badian 1984, 166–8; Toher 1985, 201–2.

[127] Compare CD. 54.7.2, for similar 'personal' grants.

[128] *IAph2007* 8.32.4–7. The language and ideological aspects are discussed in detail in Chapter 2 *infra*. Jehne 2015, 309–10.

immunitas. As an assertion of a general principle this could not be clearer, even if exceptions existed. Both details highlight the evolution of the Roman state.[129] The unique, unequalled position of the Princeps approached that of Hellenistic *basileis* transforming the nature of provincial administration. Though the Republican framework of rule persisted, the introduction of an autonomous player at the pinnacle of the state hierarchy greatly affected the practicalities of Roman rule.

However, no major innovations appear to have taken place in the fiscal sphere. Though Brunt contended that the introduction of *procuratores* implies a shift in state collection practices, moving from the extraction of a lump sum to a percentage cut of farmed taxes, it is unlikely that this occurred under Augustus.[130] The *publicani* continued to collect the *portoria*, and perhaps the *decuma* and *scriptura*, from extra-civic territories.[131] Similarly, sources attest to the continuation of communal assessment and local collection of civic taxes.[132] There is no reason to assume that the level of corruption on an individual level decreased to any significant degree, though the state now had greater leverage and stronger interest in controlling it.[133]

Augustus interfered in *provincia Asia* irrespective of a distinction between *provinciae publicae* and *Caesaris*. This reflects the way in which the *res publica* had fundamentally changed and continued to evolve. Augustus' position was unprecedented and over the course of his reign became institutionalized through praxis. Consequently, the observable tension between imperial and gubernatorial powers and jurisdiction makes sense. Moreover, it seems clear that cities and the increasingly assertive *koinon* also took advantage of structural ambiguities to enhance their own position vis-à-vis the organs of the Roman state. That said, the longevity of Augustus helped to stabilize a particular mode of power relations, which then laid the foundations for the subsequent evolution of the Principate.

Asia and the Construction of an Imperial Province

In this section I have argued that *provincia Asia*, at its inception, was not a single contiguous territorial entity. Instead, after 133, the Attalid kingdom became a patchwork of *ager publicus* and autonomous, allied cities. Put simply, the evidence suggests strongly that the Roman state had limited ambitions within Asia. While

[129] Bernhardt 1980, 192. This implies that the divorce of *libertas* and *immunitas* post-dated the conquest of Egypt, which fits neatly with a view that Augustus was responsible for this decision. Given the Princeps' involvement with state finances and his control over grants of privileges he had a strong motive to do so, and the emphasis placed on revenue here hints at a broader concern. From a practical perspective, Augustus may have implemented this change after the conquest of Egypt, in the settling of the eastern empire while returning to Rome, though this remains a hypothesis.

[130] Eich 2005, 105, 119–20; *pace* Brunt 1990b, 384–6.

[131] De Laet 1949, 370–83; Brunt 1990b, 390–1. See *AÉ* 1968, #483.

[132] Strabo 10.5.3; 14.2.19.

[133] Brunt 1961, 198–223; Tan 2017, 62–6.

Roman magistrates were often present, the scope of their administration was narrow. They had jurisdiction over Roman citizens and individuals without a *polis* citizenship but had no fiscal responsibilities vis-à-vis the cities. The new *provincia* presented a unique challenge as both Roman and local actors needed to find and negotiate the limits of civic freedom and gubernatorial authority. While the *publicani* were present, lobbying commanders and actively seeking to maximize their revenue, the institutional structure established by M'. Aquillius sought a limited 'hegemony'—to follow Kallet-Marx—and evidence implies that the Senate and individuals did intervene to protect the civic rights. Though clearly tensions could be high, during this early period, comparatively, the *publicani* and Roman governors represented an annoyance rather than a scourge to the cities of Asia.

The events of the First Mithridatic War formed a critical juncture for Roman administration in the region, however. The existing template of hegemony was swept away in the invasion and subsequent massacre of Italians in 88. This collaboration of many *poleis* with Mithridates offered Sulla an opportunity to reset the relationship between Rome and the province. Constrained by his own immediate needs, the commander took two specific actions which had a massive impact on the subsequent development of Roman administration in Asia: stripping most *poleis* of their ἐλευθερία and imposing a 20,000-talent fine. This was not the result of careful fiscal planning, but rather the contingent circumstances of civil war. Nevertheless, these decisions subjected the bulk of the region's civic communities to the jurisdiction of Roman magistrates and taxation by the Roman state for the first time. Consequently, the Senate and magistrates sought to regularize the newly extended political and economic elements of state power in the region, constrained by roads already taken. The post-Sullan Republic was formative for later institutions of *provincia Asia*, including the tax-farm for the *decuma*, the *conventus*, and the provincial *koinon*, but these did not spring into being fully formed. Rather, they emerged slowly and dynamically from pre-existing circumstances and continued to evolve across the period in response to changing political conditions at Rome and locally.

The eruption of Mediterranean-wide civil war sparked another crisis of central institutions. Caesar's stunning successes concentrated enough power and authority in his person to disrupt existing frameworks of governance. His removal of the *publicani* from the collection of the *decuma* and apparent emphasis on enshrining the rights of free cities in treaties highlight the innovation his unparalleled position made possible. His political heirs, the triumvirate, continued to oversee a concentration and personalization of state power, which altered the balance between the bodies of the central state and its leaders in establishing and implementing policy, perhaps accounting for the relative absence of provincial governors from the literary and documentary evidence of the period. Even so, the uneasy alliance between Antonius and Octavian came to a swift and summary end at Actium in 31.

Augustus' accession to supreme authority within the Roman world afforded the communities of Asia more certainty in the field of policy developments. The institutionalization of his control and influence had a significant impact on the practice of provincial government. The use of imperial *procuratores* alongside governors introduced new actors into the world of governance, while the establishment of the imperial cult cemented both the ideological basis of Augustan power and the role of the provincial *koinon* in local affairs. Though the institutions of provincial administration continued to change across the reign of the first Princeps, they shifted back into a more normal rhythm of incremental, rather than abrupt, developments. The longevity of Augustus and his pre-eminence provided a central stability which, irrespective of the tangible impact of his rule, allowed local administrative conditions to settle into their new pattern of evolution.

Overall, I have sought to demonstrate that the cognitive shift which took Roman hegemony in Asia to empire resulted from the unintended consequences of—and circumstances after—Sulla's settlement. There was initially no state-directed drive to exploit the new province. Indeed, the instability at the heart of the Republic made the development of coherent institutional approaches difficult. As the field of authoritative actors narrowed across the first century, the motivation for leaders to develop structures to efficiently govern—balancing fiscal extraction against local resentment—became more pronounced. However, institutions present only one element of Roman government in Asia. Its correlate, the ideological bases of power, are considered in Part Two.

PART TWO

ROMAN HEGEMONY, POWER, AND LOCAL AGENCY

5
Hegemony and the Discourse(s) of Power in Roman Asia

'Speech-acts' and Roman Hegemony

Thus far, I have focused on the formal institutions which shaped, developed, and created Roman hegemony within *provincia Asia*. These structural factors were crucial in framing and constructing the realities of imperial power. However, they do not represent the whole picture. This section redresses the balance by analysing the discursive elements of Roman administrative hegemony. Specifically, it poses the questions of how a discourse of Roman governance emerged in Asia during this formative period and what implications this had for the local experience of Roman rule.

Analyses of relationships between ancient imperial rulers and the subjects have frequently invoked 'speech-act' theory. For example, Millar, reflecting on his 'petition-response' model of Roman imperial governance, emphasized the action performed by 'utterances' of the Princeps, whether *subscriptiones*, letters to communities, *decreta*, or *edicta*.[1] Concentrating on the Seleucid dynasts' correspondence with communities and rulers within their sphere of influence, Ma has similarly shown that conscious engagement with this theoretical tradition can shed light on how discourse shaped and even instantiated the realities of empire.[2] Central to 'speech-act' theory is the principle that in order to fully succeed, any 'act' must be understood and accepted as legitimate by its intended audience. That is, the assertion of power through speech-acts is open to a range of potential responses: it can always be subject to misunderstanding, contest, or negotiation.

Moving beyond single 'speech-acts', the concept of a 'discourse'—a framework of acceptable and accepted language and forms, which provides common ground for interlocutors of holding asymmetric power to negotiate safely—becomes crucial. Ma's model describes the relationship between the Seleucid *basileis* and the communities of Asia Minor as a sophisticated cultural complex. Drawing on Pocock's conceptualization of discourse as a 'language'—with its own grammar, syntax, and rhetoric—he demonstrated that, despite the significant administrative and coercive power of the Seleucid state, the correspondence of its rulers with the

[1] Millar 1992 [1977], 636–7.

[2] Ma 2000. Compare Burton 2011, 24–5.

Imperial Power, Provincial Government, and the Emergence of Roman Asia, 133 BCE–14 CE. Bradley Jordan, Oxford University Press. © Bradley Jordan 2023. DOI: 10.1093/oso/9780198887065.003.0006

poleis of western Asia Minor operated in dialogue with civic honorific decrees. While these two genres were distinct, each responded directly to the other, depending upon common assumptions, addressing similar concerns, and utilizing a shared, limited syntax.[3] This restricted repertoire of reproducible terms allowed both parties to understand the terms of engagement, while presenting room for negotiation in differing interpretations. Extending civic honours to the *basileus* allowed *poleis* to aggrandize their own position, asserting their agency vis-à-vis the hegemonic power. However, by engaging directly with the ruler in honorific terms and requesting privileges from him, communities validated and legitimized the imperial regime.[4] Millar's 'petition-response' model presents a similar picture, with a common understanding of the accepted process and language for communication with the Princeps providing a framework for engagement.[5] Indeed, as Millar observes: 'the ritual of the passing of a decree, despatch of ambassadors, and the presentation of the decree with an accompanying oration, was perhaps the most fundamental contribution of Hellenistic diplomacy to the shaping of imperial rule, and survived effectively unchanged through and beyond [the Principate]'.[6]

However, the establishment of a common discourse and with it the building blocks of Gramscian hegemony between interlocutors from different cultural and institutional backgrounds was a complex process. Dialogue, learning, and negotiation must take place to establish the understanding necessary for a shared framework to exist.[7] In the remainder of this work, I argue that this process was lengthy and beset by structural problems, compounded by lack of pre-existing familiarity on both sides. To abuse a well-known Gramscian bon mot, this ideological crisis 'consiste appunto nel fatto che il vecchio muore e il nuovo non può nascere'. Often taken out of context, Gramsci here refers to the contemporary collapse of Italian liberalism, which he saw as a process caused by tensions and contradictions in the social fabric, based on the alienation of the social groups from their representatives, resulting in violence, extremism, and discontent.[8] In a similar way, I hope to demonstrate that the establishment of a commonly recognized discursive framework was hindered by failure of the Roman state to establish a coherent language in communicating with communities in Asia. The existence of multiple, parallel types of administrative utterance, each with distinctive traditions, formats, and language, presented a confusing tableau for civic leaders, problematizing their engagement with—and attempts to exploit to their own advantage—Roman power.

[3] Pocock 1987, 19–23; Ma 1999, 179–206.

[4] Ma 1999, 214–42, esp. 235–42. Welles (1934, xl) and Bencivenni (2010, 154–61) see an honorific element to the publication of royal missives.

[5] Millar's petition-and-response model (esp. 2002 [1966], 271–91, 2004 [1967], 3–22]). Compare Lenski 2017 on Constantine's interactions with fourth-century CE communities.

[6] Millar 1992 [1977], 618. [7] Pocock 1987, 29–38; 1987a, 30–3. [8] Gramsci Q3§34.

This chapter focuses purely on the Roman side of this discursive equation: the official utterances of the Roman state and its representatives. It concentrates on the structure, style, and language of these documents, tracing changes over the period and analysing how these documents collectively generated a discourse of Roman governance. Like Part One, it focuses in turn on the *provincia* before the First Mithridatic War, the period between Sulla's settlement and the assassination of Caesar in 44, the civil war period, and the supremacy of Augustus. It also highlights some of the problems posed by this process for communities, though a more complete analysis of their responses is seen in the following chapters.

The Hellenistic Framework and Roman Responses

Modern scholars often emphasize that Roman magistrates drew on the structure and language of Hellenistic royal letters in their own correspondence. However, this appropriation of existing models was not seamless. Ma identifies four themes central to the language of Seleucid royal letters: continuity, breadth of community, moral consistency, and cordiality. He emphasizes that benefactions offered Seleucid rulers are grounded in a generalized past, a continuous and consistent relationship, marked by words and phrases such as *διὰ παντός*, *ἀεί*, *συναύξειν*, or *διατελέω*.[9] The decisions and grants of the ruler are often framed as benefitting the broader community of *οἱ Ἕλληνες* ('the Greeks'), as well as the given community. Moreover, the agency of the ruler is amplified, both through the recurrence of words expressing choice (e.g., *αἵρεσις*; *προαίρεσις*) and through the use of often extensive motivation clauses to explain the grant. Finally, the use of overtly diplomatic language, emphasizing the rulers' care for and kind disposition towards his interlocutor, serves to veil the institutional power exercised by the former over the latter. Collectively, this language was specific to the situation of a Seleucid *basileus* communicating directly with a community.

Royal letters also shared structural elements, starting with a preamble which referred to the reason for the letter, almost always the reception of a civic embassy. This was followed by the decision, grant, or benefaction offered by the ruler, supported by a series of motivation clauses, often overtly framed with emotional or cordial language. Finally, these missives often concluded with an explicit reminder of the reciprocity inherent to this exchange. Benefactions were framed against precedent and conditionally offered for the future through 'contract clauses', to use Ma's term, which explicitly linked the continual goodwill (*εὔνοια*) of cities to the prospect of further privileges, reaffirming the

[9] Ma 1999, 182–94, with references.

centrality of this system which bound together the overt institutional elements of Seleucid rule.[10]

Though Attalid monarchs held different levers of power, they employed similar strategies vis-à-vis civic communities within their kingdom: Eumenes II and his successors solved the critical problem of their legitimacy by consciously retreating from military prowess as a basis for charismatic leadership, instead emphasizing their role as general *εὐεργέται* to the Hellenic world.[11] Given their subordination vis-à-vis Rome, the Attalids relied on a claim to moral excellence, exemplified through their benefactions, to legitimize their kingship.[12] This ideological development arose out of the same *do ut des* premise manifest in Antiochus' correspondence. However, due to this shift, obvious contract clauses appear less often in Attalid correspondence: many letters end with no explicit extension of the exchange into the future; with instructions, rather than dialogue.[13] Nevertheless, the basic relationship between monarch and community perpetuated Seleucid models. Despite changes in emphasis, *basileus* and *polis* continued to trade *εὐεργεσία* for the veneer of legitimacy, received through increasingly grandiose honours.[14] Consequently, when Roman actors first entered western Asia Minor, the pattern of imperial interactions with communities had a well-established format: a reciprocal, continuous dialogue which granted concessions to civic communities in return for honour offered to the ruling power through local decrees. The system was flexible: local agency and autonomy were preserved while the tacit acknowledgement of the monarch's pre-eminence and legitimacy satisfied both parties. A formal vocabulary and syntax allowed discourse to be habitual, reproducible, and consistent.[15] Negotiation through embassies remained inherent to this process and a common understanding of the 'rules of the game' allowed a significant continuity between Seleucid and Attalid rule.

By contrast, Roman institutions were fluid and multifarious; the political organs of the *res publica* held overlapping powers.[16] Generally, Roman magistrates

[10] See Ma 1999, 179 nn.4–5 for references. E.g., *I.Mylasa* 963.7–11: *τὴμ πᾶσαν πολυωρίαν ποη|σόμεθα ὑμῶν ὅσωιπερ ἄν εὐ|ν[ο]έστεροι καὶ προθυμότερο[ι] | φαίνησθε εἰς τὰ τῶι βασιλεῖ | Ἀντιόχωι συμφέροντα* ('we will show all consideration to you, insofar as you show yourselves to be better disposed and more eager towards the interests of *basileus* Antiochus').

[11] Thonemann 2013.

[12] Robert 1937, 83–9; Zuiderhoek 2009, 71–8; Thonemann 2013, 35–44; Gotter 2013, 211–13. Erskine (1997, 32–3) notes that Rome did not initially sponsor Hellenic culture in this way, but sees references to *Ῥωμαῖοι οἱ κοινοὶ εὐεργέται* (collected by Ferrary 1988, 125–8, building on Robert 1969a, 57–61) as evidence for communities treating them as successors to the Attalid tradition. On this epithet, generally: Wehrli 1978, 479–96; Ferrary 1988, 124–32; Erskine 1994, 70–87.

[13] Only eight contract clauses appear in sixteen surviving letters (see Bencivenni 2014, 169–71). Eumenes II's letters to Toriaion (*I.Sultan Daği* 1.393), for example, retain them, though the creation of a new community is precisely the moment for a monarch to define the terms of a relationship (cf. Dmitriev 1999, 410–11; Ma 1999, 248). Compare Virgilio (2013, 251–3) who sees growing absence of 'diplomatic' language in Attalid correspondence.

[14] See *OGIS* 332, with Chin 2018, 121–36.

[15] Ma 1999, 191–4.

[16] Lintott 1999; Boffo 2003, 231. Compare the distinction between early modern monarchic empires and their contemporary, the Venetian republic: Elliot 1992; O'Connell 2009.

possessed immense power within their *provincia* through their *imperium* and *iurisdictio* but their time-limited terms and their vulnerability to later prosecution served as a slight check on their activity.[17] Meanwhile, the Senate, generally responsible for diplomatic activity in the Late Republic, *stricto sensu* had only an advisory function.[18] Statutory law passed independently by the assemblies was less common and usually more limited in scope.[19] The dynamism of this period notwithstanding, communities were faced with the dissolution of the simple hierarchy of a monarchy, possessing a single figurehead and his nominated aides as a focal point for communicative action, into a morass of different functions, authorities, and interest groups.

The earliest extant letter from a Roman magistrate to a Hellenistic city, dating to 193, is often taken as paradigmatic. After to a request from Teos, which sought the Senate's recognition of their city and territory as *ἱερὰ καὶ ἄσυλα* ('sacred and inviolable'), the praetor M. Valerius Messalla responded on behalf of the Senate, the magistrates, and the tribunes of the *plebs* in the affirmative.[20] The document contains strong structural parallels with Hellenistic royal correspondence: it begins by acknowledging the Tean embassy and praising the ambassador; it moves to discuss Roman motives and their decision, before ending with a clear contract clause.[21] The text contains two unusual features: first, it places significant weight on Rome's unique piety (*εὐσέβεια*); and second, it explicitly confirms Teos as *ἀφορο|λόγητον ἀπὸ τοῦ δήμου τοῦ Ῥωμαίων* ('free from tribute to the *demos* of the Romans'), despite the city never having been subject to Roman power.[22] However, through comparison with a letter of the Athamanian rulers confirming Tean *asylia* and correspondence of Antiochus III, Driediger-Murphy has persuasively argued that Messalla consciously adopted or copied an *exemplum*, probably the original response of Antiochus to Teos.[23] This further explains the appearance of an explicit contract clause, which is unparalleled in other Roman documents. Messalla's letter also shows the first clear evidence of a Greek *polis* treating Rome, embodied by the Senate, as a Hellenistic ruler and, vice versa, the Senate responding to a civic petition in Hellenistic royal language. In this, the earliest

[17] Threat of prosecution was ineffective at ensuring good governance (e.g., Brunt 1961, 189–96; Morrell 2017, 11–13).

[18] Pina Polo 2013, 247–8.

[19] Meyer 2004, 98–9, 111. The *comitia* could, and often did, ratify senatorial decisions (e.g., *RS* 19; *SEG* 55.1452; Kunkel & Wittmann 1995, 617–25).

[20] Two other examples of letters written by a magistrate explicitly on behalf of the Senate and tribunes of the plebs exist: *RDGE* 38 and 39, in 189 and 186 respectively; though the *lex de provinciis praetoriis* (*RS* 12.Cnidus.3.28–41. Delphi.B.8–14) mentions consular letters on behalf of the *SPQR*. The appointment of a praetor to draft the letter reflects the necessity of speaking with a single voice. By contrast, the tendency for the senate to issue *senatus consulta* in response to requests for honours or decisions reflects a more complex process of debate and drafting involving multiple participants (Bonnefond-Coudry 1989, 439–44, 570–3): e.g., *RDGE* 7, 9, 10. *RDGE* 34; Rigsby 1996, #153.

[21] Piejko 1991, 24.

[22] Welles 1934, 155; Brunt 1979, 165; Ma 1999, 101, with *RDGE* 34.20–21.

[23] *SEG* 38.1227. Driediger-Murphy 2014, 116–18 contra Errington 1980, 279–84. See further: Ferrary 1988, 153 n.88; Rigsby 1996, 283 n.19, with literature and discussion.

engagement in Asia Minor, the Roman state adopted pre-existing, local practices of power.

Roman commanders on the ground in the early second century also borrowed from Hellenistic practice. However, they did so in markedly different ways. For example, the letter of L. and P. Cornelius Scipio to Heraclea-under-Latmos, only a few years later in 190, reproduces local language: the brothers articulate their εὔνοια towards the Heracleans specifically, before emphasizing the timelessness of this attitude and extending it to all the Greeks. The Scipiones restored ἐλευθερία, αὐτονομία, and the possessions of the Heracleans after their surrender, in full keeping with the surrender-grant model underpinning Seleucid, and indeed Roman, power.[24] However, the nature of the relationship expressed through this language had fundamentally changed. The authors state twice that πειρασόμεθα εὐχρηστοῦντες ὑμῖν ἀεὶ τινος ἀγαθοῦ|[παραίτ]ιοι γίνεσθαι ('we will always try to be the authors of some good for you [the Heracleans]'), but link this directly to the community's passing into their power, framed as πίστις: a translation of the Latin *fides*, a complex combination of loyalty, trust, and protection.[25] Other surviving letters of Roman magistrates from this period frame their desire to advance the interests of their interlocutors in similar terms.[26] As Rawson demonstrated, Roman magistrates had no qualms about regarding themselves as peers to Hellenistic monarchs.[27] While maintaining a resemblance of reciprocity, this shift in language highlighted the power imbalance between Rome and its interlocutors, revealing what the Hellenistic transcript kept hidden. Rather than seeking civic εὐνοία, Roman actors demanded loyalty.[28]

However, the Scipiones, by using the conative πειράσθαι, also emphasize the comparatively limited nature of their personal agency vis-à-vis the Heracleans. Unlike a Hellenistic monarch, who could make credible promises of future benefactions—thereby rendering explicit, ongoing, and contingent reciprocity a viable means of maintaining and constructing a concrete relationship—Roman commanders had limited terms and were accountable to the Senate and *populus* on their return. Gubernatorial decisions were neither unconstrained nor immutable: decisions were underpinned only by the *auctoritas* of their issuer, and not of the *populus Romanus*. They could be altered by *lex*, *senatus consultum*, or even a successor's decision.[29] Consequently, Republican commanders commonly

[24] See Chapter 2, 'Civic Freedom in Republican *provincia Asia*'.

[25] *RDGE* 35.13–14, echoing 6–10. πίστις is plausibly restored at ll. 9 and 15. Chaniotis 2015, 95–6.

[26] E.g., *RDGE* 37.8–9 (with Piejko 1985, 617); 38.22–23.

[27] Rawson 1975, 150–6. [28] Chaniotis 2015, 90–9.

[29] Yarrow 2012, 177–83. Two instructive examples: Verres' decision to ignore the *lex Rupilia*'s rulings on Sicilian judges (*Verr.* 2.2.39–40); and Cn. Pompeius Magnus' reversal of several decisions made by Lucullus during the Third Mithridatic War (Plut. *Luc.* 36.1; *Pomp.* 31.1–5, with Tröster 2008, 143–8). Decisions made in a judicial context appear to have been binding, provided the process was completed within the governor's term of office (Gai. *Inst.* 4.104–105, with de Zulueta 1953 2.277–278), though note the complication of when *imperium* ceased to be valid: Cic. *Att.* 5.16.4; *Fam.* 3.4; Marshall 1972, 895–8; Delrieux 2010, 515.

emphasized their personal and limited capacity to act.[30] While strongly 'factional' interpretations of second-century politics should be rejected, the sources present numerous examples of strong debates within the Senate on matters of 'foreign policy'.[31] Irrespective of a comfortable elite consensus around key elements of government, individual senators held strong opinions and debated questions of policy which had a significant impact across the Mediterranean.

Increasing Roman participation in political dialogue brought problems of its own. The discrepancies between language and forms of communication required that communities learn a new means of managing their relationship. The power of Rome, which prima facie resembled a *polis*, placed it in the same bracket as a Hellenistic monarchy, but the problem of relatability remained prominent.[32] The Senate often received embassies, but it possessed two means of responding: by letter or a *senatus consultum*. The former required designating an individual to draft a response, as in Messalla's case. However, in these examples, the magistrate assigned the task tended to simply report the decision of the Senate, even if the single, named author occluded that collective source. By contrast, *senatus consulta* more clearly resulted from a formal process of co-operative drafting. They report a collective decision and carry the weight of influence from the assembled body of ex-magistrates. The three extant examples of letters by magistrates on behalf of the Senate all date to the early second century. After this, our examples imply that *senatus consulta* were directly sent on to relevant parties. This makes sense, since the intermediate process of a letter added nothing to the actual outcome. Providing the text of the *senatus consultum* allowed direct interpretation of the Senate's words. However, this marked a significant change in practice, as *senatus consulta* are candidly decisions, rather than part of an ongoing dialogue. Even where elements of the diplomatic process were preserved, as in the *senatus consultum de agro Pergameno*, the appearance and language of the decree placed it in a distinct genre, carrying connotations of command rather than negotiation.[33]

This is also true of other normative texts, such as the *edicta* of magistrates and *leges* passed in different assemblies. Representing pronouncements made by magistrates or the various subsets of the Roman citizen body, they were not couched in terms of dialogue, but of command.[34] That said, Ando convincingly identifies a communicative function in the despatch of these 'administrative' decisions to provincial communities. The wide range of topics covered by the surviving corpus, for example, hints that it became increasingly standard to

[30] E.g., M'. Acilius Glabrio to Delphi in 190: *πειράσο[μαι ἐν Ῥώμῃ (?) κατὰ | τ]ὰ ἐμ[α]υτοῦ φροντίσαι ἵνα ὑμῖν κατάμονα ἧι τά ἐξ ἀρχῆς ὑπάρχοντα πάτρ[ια σωζομένης (?) τῆς] | τῆς πόλεως καὶ τοῦ ἱεροῦ αὐτονομίας* ('I shall try, in Rome, with all my power, to ensure that your ancestral rights that existed from the beginning will be yours forever, and the autonomy of your city and temple protected'). *RDGE* 37. 8–10.

[31] E.g., Eckstein 2006, 226–9. Cf. Gruen 1984, 391–8; Sherwin-White 1984, 13–14.

[32] Erskine 1997, 30–5; Davies 2013, 417–19.

[33] Ando (forthcoming).

[34] E.g., *RS* 19; *I.Sagalassos* 3. Ando (forthcoming).

inform local political elites of relevant decisions.[35] However, each type of decision had its own set of norms, standards, and language, alien to communities brought into the Roman world. The process of learning these multiple new cultural codes was not automatic: only repeated exposure and engagement with the various types would allow successful strategies of reading and responding to be developed.[36] The existence of competing authoritative media with distinctive traditions inevitably complicated this process. Having several genres made the cognitive effort required to understand and engage effectively with imperial documents much greater: the reproducibility and repeatability of language and structure inherent to the Seleucid model ran contrary to existing Roman practice. These core institutional barriers to creating one coherent discourse in the manner of Seleucids raise the question of how intentional this consistent communication was.[37]

Consequently, as Roman magistrates came to be more involved in the region, communities had to adjust to a new language of power. Roman hegemony presented structural challenges for local communities beyond the potential for cultural and linguistic misunderstanding. Established means of communicating with the dominant power were rendered inadequate and inappropriate. Though most *poleis* could count on courtesy from magistrates and the organs of the Roman state, through their formally free status, the finely balanced mechanics of reciprocity were upset. As Roman attention concentrated on western Asia, communities were forced to adapt to new imperial discourses of power.

The Sources

The nature of the evidence poses some problems: the surviving material corresponds to only a tiny proportion of the total number of documents issued by the Roman state and its magistrates, and the question of how representative the corpus is merits consideration. A conservative estimate of the available documents with sufficient text to securely date and ascertain their nature identifies around sixty texts from the period of study. However, these are unevenly distributed both typologically and chronologically. There are only four *leges*, of which three date to the Republican period and one was promulgated under the *tresviri*. Only a tiny subset of comitial statutes (i.e., *leges rogatae*) affected provincial communities. Indeed, among surviving texts only the *lex de provinciis praetoriis* was not subsequently confirmed *ex senatus consulto* or by treaty.[38] By contrast, the Senate frequently entertained civic embassies seeking intervention by the organs

[35] Haensch 1992, 215–19, 245–54; Nicolet 1994; Ando 2000, 81–3.

[36] Meyer 2004, 44. Compare Ma 1999, 191–4, 211–14; Ando 2000, 101–17, 131–8, 175–90, 352–62.

[37] Ando (2010, 20–2; (forthcoming)) interprets this as deliberate policy aimed at creating an informed elite (and thereby populace).

[38] Williamson 2005, 36–46.

of the Roman state.[39] Simply put, the Senate dealt more commonly with requests from provincials requiring action and thereby generated relevant documents at a higher rate.[40] Indeed, there are at least thirteen firmly identified *senatus consulta*, which though clustered around moments of political tension, date across the whole period.

However, magistrates in their province likely produced most documents. Embassies to Rome were costly and time-consuming exercises, involving real danger for the participants. In situations where gubernatorial authority could be leveraged, there were strong reasons for a *polis* to attempt this first. A key element of this dynamic was the physical presence of the governor in the region. On the provincial side, communities had to balance the relative expense of each option against the likelihood of success and the potential durability of the decision. A Prienean decree for Crates, for example, suggests several attempts to engage governors before approaching the Senate.[41] Responses to embassies were rarely limited to the verbal, but usually accompanied by a written decision, in both Hellenistic and Roman practice.[42] For commanders on the ground, their access to information and capacity to wield authority precisely were much improved, enabling them to intervene directly without necessarily relying on prompting from local agents. That said, given that the overwhelming majority of documents survive as public inscriptions, these tend not to be routine communications but exceptional and, as Burton noted, privilege the reactive capacity of magistrates and Principes over their normative function.[43] As such, we have only seven *edicta*, utterances with general force issued by magistrates, which all date to after the outbreak of civil war in 49, in comparison to over thirty-five letters largely though not exclusively issued in response to a local embassy. Despite its idiosyncrasies, the corpus is sufficiently broad and diverse to enable a careful analysis of trends across the period. As the institutional structure of the *res publica* transformed, so the discourse wielded by its rulers evolved separately in response.

Rome and the Free Cities

Official documents from the immediate post-Attalid period are limited: elements of three letters from Roman magistrates to communities in *provincia* Asia survive, as well as three *senatus consulta* relating to the *provincia* and the unique *lex de*

[39] E.g., territorial disputes: *RDGE* 7; status of the community: *RS* 19; status of sub-groups: Joseph. *AJ*. 14.241–2, 244–6.

[40] Burton 2002, 249–51; Ando (forthcoming). Burton (2002, 251–64) also provides quantitative analysis, see Eck (2014, 127–36) on bronze documents. Rate of embassies: Millar 1992 [1977], 410–34; Eck 2009, 197–8.

[41] *I.Priene*² 67, with Wallace 2014, 50–6.

[42] E.g., *SEG* 41.1003 (Antiochus III to Teos) with *IAph2007* 8.2 (Oppius' response to Aphrodisias).

[43] Burton 2002, 249–51.

provinciis praetoriis. The earliest letter, from Q. Mucius Scaevola to Pergamum, Ephesus, and Sardis, between 99 and 97, introduces a treaty agreed between the latter two.[44] While the lacunose text prevents detailed analysis of the language, the surviving motivation clauses emphasize that Scaevola intervened directly, unprompted by local request, in the dispute between two communities.[45] Similarly, the letter from L. Cassius Longinus to Nysa in 88 was unprompted by an embassy and simply informative, not acting, whether through instruction or affirmation of a shared principle.[46] While cordial in tone, referring to Chaeremon's actions as *καλῶς* and *ἡμεῖς χάριτα* ('right'; 'pleasing to us'), unlike earlier magistrates Cassius does not provide a clear rationale for an ongoing reciprocity.[47] The bluntness and multiple Latinisms within the text prompted Sherk to assume that either Cassius or a member of his *consilium* produced the translation rather than a local.[48] In its word-choice, style, and content, Cassius' letter finds no precedent in the corpus of Roman documents, while Scaevola's also has no easy parallel. Together, they illustrate the fact that the letters of individual magistrates could vary considerably in subject, structure, and language.

Important comparanda, demonstrating this unpredictability in the form and language employed by Roman magistrates in communicating with eastern *poleis*, exist in two contemporary letters from L. Cornelius Sulla and L. Licinius Lucullus, to Mopsuestia, a Cilician *polis* subject to the Seleucid dynasts. These respond to the community's *ἀσυλία*-request for their temple of Isis and Sarapis in 87, with Sulla stating his decision in their favour following the recommendation of his *quaestor*, Lucullus, followed by a letter from Lucullus himself.[49] It is likely that this responds to a request made by a Mopsuestian embassy in Greece in 87, however, the extant text does not mention this, moving straight to the crux of the decision and Lucullus' agency in effecting it.[50] The omission reflects the documents' concern with process and outcomes over cordiality. Sulla invokes both the *παράκλησις* ('exhortation' or 'recommendation') of his *quaestor* and the earlier decisions of Seleucid rulers, presumably invoked by the ambassadors, as informing his own grant.[51] Meanwhile, Lucullus explicitly frames his own intervention as a decision (*κ[εκρίκα]*, l. 17, 'I decided'), while acknowledging it followed those of his superiors (*οἱ π̣[ρ]ὸ̣ ἡμῶν αὐ[τοκρά]|τορ̣ες*, 'the *autokratores* before us').[52] The text implies that Lucullus encountered the Mopsuestian embassy, which asked

[44] Laffi 2010a, see Chapter 1, 'Gubernatorial Jurisdiction and the Free Cities'.

[45] Laffi 2010, 2A+B.1–8. [46] *RDGE* 48.

[47] This letter was inscribed in an honorific context, accounting for the unusual content of the letter compared to comparanda: it was selected to show Chaeremon's, rather than Nysa's, loyalty to Rome. Quass 1984, 211; Rigsby 1988, 152; Santangelo 2007, 55; Campanile 2014, 233.

[48] Sherk 1969, 262 for a full list. Compare now: *SEG* 64.492 with Bouchon 2014, 494–5.

[49] *SEG* 44.1227. Thonemann (2004, 80–2) noting Lucullus' title as *ταμίας καὶ ἀντιστρατηγὸς* (*quaestor pro praetore*) argues persuasively that the letter must date to the year of his quaestorship, that is, 87 contra Sayar, Siewert & Täuber 1994, 118–20; Kreiler 2006, 73–82.

[50] Jordan 2022, 491–5. [51] *SEG* 44.1227.5–7.

[52] The *autokratores* are Sulla and L. Licinius Murena, *pro praetore* in Greece. Jordan 2022, 498.

him to approve Mopsuestia's claim on Rome's behalf as a quasi-*basileus*. Lucullus referred this to his commander, Sulla, while making clear his own support. In this sense, his position is similar, though not analogous, to that of subordinates to the Hellenistic kings such as Zeuxis, who wielded authority over western Asia Minor in the late third century. However, such self-aggrandizing language does not survive in the letters of non-royal Hellenistic administrators.[53] Unlike earlier Roman grants of *ἀσυλία*, these letters stress the decision-making capacity of the magistrates on the ground, possibly reflecting the unprecedented civil strife between Sulla and the Senate, such as it was, in Rome. Even so, the conspicuous absence of the Mopsuestian embassy and the discussion of Diodotus' honours are unparalleled in Hellenistic or contemporary Roman correspondence. Though they concern a community outside of the Roman *provincia* of Asia, during a particularly chaotic period, these letters nevertheless emphasize the high variability of Roman epistolary practice.

Of the surviving corpus, Q. Oppius' letter to Plarasa-Aphrodisias most resembles Hellenistic royal and early Roman models. First, Oppius responds directly to an embassy, which presented him with an honorific decree.[54] The proconsul gives an account of Aphrodisian loyalty during the recent conflict, both to him personally and Rome. This serves as the rationale for a decision clause:

> *δι' ἃς αἰτίας, vac | φροντίζω [καὶ ἐν ἀρ]|χῇ καὶ ἰδιώβ̣[ιῳ], vac [ὅ]|περ ἂν σωζομέν̣[ης] | τῆς ἐμῆς πίστ[ε]|ως, ποιῆσαι ὑμεῖν δύ|νωμαι τοῖς τε δημο̣|σίοις πράγμασιν ὑ̣[μ]ε|τέροις εὐχρηστῆσαι | καὶ ἀεί τινος ἀγαθοῦ | παραίτιος γενέσθαι, | ὅπως τε τῇ συνκλήτῳ | τῷ τε δήμῳ τὰ ἀφ' ὑμῶν | πεπραγμένα ἐστίν | ὅταν εἰς Ῥώμην παρα|γένωμαι διασαφήσω* ('For these reasons, I am taking care, both as magistrate and in a private capacity, to do what I can, while preserving my good faith, to help you and your public affairs, and always preserve your advantage; and shall see to it that after I come to Rome, I make clear to the Senate and People the things, which have been done on your part').[55]

This is the most overt example of a Republican magistrate responding to an honorific decree with a promise of personal support, and, superficially at least, represents a return to more traditional approaches. Oppius emphasizes his personal decision to help the community deal with various organs of Roman government, while prudently stressing his limited influence. Oppius explicitly links his present and future concern for the Aphrodisians to their past actions, rather than making them contingent upon an ongoing exchange. Indeed, his use of *ἀεί* ('always'), disingenuous or otherwise, generalizes his commitment to this specific community. The final clause, however, denotes a significant shift in how

[53] On Zeuxis and his position, Ma 1999, 123–30, with references.
[54] *IAph2007* 8.2.i.11–12.
[55] *IAph2007* 8.2.ii.34–49.

representatives of Rome related to communities in the Greek-speaking East in this period:

> *οἱ αὐτοὶ πρεσβεῖς παρε|κάλεσαν ὅπως ἐξῇ τῇ | [ἐ]μῇ πατρωνήᾳ καὶ ὑμεῖν | χρῆσθαι τούτους ἐγὼ | ἀνεδεξάμην καταλο|γῆς ἕνεκεν τῆς ὑμετέ|ρας πόλεως, ἐμὲ τοῦ δή|μου τοῦ ὑμετέρου πα|ṭρωνα* vac *ἔσεσθαι* vac ('The same ambassadors also asked that it might be possible that you should enjoy my patronage and I accepted those men, on account of my regard for your city so that I (undertook) to be *patron* of your people').[56]

According to the text, the ambassadors further requested from Oppius that he act as the city's *patron*. Civic patronage was, fundamentally, a Roman institution.[57] Though it shared with royal practice the establishment of a personal relationship between an individual and a particular community, the heterarchic nature of Republican politics ensured that the potential benefits for communities were, practically, much more limited. Chaniotis asserts that this suits the vocabulary of subordination he detects in the civic decrees from this period. However, it is not clear that the request for Oppius' patronage should imply a subordinate role for Plarasa-Aphrodisias.[58] Patronage was a formal, consensual, if hierachical relationship; Oppius' letter shows unambiguously that honours were not given to the governor in expectation of benefactions during his command: rather, the opposite was true.[59] Other early examples from the East support this, presenting ambassadors as actively negotiating in Rome to engage their *patroni*.[60] Nichols argues that the exchange between community and civic patron was couched in vague terms to emphasize the anticipated continuity of benefaction and honour.[61] However, patronage cannot be seen as an effective continuation of royal practice by other means, or the appropriation of previously royal roles by magistrates, since patrons were often not magistrates when acting as on behalf of their client *poleis*. As Oppius pointedly stresses, he will act in the interests of Aphrodisias, both as a magistrate and as a *privatus* within the Senate.

[56] *IAph2007*.8.2.2.16–24.

[57] On patronage, note esp. Badian 1958, 1–14; Brunt 1988a, 382–442; Eilers 2002, 1–17; Nichols 2014, 70–5, 207–24.

[58] Chaniotis 2003, 252.

[59] Eilers 2002, 28–32; *pace* Nichols 2014, 72–3.

[60] *Syll.*³ 656.20–27; *SEG* 39.1243.2.24–31; *SEG* 39.1244.3.5–13. The *editio princeps* dated *Syll.*³ 656 to the aftermath of the Third Macedonian War (*c.*166, Diod. Sic. 30.6.1; Livy 43.4.8–10; Pottier & Hauvette-Besnault 1880, 52–4). While Chiranky (1982, 461–81) and Eilers (2002, 114–19), inter alios, argued robustly that it should be re-dated to early first century, the recent publication of a new Abderan decree at Teos provides strong support for the early date (Thonemann & Adak 2022, 187–95, with discussion; cf. *SEG* 47.1646, with Marek 1997, 173–7). Crucially, the circumlocution to describe the Roman custom of *salutatio* and the employment of the unparalleled loanword *ἀτρίον* (*atrium*) suggest a lack of familiarity with Roman culture which suits an earlier context (Ferrary 1978, 761; Bloy 2012, 168–201; Erskine 1994a, 49–51; Chaniotis 2015, 101–2; Ito 2021, esp. 142–51).

[61] Nichols 2014, 314.

Crucially, Oppius' letter is our only Republican evidence for a process by which civic patronage came about. Though Mitchell saw the patronage request as an afterthought, Eilers conclusively demonstrated that the document's structure outlines its centrality to the embassy.[62] Oppius presents patronage as an independent issue, complete with its own request, motive, and decision clauses: it is treated as a serious and deliberate political choice exercised by the *polis*, and assessed on its own merits.[63] However, Eilers' employment of this text paradigmatically cannot be accepted in light of the degree of institutional flux in this period, and the lack of other evidence. Nevertheless, Oppius' letter drives home the distinctiveness and variability of documents between Roman actors and communities in Asia Minor.

The structure and language of these letters individualizes the relationship between cities and officials, collapsing the paradigm governing earlier relationships. The Senate is absent from these texts, intimating that a Republican heterarchy replaced Hellenistic royal discourse with a cacophony of distinct narratives, to which cities, in turn, were forced to react. Where Cassius' and Scaevola's letters are directly informative, relaying information to communities, Oppius revivifies an earlier schema by which magistrates engaged with *poleis* in an honorific exchange, albeit framing it in a new, and peculiarly Roman, way. Collectively, these letters show little homogeneity in the use of language and structure and imply the absence of a consistent linguistic repertoire.

Normative documents issued by central institutions played a major role in constructing an imperial discourse. However, despite having a significant impact on communities, they were administrative documents which, in the first instance, gave instructions to commanders; their provisions were not directed at communities. Even where these texts resulted from a community's direct petition, as in the case of the *senatus consultum de agro Pergameno*, reflections of Hellenistic practice are limited. Though ambassadors from Pergamum were referred to at the outset in typical diplomatic language, unlike on earlier occasions, when the Senate's opinion was sought to settle disputes between *poleis*, the arguments put forward appear to have been omitted.[64] Instead, the text consists largely of detailed instructions to Roman magistrates regarding the Senate's decision.

Other extant contemporary *senatus consulta* were unilateral decisions: the so-called *senatus consulta Popillianum* and *Licinnianum* were not aimed at an audience of provincial communities.[65] Though these documents neither constituted a direct grant of privileges or a response to local petition, both carried a perceptible authority by virtue of their source, the Senate. Communities were familiar with this body as the normal recipient of embassies and consequently, the

[62] Eilers 2002, 23–7 contra Mitchell 1984, 291–7.

[63] Eilers 2002, 28–32; Zuiderhoek 2004, 265.

[64] E.g., *RDGE* 9. Snowdon 2014, 425–8.

[65] *RDGE* 11, 13 (with Famerie 2021).

decision-maker on issues referred to Rome.[66] The *senatus consultum Popillianum* demonstrated to provincial representatives that the Senate's decrees shaped magistrates' decisions rather than vice versa. The format of these documents framed senatorial decisions recognizably, emphasizing both the individual role of the proposing magistrate and the collective decision of its membership. Unlike the letters, stylistic consistency is obvious. Consequently, even where a decision did not refer to a specific privilege, the weight of senatorial *auctoritas* could be invoked in a similar fashion to a royal grant or decision. As a medium, *senatus consulta* presented a more uniform and Roman form of communication with few concessions to Hellenistic convention. However, by 133, *senatus consulta* were already a familiar document within western Asia Minor. Following their own format, they offered clarity in terms of the proposal, its author, and the final decision. They were comprehensible and useful documents to communities. However, the existence of competing bodies with influence, institutional authority, and legitimacy complicated the situation.[67]

The *lex de provinciis praetoriis* underscores the confusing nature of the Republic's political structure for provincials. *Leges*, binding statutes issued by the assembled populace, differed markedly from *senatus consulta*. Most obviously, the assemblies comprised significantly different political bodies, representing a broader range of interest groups than the Senate, including *publicani*, *negotiatores*, and the urban populace. These bodies had less exposure to embassies, since traditionally these approached the Senate. The conventions of drafting also differed markedly: where *senatus consulta* could reach a high level of specificity, *leges* could be particularly complex.[68] Adding to problems of interpretation, the promulgator of this statute was almost certainly opposed to the principle of senatorial primacy in provincial administration.[69] The scope is significantly wider than that of a typical *senatus consultum*: the surviving text covers issues ranging from imposing tax collection at the edge of *provincia Macedonia* to assigning a praetor to *provincia Cilicia*. Finally, uniquely among surviving texts from this period, the *lex de provinciis praetoriis* includes a clause requiring the dissemination and publication of related information to the cities of *provincia Asia*. One possible reason for publication within Asia specifically is that the vast majority of *poleis* within the *provincia* remained, formally, free allies of the Roman people, rather than subordinated to a Roman commander: they may have merited explicit notification. The statute's overt justification of the administrative decision to create a *provincia Cilicia* underscores the promulgators apparent concern with appearances.[70] It suggests an author conscious of the necessity to

[66] E.g., *I.Priene*² 11–12; *RDGE* 7, 9. Gruen 1984, 96–131; Kallet-Marx 1995, 161–83. Walser (2021, 154–6) plausibly argues that the text was amended to simplify its outcome for readers.

[67] E.g., proconsular decisions (*I.Priene*² 67.14–15, 21–22) or *leges* (*RS* 19).

[68] Williamson 2005, 80–2, commenting on the *lex agraria* of 111 (*RS* 2). Compare Lintott 1999, 64.

[69] Ferrary 1977, esp. 654–60; Crawford 1996, 237.

[70] *RS* 12.Cnidus.3.28–37.

engage in a dialogue with his audience, giving motivations for its decisions, rather than acting in a purely declarative fashion. Nevertheless, this document presents a fait accompli; it does not invite dialogue. Overall, these normative documents emphasize the keen engagement of Asian *poleis* with the pronouncements of the Roman state and the significant break in continuity with previous models of interaction in the region.

The existence of a wide body of normative material in civic archives, including Roman statutes, *senatus consulta*, and the correspondence of magistrates on a range of issues, highlights the co-existence of multiple imperial discourses within the documents issued to any given community. Given that the diffusion and acquisition of new 'languages' entails a process of learning, the existence of numerous traditions undermined the establishment of a single comprehensible hegemonic discourse.[71] The fragmentation of dialogue between multiple parties hindered the capacity of Asian communities to protect and increase their privileges. Both the Hellenistic royal model and its imperial Roman successor depended on a continuous reciprocal dialogue between the ruler and community, which offered honorific capital and legitimacy in return for tangible privileges. The cohesiveness of imperial society and the capacity of communities to exert agency arose, in both cases, from a common understanding of 'the rules of the game'.[72] The absence of such an understanding plausibly implies a deterioration of both.

Under the Republic, the personal link to the decision-maker necessary to maintain the Hellenistic model dissolved as the most powerful administrator was no longer an individual but a large political body, the Senate, which contained several hundred members with competing preferences and interests.[73] Civic embassies were forced to navigate a complex, foreign political ecology full of individuals with which they had little, if any familiarity. Though repeated exposure and civic patronage could provide knowledge over time, the dispersed nature of Roman power greatly complicated this process. Reversing the perspective, individual Romans were disincentivized from simply taking the place of Hellenistic rulers in their exchanges with communities. For members of the Senate, recognition of that body's legitimacy remained important. For individual magistrates and ex-magistrates, the stakes were lower. This does not mean that embassies were despatched less frequently than in other periods, or that the Senate did not vote to protect or increase privileges for some *poleis*; rather structural disincentives existed for the Republican government vis-à-vis its monarchic counterparts in engaging in a beneficent relationship with individual communities. Roman rule fundamentally disrupted the existing cycle of

[71] Pocock 1987, 34–8.

[72] Ma 1999, esp. 211–14; Ando 2000, 41–2, cf. 373–85. Cf. Pocock 1987, 20–38.

[73] E.g., Ferrary (2007, 113–22) emphasizes the importance of magistrates in shaping senatorial policy. Pina Polo (2011, 276–84; 2013a, 434–44) extends this to magistrates designate.

reciprocal honour and benefaction sustained by Hellenistic royal discourse and the institutional structure of the *res publica* precluded its easy replacement. The separation of authority and the capacity to communicate directly with communities between diverse bodies and magistrates, each with their own 'language' hindered the development of a working understanding of the 'rules of the game' and therefore of effective strategies to protect their own interests in their interaction with the state.

Roman Documents after the Mithridatic Invasion

In 88, Mithridates' invasion forced the Romans out of Asia Minor entirely for a short period. As argued in Chapter 2, after peace was agreed at Dardanus Sulla established a new basis for provincial government in Asia. Importantly, in the context of his civil war he fundamentally altered the nature of the Roman relationship with communities and the *provincia*, not to mention reshaping central institutions upon his final victory in 81. Named dictator, he held *imperium maius* vis-à-vis other magistrates and legislated extensively, shifting the balance of policy-making power from the *comitia* to the Senate.[74] A *lex Valeria* promulgated by the *interrex* L. Valerius Flaccus ratified all his *acta* between 88 and 82.[75] Even so, several *senatus consulta* confirming his grants survive, conferring greater legitimacy in specific cases, and this probably reflected a broader practice.[76] Though Sulla's position ensured none could gainsay him, this fact re-emphasizes the interrelationship between magistrates and the other bodies in authority and perceived legitimacy from the Roman side.

Although many cities suffered direct subjection to Roman *imperium*, some which offered consistent support to Roman interests were granted extensive privileges by Sulla. A *senatus consultum* of 81 introduced by letters from the dictator confirmed these for Stratonicea in Caria.[77] This document takes a familiar form, starting with the acknowledgement of the Stratonicean embassy and an account of their requests, before giving a series of motivation clauses, followed by the resolution granting eleven specific privileges to the community. In form and language, this document is unexceptional; in the scale of the grant and in the primacy accorded to Sulla, however, a seismic shift appears. The *senatus consultum*, while formally sanctioning the privileges offered within it, explicitly delegates to Sulla the right to decide the extent to which revenues from subordinate

[74] On Sulla's programme, for example, Keaveney 1982, 169–81; Hantos 1988, esp. 69–161; Hurlet 1993, 135–64.

[75] Cic. *Leg. agr.* 3.2.5. Vervaet 2004, 43–4 contra Keaveney 1982, 160.

[76] E.g., *RDGE* 18 discussed below; compare the fragmentary *RDGE* 17 & 19, for Tabae and Cormi respectively.

[77] *RDGE* 18 with *SEG* 52.1059. Jones 1939, 112–15; Magie 1950, 233–5; Santangelo 2007, 50–4.

communities were directed to Stratonicea, should he have chosen to accept.[78] The document reconfigured senatorial authority around the will of the dictator. Rather than acting as a check on magisterial action (or inaction) in the region, the Senate explicitly confirmed any decision Sulla wished to make on these matters.[79] The diametric shift in how different organs of state power interacted must have disrupted local understandings of Roman power. Though Sulla's dictatorship was a high-profile and, ultimately, brief anomaly, his constitutional reforms fundamentally altered the relationship between political bodies and magistrates across the following decade.[80] The construction of new forms of legitimacy based around the dictator foreshadowed both the rise of powerful proconsular commanders, such as Pompeius and Caesar in the 60s and 50s, and the eventual dictatorships of the latter.

Sulla's letters also reveal subtle changes in emphasis. The first starts abruptly, reporting the words of the Stratonicean embassy regarding the *polis*' ancestral loyalty, their recent resistance to Mithridates, and the dangers which it caused them.[81] Sulla stresses the εὔνοια shown by the *polis* in sending embassies, probably to other *poleis* in Asia. While the text breaks off, the letter exemplifies the *in medias res* style typical of the period. Again, εὔνοια formed the moral basis of the relationship between local community and Rome, here joined to δικαιοσύνη.[82] The second letter simply reads: 'I have given this decree to your ambassadors', followed by the text of a *senatus consultum*. In its brevity, it reveals a different attitude to conventional Republican government. As dictator, Sulla held an unprecedented position at the apex of Roman politics. Earlier comparanda focus, like most magisterial correspondence, on the personal agency of the official. However, this mostly occludes their involvement in the decree itself.[83] In these examples, though the pre-eminent position of Sulla caused a radical shift in relative power between central institutions of the *res publica*, an interrelationship between Senate and dictator remained central to legitimacy and authority. Despite Sulla's unchallenged position, senatorial sanction retained its value as a means of further guaranteeing the measures which he had enacted as commander in the East.

Unusually, two Roman *leges* with relevance to *provincia Asia* are known from the period following Sulla's dictatorship. First, the earliest section of the *lex portorii Asiae*, which, in content and language, appears unexceptional. It begins by describing the geographic limits of its effects, defining these negatively through the neighbouring kingdoms of Cappadocia, Galatia, and Bithynia, before explicitly

[78] *RDGE* 18.103–112. Kallet-Marx (1995, 270–3) on the widespread phenomenon of embassies to confirm privileges (e.g., *RDGE* 20; *RDGE* 70, with Bitner 2014, 641–8).

[79] Recalling the *lex Valeria*: Vervaet 2004, 49–50, n.46.

[80] E.g., Santangelo 2006, 7–22; Santangelo 2014; Pina Polo 2011, 225–48; Steel 2014a, 657–68.

[81] Chaniotis (2015, 90–1) argued persuasively that such summaries were an important interface for cultural transfer between sender and recipient.

[82] *RDGE* 18.5, 15.

[83] E.g., *RDGE* 7; see also *RDGE* 20, 23.

including the territories (*χῶραι*) of Byzantium and Calchedon.[84] It then succinctly summarizes the basic premise of the statute through exhaustively listing potential authorities and using a third-person imperative:

> *ἐν οἷς τόποις κατὰ δόγμα συνκλήτου ἢ κατὰ νόμον* | [*ἢ κατὰ δήμου κύρωσιν δεῖ τειμευτὴν ἢ ὕπ*]*ατ̣ον* [*τ*]*ε̣λ̣ω̣νεία̣ν ἐκμισθῶσαι, ἐν τούτοις τοῖς τόποις, ἃ ἂν κατὰ θάλασσαν εἰσάγηται, ἐξάγηται κατὰ πέραν* | [*καὶ ἃ ἂν κατὰ γῆν εἰσκομίζηται, εἰσελαύνηται κ*]*αὶ ἃ ἂν κατὰ γῆν ἐκκομίζηται ἐξελαύνται, ἐξάγηται, τὸ τεσσαρακοστὸν μέρος τῶι τέλωναι δίδοτω*{*ι*} ('in whatever places by *senatus consultum* or by *lex* [or by plebiscite *it is obligatory for a censor or consul*] to lease out the *portorium*, in those places, whatever is imported by sea or exported overseas, [whatever is conveyed in or driven in by land], and whatever is conveyed out, driven out, or exported by land, let them give a fortieth part to the collector').[85]

Following Rowe, the emphasis on different sources of authority is not egregious, exemptions to customs legislation were authorized by several groups during the first century.[86] Such clauses subsumed various bodies of law within a single framework but cannot have assisted provincial understanding of the discourse or practice of Roman governance. After this, the text focuses on specific elements, exemptions, and practicalities of implementation. Like other Roman statutes its language is carefully generic, affording the broadest possible latitude to interpreting magistrates, while third-person imperatives are employed throughout. The *lex* is an administrative document of value primarily to magistrates. The compilation of the document in 62 CE and its publication at Ephesus does seem to have been based on its informative capacity, though the imperial context provided different impetus than its Republican antecedent.[87] Like earlier documents, the *lex portorii Asiae* underscores the complex interrelationship between competing sources of legitimate authority within the *res publica*.

By contrast, the *lex Antonia de Termessibus* is especially abrupt. After the initial formula introducing the *rogatores*, led by C. Antonius, and the abbreviated formula *de s(enatus) s(ententia)*, the text immediately proceeds to a series of detailed clauses outlining the new status of Termessus. The initial *senatus consultum* seems, based on internal dates, to have been passed in 72, under the consuls L. Gellius Poplicola and Cn. Cornelius Lentulus Clodianus. Senatorial

[84] Cottier et al. 2008, ll.7–9.

[85] Cottier et al. 2008, ll.9–11, following Crawford's suggestion *ad loc.*

[86] Rowe 2008, 240–1; e.g., *RDGE* 23 (Oropus; Senate & dictator, with *senatus consultum*); *SEG* 31.952 (Ephesus, *senatus consultum* or *edictum*); *IAph2007*.8.27 (Aphrodisias, *senatus consultum* and *lex*); *RS* 36 (Cos, *edictum*, then *senatus consultum* and *lex*); Raggi 2006 (Rhosus, *edictum* with pre-authorization by *lex*).

[87] Rowe 2008, 243–8.

involvement in similar decisions is attested elsewhere and underscores the close interconnection between these two political bodies in normal circumstances.[88] However, the full restoration of tribunician powers in 70 perhaps offered a further practical reason to enshrine the decision of the Senate in statute.[89] While this copy was found in Rome, we should imagine that the community itself received a copy.[90] The *lex Antonia* and *senatus consulta* confirming various *acta* of Sulla perform similar functions but present their decisions differently. Each aligns perfectly with the conventions of their medium and the changes in the political scene between 81 and 68 account for the use of different processes. Nevertheless, this serves to highlight the diversity of communicative acts despatched to cities in the provinces in this period. The use of diverse media naturally hindered the development of familiarity with form, style, convention, and language of Roman public communication.

Overall, the documents from post-Sullan Asia Minor represent several genres, each with their own traditions and conventions. Throughout, however, a strong sense of interrelationship between the various elements of Republican government is detectable. Through Sulla's employment of *senatus consulta* to reinforce his *acta* as proconsul and the *lex Antonia* confirming provisions laid out in a *senatus consultum*, a preference for employing multiple sources of legitimate authority emerges. Partly on account of the evolving political situation, the institutions employed in each case varied significantly. This attests to the flexibility of Republican government—also witnessed in the typical framing of *leges* as authorizing several magistrates or political bodies to implement its provisions—but simultaneously created ambiguities in decoding imperial discourse.[91] The situation as the *res publica* slipped into civil war exacerbated this tendency, forcing magistrates to adapt to shifting realities in novel ways, and take on more personal responsibility in the absence of functioning central institutions.

The Personalization of Imperial Discourse: From Caesar to Civil War

The outbreak of civil war between the partisans of Caesar and Pompeius in 49 corresponds with a marked increase in the number of attested Roman 'speech-acts' in the Greek East. Writing in the first century CE the Jewish historian Josephus reproduces several documents issued by magistrates concerning Jewish communities in Asia Minor in the early 40s, providing further evidence for

[88] *RS* 19.1–4. Compare *RS* 36.4–5, with Mattingly 1997, 77.

[89] Sulla dramatically reduced the legislative powers of the tribunes of the *plebs*. Livy, *Per.* 89; App. *BCiv.* 1.60. For their restoration: Cic. *Leg.* 3.22, 26; Sall. *Cat.* 38; App. *BCiv.* 2.29. Kondratieff 2009, 334–47.

[90] Compare *IAphr2007* 8.25.23–33.

[91] Davies 2013, 417.

competing modes of discourse. Though their authenticity has been questioned and the list is chronologically confused, their formulae reflect Roman practice, they can be corroborated from other sources, and the details are plausible.[92]

This is an intriguing corpus as the documents are addressed to civic communities concerning the rights of a subset of those communities. Moreover, they date to a particularly fraught period during which republican institutions were breaking down, highlighting the flexibility inherent to Roman administration in Asia. A consular *edictum* of L. Cornelius Lentulus Crus (*cos.* 49), which permitted Jews with Roman citizenship at Ephesus to avoid military service, repeatedly recurs through Josephus' narrative. This unusual example of a consular *edictum* in a provincial context, where a *senatus consultum* might be expected, was likely prompted by Lentulus' personal presence in Asia, levying troops.[93] Alongside this, Josephus notes a letter to Ephesus from T. Ampius Balbus, *legatus pro praetore* in 49, who had previously served as proconsul in Asia in 58, possibly explaining his intervention.[94] The document, concerning a subset of the civic population, Jewish inhabitants with Roman citizenship, is addressed explicitly to the archons, *boule*, and *demos*, underscoring the crucial role of these bodies in implementing Roman instructions.[95] Balbus notes the consent of the consul Lentulus, the incoming governor, C. Fannius, and L. Antonius, *pro quaestore pro praetore*, to his request on behalf of the Jewish community.[96] He concludes by reaffirming his own wish (*βούλομαι*) that the Jews be left undisturbed. The courtesy shown through the avoidance of terms of command might indicate a deliberate choice to employ diplomatic language; however, it might equally reflect Balbus' incapacity to interfere in Fannius' *provincia*.[97]

Josephus also records letters of Fannius himself, to the archons at Cos, and L. Antonius, to the archons, *boule*, and *demos* at Sardis, both affirming support for the rights of Jewish communities within Asia. L. Antonius, despite his junior status, even explicitly bases his decision on his own personal authority: *τοῦτό τε αἰτησαμένοις ἵν' ἐξῇ ποιεῖν αὐτοῖς τηρῆσαι καὶ ἐπιτρέψαι ἔκρινα* ('since they requested that they be permitted to do these things, I decided that they might be maintained, and permitted them to do so').[98] Taken together, the documents preserved by Josephus highlight the complexity of official communication in the early civil war period, with Republican officials continuing to draw on distinctive

[92] Bikerman 1980 [1955], 24–43; Pucci ben Zeev 1996, 3–5, 359–68; Eilers 2009, 306, 309–10. Commentary in Pucci ben Zeev 1996, 22–356.

[93] Joseph. *AJ.* 14.228, 232, 234, 236, 238. Cf. Caes. *BCiv.* 3.4.1; *RRC* 445.3.

[94] Joseph. *AJ.* 14.229. On Antonius: *MRR* 2.260; Fannius: *MRR* 2.262; and Balbus: *MRR* 2.266.

[95] Pucci ben Zeev 1996, 151–2.

[96] Pucci ben Zeev 1996, 165–6.

[97] The *lex Pompeia de provinciis* of 52 set term limits beyond which commanders were expected to vacate their *provincia* and cease exercising their *imperium*. Cic. *Att.* 5.16.4; *Fam.* 3.6.4; 8.8.8. Marshall 1972, 890–900; Steel 2012, 91, n.38.

[98] Joseph. *AJ.* 14.235.

genres to give prominence and legitimacy to decisions to which local communities were expected to adhere.[99]

Caesar and Reconstruction

The dictatorships of C. Iulius Caesar, like those of Sulla before him, fundamentally reframed the languages of Roman power. Throughout the surviving record, Caesar's correspondence employs what modern scholars term a *formula valetudinis*: 'If you are well, it is good, I and my army are in good health.'[100] While such invocations were common in official correspondence between commanders and the Senate, Caesar's letters to Pergamum and Mytilene in 48/47 represent their earliest occurrence in documents intended for Asian *poleis*. This may imply that Caesar sought to maintain an aura of military command while in the field, providing a contrast with Sulla's frank acknowledgement that his dictatorship was Rome-centric, focused on restoring the central institutions of the *res publica*. While the former letter is extremely fragmentary, the latter preserves significant detail.[101] After the health formula, Caesar immediately moves to discuss his motives in terms reminiscent of Hellenistic rulers:

> [βουλόμενος] εὐεργετεῖν τὴν πόλιν καὶ οὐ μό[νον | φυλάττειν τὰ φιλάνθρωπα ἃ διεπράξ]ασθε δι' ἡμῶν ἀλλὰ καὶ συναυ[ξάνειν | αὐτὰ———]ΟΣ τὴν ἡγεμονίαν, φιλίας δόγ[ματος | τοῦ ἡμιν συγκεχωρημένου δι]απέπομφα πρὸς ὑμᾶς τὸ ἀ[ντίγραφον] ('[wishing] to benefit your city and not only | [to protect the privileges which you acquired] through us, but also to assist in increasing | [them———] leadership, | I have sent you a [copy] of the decree of *amicitia* [which has been passed]').[102]

Caesar explicitly cites the *senatus consultum* as evidence of his goodwill towards the *polis*, subsuming the functions of the state into his own personal sphere of action.[103] The *senatus consultum* follows, before Caesar concludes the letter by referring to a previous exchange with the *polis*, in which he had promised to prevent individuals claiming immunity from local taxation. Reminded of this by

[99] Joseph. *AJ*. 14.233, 235. Quaestors generally, despite their juniority, do not seem to have been shy about flaunting their authority: Jordan 2022, 496–8, with references.

[100] E.g., Cic. *Fam*. 15.1, 2: *s(i) v(aletis) v(os) b(ene est), e(go) e(xercitus)q(ue) v(alemus)*. The earliest example in Roman official correspondence is the truncated version in the introductory letter to the *senatus consultum de Oropiis* (*RDGE* 23.2): εἰ ἔρρωσθε, εὖ ἂν ἔχοι. Sherk 1969, 189. The occurrences of ἐρρῶσθε in Welles' collection of Hellenistic Royal letters (1934, 399, s.v. ῥώννυμι) shows that *basileis* tended to use the *formula valetudinis* only in personal correspondence.

[101] Ambitiously restored at *RDGE* 54.

[102] *RDGE* 26.b.9–12.

[103] Rowe 2002, 140 (incorrectly citing column a).

the envoys, Caesar positively affirms his position, before concluding, like earlier Roman magistrates, with a unilateral declaration of his *euergesia*.[104]

Two recently published fragmentary letters from Caesar at Aezani further elucidate this trend. While the former is clearly issued to the *polis*, the latter is addressed to an [ἀντι]ϛτρạτηγός, firmly identified as P. Servilius Vatia Isauricus, governor of Asia from 46–44.[105] This text shows that an Aezanetan ambassador persuaded the dictator to make concessions related to the local temple of Zeus. Neither document has space for a *formula valetudinis*, though both seem to end with a cordial farewell, potentially due to Caesar's presence in Rome as consul. The pair of documents also provides an intriguing window into the relationship between Caesar, as dictator, and provincial commanders. Aside from the addressee, little separates the language of the second letter from those sent directly to communities. The apparent use of θέλω (l.16) and the participle of συγχωρέω (l.17) recalls the typical language of command employed by Roman officials.[106] The later monumentalization of this missive, likely originally written in Latin, implies its inclusion in the civic archives of Aezani, itself surprising. It emphasizes the extent to which Caesar demonstrated his concern through publicizing his instructions to the responsible magistrate.

This reveals a significant shift in the presentation of Roman rule. Caesar's consular colleague in 48, Vatia, had an established record of interest in the welfare of provincial communities.[107] That the language of command is employed by Caesar, in public-facing but essentially private instructions to a magistrate with consular *imperium*, stresses the increasing normalization of his position at the head of the *res publica*. The letters' structure, granting privileges to the *polis* of Aezani, presents a new hierarchy of authority, framing the dictator as the legitimate source of grants, without senatorial confirmation. These are enacted by the provincial governor, Servilius, as his predecessors would enact the instructions of the Senate and People. The language reflects and draws attention to that shift. In this letter we observe central and provincial exercise of power coalesce with the personalization of central authority, fitfully developing with the breakdown of Republican constitutional norms.

Caesar's *edictum* at Sardis, found on a boundary stone for the temple of Artemis, might hint at his intentions for the future. Intriguingly, this *edictum* makes no reference to his consulship, unlike earlier letters, instead focusing on his recently commenced dictatorship *perpetuo*, and might echo broader changes in progress to the constitution of the Roman state. It is unclear exactly how his dictatorial *imperium* would apply in a province assigned to a proconsular

[104] *RDGE* 26.b.27–34.
[105] *AÉ* 2009, #1429.1–2, 13–14; Wörrle 2009, 413–18.
[106] Ando (forthcoming).
[107] Morrell (2017, 149–51) goes too far in denying any role for Caesar in provincial reform, though Kirbihler's (2011, 250) insistence on Vatia's subordination to the dictator's policy aims lacks nuance.

governor, but it perhaps emphasizes his unprecedented position and foreshadows the practices of the *tresviri rei publicae constituendae*.[108] The erasure of twenty lines on the stone between the heading and Caesar's letter, seemingly referring to Antonius, together with the final paragraph—restating Caesar's grant in the third person—may indicate that this was an act confirmed after his assassination, without senatorial confirmation.[109] The ἐπεί-clause encapsulates a universalizing discourse: Caesar's decision is premised on general agreement (συμφωνεῖται) that Sardis has always (διὰ παντὸς) been in friendship and alliance (φιλία, *amicitia*) with the Roman people, and shown good faith (πίστις, *fides*) towards the Senate and People.[110] He also refers explicitly to 'the deeds brought about for the leadership of the Romans' (πεπραγ[μέ]|νων εἰς τὴν ἡγεμονίαν Ῥ[ω]μαίων).[111] Caesar elides the civil war and envisions Sardis' attitude as continuously loyal to the state. In doing so, he continued to promote a Roman framework, prioritizing consistent loyalty over reciprocity, even where his own policy of pardoning his enemies' supporters ran counter to this.[112] This echoes Sulla's earlier emphasis on *fides* to Rome during the First Mithridatic War. The situation was, however, fundamentally different. Where Sulla distinguished between individual cities on the basis of their actions vis-à-vis Mithridates between 88 and 85, it is unlikely that Sardis offered any tangible support to Caesar or resistance to his opponents before his victory. Consequently, we likely see here a conscious choice by the dictator to overlook this complex period, in which two parties claimed to be the legitimate representatives of the *res publica*. If so, the exigencies of war led to the wholesale rejection of this attitude in the aftermath of his assassination. The corpus of documents issued under Caesar's dictatorship collectively show a movement towards language emphasizing the personal nature of grants made and the new hierarchy imposed on the Roman world.

The Triumvirate and the Personality of Imperial Hegemony

The chaos after Caesar's assassination further weakened central institutions and facilitated the rise of a new cabal of *imperium*-holders, the *tresviri rei publicae constituendae*: Octavian, M. Antonius, and M. Aemilius Lepidus. Wielding authority by virtue of their connections to the slain dictator and the troops under their command, they remade the political institutions of the *res publica* in their own interests. In Rome, magistracies and commands became their gift, while each took responsibility for a separate set of provinces; broadly, Octavian the

[108] *SEG* 39.1290.31–3; contrast Joseph. *AJ*. 14.211. Herrmann 1989a, 139–41; Fernoux 2011a, 91.
[109] See Chapter 3, 'Sardis and the Last Days of Caesar'.
[110] *SEG* 39.1290.33–7. Herrmann 1989a, 141–2.
[111] *SEG* 39.1290.42–3.
[112] Chaniotis 2015, 90, 98–9.

western Mediterranean and Italy, Antonius, the eastern Mediterranean, and Lepidus, Africa. The invention of the triumvirate had a significant impact on relationships between the state and communities. The introduction of a new college of magistrates, holding *imperium consulare* but with wider scope for action and increased *auctoritas*, added a further layer of complexity to the administration. However, the concentration of effective executive power among a small group of commanders with longer tenure allowed the winnowing of some competing discourses. Though the triumvirate disintegrated within scarcely more than a decade, this period provides numerous documents for analysis, including eleven letters from *tresviri* or other magistrates, three *edicta*, two *senatus consulta*, and fragments of an unusual *lex*. While these are concentrated unevenly within the *provincia* and cannot be considered a substantial corpus, nevertheless they offer sufficient texts to elucidate changes in language, structure, and framing during the era of civil wars.

The continuing complexities of Roman authority emerge from a document at Ephesus. Initially interpreted as an *edictum* from one of the *tresviri*, Bringmann alternatively suggested that the stone preserved extracts from three interrelated *senatus consulta*.[113] The document was monumentalized in the Trajanic period, but a reference to *portoria* in Italy provides an original date of 42–39.[114] From autopsy, Laffi argued the two fragments do not join, proposing a gap of at least nine lines, and that both a *senatus consultum* and an *edictum* could be contained. This debate highlights how much we depend on formal elements to identify document types. Laffi's emendation at line five created a clause instructing consuls, praetors, or tribunes to refer a matter to the *populus* or *plebs*.[115] These instructions to magistrates suit the context of a *senatus consultum*, as even under the triumvirs *edicta* seem to be more circumspect. Finally, each fragment mentions a *διάταγμα* (*edictum*): however, in the first instance the text speaks of a future conditional: *ὅταν τις τῶν τριῶν ἀνδρῶν | ἐπὶ τῆς καταστάσεως τῶν δημοσίων πραγμάτων | ἐπι⌜χω⌝ρῴη διατάγματι δηλῶσαι δεδόχθαι*...('if ever one of the *tresviri rei publicae constituendae* should consent to make known with an edict...').[116] By contrast, in the second fragment, the mode has shifted: *[ὅ]|πως περὶ τούτου τοῦ πρ[άγματος δια]τάγματι δηλώσο|μεν καλῶς ἔχον ἐστίν* ('so that, concerning this matter, *we will make clear* through an edict what is right').[117] This should be taken as self-referential and indicate a triumviral edict. This association of *edictum* and *senatus consultum* recurs on the Potamoneion, with the two documents framed by a letter of Caesar to the Mytileneans. In both cases the Senate explicitly invited powerful magistrates, the dictator or the *tresviri*, to act, providing an overarching and pre-emptive legitimacy should they have

[113] Bringmann 1983, 53–69 contra Knibbe 1981, 1–10.
[114] *SEG* 56.1219.15–17. Bringmann 1983, 71–2. [115] Laffi 2006, 468–84, 490.
[116] *SEG* 56.1219.7–9. [117] *SEG* 56.1219.12–14.

chosen to.[118] Accordingly, the dossier contained two different contemporary documents, and in this case suggests that the *tresviri* showed some respect for the Republican administrative framework.[119]

Another triumviral *edictum*, likely issued by Octavian and Antonius, appeared on the archive wall at Aphrodisias. Here, their title and the operative verb (*λέγουσιν*) are unambiguous.[120] The joint *edictum* again underscores the bolstering of individual authority through consensual decision-making and shows the two most powerful actors in the Roman world operating together. Moreover, the rationale offered for the grant highlights changing relationships after the period of civil war. The motivation clause of the *edictum* notes the zeal (*σπουδή*) of the subjects for the empire (*[ἡγε]μονίας*) of the Roman People and, prominently, their attachment to 'our faction' (*μ[ά]λ̣ι̣σ̣τα τοῖς ἡμετέροις μέρεσι[ν]*).[121] Assimilating their own interests with those of the Roman People, the *tresviri* did not shy away from the reality that the rewarded communities were loyal primarily to their group. This public declaration demonstrates that the benefactions result from past choices to support their alliance in a civil war—that is, demonstrating *πίστις* or *fides* towards them personally—and, while no overt claim to future actions is made, it extends the possibility of similar rewards to other communities for personal loyalty. The choice of an *edictum* helps clarify the message. It presents the words of the two men collectively and directly. There is no mediation through another body. The two *edicta* used differing strategies to construct legitimacy; where the former consciously interacted with existing modes of discourse, the latter forewent these and emphasized the consensus of the new rulers of the Roman world. This experimentation and inconsistency are characteristic of the material for this period and stress the degree to which institutions remained in flux.

The *senatus consultum de Aphrodisiensibus* further illustrates the dramatic shifts under the *tresviri*. First, though the consuls spoke concerning the matter under discussion, the resolution is overshadowed by Octavian and Antonius. The consuls were responsible for the final section of the *senatus consultum* dealing with hospitality and honours for the ambassador but the substantive issues, the freedom and immunity of the city and other key privileges, are explicitly framed as arising from proposals by the two *tresviri*.[122] The Senate's role was simply to agree and confer additional legitimacy.[123] Contrasting with earlier practice, the Aphrodisian requests are extremely compressed, in favour of a lengthy exposition

[118] App. *BCiv*. 5.75. Laffi 2006, 503–4. [119] *SEG* 56.1219.13–15.

[120] *IAph2007* 8.26.1. The text of Reynolds has Octavian referred to as Augustus (*[Σ]εβαστός*), which she explains as an editorial choice at the inscription of the text in the mid-third century CE (1982, 49–50). However, Bowersock (1984, 51–2) and Kokkinia (2015–2016, 25) convincingly argue that this fragment is misplaced. In any case, note Lepidus' exclusion from this process: see CD. 48.22.2.

[121] *IAph2007* 8.26.2–3. Contrast with the decree of Aphrodisias from 88 (*IAph2007* 8.3), discussed in Chapter 6.

[122] *IAph*2007 8.27.26–32. Osgood 2006, 228–9.

[123] E.g., *IAph2007* 8.27.39, 42.

of the senatorial process and decision, presumably, in part, to highlight the role played by the two key leaders of the Roman world. Critically, the Senate appeared to grant carte blanche to Octavian and Antonius to make future grants, to be treated as if authorized by a senatorial decree.[124] This went beyond the right to decide on minutiae afforded to Sulla in the case of Stratonicea. According to the literary sources, the *lex Titia* already granted *tresviri* a general right to issue *edicta* with statutory force, as well as more specific *iura extraordinaria*.[125] However, the additional confirmation of this fact gave further legitimacy to the provisions of the decree.

Another *senatus consultum*, relating to Stratonicea, underscores both the destructiveness of the Parthian conflict and the multiple levels of authority operating in this period.[126] The first section includes the prescript of the decree, dating it to 15 August 39 under the consuls L. Marcius Censorinus and C. Calvisius.[127] It lists the ten witnesses present at the drafting, following earlier examples, giving an impression of senatorial consensus. References to the city's loyalty (*πίστεως*) and endangerment during the war (*ἐν ῷ πολέμῳ τά τ[ε] μέ[γιστα κεκινδυνευ]|κότες*) suggest that the embassy sought privileges to relieve the difficult situation, such as the tax relief recently granted to several cities.[128] The second fragment confirms earlier benefactions and refers directly to the Temple of Zeus at Panamara, most likely confirming *ἀσυλία*.[129] The linguistic parallels with both the *senatus consulta de Stratonicensibus* (81) and *de Aphrodisiensibus* (35) are striking and demonstrate the extent to which the framework of senatorial action remained intact.[130] This may show institutional memory in action at Rome; the survival of praxis among the *scribae* involved in assisting magistrates with administrative tasks, for example.[131] In any case, this document further underscores how, despite the increasing personal power of the *tresviri*, the institutions of the *res publica* interacted in traditional ways with provincial communities.

Correspondence relating to Octavian's relationship with Aphrodisias further illustrates shifts in praxis and discursive strategies. Of five surviving letters, however, only one was personally addressed to the *polis* by Octavian. Dated to 39/38, it follows a familiar format: after addressing the archons, *boule*, and *demos* of Plarasa-Aphrodisias, and including a *formula valetudinis*, Octavian turns to the ambassador, Solon.[132] Here, however, the language becomes unusual. Rather than praising Solon's zeal and eloquence in putting forward his city's case, Octavian stresses his attention paid to the matter at hand (*ἐπι|μελέστατα*) and focuses on

[124] *IAph2007* 8.27.48–51.

[125] App. *BCiv* 5.22, 67; CD. 46.55.3. Vervaet 2020, 34, 36–8, with additional references. Compare Reynolds 1982, 83.

[126] *Ambascerie* 453b, c. Canali de Rossi (1997, 399) argued convincingly against Hatzfeld's (1927, 59–61) separating them.

[127] *Ambascerie* 453b.3–4.

[128] *Ambascerie* 453b.19, c.8–10, 15. Sherk 1969, 161; Osgood 2006, 225.

[129] *Ambascerie* 453c.15–17. Rigsby 1996, 426–7.

[130] Sherk 1969, 173.

[131] Purcell 2001, 647–54; 671–2, on their desuetude.

[132] *IAph2007* 8.25.11–33.

the substance of his requests. Noting Solon's satisfaction with the 'administrative arrangements' (οἰκονο|[μή]μασιν) decided, Octavian highlights the further request for documents relating to Plarasa-Aphrodisias: ἐπι|κρίματος καὶ δόγμα|τος καὶ ὁρκίου καὶ νό|μου (*edictum*, *(senatus)consultum*, *foedus*, and *lex*). The requests themselves (ἐφ' οἷς) appear to prompt Octavian's praise of Solon.[133] Moreover, the framing of his success is non-standard: the *triumvir* grants him privileges and regards him as an 'acquaintance' (γεινωσκόμενοις).[134] This underscores the increasing personalization of power under the *tresviri*, emphasizing how personal knowledge and access to individual rulers could itself become a valuable honour; one worth recording in an official letter from a magistrate to a *polis*. These γεινωσκόμενοι need not represent a formal group with a defined membership and specific privileges. The very informality and variation in language between letters reinforce the extent to which this was a period of experimentation.

Critical to interpreting the dossier is a semi-private letter from Octavian to Stephanus, a representative of Antonius operating from Laodicea-on-the-Lycus.[135] Stephanus appears to have acted as representative of Antonius in western Asia though the extent of his authority cannot be established. Given his lack of *tria nomina*, he is likely not a citizen; his position was necessarily informal, foreshadowing the *procuratores* of the early Principate, his power deriving fully from his personal relationship with the *triumvir*.[136] Within Antonius' sphere of responsibility, letters represented Octavian's main form of agency. Even so, the permanent presence of a representative in the person of Stephanus in the vicinity of Plarasa-Aphrodisias allowed actions implemented efficiently, by either *triumvir*. The text reads:

> *vac* Καῖσαρ Στεφάνῳ *vac* χαίρειν· *vac* | ὡς Ζωΐλον τὸν ἐμὸν φιλῶ ἐπίστασαι τὴν πατρίδα αὐτοῦ ἠλευθέρωσα καὶ Ἀντωνίῳ συνέστησα | ὡς Ἀντώνιος ἄπεστιν δὸς ἐργασίαν μή τις αὐτοῖς ἐπιβάρησις γένηται μίαν πόλιν ταύτην | ἐξ ὅλης τῆς Ἀσίας ἐμαυτῷ εἴληπφα τούτους οὕτω θέλω φυλαχθῆναι ὡς ἐμοὺς πολείτας· | *vac* ὄψομαι ὡς τὴν ἐμὴν σύνστασιν ἐπὶ πέρας ἀγάγῃς *vac* ('Caesar to Stephanus, greetings. You know of my affection for my *amicus* Zoilos, I have freed his home city and recommended it to Antonius. Since Antonius is absent, give your attention that

[133] *IAph2007* 8.25.33–42.

[134] Reynolds (1982, 46) drawing on Robert (1989 [1966], 46 n.1; referring to 1937, 227–8) noted the repeated use of γιγνώσκειν and cognates to mean 'official acquaintances', tracing it to Hellenistic court practice. She adduced the parallel of *notus* in Latin and emphasized Seneca's reference to C. Gracchus hierarchizing his friends for the *salutatio*, suggesting that this was the earliest attestation of a common practice. Compare Paterson (2007, 129–31) on Hellenistic practice.

[135] Reynolds 1982, 97, 99–100; De Chaisemartin 2017, 333.

[136] Reynolds (1982, 99–100) posited that he is Antonius' freedman, or a local; Badian (1984a, 160–1) preferred to view him as a slave. Note the employment of other agents by Antonius: Dalla Rosa 2017, 107–10.

no burden falls on them: this one city from all of Asia I have taken for my own. I wish for these people to be protected as if they were my own townsmen. I will see that you carry out my recommendation to the full').[137]

This letter employs an unambiguously commanding tone throughout, unsurprising given Stephanus' (lack of) status as a Greek agent vis-à-vis Octavian. The imperative (δός, l.3), use of θέλω (l.4), and implication of close observation (l.5) emphasize the simple hierarchical relationship. Octavian as *triumvir*, though *sans* title, commanded, and Stephanus obeyed.[138] The letter's subject is Aphrodisias' ongoing well-being; however, the two ὡς-clauses at the missive's opening contextualize the later instructions. Octavian privileges (Gaius Julius) Zoilos, likely Caesar's freedman and a well-attested civic benefactor at Aphrodisias, as the reason for his interest.[139] Crucially, Octavian uses the unambiguous φίλος/*amicus* rather than the more oblique 'acquaintance'. Octavian's attention is on the *polis* for the sake of individuals, rather than on the political community writ large, marking a radical change from the *senatus consultum de Asclepiade* issued in 78, which makes no suggestion that the beneficiaries would form a continuing link with the imperial centre to their homeland's benefit.[140]

The document's language emphasizes both the author's agency and the communities' position as passive recipients of imperial favour. First, the singular ἠλευθέρωσα frames the freedom of Aphrodisias as a personal action, where the *senatus consultum* privileged the involvement of his colleague, Antonius, and the Senate: the choice to present the outcome thus reflects the personalization of power and discourse under the *tresviri*.[141] The strong personal voice continues throughout the letter, climaxing in the declaration that μίαν πόλιν ταύτην | ἐξ ὅλης τῆς Ἀσίας ἐμαυτῷ εἴληπφα ('this one city from all of Asia I have taken for my own'). The primary meaning of λαμβάνω suggests ownership or seizure but underscores the reality that Plarasa-Aphrodisias was territory to be owned or ruled, irrespective of the 'freedom' bestowed.[142] The communiqué's personal nature may account for the more overt language, which does not reflect a broader trend. Nevertheless, its appearance on the archive wall demonstrates that a copy

137 *IAph2007* 8.29.

138 Compare his own letter to Aphrodisias: *IAph2007* 8.30. Osgood 2006, 230.

139 For Zoilos' life and activity: Robert 1989 [1966], 32–56; Reynolds 1982, 156–64; Smith 1993, 4–13; Heller 2011, 229–34. *IAph2007* index 'Names attested at Aphrodisias' s.v. Ζωΐλος. De Chaisemartin 2017, 337. Compare Solon, who does not seem to have received similar benefactions: Laignoux 2017, 230.

140 Osgood 2006, 276; Heller 2011, 234–7; *pace* Badian 1984, 158.

141 *IAph2007* 8.29.2. Badian 1984, 162–3. Compare the use of first-person plural in the joint *edictum* offering Plarasa-Aphrodisias privileges elsewhere: *IAph2007* 8.26.6, 9, 13. Osgood 2006, 229.

142 Frija 2017, 198. Note Chaniotis' (2003, 253–4) perceptive observation that this creates a distance between Aphrodisias and other *poleis* in Asia.

could later be found in the civic archive.[143] While Badian noted that the public-facing language suggests that the letter was intended as a public document, it does not automatically entail that Stephanus would forward it on.[144] Intended and likely audiences must remain distinct. That Plarasa-Aphrodisias may have received the letter had obviously occurred to Octavian but probably was not his object.

Octavian's letter to Ephesus reveals further elements of personalizing discourse. This text's catalyst is a report from Solon to Octavian concerning the damage to Plarasa-Aphrodisias during the Parthian War of 40/39.[145] Octavian explicitly notes that he has sent letters (*ἐντολαί*) to Antonius about Aphrodisias, drawing perhaps on his colleague's more present authority. Similarly, in urging Ephesus to assist Plarasa-Aphrodisias, Octavian avoids the language of command, or even an overt suggestion, noting only that they are *εὐκαίρον* ('well-situated') to help.[146] A golden statue of Eros complicated the situation: originally dedicated by Caesar in the temple of Aphrodite at Aphrodisias, it had been looted by Labienus and the Parthians, and later rededicated as an offering to Artemis at Ephesus. How the Artemision acquired it is not stated. The circumspect nature of Octavian's language may be explained through his intervention in his colleague's *provincia*. Instead, he offers moral capital as a motive, suggesting that the Ephesians would *καλῶς ποιήσετε καὶ ἄξιος* ('act well and rightly') to return the statue, and even offering the ironic suggestion that Eros was an inappropriate offering to Artemis.[147] Drawing on the repertoire of civic virtue, Octavian sought to leverage reasons beyond political authority to ensure success.

The letter concludes with an unusually overt declaration of Octavian's own motives, hearkening to royal models: *ἀνάνκη γάρ μοι [[Ἀφροδεισιέων]] ποιεῖσθαι πρόνοιαν οὓς τη|λικαῦτα εὐεργέτηκα ἣν καὶ ὑμᾶς ἀκούειν νομίζω* ('for it is necessary for me to show care for the Aphrodisians, upon whom I have conferred such benefits, about which I judge you too have heard').[148] The force of this sentence lies in the opening phrase: Octavian is constrained to act on behalf of the Aphrodisians, due to his role as *εὐεργέτης*. This should not be considered a form of patronage in a technical sense, nor a legal bond.[149] Rather, Octavian invokes moralizing language to give force to his actions. He constructs himself as a

[143] Ando 2000, 85–6. See Coudry (1994, 66–70) on senatorial documents; magistrates' correspondence may have been a grey area: though official, it remained the responsibility of the individual. The utility for the administration of empire is obvious, but we cannot assume it was collected for public use.

[144] Badian 1984, 158–9. [145] *IAph2007* 8.31.4–6, 13–18.

[146] *IAph2007* 8.31.7–12. Reynolds 1982, 102–3 *contra* De Chaisemartin 2017, 334. We should not see this as reflecting the high imperial use of this word to describe imperial *mandata* delineating the governor's responsibilities and how administration should be carried out. The term likely reflects evolving practice: like *procurator*, *mandatum* had a private meaning before being taken into the public sphere (Buckland 1963³, 514–21).

[147] *IAph2007* 8.31.16. Reynolds 1982, 103; Osgood 2006, 230. Note the tensions between Aphrodisias and Ephesus: Pont 2012, 322–3.

[148] *IAph2007* 8.31.19–20. [149] *Pace* Reynolds 1982, 103; Badian 1984, 163–5.

protector of the interests of *his* city and invites the Ephesians to consider his actions towards the Aphrodisians as consistent, repetitive, and morally correct. In this, he returns openly to a more regal style of communication. Despite or perhaps due to his relative weakness vis-à-vis Antonius, Octavian engages in a meaningful dialogue with Ephesus, presenting his wishes and offering reasons for the *polis* to comply. In this sense, the letter is something of an anomaly, though its record at Plarasa-Aphrodisias attests his success.

Documents relating to two separate grants of citizenship in the East: (i) to Seleucus of Rhosus by Octavian; and (ii) an unnamed resident of Cos under the so-called *lex Fonteia* illustrate the institutional and discursive uncertainty of the triumvirate. The Rhosus dossier includes an *edictum* recording that Octavian [*κατὰ ν*]*όμον Μουνάτιον καὶ Αἰμίλιον πολιτείαν καὶ ἀνεισφορίαν πάντων τῶν* | [*ὑπαρχόντ*]*ων ἔδωκαν εἰς τούτους τοὺς λόγους* ('in accordance with the *lex Munatia Aemilia*, gave citizenship and tax-exemption on all property, in these words').[150] Octavian's covering letter demonstrates that the document's purpose was to provide a record for the civic archive. Consequently, the absence of a ratifying statute implies that such a document was—after Actium, at least—no longer considered for inclusion, reinforcing the personal link between Octavian and the beneficiary.[151] By contrast, the *lex Fonteia* found at the Asklepieion on Cos appears to have been a *lex populi Romani* promulgated by C. Fonteius Capito between 41 and 34, confirming an earlier *senatus consultum*.[152] Fonteius' description in the prescript as *pontifex* rather than magistrate presents a constitutional riddle. However, the motivation clause refers to the opinion (*γνώμη*) of a *triumvir*—the name erased—with his *consilium* and, later, Antonius' judgement (*τὴν Ἀντωνίου κρίσιν*). Most likely, Fonteius presented the measure on Antonius' behalf, emphasizing the latter's central role in the bill.[153] Like other *leges*, the language is formulaic and comprehensive, with no discernible personality. The privileges are consistent with those granted to Seleucus, emphasizing the exemption of the recipient (and his descendants) from customs dues on goods export from or imported [*εἰς ἐπαρχεί*]|*αν Ἀσίαν ἤ νῆσόν τινα Ἀσία*[*ς*] ('to *provincia Asia* or any island of Asia'), as well as the choice of juridical procedure if arraigned.[154] Notably, in conjunction with the *senatus consultum de Asclepiade* and the Rhosus dossier, we possess a complete set of potential granting bodies of Roman citizenship within a (broadly) Republican framework: a *senatus consultum*, a *lex*, and a

[150] Raggi 2006 ll.9–11. Raggi (2006, 98–9; already, Reynolds 1982, 23, 45) noted that the edict, beyond the prescript, is consistently in the first-person plural, where the three letters use the singular and concludes that the *edictum* was issued on behalf of all the *tresviri*. See Raggi 2006 19–23, with references for previous editions.

[151] Raggi 2006 ll.5–8. [152] *RS* 36.1.4–5.

[153] *RS* 36.1.8, 12. Crawford et al. 1996, 504; Buraselis 2000, 25–30. On Fonteius: Ferriès 2007, 401–3, speculating that he held the tribunate.

[154] *RS* 36.2.1–24. Buraselis observed (2000, 28) that Cos must have held free status at the time of the *lex*'s passage.

magistrate's *edictum* (empowered by a *lex*). As noted, the *lex Aemilia Munatia* gave the *tresviri* the authority to unilaterally create *cives Romani*: a simple pronouncement outlining the scope of privileges would suffice.[155] The motivation behind recourse to a *senatus consultum* and *lex*, when the decision of Antonius had the same legal force, must reflect a desire to ratify the privileges through the consensus of the *populus* and Senate.[156] Again, powerful actors invoked the central institutions of the *res publica* to give further legitimacy to their actions. Though the lacunose text does not allow speculation whence the impetus of the *lex Fonteia* emerged, local interest in securing of their privileges against central instability plausibly played a role.[157] Together, the examples of Seleucus and the *lex Fonteia* emphasize experimentation with the format of official decisions relevant to provincial communities and the continuing overlap and complexity between central institutions of the *res publica*.

Octavian's letter to the *koinon* and *conventus* centres of Asia reinforces the discursive evolution after Actium. The text evokes a similar generalizing and moralizing tone to Hellenistic royal correspondence. The central concern of the remaining text with the ἀναιδεία ('shamelessness') of certain unnamed individuals contrasts strongly with the care (ἐπιμελῶς) taken on behalf of the letter's author to protect his settlement. This corresponds well to Octavian's post-Actian arrangements in Asia.[158] The unusually prescriptive publication clause further shows the unique nature of this document: the author requires that each *polis* despatch copies of his letter to the other communities in their διοικήσις, the earliest employment of this administrative term in a Roman epigraphic context, and display the letter: ἔν τε τῶι ἐπ[ι]|φανεστάτωι τόπωι ἐν στυλοπαραστάδι ἐπὶ | λίθου λευκοῦ ἐνχαραχθῆναι ('engraved in the most conspicuous places, on a stele of white stone').[159] While this instruction is paralleled for earlier *senatus consulta*, the explicit requirement to display a letter is unusual.[160] The motivation clause stresses the broad context considered by the author: ἵνα κοινῶς πάσηι τῆι ἐπαρχεία[ι τὸ] | δίκαιον ἑσταμένον ἧι εἰς τὸν αἰεὶ χρόνον, αἵ τε ἄλ|λαι πᾶσαι πόλεις καὶ δῆμοι τὸ αὐτὸν παρ' αὐτοῖς | ποίησωσιν ('so that in common for all the province justice might be established for all time, and that all the other cities and peoples might do the same things among themselves').[161] The emphasis on

[155] E.g., *RDGE* 58.2.9–72. [156] *RS* 36.1.1.3–7.

[157] Herzog (1922, 212) presented it as a loss of sovereignty for the tyrant Nicias of Cos, Antonius may simply have been as more concerned with the appearance of institutional legitimacy than Octavian.

[158] *I.Priene*² 13.41–42. Compare *I.Mylasa* 602 (with Sherk 1969, 311; Millar 2002a [1973], 254; Osgood 2006, 226).

[159] *I.Priene*² 13.47–49.

[160] *Pace* Ando 2000, 83. Ulpian (*Dig.* 14.3.11.3; cf. Valerius Probus, *de iuris notarum* (Keil *GL* 4, p. 273)), in a third-century CE juristic context, demonstrates that the formula *unde de plano recte legi possit* had wider application, but the requirement of inscription is unusual.

[161] *I.Priene*² 13.50–53.

the timelessness of his judgement sits uneasily with the temporary nature of a commander's position and the contingent nature of his decisions, further suggesting an author of greater authority.[162] This passage contains several generalizing phrases, extending the justice of the decision rendered to the whole *provincia* for all time and 'all the other cities and peoples [sc. in Asia]'. The adverbial *κοινῶς* hearkens to Hellenistic models, but these earlier uses emphasized the distinction between a *polis*, as a civic community, and individual citizens.[163] Here the author widens that sense of community to include the whole province, that is, the group of communities subject to the commander in Asia, establishing a single Roman standard. This interfaces neatly with the use of the *koinon* as a conduit to facilitate communication between the imperial centre and local *poleis*. Such sentiments are unparalleled in earlier examples and suggest the author's conscious intent to frame the inhabitants of the whole *provincia* as a single unit. Finally, the explicit foregrounding of the author's own use of the Greek language, 'to avoid confusion', provides a hint that in normal circumstances official communication from Roman magistrates in Asia to local communities was conducted in Latin.[164] However, exceptions clearly occurred: P. Licinius Crassus allegedly conducted his tribunals in Asia in whatever dialect the petitioner used.[165] More intriguing is the acknowledgement here that misinterpretation of central instructions could be a problem.

Though the triumviral period saw a personalization of communication between communities and the Roman state, various genres of document persisted through the period. We have examples of *senatus consulta* and *leges*, though most extant normative documents are admittedly more direct, *edicta* and letters. The mutual reinforcement of the various genres witnessed throughout the Republican period continues, despite the instability of central institutions resulting in greater experimentation. The prominence of Octavian within the material presents another change, likely on account of his later success. We have sufficient surviving texts issued by him to construct a view of his style, and it is striking that even within his own correspondence we witness a distinctive lack of consistency, reproducibility, and uniformity. A common element across the period is the increasing emphasis on the importance of local individuals and their relationship to powerful Romans as a layer of mediation between Rome and communities. Though perhaps an accident of our material, it is notable that our evidence for civic patronage seems to decline.[166] Overall, the official utterances of the Roman state during this period of internal flux continued to move towards an individualized basis, though coherence in scope, language, and format failed to materialize.

[162] Kokkinia 2009, 192. [163] Compare Ma 1999, 188, with examples n.35.
[164] *I.Priene*² 13.54–57. [165] Val. Max. 8.7.6. [166] Eilers 2002, 160–5, 172–81.

A New Form of Administration?

Octavian's success at Actium and the subsequent conquest of Egypt left him without rivals. Over the following twelve years he acquired a series of powers which cemented his position at the apex of Roman society. The Republican constitution was radically redesigned, placing the newly entitled Augustus and his family at the centre of the state. In outline, the consolidated Augustan Republic came to resemble the Hellenistic kingdoms: power flowing from a limited in-group around the Princeps, down into a hierarchical court structure around the Imperial household. Though the Senate and other social groups such as the *equites* and *plebs urbana* retained formal influence and prestige, provincial communities increasingly relied on their relationship with the Princeps, mediated through governors or, occasionally, the Senate.

The honorific monument for Potamon of Mytilene, which displayed several official documents relating to his career, including *senatus consulta* and letters from magistrates, provides an early example of Augustan processes.[167] While the texts were selected to aggrandize Potamon's reputation, rather than illustrate the relationship between Rome and Mytilene, they shed important light on the language, structure, and use of official documents in this period. Among the preserved material are two *senatus consulta* dated securely to 25.[168] The first responds to a Mytilenean embassy requesting a treaty with Rome, and is structurally consistent with earlier examples, noting the consuls, date, and location of the meeting, as well as the senators present at the drafting of the decree.[169] The second, framed as an addendum to the first, omits the consuls and begins with the date and drafters alone.[170] In both cases, the consul M. Iunius Silanus gave the *relatio*, though Augustus' absence in Spain facilitated his exercise of traditional consular prerogatives.[171] However, these documents illustrate the sea-change in political practice at Rome under the early Principate. In the first decree Silanus recommends that: *[ἐπὶ Αὐτοκράτορα Καίσαρα Σεβασ]|τὸν [τ]ὸν συνάρχοντα γράμμ[ατα δεῖν πεμφθῆναι]* ('letters should be sent to Imperator Caesar Augustus, his colleague').[172] This explicit intent to consult Augustus vis-à-vis the acceptance of the Mytilenean request for benefactions, including a treaty, despite Augustus' symbolic return of the *fasces* in 28 to his consular colleague, Agrippa, demonstrates the evolution of the exercise of Roman power. It emphasizes the Princeps' centrality to decision-making in an ongoing transitional period. It remained unclear in the mid-20s how the Roman state would sort itself out and the Mytilenean ambassadors' initial approach to the Senate

[167] On the monument: Parker 1991, 115 n.2. Sherk (1969) collects the Roman documents as *RDGE* 25–6, 51, 73–8. On Potamon's career and family: Robert 1969b, 740–5; Parker 1991, 115–21.

[168] *RDGE* 26.B.i.36–C.26. [169] *RDGE* 26.B.i.37–44. [170] *RDGE* 26.C.9–16.

[171] Labarre 1996, 111–12; Arrayás Morales 2010, 138, with references. [172] *RDGE* 26.C.1–2.

illustrates the confusion which the evolving regime created for its interlocutors. The promulgation of the two decrees closely followed one another: the first must date between 16 May and 13 June 25, the second to 28 June 25. Evidence from the monuments' other documents and the presence of Crinagoras, another Mytilenean ambassador in Tarraco implies that the embassy travelled directly to consult the Princeps.[173] This additional journey went unmentioned in the text of the decree which focuses explicitly on the obligations and actions of the Senate and magistrates. Even allowing for the overt deference showed to Augustus, the practical scope of these *senatus consulta* does not appear to have altered vis-à-vis earlier documents.

Outside of Asia, Augustus' fifth Cyrene edict and its enclosed *senatus consultum* highlight the construction of a new world order. Critically, though the latter does the heavy lifting, supplying the legislative specifics, it is given weight through Augustus' *edictum*. Noting his own presence and involvement in the drafting process, Augustus claims that he was motivated to demonstrate his (and, less importantly, the Senate's) concern for provincials' well-being.[174] This *senatus consultum* was a general change in legislation affecting every province, apparently extending the scope of *repetundae* to cover any appropriation of property. The framing of this decree as the product of the Senate and Princeps in concert presents a fundamental shift from the imperial discourse of the Republic. This practice of embedding senatorial pronouncements in imperial *edicta* became commonplace under the later Principes, though this never became an exclusive practice.[175] The Princeps' position as the incontestable source of legitimate authority, while in its infancy in the last years of the millennium, simplified the situation for *poleis* in understanding and responding to imperial power.

The dossier of Paullus Fabius Maximus provides an example of a governor using an *edictum* rather than correspondence to effect his will.[176] The document opens with a lengthy panegyric praising Augustus for rescuing the state from civil war.[177] Consequently, Paullus suggests that: *πασῶν τῶν πολειτηῶν εἶναι μίαν καὶ τὴν αὐτὴν νέαν νουμενίαν | τὴν τοῦ θηοτάτου Καίσαρος γενέθλιον, ἐκείνῃ τε πάντας εἰς τὴν | ἀρχὴν ἐνβαίνειν* ('all the communities celebrate the new year on one and the same day, the birthday of the most divine Caesar, and that all magistrates enter office on that day').[178] The introduction of the new calendar had the effect of 'Romanizing' time for provincials, collocating the local past and imperial present. The regularization of time across the *provincia* in ideologically

[173] *IG* 12.2.44; Quint. *Inst.* 6.3.77; *Anth. Pal.* 9.419, 516, 599. Arrayás Morales 2010, 144–5. On Crinagoras: Gow & Page 1963, 2.210–13; Bowersock 1965, 36–7, see Chapter 7 'The Institutionalization of Personal Relationships'.

[174] *RDGE* 31.72–73.

[175] E.g., the *senatus consultum de Cn. Pisone patre* in 29 CE (Eck, Caballos, & Fernández 1996).

[176] *RDGE* 65. Further commentary in Laffi 1967, 5–98; see now Dreyer & Engelmann 2006, 175–82.

[177] *RDGE* 65.A.1–9.

[178] *RDGE* 65.A.21–23.

charged terms echoed the unity of imperial rule, while Stern has highlighted the parallels between the simplicity of autocratic rule and the predictability of the Julian calendar.[179] However, this outcome does not require that Roman actors were motivated in similar terms. As Burrell notes, the edict's tone is 'hortatory rather than imperative'.[180] Paullus does not, or cannot, require that the *poleis* alter their calendars, but justifies his proposition by reference to Augustus' manifest good qualities. Through the *καὶ ἐπεὶ* clause, Paullus attempts to establish not only that Augustus' birthday is a day of good fortune, but also that the change involved would not be that great.[181] Paullus frames his decision as a proposal rather than a command (*δοκεῖ μοι*), noting that the impetus and process should come from the *koinon*: *ψήφισμα δὲ ὑπὸ τοῦ κοινοῦ τῆς Ἀσίας δεή|σει...ἵνα τὸ ἐπινοη|θὲν ὑφ' ἡμῶν εἰς τὴν τειμὴν τοῦ Σεβαστοῦ μείνῃ αἰώνιον* ('a decree of the *koinon* of Asia is necessary...so that our plan for the honour of Augustus may remain forever').[182] The proconsul's decision is mediated through the *koinon*'s action.[183] Overall, Paullus' *edictum* places the commander in an intriguing position. While the communal response is analysed in Chapter 8, Paullus unambiguously frames this decision as beyond his own remit and connives at elevating Augustus' reputation within the *provincia*.[184]

The *edictum* of Sex. Sotidius Strabo Libuscidianus, *legatus pro praetore* of Galatia, most likely from 14–15 CE, concerning the requisitioning of transport by public officials, provides a useful comparandum for the ideological changes associated with the Principate.[185] Sotidius' decree reasserted that the *polis* of Sagalassos was required to provide transportation in specific cases, in return for a fixed rate of payment. The text implies that prior to his intervention private individuals were insisting on their right to use the service, while others were refusing payment. The imperial authorities on the ground reacted to information rather than spontaneously implementing policy.[186] The text appears in both Latin and Greek translation and provides instructions for its display in the *πολεῖς καὶ κῶμαι* of Sagalassos' territory. Indeed, the governor explicitly links knowledge of the *edictum* to its observation.[187] Crucially, the text overtly draws on the Princeps and his predecessor to bolster gubernatorial authority:

179 Stern 2012, 222–7; Heller 2014, 228; Dench 2018, 134–5.

180 Burrell 2004, 371.

181 Thonemann (2015, 123–4) notes that the *koinon* decrees assume calendars of Asia were already synchronized, something demonstrably untrue.

182 *RDGE* 65.A.26–28.

183 Heller 2014, 225.

184 E.g., the inclusion of the adjective *θειότατος* to describe Augustus in the Greek copy (Sherk 1969, 337).

185 On the date: Mitchell 1976, 113; contra Coşkun (2009, 159–61) who favours a date after 20 CE.

186 Mitchell 1976, 111–12.

187 *SEG* 26.1392.5–6=29. This copy seems to have been displayed in such a secondary context, *pace* Mitchell 1976, 110–11, 116.

> *ὅν τη|ρήσω οὐ μόνον δι᾽ ἐμαυτοῦ, ἀλλὰ ἐὰν δεῇ καὶ τὴν τοῦ σωτῆρος Σεβαστοὺ δεδωκότος μοι | περὶ τούτων ἐντολ[ὰς] προσπαραλαβὼν θειότητα* ('which I will ensure not only with my own [*potestas*] but, if this is neglected, bringing in as support the *maiestas* of the saviour Augustus, who gave me *mandata* concerning these things').[188]

Sotidius states his reluctance to intervene at all in the prescript to his pronouncement, noting the 'injustice' (*iniquissimum*/*ἄδικον*) of his tightening of regulations which are already cared for diligently by *Augusti alter deorum alter principum | maximus* ('the *Augusti*, one the greatest of gods, the other of *Principes*').[189] Instead, he offers a clear hierarchy of administrative practice and imperial authority. Both Augustus and Tiberius have shown the greatest care about the provision and use of vehicles, implying that a pronouncement or *edictum* had been issued to regulate practice.[190] The current Princeps had also issued *ἐντολαί* (Lat. *mandata*, Eng. 'instructions') to the commander delineating his responsibilities and how administration should be carried out. The Greek, at least, implies specific reference to this issue (*περὶ τούτων ἐντολ[ὰς]*).[191] Finally, the commander himself, in the *provincia*, has seen that these regulations are not being enforced adequately, and has issued this *edictum* to clarify matters, while ensuring that the specifics of his decision are publicly displayed in several places throughout the relevant civic territory.

Unlike earlier commanders, Sotidius emphasizes the legitimacy of his right to decide on this issue, invoking the Principes deliberately. This might indicate a tendency for aggrieved individuals to appeal gubernatorial decisions to central authorities. Domitius Corbulo's letter to Cos, under Claudius, similarly attempted to head off potential appeals by underlining the crucial role of the Princeps in crafting imperial policy.[192] While proconsular commanders maintained *stricto sensu* the same *imperium* and *iurisdictio* as their Republican counterparts, that is, their right to make legally binding decisions within their *provincia*, the realities of the Princeps' unchallenged authority created problems of legitimacy within the provincial context. For *legati*, this situation was exacerbated by their direct, legal subordination to the Princeps: their receipt of their *imperium* by delegation under his *auspicia*.[193] Though provincial communities had a long history of appealing to the Senate, they appear to have quickly adjusted to the Princeps' central position. The perception that legitimate power proceeded from Augustus and his successors provoked a shift in emphasis from magistrates and appointed officials. Rather

[188] *SEG* 26.1392.29–31; compare ll.6–7.

[189] *SEG* 26.1392.3–4.

[190] Edmondson 2014, 133.

[191] This is the earliest example of a magistrate referring to imperial *mandata* in his own *edictum*, but it seems reasonable to extend this practice further back into Augustus' reign, at least for his *legati*: Mitchell 1976, 116.

[192] *SEG* 29.751.6–10.

[193] Vervaet 2014, 20; Drogula 2015, 355–6.

than issuing ordinances secure in their own authority, increasingly they appealed to their relationship with the Princeps. In turn, this institutionalized the situation, further marginalizing provincial commanders.[194]

We witness this transformation in action through the Cyme dossier, already discussed in Chapter 4. The language of the consular *edictum* issued by Augustus and Agrippa is strongly prohibitive, consisting of a series of negative imperatives: for example, *μηδεὶς... αἰρέτω μηδὲ ἀγοραζέτω μηδὲ ἀπὸ μηδενὸς δῶρον λαμβανέτω...* ('let no-one take, nor buy, nor accept from someone as a gift...').[195] The topic, the restoration of sacred lands which have become privatized in the course of the civil wars, represents a specific concern of Augustus, as *Res Gestae* 24.1 shows, the only provincial act mentioned in that text.[196] Vinicius' letter to Cyme raises different issues. The elision of Cymaean institutions, in simply addressing the archons, is striking, as is the fact that letter arises out of a local disagreement. Here, however, the crucial elements are the language and formulae used by Vinicius. First, he employs the abbreviated Latin formula *e(go) v(olo) v(os) c(urare)...* ('I want you to ensure...').[197] Though precisely how this was rendered in the Greek copy remains unclear, the clause constructs an implied hierarchy between the proconsul and Cyme. Though avoiding direct imperatives, the use of *volo* leans on his authority as a Roman magistrate. It establishes a standard of behaviour based on will rather than normative documents. That said, the proconsul explicitly formulates the *edictum* as a command (*iussum*) of Augustus, suggesting that he himself regarded the text as such, binding his actions and those of the disputants.[198] Moreover, the letter ends by invoking a Roman system of justice and mediation if the local authorities wish to use them. This framework asserts linguistically the power of Roman magistrates to subvert the normal relationships between local communities and their own citizens. Both elements illustrate a shift towards a more hierarchized relationship between local political communities and Roman authorities during this period.

Intriguingly, Vinicius' instructions exceed the requirements implied by the consuls' *edictum*, raising the question of how the two documents relate to one another. The *edictum* is not specific to Cyme, though limited to *provincia Asia*, and Vinicius likely cited it in his correspondence to give weight to his own decision. However, given that the *edictum* was raised initially by the plaintiffs, the *thiasoi* of Dionysus at Cyme, it seems more plausible that the decision to include the *edictum* occurred at a local level.[199] Most interesting is Vinicius'

[194] Kokkinia 2009, 191–4. [195] Crook 1962, ll.5–8.

[196] *RGDA* 24.1. Compare Oliver's restoration of IG^2 1035.8–10 (1972, 192, accepted by Ando (forthcoming), 10).

[197] Crook 1962, l.17. [198] Ando (forthcoming).

[199] Hurlet 2006, 208; Dalla Rosa 2014, 128–9. See Chapter 4, 'Augustus as Princeps: The Cyme Dossier'.

requirement that when restored, the shrine be inscribed with *Imp. Caesar deivi f. Augustus restituit* ('Imperator Caesar, son of the god, Augustus restored [sc. this shrine]'). This echoes Augustus' rhetoric in the *Res Gestae* but does not appear in the *edictum*, suggesting the proconsul acquired these instructions elsewhere.

Other changes in administrative practice under Augustus had an impact on the discourse of Roman power. In the penultimate decade of the first century, C. Norbanus Flaccus, *pro consule* in Asia, wrote to the archons, *boule*, and *demos* of Aezani in response to an embassy from the city. In language typical of a Hellenistic dynast, Norbanus notes his reception of Aezani's ambassadors and his personal wish to increase the privileges (φιλάνθρωπα) of the city. However, unlike other examples, he received not a local decree, but a letter from Augustus.[200]

> *Ἐκ Περγάμου | Γάϊος Νωρβανὸς Φλάκκος ἀνθύπατος Αἰζανειτῶν | ἄρχουσι, βουλῆι, δήμωι vac χαίρειν· | Μενεκλῆς καὶ Ἱέραξ καὶ Ζήνων οἱ πρεσβευταὶ ὑμῶν | ἀνέδωκάν μοι Σ[ε]βαστοῦ Καίσαρος ἐπιστολήν, ἐν ᾗ[ι] | ἐγέγραπτο συνκεχωρηκέναι ὑμ̣ῖν ἐκκ̣λησίαν | συνάγε̣ι̣ν̣ Ὀφίλι̣[ο]ν̣ Ὀρ̣ν̣ᾶτ̣ον ἐπίτροπ̣ο̣ν̣ [π]ε̣ρ̣ὶ [ἀ]τ̣ε[λ]ε̣ί̣α̣ς̣ τ̣ῷ̣ι̣ [ἱε]|ρεῖ θ̣υ̣σ̣ι̣ῶ̣ν̣ ἕ̣νεκα, μ̣ὴ συνχωρήσειν δ' ἄ̣λ̣λ̣α̣ σ̣υ̣ν̣τ̣ε̣λ̣ε̣ῖ̣ν̣ τ̣ὴ̣ν̣ | πόλιν· vac ἐγὼ οὖν συναύξειν βουλόμενος τ̣ὰ φιλά[νθρω]|πα τῆς πόλεως ὑμῶν ἐπιτρέπω κατὰ τὸ συνχώρημα | τοῦ Κ̣αίσ[αρος — | —] δε δ̣ιαταξ[ιν?]*... ('From Pergamum. Gaius Norbanus Flaccus, proconsul, to the archons, council and people of the Aezanetans, greetings. Menecles, Hierax and Zeno, your ambassadors, gave me the letter of Augustus Caesar, in which he wrote that Ofilius Ornatus, procurator, had allowed your assembly to come together concerning the *ateleia* of the priest, on account of the sacrifices, but will not allow that the city offer anything further. Therefore, I, wishing to increase the privileges of your city, yield (?) to the decision of Caesar... *edictum*(?)...')[201]

This fascinating letter encapsulates the tension between traditional and novel discourses of power during the period under investigation. In its structure and the personal motivation offered by Norbanus the document closely follows the model of earlier Roman magistrates and ultimately of Hellenistic kings. However, the references to a letter of Augustus and the decision of a procurator highlight the existence of competing sources of authority. This inverts the traditional structure of civic–gubernatorial interactions. Rather than the civic community making their own resolution and engaging in dialogue with the commander, the Aezanetans or the procurator Ofilius had already consulted the Princeps directly and received a response, prompting the embassy. Nevertheless, Norbanus' response appropriates themes and language from an earlier era. He evokes his personal wish to increase the privileges of the city in the same format as second-century

[200] Compare C. Cornelius Dolabella receiving a *senatus consultum* in *c.* 80: *RDGE* 21.4.

[201] *SEG* 61.1134, updating *MAMA* 9.13.

commanders: *ἐγὼ οὖν συναύξειν βουλόμενος τὰ φιλά[νθρω]|πα τῆς πόλεως ὑμῶν* ('therefore, I wish to increase the privileges of your *polis*') and commits to uphold the concessions granted by Augustus (*ἐπιτρέπω κατὰ τὸ συνχώρημα | τοῦ Καίσ[αρος]*).[202] As already noted, the verb *ἐπιτρέπειν* has a wide semantic range. Unfortunately, the stone breaks off, leaving limited clues to Norbanus' intent. A final hint may be preserved in the final extant line with the appearance of *διαταξ*—, almost certainly *διάταξις*, possibly an *edictum* either from the imperial centre, or, more likely, from the commander himself.[203]

The letter's subject further alludes to the major administrative changes underway in this period. That a procurator interfered in the internal civic process of a *polis* subject to the *imperium* of the proconsul of Asia so early into Augustus' principate is striking. Wörrle notes that this implies not only that *procuratores* had a strong personal relationship with the Princeps which could be adduced to lend authority to their actions, but also that from the beginning of the Principate they had an implied mandate to act beyond imperial estates, offering Augustus (indirect) agency in the *provinciae* while he consolidated his power.[204] Given Tiberius' later statement that Lucilius Capito, as procurator in Asia, was restricted to operating in imperial domains, it seems clear that this was an informal development based on networks and implication than a statutorily defined capacity of the office.[205] In any case, Ofilius' decision, authorized by Augustus before offered to Norbanus for approval, demonstrates ongoing evolution in hierarchies and discourse. While his letter was published at Aezani, it stresses in practice the proconsul's excision from the decision-making process: Norbanus acts only to lend his approval to a fait accompli. By contrast, the text emphasizes his own agency so far as possible.[206] Nevertheless, this gloss cannot but reinforce the critical role played by both procurator and Princeps in deciding the fate of the civic reform. This represents a highly visible direct action by the Princeps in a small *polis* in rural Phrygia. Augustus' rise to clear supremacy had not only fundamentally altered the shape of the central Roman constitution, but also had a commensurate impact on the lived experience of Roman rule and the emissions of the Roman state in a provincial setting.

Finally, Augustus' response to the Samian request for *ἐλευθερία* reinforces the changing discourse of empire. In emphasizing the unique status of Aphrodisias, Augustus' use of the first person is not coincidental, if misleading. As noted, the Aphrodisian archive includes the *senatus consultum* granting freedom to their community, which drew on a recommendation by both

[202] *SEG* 61.1134.9–11.

[203] *SEG* 61.1134.12. Compare *TLG* s.v. *διάταξις*. Note, however, *IGR* 4.1188 and *OGIS* 484.36–37, referring to local documents and regulations.

[204] Wörrle 2011, 367–71.

[205] See Chapter 4, 'Augustan *procuratores*'.

[206] Compare *RGDE* 70.2–4, (late first century) where the governor emphasizes his 'general procedure' in judging disputes.

Octavian and Antonius.[207] Though dating this response after Actium provides a strong motive for this framing, other examples from this dossier emphasize that such personalizing discourse was already a feature of official correspondence. More importantly, from an ideological perspective, Augustus explicitly affirms a principle of reciprocity governing his decisions on matters of civic privilege, albeit rooted in a distinctively Roman framework: *οὐ γάρ ἐστιν δίκαιον τὸ πάντων μέγιστον φιλάνθρωπον εἰκῇ καὶ χωρὶς αἰτίας χαρίζεσθαι* ('for it is not right to grant the greatest privilege of all at random and without cause').[208] Freedom, including immunity from Roman taxation and removal from the *formula provinciae*, cannot be taken for granted but required commensurate displays of loyalty (*fides*).[209] The specific framing of the sack of Aphrodisias by Labienus as *ἐν τῷ πολέμῳ τὰ ἐμὰ φρονήσας δοριάλωτος διὰ τὴν πρὸς ἡμᾶς εὔνοιαν* ('taking *my* side in the war, on account of goodwill towards us, [the city] was captured by storm') personalized the experience of empire.[210] In Augustus' contentious narrative, for the consumption of the Samians at least, Aphrodisias was not rewarded for its suffering in service to Rome, but to him alone. The cue provided by this letter is unmissable. Even Livia's support was insufficient to ensure imperial benefaction. The public expression of loyalty through action must precede Augustus' euergetism. The Princeps through his correspondence established a new framework for the Samians and other communities to relate to the state; one based on personal loyalty in return for civic privileges.

Overall, Augustus' new position as the de facto head of the *res publica* inaugurated a new phase in the dialogue between the Roman state and provincial communities. Though the organs of the Republican state, the Senate, People, and magistrates, continued to exist and operate, the presence of an unambiguous authority provided a focal point for petitions, embassies, and requests.[211] The formation of new policy-making institutions around the Princeps allowed a greater consistency of language, policy, and action to develop. This marked the definitive commencement of a new type of dialogue between Augustus, representing the Roman state, and communities seeking redress or favour.

Summary

This chapter has investigated the role played by official Roman documents in formulating and supporting a discourse of provincial administration. The utterances of the Roman state were 'speech-acts', creating an ideological framework to

[207] *IAph2007* 8.32.2–3. Contrast 8.25.26. [208] *IAph2007* 8.32.4.
[209] Chaniotis 2015, 89–90. [210] *IAph2007* 8.32.3.
[211] Note the Principes' capacity for direct action and to pressure the Senate or instruct governors. Edmondson 2014, 131–7; Ando (forthcoming).

support the structural elements of administration. However, to be successful such acts must be both understood by recipients and accepted as legitimate. The advent of Roman rule disrupted existing modes of interaction between *poleis* and their rulers, but the creation of a new language of power was neither simple nor co-ordinated. At the fundamental level, the structural differences between the Roman Republic and the Attalid monarchy had a profound impact. In place of a single perceived locus of legitimate normative material, the *basileus*—and, through him, his subordinates—the *res publica* dispersed power and authority through different state institutions; the Senate, *comitia*, and magistrates. The impracticalities of co-ordinating policy and, especially, language across these institutions ensured that an emergent Roman discourse of power was slow to coalesce. A personal relationship based on reciprocity, such as that between *polis* and *basileus*, was impossible in the Republican system: the new 'rules of the game' had not yet been compiled. Crucially, the Republic itself was caught in the throes of its own evolution during this period, further complicating the task of the Asian *poleis*.

The radical transformation prompted by Sulla's reorganization of Asia had a significant impact on the official communication between the state and local communities. The evidence reveals greater interconnectedness between different genres, with extant *leges*, *senatus consulta*, and magistrates' decisions consciously interacting to create a complex composite of legitimacy and authority. This flexible deployment of Republican institutions shows, from a Roman perspective, the system working—the Senate, People, and magistrates operating collectively to authorize specific outcomes. However, from a civic perspective, such diversity continued to create problems of interpretation.

Caesar's dictatorship and the triumviral period witnessed the continued personalization of legitimate authority: though the Senate and People continued to issue administrative documents the surviving evidence increasingly takes the form of *edicta* and letters. The experimental nature of triumviral rule saw innovations in practice, and the example of Octavian shows that consistency and reproducibility of form and language was not the natural result of an increasingly circumscribed group of authors. Nevertheless, as the Principate became consolidated Augustus came to be viewed as the unambiguous, ultimate source of authoritative rulings. The relative institutional stability provided by Augustus' reign and the increasing concentration of legitimate authority in his person created conditions in which imperial discourse became coherent. This is not to comment on the administrative effectiveness of the monarchical system established after 27 BCE, but rather to note that the (re-)emergence of an unambiguous hierarchy, with a single locus of authority at its head, created conditions conducive to the development of a single discourse of power. Consequently, under the lengthy reign of Augustus, *poleis* had the time to learn a new language of engagement with Rome, the new 'rules of the game', and strategies through which to subvert them.

6

The ‘Politics of Honour’

Learning a New Set of Rules

Civic Decrees and Honorific Practices in Asia

Civic decrees, the decisions of the political institutions of a *polis*, most directly articulate the voice of the civic community. When searching for the provincial side of the dialogue with Roman power, such utterances are the logical starting point. Though decrees of the late Hellenistic and Roman period varied in their choice of language and their initiating bodies, they tended to follow a standard format. Generally, this began with preamble including a dating formula and an expression of the responsible body or bodies, sometimes naming the proposing officials. After this, the decree opened with a motivation clause, introduced by *ἐπεί* or *ἐπειδή*, giving the reasons behind the decision. Occasionally, a hortative clause followed, describing the intent of the decree in broad terms, introduced by *ὅπως* or *ἵνα*. Finally, the impersonal *ἔδοξεν* or *δεδόχθαι* presented the resolutions themselves: the collective decision of the community.[1]

While these texts purport to offer a straightforward declaration of the will of the community, as finished products they elided disagreement and debate in the process.[2] Most often, the text preserved was not the product of negotiation within the assembly but one which had been referred en bloc from the *boule*.[3] Consequently, we cannot assume that any extant decree represented a universal or enduring decision.[4] Nevertheless, as the final recorded and displayed text, the surviving documents carried the authority of civic political institutions and acted as the voice for the whole community.

[1] The framing and terminology are Ma’s (1999, 183–4); this structure persisted into the imperial period: Zuiderhoek 2008, 418–19.

[2] Compare, for example, the striking affective claim of the Aphrodisians in 88: *πᾶς ὁ δῆμος ἡμῶν σὺν γυναιξὶ | καὶ τέκνοις καὶ τῷ παντὶ βίῳ ἑτ<οῖ>μος παραβάλλεσθαι ὑπὲρ | Κοΐντου καὶ τῶν Ῥωμαίων πραγμάτων καὶ ὅτι χωρὶς τῆς | Ῥωμαίων ἡγεμονίας οὐδὲ ζῆν προαιρούμεθα* (‘our whole *demos*, together with our wives and children and all our property, is ready (?) to risk all for Quintus and the Roman cause; and that without the hegemony of the Romans we do not choose even to live’, *IAph2007* 8.3.b.2.11–4), which Chaniotis (2013, 747–55) argues sought to unify the community after a difficult debate on whether to aid the Romans against Mithridates.

[3] Rhodes & Lewis 1997, 475–97, 511; Fernoux 2011, 223–6.

[4] E.g., Livy’s account (32.22), based on Polybius, of the divisions in the Achaean assembly in 198, with the delegates from Argos, Dyme, and Megalopolis leaving the meeting. Compare Cicero *Flacc.* 16–7.

Imperial Power, Provincial Government, and the Emergence of Roman Asia, 133 BCE*–14* CE. Bradley Jordan, Oxford University Press. © Bradley Jordan 2023. DOI: 10.1093/oso/9780198887065.003.0007

Honorific decrees had multiple audiences, including the honorand themselves and equally members of the honouring community. Public recognition of an individual's worth to and within the *polis* community had significant implications. While the positive judgement of the *demos* and/or *boule* offered recipients political and social capital, its acceptance and, increasingly, permanent inscription reasserted the primacy of civic institutions as the gatekeepers of honour. At least initially, most recipients were local citizens; minor benefactors who remained members of the *demos* and were contained within it, even if tension inevitably existed between social competitiveness and the communitarian ethos of the *polis*.[5] This dialectic also proved a useful mechanism for wrangling with powerful, external figures: namely Hellenistic rulers and Romans. Ma's description of the relationship between Antiochus III and the *poleis* of Asia presents a robust paradigm for the former.[6] Despite the comparative complexity of Roman administration, the letter of Q. Oppius to Aphrodisias, often treated as paradigmatic, follows exactly this model.[7] However, traditional Roman notions of aristocratic honour tended to be more personally and less publicly constructed. Nevertheless, amid the competitive environment of the late Republican political elite, individuals did not shirk the opportunity presented by the civic honorific practice. As Roman power became increasingly concentrated and the institutions of the Principate coalesced, the civic decree became an integral part of the imperial system. The 'politics of honour', as the title of a recent volume puts it, were integral to local strategies for co-opting Roman assistance and goodwill.[8] As such, this chapter analyses the ways in which the language of honorific practice adapted to the emergence of Roman hegemony in Asia.

Patrons, Saviours, and Benefactors? Honorific Decrees and Roman Magistrates

Throughout the late Republic and early Principate, *poleis* passed honorific decrees and erected public statues for Romans, co-opting the official representatives of the hegemonic power into their existing networks of honour. However, for the most part our evidence derives not from full honorific decrees but from inscribed statue-bases which provide a truncated summary of the interaction between community and individual. The standard formula, ὁ δῆμος τὸν δεῖνον τοῦ δεῖνου

[5] Gauthier (2011 [1984], 315–40 contra Veyne 1976) and Heller (2016, 74) dating the acceleration of this practice to the mid-second century. Ma (2013, 49–55 70–5) convincingly argues that civic institutions retained a remarkable degree of control over the nature of the award into the imperial period.

[6] Ma 1999, 179–242. See now Heller & van Nijf (2017, 1–8) generally and Chin (2018, 121–37) on Attalus III.

[7] *IAph2007* 8.2.b.1.2–12. See Chapter 5.

[8] Heller & van Nijf 2017, 10–13.

ἀρέτης ἕνεκα καὶ εὐνοίας (ἐτίμησεν) ('The *demos* (honoured) X son of Y, on account of his excellence and goodwill'), tends to elide differences between the actions of individual honorands.[9] Comparatively, surviving monuments for local benefactors more often preserve the full honorific text, even where a statue was the result, thereby presenting a full civic-orientated account of an individual's career and encouraging its enduring local value as an exemplum of correct behaviour.[10] Frija argues that the relative dearth of full decrees on monuments for Roman benefactors was deliberate and that the reduced size of the honorific vocabulary employed afforded *poleis* flexibility in dealing with officials. The vague moral qualities invoked allowed them to honour a typical Roman commander simply for his administrative competence or solely on the basis of his position. In her view, these changes mark the introduction of routine honours for Romans grounded in the fact of their magistracy.[11] However, as Heller has demonstrated, the first century saw a drastic shift away from the inscription of full decrees in favour of more condensed statue-bases relying on 'titles' as shorthand for local benefactors as well.[12] Consequently, it is likely that such longer documents were almost certainly produced for both Roman and local benefactors, even if they were no longer routinely inscribed.

In form, this process echoes the spirit of the earlier dialogue between *basileus* and *polis*.[13] Critically however, unlike their Hellenistic forebears or Imperial successors, Republican commanders directly competed with one another for prestige in the form of political success at Rome. A magistrate's reputation within his *provincia* could have a significant impact on their subsequent career. Without claiming that the threat of *repetundae* charges successfully restrained rapacious governors, honorific decrees did assert the existence of a rapport between community and honorand, making later prosecution less likely. Furthermore, local honorific decrees could be adduced by a defendant as evidence that the prosecution was promoted by individual malcontents, rather than the *polis* writ large.[14] Governors had a direct interest in soliciting honours. In turn, pressure from magistrates, combined with the increasing personalization of influence through the spread of patronage, promoted innovation in the honorific system. Governors could pressure communities indirectly, through their presence, absence, and responsiveness to their petitions, or directly, through the use and abuse of their power. However, crucial to generating this climate of innovation was the competition between cities to establish and maintain meaningful relationships with

[9] Ma (2013, 45–63) and Stoop (2017, 24–5) highlight that even this bland formulation reveals something of civic agency. Compare Frija 2014, 86–90.

[10] E.g., the Claros decrees for Menippus and Polemaeus (*SEG* 39.1243–4). Santangelo 2009, 68–73.

[11] Frija 2014, 81–90. Compare Stoop 2017, 28–9.

[12] Heller 2016, 75–8.

[13] E.g., Ma 1999, 194–242.

[14] Esp. Cic. *Verr.* 2.2.154, 4.138–9; *Flacc.* 16–18, 34–8, 42–58. Compare, later, Trajan's recourse to honorific statues as a proxy for behaviour: Plin. *Ep.* 10.60. Stoop 2017, 10–15, 30–1.

governors. Levers available to *poleis* were limited to direct gifts, which were technically prohibited, or honorific decrees.[15] Given the logical proliferation of the latter, the question of how to approach governors posed itself to the communities and they responded with a variety of strategies.

The corpus of identifiable honorific inscriptions (Table 6.1) relating to Roman officials and their immediate family members originating from poleis in *provincia* Asia between 133 BCE and 20 CE amounts to 130 texts relating to sixty-four individual officials, with an increasing number of inscriptions, though not honorands, under the Augustan regime.[16] The data immediately reveals some broad trends: from 133 to the outbreak of civil war in 49 governors and their immediate family were the primary though not exclusive recipients of honorific statues, named on twenty-four occasions. By contrast, *legati* received statues on nine occasions, of which four are directly related to military commanders.[17] Finally, sixteen statue-bases survive for quaestors, though three were for Lucullus who played a role in mitigating the impact of Sulla's demands in the late 80s, and nine more date between 55 and 49. By contrast, during the civil war period, taken here as 49–30, when proconsular appointments broke down, only one governor received honorific statues, the popular Vatia Isauricus, while sixteen *legati* were recognized. Finally, under Augustus the ratio of gubernatorial to other recipients increases substantially: forty-five governors, one potential *legatus*, and only five honorific decrees for *quaestores*. The increasingly circumscribed roles for *legati* accompanying magistrates and provincial *quaestores* under the Augustan regime explain this evolution: the limited opportunities to become acting governor reduced the opportunities available to become useful to *poleis*.[18] The overwhelming majority of these inscriptions originated with the *demos*, though there are five examples of the *boule* being involved in the process and five of wider communities, re-emphasizing the extent to which civic assemblies retained control over the award and the dialogue around honour during this period.

While the issuance of honorific decrees and the erection of statues for Roman officials remained an important phenomenon across the period, the euergetic language employed and inscribed underwent noticeable changes. Prior to the outbreak of the First Mithridatic War in 88, only one of seven documents, that honouring the *legatus* M. Popillius Laenas on Cos, used a traditional Hellenistic title: that of εὐεργέτης ('benefactor'). However, even here this term was paired

[15] Cic. *Att.* 5.21.7, 11. Bérenger 2011, 174. Note also Stoop (2017, 15–18) on statues as a vehicle for financial gain.

[16] Table 6.1.

[17] Military: A. Terentius Varro; C. Sornantius Barba; C. Salluvius Naso.

[18] Erkelenz (2003, 52–5), noting his belief that the extant record for governors in the Republican period is artificially low. On *legati* and *quaestores* as interim Republican governors see, for example, Cic. *Att.* 6.4.1, 5.3, 6.3–4; *Fam.* 2.15.4, 18.2–3. The significant range of action afforded to the *quaestor pro praetore*, P. Cornelius Scipio, honoured at Messene in 3/4 CE seems to be the result of an exceptional mission (*SEG* 63.289, with Jones 2019, 40, 42–3).

with the transliterated Latin term *πάτρων* (*patron*).[19] Indeed, during the 90s BCE, a number of Greek cities chose to honour Roman magistrates with this Latin term. Eilers and Milner plausibly supply the epithet *πάτρων τᾶς πόλιος* ('*patron* of the city') in another Coan statue base, honouring the son of Q. Mucius Scaevola, and an Ephesian inscription for his wife Caelia.[20] The brothers C. and L. Valerius Flaccus were similarly honoured at Claros.[21] Two other early examples, for Popillius at Magnesia-on-the-Maeander and Scaevola, again via his son, at Nysa include no titles, simply honouring both in traditional terms for their *ἀρετή* and *εὔνοια*.[22]

Despite the small sample size, the frequent use of the transliterated Latin term *patron* rather than the existing repertoire of honorific language is significant. Neither Greeks nor Romans viewed the term as synonymous with existing Greek labels. This represented the deliberate deployment of a Roman concept to honour Roman magistrates.[23] However, *ipso facto*, this amalgamated civic honorific practice and Roman social institutions in a novel way. Patronage, for Roman aristocrats, was not in itself an honorific position: though having numerous and significant individuals in one's *clientela* demonstrated one's worth and influence within the political community, the patron–client relationship was often a formal consensual agreement. This was equally true of civic communities. Here the language of patronage was co-opted into a new concept drawing on the Classical and Hellenistic institution of *proxenia* to construct a Roman-specific honorific relationship.[24] This is perhaps unsurprising, given that the services provided by *πάτρωνες* in the earliest Greek decrees from Teos and Colophon are precisely grounded in helping ambassadors navigate the unfamiliar Roman institutional and political landscape.[25] The choice of *poleis* from the 90s to use a novel technical term *πάτρων* to honour Roman magistrates represents a negotiated outcome arising from Roman social discourse and local practice.[26] However, the upheaval generated by Mithridates' invasion of Asia in 88 disrupted these early moves towards a standard practice.

After Dardanus, communities were forced to adapt to a new administrative reality. Despite most *poleis* being subjected to gubernatorial jurisdiction and

[19] *I.Cos* 225. Compare *AÉ* 1995, #1538.

[20] *SEG* 45.1128. Eilers & Milner 1995, 78–81, 83.

[21] Though the texts are identical, the monuments differ markedly, suggesting that they were produced separately. Ferrary 2000a, 334–7. Compare *I.Magnesia* 144–46, which *pace* Erkelenz (2003), likely date to the 60s.

[22] *I.Magnesia* 123; *SEG* 57.1104. Raßelnberg (2007, 52–4) working from the large size of the latter monument convincingly suggests it honoured other family members, including the proconsul himself.

[23] Ferrary 1997, 208–12; Eilers 2002, 110–12; Bloy 2012, 181–3.

[24] *Proxenia*, though rooted in the same ideals of benefaction and reciprocity, was an inter-*polis* institution, in which one community honoured an individual from another community, who would assist their citizens in their activities within his place of residence. While often involving the grant of specific privileges, *proxenia* did gain an honorific element. Mack 2015, 22–5, 81–9; Domingo Gygax 2016, 109–14.

[25] *Syll.*³ 656; *SEG* 39.1243, 1244.

[26] Bloy 2012, 182–3.

regular taxation, their capacity to honour individuals through civic decrees remained untouched. As one of few remaining levers to generate favourable outcomes, it is unsurprising to see cities continuing to elevate commanders, who had their own reasons to encourage the practice. One fascinating consequence of this change was the revival of traditional Hellenistic honorific language.[27] Of twenty-nine extant honorific inscriptions for Roman governors between the denouement of the First Mithridatic War and Augustus' consolidation of power in the early 20s, only five use the title *πάτρων*, three of which belong to Q. Cicero: at Claros and twice at Samos. A fourth example, also from Claros, honoured L. Valerius Flaccus, his predecessor, and hereditary *πάτρων* through his father. The final example is a shadowy L. Cornelius Lentulus, attested at Labraunda.[28] All but the last were also called *εὐεργέτης*, a title which appears in nine other inscriptions, five times alongside *σωτήρ*. Honours for *legati* and *quaestores* during the same period exhibit a similar pattern, albeit including greater proportion of *πάτρωνες*. The numbers for *quaestores* and *legati* are close to identical: in the period, for each group thirteen inscriptions (of fifteen, in the former, and of sixteen in the latter case) address *εὐεργέται*; ten *πάτρωνες*; and four *σωτῆρες*. Given that these officials had less scope to materially benefit *poleis*, more substantial links might be expected.[29] In the quaestorian case, of the ten surviving inscriptions for *patroni* four belong to L. Antonius, brother of the later *triumvir* during his period of temporary governorship in 49, and two to Lucullus, which suggests the phenomenon was more limited in practice.[30]

These Hellenistic titles had diverse origins and implications, offering *poleis* the opportunity to differentiate between recipients. The generic *εὐεργέτης* originally implied admission to a category of non-citizens with privileged status within a civic community, akin to *πρόξενος*. Nevertheless, it was consistently employed as an honorific title from at least the fifth century.[31] By contrast, *σωτήρ* was originally applied to divine figures, and *κτίστης* to semi-divine or legendary founders. Both came to be applied to Hellenistic rulers in an honorific capacity.[32] Bloy suggests that this titulature allowed *poleis* to better articulate their relationship with Roman

[27] Nichols (1990, 81, 2014, 71) notes this resurgence of traditional titulature compared to civic patronage without analysis.

[28] Q. Cicero: Ferrary (2000a), #6, Kajava #24a, *IGR* 4.1713; L. Flaccus: Ferrary (2000a), #5; L. Lentulus: *I.Labraunda* 63.

[29] Table 6.1. Of the attested *quaestores*, L. Antonius served as interim governor after the departure of Q. Minucius Thermus in 50, under the terms of the *lex Pompeia de provinciis* (Marshall 1972, 898–911, with Cic. *Fam.* 2.18.2–3), while C. Scribonius Curio, who was still returning to Italy in late 53/early 52 (Cic. *Fam.* 2.6.1; *Phil.* 2.4), seems likely to have done so for C. Claudius Pulcher.

[30] With two exceptions (Lucullus in the 80s and Q. Aemilius Lepidus in 15–13), every combination *σωτήρ καὶ πάτρων* occurs between 50 and 37 and was awarded to a *quaestor* or *legatus*. This could indicate that the goodwill of a Roman official was particularly sought after in this period of instability.

[31] Gauthier 1985, 22–4, 33–9, 134–6, 141–3; Domingo Gygax 2016, 51, 111, 230–1; Heller 2020, 19–21.

[32] Heller 2020, 21–5.

magistrates: expressing a connection in terms of προξένια or εὐεργεσία became inappropriate when the power asymmetry between honorand and community became clear. While he fails to recognize the revival of Hellenistic titulature after the First Mithridatic War, Bloy's model has heuristic value.[33] The sudden deterioration of civic status in the post-Sullan era radically altered the balance of power between magistrates, their representatives, and local communities. As most cities were now directly subject to the governor's jurisdiction, the impact of each individual officeholder on civic affairs was amplified. Given this increasing significance, titles previously employed for Hellenistic rulers became appropriate for individual Romans who had contributed to the community's well-being in a tangible way.[34]

Only one Republican magistrate associated with *provincia Asia* received an honorific title outside of πάτρων, σωτήρ, or εὐεργέτης: L. Licinius Lucullus, as *quaestor* between 87 and 80, was honoured at Thyatira as κτίστης.[35] By contrast with Pompeius, similarly honoured at both Pompeiopolis-Soli in Cilicia—which he refounded—and Mytilene—to which he granted ἐλευθερία—it is unclear what Lucullus may have done to warrant this unusual honour at this early stage of his career.[36] Even during the Augustan period only one other magistrate received this title, Augustus' nephew Sex. Appuleius at Claros in the late 20s. Appuleius was widely honoured, appearing in nine extant inscriptions from Asia distributed across the province. His titles vary widely across these inscriptions. Two examples at Cyme and Pergamum declare him σωτήρ καὶ εὐεργέτης and three, two at Pergamum, one at Miletus, as simple εὐεργέτης, otherwise each decree is unique: κτίστης at Claros, πάτρων at Samos, and σωτήρ at Metropolis.[37] This variation encourages caution in approaching the evidence—if more texts for any individual governor had survived, perhaps we would observe a similar inconsistency. However, that Appuleius would be the object of special treatment would be unsurprising, both in terms of the number of honours received and their nature, given his relationship to the Princeps and position within the Augustan regime—he was *consul ordinarius* with Augustus in 29 and proconsul in Spain before his Asian command. Honours also were extended to several of his family members, including his mother, Octavia Major, at Pergamum, his wife, son, and daughter at Cyme, and his brother *inter alios* at Miletus.

In this context, civic cult honours presented another potential tool for communities to employ vis-à-vis governors. However, evidence suggests that this

[33] Bloy 2012.

[34] The rapid turnover of Roman magistrates and the diffuse nature of Roman authority inevitably contributed to honorific inflation vis-à-vis the Hellenistic period. E.g., Frija 2012, 83–90.

[35] *IGR* 4.1191. [36] *IGR* 3.869; *IG.* 12.2.140–1, 163, 165.

[37] Cyme (*I.Kyme* 18), Pergamum (*AvP* 8.2.418–20), Claros (Ferrary (2000a) #9), Samos (*IGR* 4.1719), Metropolis (*I.Eph.* 3435), Aphrodisias (*IAph2007* 12.301); Miletus (*Milet* 6.3.1123, with Kuhn 2015, 189–92).

remained an extraordinary honour during the Republic. The earliest attested example is a priesthood of M'. Aquillius at Pergamum, which served as a model for a local benefactor's cult in the 60s. Though the circumstances remain obscure, this likely arose from his role in securing Pergamene freedom while organizing the initial *provincia*.[38] As we have already seen, the *δῆμοι καὶ ἔθνη* celebrated the *Moukieia* on behalf of Q. Mucius Scaevola from the 90s onwards, while according to Appian the Cyzicenes continued to celebrate the local *Leukolleia* in the second century CE, which was established after Lucullus relieved the city from Mithridates' siege in 73.[39] Likewise, Servilius Isauricus' cult at Ephesus, probably relating to his widely praised governorship during 46–44, persisted well into the imperial period.[40] More unusually, an inscription from Mylasa dated securely to before 2 CE records a priest of L. Munatius Plancus, the governor of Asia who signally failed to defend the city from Labienus and the Parthians in 40.[41] C. Vibius Postumus' heroization at Samos, while proconsul in Asia in *c.*6–9 CE, presents a further anomaly, although given the significant realignment of social hierarchies as the Principate took hold, experimentation is unsurprising.[42] Across the whole Republican period civic festivals for governors presented a viable strategy for communities to honour exceptional commanders.

During the Augustan period, the primacy of the imperial family devalued the benefits of offering such privileges to other Romans, though again this involved a learning process: Cyme offered cultic honours to L. Vaccius Labeo, a resident Roman, which he, likely mindful of Augustus' own policies, courteously refused.[43] Indeed, civic cult for members of the imperial family became commonplace, starting with Caesar and Augustus, before extending to the wider imperial house. As Frija has shown, this innovation appears to have been driven by locals with Roman citizenship.[44] However, this does not necessarily indicate imperial involvement. The experience of an Aezanetan family may prove instructive: following Wörrle, the brothers Menecles and Metrodorus drove the establishment of one cult for Augustus, his children, Livia, Nero (Tiberius), and Drusus and another for C. and L. Caesar, Agrippa (Postumus), and Nero (Germanicus?).[45] However, this does not seem to have resulted in a grant of citizenship despite the family's continued leadership of the community in dialogue with the Principes.

[38] *IGR* 4.292.24.

[39] *OGIS* 438.3–5; App. *Mith.* 76. See Chapter 2, 'The Origins of the Provincial *koinon*'.

[40] *I.Eph.* 702, 3066. Robert 1948, 40–1.

[41] *I.Mylasa* 134. Delrieux & Ferriès (2004, 71 n.105) present several theories: that this was due to his actions in the aftermath of 40/39; for his intercession with Antonius on their behalf; or for grants made while censor in 22.

[42] *IGR* 4.963. This is among the last examples of divine honours for non-members of the imperial family. Price 1984, 51; Thériault 2001, 92–3.

[43] *I.Kyme* 19, with Kuhn 2017, 202–5.

[44] Predominantly C. Iulii, but note especially M. Antonius Meleager at Alabanda and M. Tullius Cratippus at Pergamum. Frija 2012, 34–41.

[45] Wörrle 2014, 447–53.

While Wörrle sees this as requiring explanation, it seems preferable to emphasize the limits of citizenship grants in this period. While substantially more common than during the Republic they were still rare.[46] Overall, cult presented another honorific tool for *poleis* to employ in negotiating with imperial representatives which the advent of imperial rule blunted.

More broadly, under Augustus the political revolution at the imperial centre and the consequent changes to provincial administration affected the honorific landscape. Only five officials below the level of governor were honoured; none can be dated with certainty. The *legatus pro praetore* [C. Pac]ius Balbus was honoured as πάτρων at Cos; the *quaestores* Cn. Domitius Corbulo as εὐεργέτης at Ephesus and P. Numicius Pica as πάτρων of the whole province. P. Quinctilius Varus as *quaestor* was honoured twice, without titles, at Pergamum and once at Tenos as πάτρων καὶ εὐεργέτης. Outside this group P. Vedius Pollio who may have acted as interim governor is honoured as εὐεργέτης by Miletus and without title at Ilium.[47] By contrast, forty-five inscriptions for proconsular magistrates from this period exist, twenty-seven of which produce one or more titles. Only four of these do not name their honorand εὐεργέτης, implying a standardization of honorific language. Only five record the title σωτήρ, three of which honour Sex. Appuleius, though the other two recipients, Q. Aemilius Lepidus at Cibyra and C. Marcius Censorinus at Mylasa seem less obvious candidates. Despite the well-worn narrative of decline in civic patronage under the Principate eleven individual governors in fourteen inscriptions are entitled πάτρων, including L. Calpurnius Piso in 9/10 CE, suggesting an enduring honorific value during the reign of Augustus. This forms a strong contrast with the intermediate period, where *legati* and *quaestores* were regularly attested as patrons and governors tended not to appear. In turn, we might infer that the gubernatorial patronage actually grew in symbolic importance under the early Augustan regime, in the absence of lower-ranked officials with political weight in Rome, before declining slowly as the institution's utility waned.[48] Alternatively, based on the absence of Hellenistic titulature, except εὐεργέτης, under Tiberius and his successors, the concerns of Augustus with preserving his unique authority offers another explanation. As Nichols highlights, σωτήρ and κτίστης had their roots in royal titulature and, like the award of ἰσόθεοι τιμαί, could be held to challenge the position of the new ruler.[49] Overall, under Augustus the relative number of surviving inscriptions slightly increases, but the number of individuals receiving such honours decreases, which may suit a narrative of routine two-year commands, giving governors greater opportunity to make

[46] Cf. Crinagoras of Mytilene, discussed in Chapter 7, 'The Institutionalization of Personal Relationships', *pace* Wörrle 2014, 469–70.

[47] Full references in Table 6.1.

[48] *Pace* Eilers 2002, 161–6.

[49] Nichols 1990, 86; Delrieux & Ferriès 2011, 430–8. Bowersock (1965, 119–21) suggests the retrospective nature of εὐερέγτης rendered it more acceptable.

an impact, and a regularization of the *conventus* districts, making governors more visible on a province-wide basis.

Variations in Honorific Practice

Beyond these broad trends, however, the corpus points to a vibrant ecosystem of differing epigraphic cultures and experimentation with the forms of honorific practice. For example, Erkelenz has shown that the number of extant honorific inscriptions for Romans at Ephesus sharply increased during the Augustan period and continued to grow during the Principate. By contrast, elsewhere in Asia the long-term trend from the Republican period was decline. The earliest dedication to a Roman official by the Ephesian *demos* dates to the reign of Gaius. Four earlier examples from the Augustan and Tiberian periods involve the *publicani* or private individuals on their own behalf, even if in one case they identify themselves as civic *prytanis*.[50] Inscriptions for *legati* follow this pattern: M. Cocceius Nerva was honoured twice, but by the *Italici* and *conventus c(ivium) R(omanorum) qui Ephesi negotiantur* ('the Italians and *conventus* of Roman citizens at Ephesus').[51] For Cn. Domitius Ahenobarbus the honouring body is left unstated, though he is explicitly honoured as πάτρωνα ὄντα διὰ|προγόνων τοῦ τε ἱεροῦ τῆς Ἀρτέ|μιδος καὶ τῆς πόλεως ('ancestral patron of the Temple of Artemis and the city'), setting him apart from all the other examples, except for a restoration of the same formula in a similar inscription for the *proquaestor* Lucullus.[52] One final example for the *quaestor* Cn. Domitius Corbulo in the early first century CE proves an exception, honouring him as εὐεργέτης of the city 'in all things' and authorized by the *demos* and *boule*.[53] The comparative wealth of evidence from Ephesus renders it implausible that the dearth of honours for governors there is simply a product of the evidence profile. More likely this phenomenon was a distinctively Ephesian response to the circumstances of its tense relationship with the Roman state after the First Mithridatic War.

Delos also had a distinctive local practice. Although not administered by the Roman commander in Asia, it lay on the most convenient route to the province and provides seventeen inscriptions for officials active in the *provincia*.[54] However, only two originated with the civic body: both, in the 90s, named their

[50] *I.Eph.* 659a; 706; 3022; 3023; 3024. Compare Q. Publicius, *pro quaestore pro praetore*: *AÉ* 1983, #920.

[51] *I.Eph.* 658; *AÉ* 1990, #938. On *negotiator*/*negotiari* standing simply for membership of the Roman diaspora rather than as an economic marker: Eberle 2017, 324–31.

[52] *I.Eph.* 663; 2941. On πάτρων διὰ προγόνων as 'ancestral' rather than 'hereditary' patron: Eilers 2002, 61–83.

[53] *I.Eph.* 2059.

[54] Kantor 2009, 138–49 (French summary: *AÉ* 2009, #1373); Pawlak 2016, 187–98.

recipients πάτρων τᾶς πόλιος.[55] Similarly, the *demos* at Sardis seems to have avoided public honours for Roman officials. A dedication for L. Munatius Plancus, *legatus* in the 80s, was arranged by *Italici qui Sardibus negotiantur*, while the single example of a governor being honoured, M. Plautius Silvanus in 5/6 CE, derives from the γερουσία.[56] By contrast, Caunus shows a remarkable consistency: across eleven inscriptions for various officials—including three proconsuls and three *quaestores*—between 85 and the Augustan period every honorand was titled εὐεργέτης and four named as πάτρωνες.[57] While broad trends are detectable across the period within the province as a whole, diverse practices between civic communities remained a crucial element of the burgeoning provincial culture.

Honours granted to the family members of Roman magistrates make up a quarter of the total dossier (35/130) underscoring their importance as a conduit for *poleis* to exploit.[58] Communities could thereby expand the opportunities available to them: it provided a means to increase the visual and spatial impact of honours for a given governor, without having multiple statues for the same person. However, the differences in practice between individual communities is striking. Magnesia-on-the-Maeander honoured family members alongside all three gubernatorial honorands, while relatives were associated with several Republican commanders memorialized at Caunus, Cos, Pergamum, and Samos. Outside these communities, the phenomenon was more limited. Though the prevailing view holds that female family members did not accompany their male relatives to the *provincia*, comparative evidence would suggest caution is warranted.[59] Hellenistic queens, for example, generally had real if limited agency to act beneficently in their own right, while the well-known example of Archippe at Cyme shows that local women could be honoured as benefactors.[60] As such, it is at least possible that these family members were honoured for actions in their own right, whether as empowered officials, such as *legati*, or their influence with the governor in *consilium* or in private.[61]

Moreover, a small number of texts erected outside the honouring community hint at deliberate inter-community messaging. The earliest example, a decree of Pisidian Prostanna for the *pro quaestore pro praetore* M. Antonius, was

[55] *I.Délos* 1700, 1701.

[56] *AÉ* 1996, #1453; *Sardis* 32. On the dating of Silvanus' governorship: Wörrle 2014, 443–4.

[57] See Table 6.1.

[58] This includes individual and larger family monuments like *Milet* 6.3.1123 (on which, Kuhn 2015, 189–92).

[59] E.g., Raßelnberg 2007, 53–4; Frija 2017a, 272–8. Cf. Gell. *NA*. 10.3.1–3; Tac. *Ann*. 3.33–4. Foubert 2016, 465–71.

[60] E.g., Ma 1999 #26; Van Bremen 2008, 357–82.

[61] See the frequent phenomenon of fraternal *legati* (e.g., L. Cornelius Scipio, brother of P. Africanus; L. Quinctius Flamininus, brother of T.; Q. Cicero, brother of M.). On women contributing to (and leading) politically sensitive *consilia*: Flower 2018.

inscribed at Delos.[62] Though producing the standard honorific formula, it reveals a significant expense on the part of a remote Pisidian community to honour a *quaestor*, albeit with delegated *imperium praetorium*. It indicates an interest in Roman government on the part of the community, which may have been reciprocated, raising interesting though unanswerable questions about whether or how Antonius intervened in the region.[63] Similarly, an inscription erected by the Mysian Abbaeitae before the temple of Diana at the lake Nemi in Latium honours C. Salluvius Naso, a *legatus* of Lucullus, for defending them during the Third Mithridatic War.[64] The text is bilingual, Latin followed by Greek, and speaks to the increasingly close connections between Asia and Italy during this period. The Mysian Abbaeitae are rarely attested acting as a community and their choice to make a collective dedication at Nemi, an important Latin religious centre, rather than in their own territory, raises questions of agency. Should we posit Salluvius as dictating the location, or did the community have a voice? The evidence is insufficient to draw conclusions; however, the strong Latin connection and the prominence of the shrine may indicate a strategic attempt on Salluvius' part to increase his standing within the Roman elite.[65]

The sanctuary of Apollo on Delos held global significance in the Hellenistic world and the island had a growing Roman community from the mid-second century, while the temple of Diana Nemorensis held great importance for the Latin community, if not more broadly. Location was also significant for two additional examples, a statue-base for Q. Mucius Scaevola at Olympia, offered by the *δῆμοι καὶ ἔθνη* in Asia, and an inscription at Rome for P. Numicius Pica, on behalf of the *provincia Asia*.[66] In the latter three instances, the decree emerged from a collective entity which could indicate that the site of the inscription or statue was subject to negotiation between the various members.[67] These four statues match the pattern of dedications made in Asia but suggest a deliberate concern with visibility beyond the confines of the honouring community: that is, they were in some sense outward-facing documents. Irrespective of whether the recipient solicited the grant or influenced the location, these groups chose to advertise their relationship with individual Romans in well-trafficked and highly meaningful locations. Consequently, we should view this small group of inscriptions as attempts by the dedicants to articulate publicly their relationship with Rome and its representatives.

Finally, several innovations in titulature appear from the 60s: Cn. Pompeius Magnus, for example, was honoured as *τρὶς αὐτοκράτωρ* ('*imperator* for

[62] *I.Délos* 1603.

[63] On Pamphylia and Pisidia in this period: Sherwin-White 1976, 3–4; Dmitriev 2005, 81.

[64] *OGIS* 445.

[65] Salluvius is an obscure figure, onomastic data may indicate an Apulian *origo*, though a link with the Salluvii of southern Gaul is possible. Strabo 4.1.3. Silvestrini 1996, 282.

[66] *OGIS* 439; *CIL* 6.3835. [67] Compare the processes discussed by Mackil 2013, 145–258.

the third time') across Asia Minor. Though this titulature, unique to Pompeius himself, was perfectly accurate, using it to supplant traditional forms such as ἀνθύπατος (*proconsul*) evoked a sense of distance between this commander and his rivals. Though the use of αὐτοκράτωρ or transliteration ἰμπεράτωρ as titles for Roman magistrates is not unparalleled, they occur in ambiguous contexts.[68] Strikingly, the Colophonian *demos* honoured Q. Cicero as εὐεργέτην ὄντα | τῶν Ἑλλήνων καὶ | πάτρωνα τοῦ δή|μου ('benefactor of the Greeks and patron of the *demos*').[69] The extension of honour beyond the civic body into the broader realm of the 'Greeks [sc. of Asia]' speaks to a growing sense of community between *poleis* in this period. Similarly, in 39, M. Cocceius Nerva was honoured at Teos as: τὸν κοινὸν | εὐεργέτην καὶ σωτῆρα τῆς ἐπαρχήας | καὶ τῆς πόλεως πάτρωνα ('the common benefactor and saviour of the province, and the patron of the city').[70] This again contrasts the position of Nerva vis-à-vis the province as a whole and Teos specifically. Though the contexts were significantly different—Cicero governed the *provincia* for three years during the height of the *publicani*'s influence, while Nerva as *legatus* played a key role in forcing the Parthians out of Caria—this implies that the *poleis* were happy to present the two men as serving a community beyond their own borders.[71] This could speak of the influence of the emergent *koinon* during this period. The *provincia* itself begins to honour governors during the Augustan period as this body became more institutionalized.[72] Outward-facing and innovative honorific grants highlight the strategic exploration of new ground by communities in managing their relationship to Rome and Romans. Both represent attempts to engage effectively with imperial power to the benefit of the dedicants. They illustrate the extent to which such experimentation was possible within the parameters of the traditional reciprocal honorific exchange.

The Impact of Rome on Civic Honorific Practice

Beyond civic attempts to integrate Romans into their culture of honour, the advent of Roman rule affected practice vis-à-vis local benefactors. Most obviously, in the late second and early first centuries honorific decrees came increasingly to focus on their recipients' dealing with Rome and its representatives.[73] While adhering to traditional formulae and language, as the Roman presence intensified

[68] E.g., L. Licinius Murena: *IG*. 5.1.1454; 12.1.48; *I.Kaunos* 31 and 103, with Jordan 2022, 498 n.61.

[69] *SEG* 37.958.5–8. Laffi (2010, 37), adducing as comparanda *I.Priene*² 233 (M'. Aemilius Lepidus, *c*.80/79) and honours for Caesar (*I.Eph*. 251). Ferrary (2001, 19–35) sees the *koinon* as responsible. See Chapter 2, 'The Origins of the Provincial *koinon*'.

[70] *Carie* 2.103. Compare *ILS* 8780. On Nerva: Delrieux & Ferriès 2011, 421–52.

[71] On the title of 'common benefactor' applied to individuals: Erskine 1994, 87 n.64; Delrieux & Ferriès 2011, 437–8.

[72] E.g., Antistius Vetus (*IGR* 4.778); Numicius Pica (*CIL* 6.3835).

[73] E.g., Brun's dossier (2004, 44–52) for the Aristonican War.

more decrees refer to governors or institutions, as the extensive evidence from Priene demonstrates. The texts highlight the importance of personal and institutional connections between the *polis* and its representatives, one the one hand, and Roman officials or the Senate, on the other.[74] However, after the First Mithridatic War, new trends emerged. Evidence suggests an inflation of honours for citizen benefactors took place, concurrent with a renewed emphasis on locally directed euergetism as opposed to diplomatic action. At Priene, A. Aemilius Zosimus was repeatedly honoured for achievements across a lengthy career. However, Zosimus' relationship with individual Romans or Rome goes unmentioned: on this evidence, he undertook no embassies and received no visitors.[75] The well-known dossier of Diodorus Pasparus at Pergamum reinforces this view.[76] While he served as an ambassador to Rome and drew on his personal connections to secure privileges for the *polis*, throughout his extensive dossier his localized actions including his reconstruction of the *gymnasion* and the funding of festivals are emphasized.[77] Strikingly, language and honours previously restricted to members of the Attalid dynasty are employed. The earliest decree, dated by Chankowski to before 73, granted Diodorus an ἄγαλμα, implying cultic honours, and also hailed him as εὐεργέτης and σωτήρ.[78] More significantly, he seems to have been recognized as having achieved the benefits for [πασῖν?] τοῖς τὴν ἐπαρχείαν κατοικοῦσιν (‘[all?] those resident in the *provincia*’), recalling the generalizing tone used of Seleucid benefactions and the strategic assertion by Attalid monarchs to be benefactors par excellence.[79] This claim is circumscribed by the administrative geography of the Roman *provincia*. Rather than referring to the Greeks at large, the decree focuses in on the region subjected to the same Roman official as Pergamum itself. This may partially reflect the reality that his embassy had effective implications only for those *poleis* suffering from the decisions of Sulla in the aftermath of Dardanus.[80] However, it might also reflect a growing solidarity among the communities of Asia during this period. Similarly, evidence for Theophanes and

[74] E.g., *I.Priene*² 64, 67, 71, 75 all refer to embassies to governors or the Senate and date between 133–88. Compare *SEG* 39.1243–4; *I.Ilion* 73.1–3. Santangelo 2009, 75–7.

[75] *I.Priene*² 68–70. Zosimus' status remains controversial: his *tria nomina* and filiation, *Αὖλος Αἰμίλιος Σέξτου Ζώσιμος*, led some to view him as a freedman (e.g., Magie 1950, 256) or an Italian immigrant (Kah 2012, 62–9; Blümel & Merkelbach 2014, 183). However, it was quite possible for the father of a newly enfranchised citizen to bear a Latin name through his own enfranchisement (e.g., L. Cornelius Balbus (*cos. suff.* 40) recorded on the *fasti Colotiani* as L.f. (*InscrIt* 13.1.18.16; Münzer (*RE* s.v. Cornelius 69, 1260–1)). Rumschied's claim (2002, 82) that Zosimus was a member of the Prienean elite is thereby persuasive. Though Kah (2012, 63–5) suggests an Augustan date, Hamon (*BÉ* 2013, #362) notes this is ‘pas d'argument décisif’.

[76] On the date: Jones 1974, 190–205; 2000, 6–12 contra Musti 1998; 1999, 325–33. Chankowski (1998, 194) notes that two texts seem to be copies, raising the possibility that the quantity of monuments, rather than decrees per se, was growing during this period.

[77] Personal connections: *IGR* 4.293.2.11–6.

[78] *IGR* 4.292.15–6, 32, 42. Chankowski 1998, 167–9.

[79] *IGR* 4.292.2–3, 15–16.

[80] Cf. Virgilio 1994, 303–4.

Potamon at Mytilene, though extensive, does not include civic decrees referring explicitly to their personal contact or connection with the powerful Romans who granted their *polis* privileges. Both men were widely honoured, yet within the civic space this truth remained hidden.

The relative decline of the celebration of embassies to Roman officials in decrees for citizens requires explanation. As noted, honorific decrees for citizens likely targeted a civic, internal audience.[81] Embassies may simply have become less important to *poleis* during the late Republic. However, the ample evidence for embassies at Rome during this period and the proliferation of letters and *senatus consulta* during the triumviral period and under Augustus contradicts this interpretation. Alternatively, ambassadors may have met with less success in making their requests to the Senate. But this explanation too collapses in the face of the evidence. Diodorus was clearly successful, yet the extant texts spend more space on his local benefactions.[82] Acknowledging that our evidence is insufficient to provide the requisite standard of proof, the most likely explanation is that local civic discourse had shifted due to the economic crisis provoked by Sulla's actions. Within communities, locally focused euergetism displaced ambassadorial tasks as the main driver of prestige. Zuiderhoek, focusing on Imperial Asia Minor, argued that civic euergetism provided local actors with symbolic capital, that is, political and social legitimacy. Though his model has been criticized for underplaying economic aspects, the nexus of these two elements explains the shift in local narratives.[83] The value of hard financial contributions to the upkeep of the *polis* became more important than attempts to solicit senatorial intervention. Instead, focus moved to communal attempts at persuasion alongside honorific competition for gubernatorial attention. Plutarch's account of Lucullus' palliative action frames them in the context of the *provincia* writ large.[84] Similarly, Q. Cicero's description as *εὐεργέτης τῶν Ἑλλήνων* is given greater prominence by the disappointment voiced by his brother over his treatment of Roman *negotiatores*.[85] The trend towards common approaches to Rome through collectively chosen representatives, mediated through the nascent *koinon*, rendered individual embassies less efficacious.[86] Given these practical changes, local civic discourse moved away from praise for interaction with Rome's representatives, which began to be conducted through regional organizations, and recentred themselves on the practical contributions of citizens to civic life.

[81] Compare, for example, the dispute between Aeschines (3.32–48) and Demosthenes (18.120–1) over announcing honours in front of the foreigners at Dionysia.

[82] *IGR* 4.293, 294.

[83] Zuiderhoek 2009, esp. 117–53; Heller 2020 contra Jones 2011a, 773–5; Kalinowski 2011, 148–52.

[84] Plut. *Luc.* 20. See Chapter 2, 'Roman Taxation after Sulla's Settlement'.

[85] *SEG* 37.958.5–8; Cic. *QFr.* 1.2.4–14.

[86] *IAph2007* 2.503.

Ephesus, Mithridates, and Roman Hegemony

A final, non-honorific decree from Ephesus presents an intriguing reflection of the developments in civic honorific practice. In 88, as Roman opposition to Mithridates dissolved, the city offered no resistance and participated willingly in the 'Asian Vespers' later that year.[87] In late 86 or early 85, the Ephesian *demos* declared war on Mithridates VI of Pontus. A single marble stele, broken at the top and bottom, preserves the conclusion of one decree and the beginning of another passed by the *demos* at the critical moment. The second deals with the practical consequences of the decision to oppose Mithridates. The language of unanimity is invoked in the motivation clause: *ἐπεὶ τῶν μεγίστων κινδύνων ἐπαγομένων... τὴν τε πόλιν καὶ τὴν χώραν, ἀναγκαῖόν ἐστι πάντας ὁμονοήσαντας ὑ[πο]στῆναι τὸν κίνδυνον* ('since the greatest dangers have befallen... the city and its territory, it is necessary for all with one voice to bring an end to the danger').[88] The first, strikingly, stresses the preservation of *εὔνοια* towards the Romans and frames the (current) declaration of war against Mithridates as an opportunity, the earliest possible, to provide active aid to Rome. The narrative boldly refashions Ephesus' involvement in the conflict.

> *[ἐπειδή, τοῦ δήμου | φυλάσσον]τος τὴν πρὸς Ῥωμαίους τοὺς κο[ινοὺς σωτῆρας πα|λαιὰν εὔν]οιαν καὶ ἐν πᾶσιν τοῖς ἐπιτασσομέ[νοις προθύμως | πειθαρχ]οῦντος, Μιθραδάτης Καππαδοκί[ας βασιλεύς παρα|βὰς τὰς π]ρὸς Ῥωμαίους συνθήκας καὶ συναγαγὼ[ν τὰς δυνάμεις ἐ|πεχείρη]σεν κύριος γενέσθαι τῆς μηθὲν ἑαυτῶι προ[σηκούσης | χώρα]ς, καὶ προκαταλαβόμενος τὰς προκειμένας ἡμῶν πό[λεις ἀ|πάτ]ῃ, ἐκράτησεν καὶ τῆς ἡμετέρας πόλεως καταπληξάμενος | [τῶι] τε πλήθει τῶν δυνάμεων καὶ τῶι ἀπροδοκήτωι τῆς ἐπιβολῆς, | [ὁ] δὲ δῆμος ἡμῶν ἀπὸ τῆς ἀρχῆς συνφυλάσσων τὴν πρὸς Ῥωμαί|ους εὔνοιαν, ἐσχηκὼς καιρὸν πρὸς τὸ βοηθεῖν τοῖς κοινοῖς πράγμα|σιν, κέκρικεν ἀναδεῖξαι τὸν πρὸς Μιθραδάτην πόλεμον ὑπὲρ | τῆς Ῥωμαίων ἡγεμονίας καὶ τῆς κοινῆς ἐλευθερίας, ὁμο|θυμαδὸν πάντων τῶν πολιτῶν ἐπιδεδωκότων ἑαυτοὺς εἰς τοὺ[ς | π]ερὶ τούτων ἀγῶνας* ('[Since the *demos*, preserving] the [ancient] goodwill towards the Romans, [common saviours], and in all matters [willingly] obedient to commands issued, when Mithridates, [*basileus*] of Cappadocia, [violating] the treaty with the Romans and gathering [his forces, made an attack] to become master over [lands] that did not [belong to him] and, after taking the [cities] before us [by deceit], he conquered our city, through the vastness of his forces and the suddenness of his attack; and our *demos*, preserving from the beginning goodwill towards the Romans, having the opportunity to help in common action, decided to

[87] App. *Mith.* 23. [88] *I.Eph.* 8.22–4.

declare war against Mithridates on behalf of the hegemony of the Romans and common freedom; all the citizens with one voice giving themselves over to the struggle for this end').[89]

This document presents several intriguing aspects to civic self-representation vis-à-vis the Roman administration. Though an independent actor, the Ephesians frame their *polis* as being tied by bonds of utter loyalty to Rome.[90] They assert their continuous loyalty by framing their capitulation as the seizure of a defenceless city. Emphasizing the injustice of Mithridates' designs on the Roman *provincia*, though leaving ambiguous the territorial rights of Rome, the decree dwells on the vast size of the *basileus*' forces and the suddenness of his appearance. Crucially, the authors carefully explain that the *polis* was always obedient *ἐν πᾶσιν τοῖς ἐπιτασσομέ[νοις]* ('in all things to the orders given [sc. by Roman magistrates]'). The declaration of war on Mithridates, the ostensible purpose of the decree, is de-emphasized in the extant text by the intense focus on crafting a narrative of loyalty to Rome. While rewriting history to shape civic memory provides one motive, a more immediate goal would be publicizing the *polis*' enduring support for their hegemon. As Chaniotis stressed, this decree contained no specific measures. Its sole function was to present a new narrative for the *polis* community and, Kallet-Marx has suggested, possibly Roman commanders or the institutions of the *res publica*.[91]

These Ephesian decrees prioritize their close bond with and respect for the Romans as hegemons, disingenuously or not, and the unity of the civic body. The documents' inscription suggests that they played an important and conscious role in shaping civic memory, establishing a hegemonic narrative of Ephesian loyalty to Rome. If the city did aim to assuage Roman irritation at their late defection, they were ultimately unsuccessful. Like most *poleis* in Asia, they lost their freedom during Sulla's reorganization and were explicitly subordinated to the Roman administrative framework for the first time.[92]

The surviving honorific texts from Asian *poleis* reflect the transformation of their relationship with Rome as the hegemonic power became increasingly implicated in the region. However, as the Ephesian decree demonstrates, this need not be sincere. Rather, these documents provided opportunities for elites to gloss over division and through their publication shape civic memory over the long term. Honorific decrees for Romans were also undoubtedly intended for individual magistrates. In form they resemble exchanges with Hellenistic rulers, but the framework underpinning this dialogue had fundamentally changed. The evidence

[89] *I.Eph.* 8.1–14. [90] Compare *IAph2007* 8.3.b.11–14.

[91] Kallet-Marx 1995, 284–5; Chaniotis 2013, 749–50, 2014, 152–3; cf. Kirbihler 2016, 64–8. On civic memory: Jones 2001; Ma 2013a, 7–10; Chaniotis 2014, 132–61.

[92] Magie 1950, 234–5; Guerber 1995, 388–409; Kallet-Marx 1995, 265; Kirbihler 2016, 64.

shows a diversity of practice within Asia, though the exclusive emphasis on patronage before the First Mithridatic War and the return to more diverse Hellenistic titles after this conflict is revealing, perhaps indicating the greater capacity of magistrates to impact the well-being of communities. The shifting language and structure of honours for citizens further reflects the evolution of the dynamic between Rome and local communities. Individual communities organically adapted their existing processes for negotiating with empire to the new situation, though this was far from seamless. The greater number of Roman magistrates required more frequent action and lessened opportunities to repeatedly engage with the same individual. Consequently, alternative strategies emerged. However, the speech-acts of civic bodies were only one part of the dialogue between empire and community. Negotiation was critical in dealing with the imperial centre; individuals came to the fore. The persuasive role of ambassadors formed a crucial part of interaction with Roman political actors, and it is this aspect which the following chapter addresses.

Table 6.1 Honorific inscriptions for Roman magistrates in *provincia Asia*, 133 BCE–14 CE

Date	Honouring Community	Honorand	Position	Titles	Source	Reference
113	Prostanna*	M. Antonius	Q	–	D	*I.Delos* 1603
100	Cos	M. Popillius Laenas	L	PE	D	*I.Cos* 225
100	Magnesia-on-the-Maeander	M. Popullius Laenas	L	–	BD	*I.Magnesia* 123
*c.*99–97	Ephesus	Q. Mucius Scaevola (wife)	PC	P	D	*I.Eph* 630a
*c.*99–97	Cos	Q. Mucius Scaevola (son)	PC	P?	D	*AÉ* 1995, #1440
*c.*99–97	Nysa	Q. Mucius Scaevola (son)	PC	–	D	*SEG* 57.1104
*c.*99–97	Oinoanda (Lycia)	Q. Mucius Scaevola (son)	PC	PE	D	*AÉ* 1995, #1538
95	Colophon (Claros)	C. Valerius Flaccus	PC	P	D	Ferrary (2000a), #1
92	Colophon (Claros)	L. Valerius Flaccus	PC	P	D	Ferrary (2000a), #2
post 89	Ilium	L. Iulius Caesar	CS	–	D	*I.Ilion* 71
post 89	Ilium	L. Iulius Caesar (daughter)	CS	–	BD	*I.Ilion* 72
85/84	Halicarnassus	L. Cornelius Sulla	PC	E	D	*ILS* 8771
85–81	Caunus	L. Licinius Murena	PC	SE	D	*I.Kaunos* 103
85–81	Caunus	L. Licinius Murena (son)	PC	SE	D	*I.Kaunos* 104
85–80	Ephesus	L. Licinius Lucullus	Q	PE	–	*I.Eph*. 2941
85–80	Thyatira	L. Licinius Lucullus	Q	SKE	D	*IGR* 4.1191
85–80	Synnada	L. Licinius Lucullus	Q	PE	D	*MAMA* 4.52
82	Euromos	A. Terentius Varro (mother)	L	–	D	*ILS* 8773
82	Labraunda	L. Cornelius Lentulus	PC	P	D	*I.Labraunda* #63
*c.*84–78	Priene	M'. Aemilius Lepidus	Q	E	–	*I.Priene*^{2} 233
75/74	Pergamum	M. Iunius Iuncus (father/son?)	PC	–	D	*AvP* 8.2.408
74	Ephesus	Q. Publicius	Q	E	–	*AÉ* 1983, #920
74/73	Mysia, Abbaitai*	C. Salluvius Naso	L	–	Mysians	*CIL* I^2 743
73–69	Acmonea	C. Sornantius Barba	L	–	BD	*MAMA* 6.260
73–69	Andros	L. Licinius Lucullus	PC	–	D	*SEG* 60.908
73–69	Colophon (Claros)	L. Licinius Lucullus	PC	SE	D	Ferrary (2000a) #3
73–69	Pergamum	C. Sornantius Barba	L	E	D	*AvP* 8.2.431
68/67	Pergamum	P. Cornelius Dolabella	PC	E	D	*AvP* 8.2.405

67	Miletus	L. Manlius Torquatus	L	E	–	*ZPE* 68, 275/276
67	Caunus	P. Cornelius Sulla	PC	PE	D	*I.Kaunos* 106
63	Claros	P. Servilius Globulus	PC	PE	*koinon Ionion*	*SEG* 60.1247
62/61	Colophon (Claros)	L. Valerius Flaccus	PC	P	G	Ferrary (2000a), #5
62/61	Magnesia-on-the-Maeander	L. Valerius Flaccus (mother)	PC	–	–	*I.Magnesia* 144
62/61	Magnesia-on-the-Maeander	L. Valerius Flaccus (wife)	PC	–	–	*I.Magnesia* 145
62/61	Magnesia-on-the-Maeander	L. Valerius Flaccus (daughter)	PC	–	D	*I.Magnesia* 146
61–59	Tralles	L. Aelius Tubero	L	P	*gerontes*	*SEG* 54.1171
61–59	Colophon (Claros)	Q. Tullius Cicero	PC	PE	D	Ferrary (2000a) #6
61–59	Samos	Q. Tullius Cicero (wife)	PC	–	D	*IG* 12.6.1.354
61–59	Samos	Q. Tullius Cicero (son)	PC	–	D	*IG* 12.6.1.355
60	Caunus	L. Afranius (son)	L	E	D	*I.Kaunos* 112
*c.*54/53	Caunus	C. Scribonius Curio (wife)	Q	E	–	*I.Kaunos* 108
*c.*54/53	Caunus	C. Scribonius Curio (son)	Q	E	–	*I.Kaunos* 107
54	Pergamum	L. Sestius	Q	PE	D	*AvP* 8.2.406
54	Pergamum	L. Sestius	Q	–	–	*AvP* 8.2.407
50/49	Ephesus	L. Antonius	Q	PE?	–	*I.Eph.* 614a
50/49	Magnesia-under-Sipylos	L. Antonius	Q	E	–	*I.Magnesia Sipylos* 3
55–53	Pergamum	C. Claudius Pulcher	PC	E	–	*AvP* 8.2.409
50/49	Thyatira	L. Antonius	Q	–	BD	*TAM* 5.920
50/49	Thyatira	L. Antonius	Q	PE	D	*TAM* 5.919
50/49	Pergamum	L. Antonius	Q	SP	D	*AvP* 8.2.410
50/49	Pergamum	L. Antonius	Q	SP	D	*IGR* 4.401
49/48	Apamea	P. Licinius Crassus Damasippus	L	SEP	BD	*AÉ* 1890. #76
49	Miletus	M. Pupius Piso Frugi	L	PE	D	*Milet* 1.3.173
49/48	Pergamum	Q. Caecilius Metellus Pius	L	SE	D	*AvP* 8.2.411
49/48	Pergamum	Q. Caecilius Metellus Pius (daughter)	L	–	D	*AvP* 8.2.412
49	Samos	M. Pupius Piso Frugi	L	PE?	D	*IGR* 4.1709
49–45	Nysa	Cn. Domitius Calvinus	L	PE	?	*I.Tralleis* 2.445
46–44	Pergamum	P. Servilius Isauricus	PC	SE	D	*AvP* 8.2.413

Continued

Table 6.1 *Continued*

Date	Honouring Community	Honorand	Position	Titles	Source	Reference
46–44	Pergamum	P Servilius Isauricus (daughter)	PC	SE	D	*AvP* 8.2.414
46–44	Cos	P. Servilius Isauricus (wife)	PC	–	D	*AÉ* 1934, #84
46–44	Mytilene	P. Servilius Isauricus (wife)	PC	–	D	*IG* 12.supp.60
46–44	Magnesia-on-the-Maeander	P. Servilius Isauricus (father)	PC	E	–	*I.Magnesia* 142
44/43	Ephesus	M. Appuleius (wife and father-in-law)	Q	–	–	*I.Eph.* 1547
40?	Caunus	M. Barbatius Pollio	Q	PE	?	*I.Kaunos* 110
40?	Caunus	L. Caninius Gallus	PF	SEP	?	*I.Kaunos* 109
40/39	Nysa	M. Vinicius	L?	–	?	*I.Tralleis* 2.444
c.38–35	Colophon (Claros)	M. Valerius Messalla Potitus	Q	P	D	Ferrary (2000a) #10
38/37	Lagina	M. Cocceius Nerva	L	SEP	D	*I.Stratonikeia* 509
38/37	Teos	M. Cocceius Nerva	L	SEP	D	*SEG* 4.604
38/37	Pergamum	L. Cornificius	L	E	D	*IGR* 4.420
40 or 33	Caunus	C. Fonteius Capito	L	PE	D	*I.Kaunos* 111
35/34	Colophon (Claros)	M. Titius	L	–	–	Ferrary (2000a) #7
35/34	Samos	M. Titius (wife)	L	P	D	*IGR* 4.1716
32/31	Ephesus	Cn. Domitius Ahenobarbus	L	P	–	*I.Eph.* 663
32/31	Labraunda	Cn. Domitius Ahenobarbus	L	E	D	*I.Labraunda* #62
32/31	Samos	Cn. Domitius Ahenobarbus	L	–	–	*IGR* 4.968
c.31–29	Ilium	P. Vedius Pollio*	PA	–	BD	*I.Ilion* 101
c.31–29	Miletus	P. Vedius Pollio*	PA	E	D	*I.Didyma* 146
23	Samos	C. Stertinius & C. Asinius Pollio	CN	–	D	*SEG* 1.389
23–21	Pergamum	Sex. Appuleius	PC	E	*demos Kotiaeon*	*AvP* 8.2.418
23–21	Pergamum	Sex. Appuleius	PC	E?	–	*AvP* 8.2.420
23–21	Pergamum	Sex. Appuleius (mother)	PC	SE	D	*AvP* 8.2.419
23–21	Aphrodisias	Sex. Appuleius	PC	–	D	*IAph2007* 12.301
23–21	Colophon (Claros)	Sex. Appuleius	PC	K	D	Ferrary (2000a) #9
23–21	Metropolis	Sex. Appuleius	PC	S	D	*I.Eph.* 3435
23–21	Samos	Sex. Appuleius	PC	P	D	*IGR* 4.1719

23–21	Cyme	Sex. Appuleius (& wife, daughter, parents)	PC	SE	D	*I.Kyme* 18
23–21	Miletus	Sex. Appuleius (& brother)	PC	E	D	*Milet* 6.3.1123, with Kuhn 2015
22?	Pergamum	P. Quinctilius Varus	Q	–	D	*AvP* 8.2.424
22?	Pergamum	P. Quinctilius Varus	Q	–	D	*IGR* 4.419
22?	Tenos	P. Quinctilius Varus	Q	PE	D	*OGIS* 463
*c.*22/21	Stratonicea	M. Iunius Silanus	PC	PE	?	*I.Stratonikeia* 1510
20	Cos	M. Valerius Messalla Potitus	PC	PE	?	*SEG* 58.860
21–19	Magnesia-under-Sipylos	Potitus Valerius Messalla	PC	PE	D	*IGR* 4.1338
21–19	Miletus	Potitus Valerius Messalla	PC	PE	D	*I.Didyma* 147
21–19	Pergamum	Potitus Valerius Messalla	PC	–	D	*AvP* 8.2.417
*c.*18–16	Pergamum	C. Norbanus Flaccus	PC	E	–	*AvP* 8.2.416
15–13	Cibyra	Q. Aemilius Lepidus	PC	SEP	D	*IGR* 4.901
15–13	Colophon (Claros)	Q. Aemilius Lepidus	PC	–	D	Ferrary (2000a) #12
15–13	Halicarnassus	Q. Aemilius Lepidus	PC	PE	D	*I.Kaunos* 111
12–10	Miletus	P. Cornelius Scipio	PC	–	D	*Milet* 1.9.333
9/8	Pergamum	Paullus Fabius Maximus	PC	–	D	*AvP* 8.2.421
*c.*1–3	Miletus	C. Marcius Censorinus	PC	PE	D	*Milet* 1.7.255
*c.*1–3	Mylasa	C. Marcius Censorinus	PC	SE	P	*I.Mylasa* 410
*c.*1–3	Pergamum	C. Marcius Censorinus	PC	–	D	*AvP* 8.2.422
*c.*2–4	Apamea	C. Antistius Vetus	PC	P	P	*IGR* 4.778
*c.*2–4	Pergamum	C. Antistius Vetus	PC	PE	D	*AvP* 8.2.423
*c.*2–4	Thyatira	C. Antistius Vetus (son)	PC	–	D	Robert (1937) p.128
5/6	Caunus	M. Plautius Silvanus	PC	PE	?	*I.Kaunos* 114
5/6	Sardis	M. Plautius Silvanus (wife)	PC	–	*gerousia*	*Sardis* 32
5/6	Ephesus	M. Plautius Silvanus (daughter)	PC	–	BD	*I.Eph.*707
*c.*6–9	Samos	C. Vibius Postumus	PC	HE	D	*IGR* 4.963
*c.*6–9	Magnesia-on-the-Maeander	C. Vibius Postumus (brothers)	PC	–	BD	*I.Magnesia* 152
*c.*6–9	Teos	C. Vibius Postumus (brother)	PC	E	D	*IGR* 4.1564
*c.*7–12	Andros	P. Vinicius	PC	PE	D	*IG* 12.5.756
*c.*7–12	Cnidos	P. Vinicius	PC	–	D	*SEG* 12.452

Continued

Table 6.1 *Continued*

Date	Honouring Community	Honorand	Position	Titles	Source	Reference
*c.*7–12	Smyrna	P. Vinicius	PC	–	D	*I.Smyrna* 2.1.633
*c.*7–12	Aphrodisias	P. Vinicius	PC	E	D	*AÉ* 1984, #880b
*c.*8–12	Pergamum	L. Volusius Saturninus (mother)	PC	–	D	*AvP* 8.2.427
9/10	Mytilene	L. Calpurnius Piso	PC	E	D	*IG* 12.2.219
9/10	Stratonicea	L. Calpurnius Piso	PC	PE	D	*AvP* 8.3.40
9/10	Pergamum	L. Calpurnius Piso	PC	–	D	*IGR* 4.411
9/10	Pergamum	L. Calpurnius Piso	PC	E	D	*AvP* 8.2.425
9/10	Pergamum	L. Calpurnius Piso (wife)	PC	–	D	*AvP* 8.3.19
9/10	Samos	L. Calpurnius Piso (wife)	PC	–	D	*IG* 12.1.364
9/10	Keramos	L. Calpurnius Piso (unknown relative)	PC	–	D	*SEG* 53.1203
1st C	Tenos	L. Quinctius Rufus	PC	SE	–	*IG* 12.5.924
Aug.	Asia	P. Numicius Pica Caesianus	Q	P	*provincia Asia*	*CIL* 6.31742
Aug.	Cos	[C. Pac?]ius Balbus	L	P	D	*AÉ* 1934, #85
Aug.	Ephesus	Cn. Domitius Corbulo	Q	E	BD	*OGIS* 768

* indicates displayed outside of honouring community

Key:

Position: Q(uaestor); L(egatus); P(ro)C(onsul); C(en)S(or); C(o)N(sul)

Titles: P(atron); E(uergetes); S(oter); K(tistes); H(eros)

Source: D(emos); B(oule); G(erousia); P(rovince)

7
Speaking to Roman Power
Diplomacy and Civic Privilege

Diplomatic activity was crucial to shaping the relationship between the cities of Asia and Rome. Formal embassies, conducted by πρεσβευταί ('ambassadors') appointed by the *demos*, brought the voice of the community to the Roman state and its representatives. They could convey civic decrees and speak in their support, but also had the capacity and authorization to innovate and negotiate.[1] Ambassadors remained central to the relationship between individual communities and the imperial centre, throughout the period of this study and well beyond.[2] However, informal contacts and exchange were critical to communities' strategies for dealing with Roman power. This chapter focuses first on the nature of official embassies, their objects, and their targets. How did Greek communities draw on existing frameworks to interact with the new hegemonic power? What were they concerned with acquiring and how had this changed from earlier periods? What relationships did they manage to construct with permanent Roman institutions? How much agency did *poleis* have in the process of articulating these relationships? It then turns to how private individuals formed personal relationships with Rome and Romans to the benefit of their home *polis*, asking to what extent these figures cultivated such contacts with a view to local rather than imperial issues. Overall, this chapter elucidates the diplomatic strategies employed by communities in Asia to relate to Roman power.

Civic Embassies: Public Voices of the City

Embassies were the most common means by which civic communities engaged with Roman institutions and officials. Asian *poleis* had a lengthy history of communicating via ambassadors and the establishment of Roman hegemony did not lessen their enthusiasm for the medium. Diplomatic contact between Rome and the communities of Asia existed from the late third and early second centuries. However, the extinction of the Attalid line and establishment of a permanent *provincia Asia* altered the dynamic. Literary sources from the Late

[1] Conveying decrees: *Syll.*[3] 601; *IAph2007* 8.2. Negotiating: *Syll.*[3] 656; *SEG* 39.1243/1244.
[2] E.g., Millar 1992 [1977], 375–85; Eck 2009, 193–207; Lenski 2017, 15–16.

Imperial Power, Provincial Government, and the Emergence of Roman Asia, 133 BCE–14 CE. Bradley Jordan, Oxford University Press. © Bradley Jordan 2023. DOI: 10.1093/oso/9780198887065.003.0008

Republic give the impression that the Senate was besieged by Greek embassies, especially during the month of February, set aside for managing diplomatic missions.[3] The epigraphic record, though fragmentary, offers some corroboration with embassies attested for a wide range of cities from across the province.

Embassies to Roman Commanders in Asia and Beyond

While the evidence emphasizes embassies to the Senate, there are several examples of approaches to provincial commanders. These embassies stand apart from general requests for military aid, of which several are attested. Two early decrees, for Machaon at Cyzicus and Menas at Sestus, praise the honorands for missions seeking assistance from the Roman commander in Macedonia during the turbulent transition from Attalid to Roman control.[4] These fit into a broader category of embassies to powerful regional actors in perilous circumstances, resembling approaches to Roman commanders in the region during the early second century.[5] An honorific decree from Mysia Abbaeitis also fits into this group, while the military exploits of Apollonius of Bargasa in the war against Aristonicus are mentioned alongside his embassy to dissuade the consul M'. Aquillius from billeting his troops on the city.[6] Finally, the embassy of Plarasa-Aphrodisias to Q. Oppius when besieged at Laodicea-on-the-Lycus, already discussed, was also a practical strategic decision.[7]

Our best evidence for gubernatorial embassies comes from several honorific inscriptions found in Priene's so-called sacred stoa, which begins before a formal Roman administrative framework. The prominent Moschion, whose career included embassies to the Seleucid kings Demetrius I (r. 160–152) and II (r. 145–139, 129–126), was sent to Pergamum in 130 after M. Perperna had written to the *demos*.[8] Another Prienean decree honours an unknown citizen for his missions to several Roman officials present in Asia in the late second century. Significantly, the Roman embassies are given prominence here, though a subsequent list of his embassies to Greek *poleis* provides context. Though the text implies each Roman official received one embassy, the honorand visited nearby Miletus and Magnesia-on-the-Maeander, πολλάκις ('often'), and the text provides a list of specific missions undertaken to a range of cities.[9] Neither example provides reasons for the embassies, but together they imply that Roman governors were worth engaging with on a regular basis.

[3] See section 'Embassies to the Senate' in this chapter.
[4] *IGR* 4.134.9–11; *I.Sestos* 1.16–23.
[5] E.g., Champion 2007, 265–70; Burton 2011, 84–8, 229.
[6] *SEG* 34.1198, 8–13; 51.1495.18–21.
[7] *IAph2007* 8.3.
[8] *I.Priene*² 64.227–31. Perhaps accompanied by one Herodes (*I.Priene*² 65.91–4).
[9] *I.Priene*² 75.24–35.

Two later decrees further underscore the relative importance of gubernatorial embassies compared with trips to Rome. The first, honouring Crates, mentions embassies to at least two Roman commanders, to C. Iulius Caesar and L. Lucilius. The second, for Heraclitus, mentions another embassy to Caesar.[10] The dating of Caesar's command remains controversial. Fragments of an Augustan *elogium* appears to place his governorship before his service on a Saturninan agrarian commission, that is, before 101.[11] However, based on the references to three separate stephanophorates separating references to Caesar in the Crates decree, Sumner argued forcefully that Caesar was Lucilius' immediate predecessor, governing for at least two full years from 93/92.[12] What can be asserted with confidence is that Crates undertook at least four embassies to two Roman commanders in Asia and the Senate, across three different Prienean years concerning disputes with the *publicani* and Miletus.[13] After Lucilius referred the former case to the Senate, Crates went to Rome to speak for the *polis*.[14] Heraclitus, similarly, was involved in two embassies to Caesar.[15] Together, these examples, even allowing a high date for Caesar's command, emphasize the frequency of embassies to commanders and highlight two key themes: disputes with their neighbours and rapacious behaviour by Roman citizens.

The reaction of both Roman governors to the entreaties of Crates and Heraclitus shows their reluctance to close cases in favour of the cities on their own authority. As already argued, these decisions were consistently referred to the Senate, probably due to the structural weakness of praetorian commanders vis-à-vis the *publicani*. Although Caesar and Lucilius released territory back to Priene in the interim, it seems likely that this decision was not strongly enforced.[16] As far as commanders were concerned, referral to Rome may have bought time for their term to expire, making the fallout their successors' problem.[17] Cicero reveals another dynamic provoked by Verres' pillaging of the Samian Heraion. Ambassadors sent by Samos to the commander in Asia, C. Claudius Nero, were informed: *eius modi querimonias, quae legatos populi Romani pertinerent, non ad praetorem sed Romam deferri oportere* ('complaints of this sort, which pertained to *legati* of the Roman People, ought to be brought not before a praetor, but to Rome').[18] Even had Nero wanted to punish Verres, he had little authority over his colleague's *legatus*. The only recourse in this instance was

[10] *I.Priene*² 67.14, 21, 136, 147; 71.48–9. Though, note the reference to a proconsul at 71.17. Wallace 2014, 45–6. *Pace* Rousset (*BÉ* 2016, #98), there is no reason to reject the overlap in the careers of the two men at this point.

[11] *Inscr. It.* 13.3.75a. Ferrary 2000, 175–9. Earlier Frank 1937, 89–93.

[12] Sumner 1978, 145–50; Wallace 2014, 39–42. Earlier: Broughton 1948, 323–30; Badian 1964, 87–8.

[13] Note, with caution, the discussion of Wallace (2014, 48–53) of the relative chronology of the disputes.

[14] *I.Priene*² 67.136–43.

[15] *I.Priene*² 71.20–1, 45–7.

[16] *I.Priene*² 67.116, 136–43.

[17] Compare Cicero's deferral of Salamis' dispute with M. Scaptius in 51/50 to his successor. Cic. *Att.* 5.21.12.

[18] Cic. *Verr.* 2.1.50.

a trial in Rome. This underscores the key theme of the Roman Republic's distributed power and the problems it could cause for communities. While the governor had the capacity to resolve most problems, the influence wielded by the Senate and internal dynamics of Roman society frequently prompted them not to intervene.

The decrees for Polemaeus and Menippus at Claros shed additional light on this phenomenon. Polemaeus was explicitly honoured for two embassies to Roman commanders in Asia. On both occasions his presence before the magistrate is made explicit. First, he convinced a magistrate to overturn a judgement made against a Colophonian citizen, contrary to normal practice. Second, he persuaded another magistrate not to issue an *edictum* which would have abrogated Colophon's local laws.[19] In both instances, the rhetoric employed in the decree is striking and framed the *polis* as an equal participant in dialogue with the Roman governor. Menippus' decree parallels that of his older contemporary. His five embassies to Rome and the Senate are central: visits to Roman commanders and *quaestores*, as well as those to Attalid *basileis* and other cities, are explicitly subordinated to his senatorial missions.[20] By contrast, these are explored in detail. During the first two: τηρήσας ἄθραυστα τὰ τοῦ δήμου φιλάνθρωπα ('he preserved, undiminished, the privileges of the city').[21] The third concerned a territorial dispute, the antagonist in which is unclear but could plausibly be Roman *publicani* contesting the boundaries of civic territory.[22] The last two dealt with issues of jurisdiction, culminating in the recognition by the Senate that Colophon lay outside of the power of Roman promagistrates and could administer its own laws over Romans accused or accusing Colophonian citizens.[23] Both men undertook embassies on similar topics. However, Polemaeus was able to wrangle a decision directly from the commander on the ground, where Menippus was forced to undertake multiple journeys to Rome. One explanation would see both Romans and locals adapting to regular interaction. As the *publicani*'s exploitation of *ager publicus* became more pronounced and the Roman diaspora within Asia burgeoned, the potential for Roman citizens to invoke the governor grew. The unusual situation within Asia where most *poleis* were ἐλεύθεραι exacerbated ambiguity as to the limits of Roman jurisdiction, which citizens could exploit. The increasing leverage of the Roman diaspora and *publicani* after 123 must also have played a role. Consequently, over time, several factors led to an increasing emphasis on the Senate as the object of civic entreaties.

[19] *SEG* 39.1243.51–61. See Chapter 1, 'Gubernatorial Jurisdiction and the Free Cities'.

[20] *SEG* 39.1244.1.13–9. On the odd formulation of τὴν Ἀτταλικὴν βασιλείαν, see Robert & Robert 1989, 69.

[21] *SEG* 39.1244.1.21–2.

[22] Robert & Robert 1989, 71–85, on the territory referred to. Comparanda at Wallace (2014, 56–62, with references), though his subsequent citation of the *senatus consultum de Oropiis* is misleading.

[23] *SEG* 39.1244.1.37–48.

A final example offers a distinctive view on the strategies for engaging directly with Roman commanders. An honorific decree of the Otorkondeis at Mylasa, for Iatrocles dated tenatively to *c*.100 provides a novel reason for his service:

> *πρεσβευτής τε αἱρεθεὶς καὶ αὐτὸ[ς πρὸς] | Μᾶρκον Ἰούνιον Δεκόμου υἱὸν Σιλανόν, στρατηγὸν, πάτρωνα τῆς πόλεως, διαβαίνοντα ε[ἰς τὴν] | Ἀσίαν, ἐξῆλθεν καὶ ἔπεισεν ἐλθεῖν εἰς τὴν πόλιν ἡμῶν τὸν ἄνδρα καὶ ἐποίησεν εὐεργε[τικώ]|τερον διατεθῆναι πρὸς τὸν σύμπαντα δῆμον, αὐτόπτην γενόμενον τῆς σπουδῆς τῶν [πολι]|τῶν τῆς εἰς αὐτὸν τε καὶ τὸν Ῥωμαίων δῆμον* ('He was also chosen as ambassador and he went to Marcus Iunius, D.f., Silanus, praetor, patron of the city, who was arriving in Asia,[24] and persuaded the man to come to our city and made him more beneficently disposed towards the whole people, so that he became a witness to the esteem of the citizens towards both him and the Roman people').[25]

Iatrocles' embassy appears to have had the sole purpose of persuading the governor to visit Mylasa. This provides an interesting twist on the typical narrative of gubernatorial visits as something to be endured by allies rather than celebrated, demonstrating that the presence of the governor could be actively sought in order to make a positive impression.[26] It seems Silanus already had ties to the city, named here as *πάτρων*, and perhaps *polis* representatives sought to re-affirm these personal ties with the praetor. Why Silanus required persuasion to visit Mylasa has implications for understanding the administration of Asia. The *polis* was a *conventus* centre by 29 at the latest, though it had lost this privilege by 17.[27] Most scholars assume that the list of cities within which proconsuls held assizes remained relatively stable, leading to the plausible view that Mylasa was one of the original cities designated as such.[28] Although during the Republic a fixed schema for a gubernatorial assize tour can be ruled out, this status would imply that Mylasa was more frequently visited by Roman commanders than other communities which did not host the *conventus*. Two possible reasons for Iatrocles' embassy arise. First, if the decree pre-dates the First Mithridatic War, Mylasa, like most of southern Caria, lay beyond the formal scope of the Asian command and *conventus* structure. Second is Silanus' position as civic patron. The decree also implies that he already held this position before arriving in Asia as governor. One explanation would suggest Mylasan ambassadors to Rome had

[24] For this meaning of *διαβαίνω*: Robert 1940, 54–5, with comparanda; add now, *SEG* 39.1243.49–51.

[25] *I.Mylasa* 109.14–18. On the date: Ferrary 2000, 172–4, esp. n.61 contra Eilers 1999, 80–6.

[26] Compare the self-conscious claims of Cicero of his own moderation: for example, *Att.* 5.16.3; 21.4, 7.

[27] *I.Priene*² 13.44–5; Cottier et al. 2008, ll.88.

[28] E.g., Burton 1975, 92–3; Habicht 1975, 67–70; Mitchell 1999, 22–8; Kantor 2013, 156.

engaged his assistance in an earlier matter, though the nature of this connection must remain obscure. The existence of *patroni* for nearby Teos from the mid-second century shows that an ongoing relationship could exist without necessarily arising from a prior visit.[29] It also speaks to the importance of a governor's presence for communities to effectively demonstrate their regard to the individual and Rome.[30] Physical presence was a crucial element to official communication between state representatives and local communities. Roman magistrates in *provinciae* were rarely static. Polemaeus' inscription emphasizes the corollary of this point: he was honoured for taking on the expense of hosting the governor Q. Mucius Scaevola and his entourage when they arrived at Colophon.[31] The movement and presence of governors had a practical and ideological significance. It facilitated communication between the governor and the local populace: Bérenger emphasizes that a commander could only effectively mediate between the distinct interest groups active within a *provincia* with local contacts. Visiting communities and being hosted facilitated more intimate contacts on a larger scale.[32] At a practical level, the proximity or otherwise of the governor allowed *poleis* in dispute with one another to pre-empt or out-petition their rivals.

The turnover of Roman governors highlights another important factor. Unlike powerful Seleucid officials—such as Achaeus or Zeuxis, regent-like figures responsible for administering most Seleucid territory in Asia Minor—Roman magistrates, at least initially, expected to exercise authority within the smaller boundaries of the former Attalid kingdom. By contrast, Attalid officials were more limited in their mandate, as their rulers inverted the pre-existing Seleucid power structure to place more emphasis on localized authorities.[33] As such, the transition to Roman rule made powerful officials more accessible than under previous regimes, due to these spatial factors. The absence of established places associated with the exercise of Roman power, an administrative capital, meant that commanders were more likely to travel directly to trouble spots. Over time, consistent association of Roman commanders with fixed locations, often major *poleis* with significant communities of Roman citizens, began to form the basis of an administrative geography.[34] That said, problems with information flow between governor and city should not be under-emphasized. It was not always possible for communities to have up-to-date information on magistrates' whereabouts, which may explain Iatrocles' embassy to Silanus.

[29] *Syll.*³ 656.20–7. [30] E.g., Quass 1993, 138–9.

[31] Compare *I.Cos* 180, in which the priest of Heracles Callinicus is exempted from 'providing hospitality to the Romans' and *Syll.*³ 748, on the Cloatii at Gytheum entertaining *legati* of the governor. Hennig 1997, 363–8.

[32] Bérenger 2011, 171–6. [33] Thonemann 2013, 11–17. [34] E.g., Cic. *Flacc.* 68, 71.

Embassies to the Senate

By contrast, embassies to the Senate were a more significant undertaking, involving greater time, expense, and danger. Nevertheless, several factors prompted communities to attempt resolution at the heart of the Roman state. Foremost among these was the phenomenon of commanders on the ground referring disputes to senatorial oversight. Roman citizens could also draw on their personal connections to force cases to Rome. The summoning of Pericles of Ephesus to trial in Rome by M. Aurelius Scaurus for resisting the latter's violation of the Artemision's asylum provides a key example.[35] Similarly, Cicero wrote to Q. Minucius Thermus, during the latter's governorship of Asia, asking him to compel several *poleis* to send *ecdici* to Rome to settle a dispute with Cluvius of Puteoli.[36] However, communities could also take their grievances and requests to the Senate of their own accord. The example of Menippus, cited above, and several attested disputes with the *publicani* do not suggest earlier attempts to solicit decisions from magistrates in Asia.[37] Consequently, while many embassies could be referred by governors to the Senate, the sheer volume seen under the Late Republic makes it more likely that most requests were despatched to Rome directly.

Cicero's correspondence emphasizes both this frequency and the variety of topics which embassies addressed in the late 60s and 50s. Writing to his brother during the latter's command in Asia from 61–59 he lists ambassadors from five *poleis* whom he claims to have appeased despite Quintus' intemperate actions.[38] By contrast, he reports in 54 that ambassadors from Magnesia-under-Sipylos visited him and praised Quintus' decision in their favour on a suit brought by a Roman citizen. In neither case can we reconstruct the specific catalyst of diplomatic action and the meetings took place outside of the Senate. Perhaps in the former case the embassies intended to address the Senate on Quintus' conduct, but the latter example demonstrates that the Magnesians acted directly to build goodwill with an influential consular. In the same letter, Cicero mentions that a delegation from Tenedos had lobbied the Senate for a grant of *libertas* and been rejected out of hand, despite support from himself and M. Calpurnius Bibulus.[39] Cicero also refers to embassies from Caunus, seeking to be removed from subjection to Rhodes and integrated into the province of Asia, and a delegation of *legati* sent from Mylasa to deal with a fiscal dispute.[40] These incidental references in Cicero's letters emphasize the extent to which

[35] Cic. *Verr.* 2.1.85. See Chapter 1, 'Gubernatorial Jurisdiction and the Free Cities'.

[36] Cic. *Fam.* 13.65.

[37] E.g., *RDGE* 12; Strabo 14.1.26.

[38] Cic. *QFr.* 1.2.4–5: he mentions delegates from Dionysopolis, Apamea, Antandros, Smyrna, and Colophon. On this passage, Jordan (forthcoming b).

[39] Cic. *QFr.* 2.11.2–3.

[40] Caunus: Cic. *QFr.* 1.1.33; Mylasa: *Fam.* 13.56.1.

Asian cities would send ambassadors to Rome to interact with individuals and the Senate during this period.

One final example shows Cicero anticipating delegates from various *poleis* responding to a disagreement about *portoria* which Quintus had referred to the Senate. Cicero assumes that multiple embassies would arrive to complain about the actions of the *publicani*, who were charging *portoria* twice on goods which had been brought into one port and then moved to another.[41] This phenomenon might explain Strabo's report that Xenocles of Adramyttium defended the province against accusations of Mithridatism before the Senate. The text does not suggest that Xenocles represented the nascent *koinon*, the collective body of the province. Instead, he may have appeared in Rome as ambassador for an individual *polis*, probably Adramyttium, and launched a general defence of provincial communities when challenged in the Senate.[42] The members of the Milesian embassy co-opted by Cicero as witnesses against Verres provide a strong parallel.[43] More ambiguous is Diodorus Zonas from Sardis—who *floruit* in the Mithridatic period—whom Strabo describes as ἀνὴρ πολλοὺς ἀγῶνας ἠγωνισμένος ὑπὲρ τῆς Ἀσίας ('a man who spoke in many cases on behalf of Asia').[44] Diodorus Pasparos was honoured at Pergamum not only for his advocacy on behalf of his home *polis* but also ṭοῖς τὴν ἐπαρχείαν κατοικοῦσιν ἑκά[στωι] ('for each inhabitant of the province').[45] Finally, the decree of the *koinon* honouring Dionysus and Hierocles shows that they spoke at Rome on behalf of the collective, likely in the late 60s or 50s.[46] These examples stress the unpredictability of the ambassador's task when speaking to Roman power and the continued growth of collective identity among communities in Asia after Sulla's reorganization of the province.

Cicero's blunt admonishment of Quintus over his treatment of certain *poleis* highlights the phenomenon of civic embassies complaining about governors' conduct to the Senate, which often escalated to legal action.[47] A well-known Samian inscription honouring Cn. Domitius Ahenobarbus as τοῦ δοθέντος ὑπὸ συνκλήτου πάτρωνος τῶι δήμωι ('*patron*, assigned to the *demos* by the Senate') must derive from a legal context: likely referring to Ahenobarbus' appointment as a prosecutor in a *quaestio*, perhaps in a *repetundae* case.[48] Allowing this, it must pre-date the *lex Sempronia de repetundis* in 123, which fits into the general picture that even in the earliest stages of Roman commands in Asia embassies from *poleis* would address the Senate directly with complaints about gubernatorial conduct.[49]

[41] Cic. *Att.* 2.16.4. Cottier et al. 2008 ll.16–19. [42] Str. 13.1.66.

[43] Cic. *Verr.* 2.1.90. The characterization of the ambassadors as *mensem Februarium... exspectant* shows that they had official business beyond the Verres case.

[44] Strabo 13.4.9. [45] *IGR* 4.292.3, 5–6, 15–16. [46] *IAph2007* 2.503.

[47] Cic. *QFr.* 1.2.4. [48] *IGR* 4.968. Eilers 1991, 167–9; more cautiously, Ferrary 1997a, 105–7.

[49] E.g., Cic. *Flacc.* 98 (with Maselli 2000, 196 n.187); Gell. *NA.* 10.3.5; App. *BCiv* 1.92.

Personal, Political, or Public?: Witnesses in *repetundae* Trials

This leads to the related problem of whether witnesses in *repetundae* trials were considered official ambassadors. The key evidence appears in Cicero's forensic speeches, especially *in Verrem* and *pro Flacco*. Cicero consistently uses the Latin *legati* and *legatio* to describe the witnesses despatched by *poleis* to give evidence.[50] Between the two texts, Cicero gives positive and negative views of their appointment, varying his argument based on his clients, the wronged provincials in the former case and the accused governor in the latter. In his prosecution of Verres, Cicero carefully explains that whole communities repudiated the honorific statues and embassies they had disseminated during Verres' command in Sicily. He stresses that *senatus decrevit populusque iussit* ('the *boule* decreed and the *demos* commanded') that *Romam mandata legatosque misissent* ('letters and ambassadors be sent to Rome') to testify.[51] However, in defending Flaccus, a governor of Asia, Cicero emphasizes the role played by prosecutors in encouraging these embassies. Contrasting his own case against Verres with that of his young adversary, D. Laelius, he states: *ego testis a Sicilia publice deduxi: verum erant ea testimonia non concitatae contionis, sed iurati senatus* ('I myself summoned witnesses from Sicily at public expense: but truly this was evidence not from an excited public meeting but sworn to by *boulai*').[52] He underlines the relative influence of prosecutors in assembling a case.

> *Adulescens bonus, honesto loco natus, disertus cum maximo ornatissimoque comitatu venit in oppidum Graecorum, postulat contionem, locupletis homines et gravis ne sibi adversentur testimoni denuntiatione deterret, egentis et levis spe largitionis et viatico publico, privata etiam benignitate prolectat.* ('A virtuous youth, born of honourable rank, and eloquent arrives, with a very large and distinguished company, in a town of the Greeks. He demands a *contio*; he terrifies the wealthy and men of authority from opposing him, by summoning them to testify; he incites the needy and insignificant through hope of largesse and of travelling expenses on the public purse, or through his private benevolence').[53]

The crux of Cicero's argument is that the 'embassies' against Flaccus are not legitimate representatives of the civic community, as they are appointed by

[50] E.g., Cic. *Verr.* 2.2.13 (only one city sends *publice legati* to support Verres), 114 (cities accuse Verres *publice litteris, legationibus, testimoniis*); 120 (lists four cities by name—Centuripa, Halaesa, Catina, Panormus—and others as sending embassies); 156 (Hortensius' accusation that Artemo of Centuripa was not a *legatus* but *accusator*).

[51] Cic. *Verr.* 2.2.161. Generally, Stoop 2017, 10–15.

[52] Cic. *Flacc.* 17 (with Maselli 2000, 162). On Laelius: Steel 2016, 216–17. On Cicero's own collection of evidence: Lintott 2008, 86–7. Thirteen embassies spoke at the *actio prima*, seventeen more are attested as present in the *actio secunda*, see: Lintott 2008, 93, n.44 for references.

[53] Cic. *Flacc.* 18.

assemblies alone without the oversight by the *boule*. He warms to this theme when treating the specific charges levelled against Flaccus, highlighting the absence of respected, for which we may read aristocratic, voices from the Trallian delegation and stressing the exclusive and unrepresentative nature of the embassy from Temnus.[54] This echoes his attempt to dismiss the supporters of Verres as those *iniussu populi ac senatus* ('uncommanded by *demos* and *boule*').[55] Though Cicero's ulterior motives must be acknowledged here, this speaks to a set of expectations on the part of Roman jurors as to how witnesses could be deemed 'official'. Cicero consistently asserts that a vote of the *senatus* and *populus*, that is, the *boule* and *demos*, would distinguish witnesses as representing the community. This corresponds to expectations surrounding embassies to the Senate, which, when referred to in these works, are described in exactly the same language of *legati* and *legationes*.[56] Cicero would suggest that witnesses in *repetundae* trials, for the post-Sullan period, shared descriptors and a status with ambassadors to the Senate.

The Personalization of Official Embassies

Through the latter part of the period, communities increasingly sought benefactions directly from powerful individual Romans. Though Caesar and Augustus both held official status, their power, authority, and influence lay outside the traditional *cursus honorum*. This phenomenon is particularly obvious after Pharsalus, when Caesar's pursuit of Pompeius through the eastern Mediterranean was besieged by embassies from his opponent's erstwhile supporters. His lenient treatment of Mytilene may have encouraged other *poleis* to seek absolution.[57] During Caesar's Alexandrian sojourn the governor of Asia, Servilius Isauricus, a directly appointed representative, formed the focal point of diplomatic activity rather than the Senate.[58] Under Augustus this became the norm. The Mytilenean embassy seeking a renewal of their treaty in 25, after reaching the Senate, then approached the Princeps in Spain directly.[59] By 6, Augustus could describe his encounter with a Cnidian embassy in terms typical of a Hellenistic *basileus*: *οἱ πρέσ|βεις ὑμῶν… ἐνέτυχον ἐν Ῥώμῃ μοι καὶ τὸ ψήφισμα ἀποδόντες* ('your ambassadors…met me in Rome and gave me your decree').[60] One reason was practical. As the power dynamics of the Roman state evolved, it behoved communities to seek favours first from the most authoritative actor possible. Furthermore, the institutions of the *res publica* itself changed during this period to place Augustus, and

[54] Cic. *Flacc.* 42–3, 52–3. [55] Cic. *Verr.* 2.2.14. [56] E.g., Cic. *Verr.* 2.2.50.
[57] Caes. *BCiv.* 3.102.4; Plut. *Pomp.* 75.2. [58] Kirbihler 2016, 88.
[59] *IGR* 4.38; Gow-Page *GP* #16, cf. *RDGE* 26.c.1–5. [60] *RDGE* 67.5–7.

subsequently the imperial house, at the centre of the ideological as well as the practical networks of power.

The advent of the Triumvirate and, eventually, the Principate fundamentally altered the nature of the dialogue between the Roman state and Asian *poleis*. While, strictly speaking, the Senate, *populus*, and magistrates continued to perform their venerable functions, the reality of power increasingly concentrated in the hands of a few individuals did not go unrecognized by local actors. For example, as already noted, the *senatus consultum de Aphrodisiensibus* refers to an embassy which approached the Senate in entirely traditional terms, before granting several privileges moved jointly by the *tresviri* Octavian and Antonius.[61] A separate letter from Octavian to the *polis* personalizes this context: he notes his own relationship with the ambassador, Solon, praising his diligence, and a request made for copies of several documents, which he has provided.[62] Similarly, Octavian's unsubtle emphasis of his personal regard for Seleucus in his communication with Rhosus was unlikely to avoid 'correct' interpretation for long.[63] As the nature of Roman power swiftly changed, it is unsurprising to find communities innovating in their attempts to improve their situations.

The Augustan proconsular letter to Chios provides an important example of local adaptation, specifically, the Chians' strategy in achieving their goal. Initially, an embassy approached the governor, C. Antistius Vetus, who gave a decision against them. Undeterred, the Chians sent a second embassy to his successor, after his departure. This too was brushed aside, as the governor took a conservative line on decisions rendered by his predecessor. However, he allowed both parties to present their arguments with ἐπιμελέστερα γεγραμμένα . . . ὑπομνήματα ('more carefully written documents') to support them. Normally, ὑπομνήματα would mean documents held by the court or magistrate, that is, *memoranda* in Latin; though Bitner accepts this reading, he admits that it is unparalleled.[64] Nevertheless, the Chians took advantage of this request to present at least two Roman normative documents which offered specific and detailed conditions of their freedom, regulating their relationship with the Roman state. The first of these, described as 'a sealed copy of a very old *senatus consultum*', dating to 80, rewarded the islanders for their resistance to Mithridates, confirmed their enjoyment of their laws, customs, and rights (as they stood when they came into the friendship of the Roman people), guaranteed their freedom from written instructions of Roman magistrates and, contentiously, made Romans subject to Chian law.[65] The second document's provisions, a letter of Augustus in 26, are largely unpreserved.[66] These were demonstrably not arguments or records but new, and

[61] *IAph2007* 8.27.16–23. [62] *IAph2007* 8.25.16–39, 55–9. [63] *RDGE* 58.81–4, 92–3.

[64] *Memoranda* normally translates as γράμματα or ἐπιστολαί. Bitner 2014, 656–7.

[65] *RDGE* 70.11–13.

[66] *RDGE* 70.18–20. Bitner's claim (2014, 663) that this may not have resulted from an embassy is unlikely.

apparently convincing, evidence to be adduced. Bitner questions why, were this the case, they had not been brought forward at an earlier stage, suggesting plausibly that the initial decision against the Chians took place through a written response to a Roman citizen's petition.[67] However, the *senatus consultum* explicitly states that Chios was to remain immune from any decision by a Roman magistrate, implying that neither Antistius, nor his successor, were initially aware that Chios held this privilege. The Chians, who appear to have held this right continuously since 80, may have simply assumed the Romans were conversant with their situation. If true, this could suggest that the Chians themselves originally sought the aid of Antistius in enforcing a local ruling on a Roman citizen resident, as per their privileges under the *senatus consultum*.[68] While Bitner astutely presents the judicial processes through which the case proceeded, I contend that what we are dealing with here is a Chian sleight of hand, together with a lack of understanding by the Roman governor. If the *senatus consultum* and letter of Augustus were as unambiguous as they appear, and were well known, how could Antistius and his successor decide in favour of their opponents? This suggests rather that the original embassies did not travel with documentary evidence of Chios' status; rather, the governor(s) may initially have been petitioned by Roman residents, resulting in a favourable decision which the Chians sought to overturn. At a request to submit more careful documents, the Chians took the opportunity to locate and add their documentary evidence. As Bitner concludes, 'the Chians used their knowledge of Roman... legal documents... to gain an advantage'.[69] At the third time of asking, the Chians understood and chose to submit as evidence documents in line with Roman legal practice, appealing to the strong Roman preference towards following precedent.[70] Allowing this reconstruction of events emphasizes the extent to which communities had to learn and adopt Roman modes of thinking to successfully achieve their goals.

Norbanus' letter to Aezani provides a further example of the realignment of civic strategies for engaging with Roman magistrates in the Augustan period. Though redolent of Hellenistic royal language, Norbanus' communiqué responds to a letter of Augustus presented to him by the ambassadors, rather than an honorific decree.[71] The Aezanetans cite Augustus, as in the Chian example, as a source of authority vis-à-vis the governor. However, by contrast, the Aezanetans appear to have deliberately solicited the Princeps' confirmation of a decision made on the ground by the procurator Ofilius; the earliest example of a procurator interfering in the internal, fiscal affairs of a *polis*.[72] This letter further demonstrates

[67] Marshall 1969, 264–5; Bitner 2014, 661–2.
[68] Marshall 1969, 258–9.
[69] Bitner 2014, 664; *pace* Meyer-Zwiffelhoffer 2002, 269.
[70] Meyer 2004, 122, 169–206; Bitner 2014, 662–4.
[71] *AÉ* 2011, #1303.
[72] CD 53.15.3. Wörrle 2011, 365–70.

awareness among Asian *poleis* of competing sources of Roman authority. The first was the procurator himself, whose decision precipitated the entire diplomatic exchange. Indeed, how and why Ofilius issued instructions to Aezani requires careful consideration. The text implies that, in Norbanus' view, the concession of civic autonomy to grant ἀτέλεια to the priest was a privilege, which might reflect an earlier instruction to desist from making such grants.[73] Alternatively, Ofilius may have been given explicit instructions to regulate civic finances within the region, as Vedius Pollio appears to have been given oversight of the finances of the Artemision at Ephesus.[74] In either case, the Aezanetans treated the procurator's decision seriously. However, it does not seem to have been regarded as secure. The existence of Augustus' letter suggests, though does not prove, a civic embassy was despatched to the Princeps to confirm Ofilius' action before approaching Norbanus. This recognition of the overarching authority of Augustus echoes both his invocation at Chios and the language of proconsuls themselves, as shown in Chapter 5. Finally, after receiving a written response, the Aezanetan embassy witnessed in the letter visited the governor directly. Given that he held his position under the Senate's authority, one would expect that he held unchallenged authority within his *provincia*, and his insistence on his personal wish to benefit the *polis* emphasizes his own agency. As mentioned, his choice of the verb ἐπιτρέπειν to concede approval could support this point. Overall, the complex manoeuvring seen in this text point to a growing understanding by the inhabitants of one *polis* of the tensions between the structural elements of Roman power. It seems that Aezani intended to confirm the grant of privileges by an imperial procurator with the Princeps before raising the issue with the relevant authority, the proconsul of Asia. The unprecedented primacy of Augustus offered new opportunities for leverage within imperial governance, and communities were not hesitant to utilize them.

Civic diplomatic missions across the period were multifarious and diverse, but some general comments are possible. Largely, they were proactive, strategic, and targeted. While our evidence represents a meagre fraction of the original material, difference in attitudes and approaches are detectable both over the period and from *polis*-to-*polis*. This complements a second observation: almost all the surviving evidence pertains to individual communities acting in their own interests. A few examples of collective action exist for the Late Republic; the decree of the *koinon* from Aphrodisias, and ambassadors, such as Diodorus Pasparos and Diodorus Zonas, did speak on behalf of the province. While not denying that communities often co-operated when it was in their interests—embassies from different *poleis* were essential in *repetundae* cases, such as that against L. Valerius

[73] Compare Caesar's instruction to Mytilene during his third dictatorship: *RDGE* 26.27–9.
[74] Wörrle 2011, 371–2; Kirbihler 2017, 133–4.

Flaccus, for example—the evidence suggests that, first and foremost, each city engaged in direct dialogue with Rome and its representatives.[75]

Informal Contacts: Diplomacy through Personal Relationships

Beyond formal diplomatic missions, communities and individuals could employ less-formal ties to their own advantage. The rise of Roman power brought about fundamental structural changes to the ways in which *poleis* could engage with the hegemonic state. Most obviously, the existence of a granular and constantly evolving administration, by comparison to Hellenistic kingdoms, provided opportunities and challenges.[76] Where royal benefaction could ultimately depend upon the mood of a single individual, the distributed power structure of the Republic required the formation of coalitions within the senatorial elite to realize preferred outcomes. The Romans did not engage with the Greek institution of *προξενία*, through which *poleis* would establish relationships with a network of individuals based among their peer-polities, who could assist their citizens on public or private business. However, this may have provided a cognitive framework for communities interacting with specific Romans.[77] Over time, alternative tools such as formal civic patronage became more significant as levers. However, the corollary was the increasing prominence of personal connections for informing Roman attitudes towards provincial communities. Though these informal contacts did not represent public or, necessarily, officially sanctioned exchanges, they had significant effects on the well-being of communities. Important questions include: to what extent these were publicly minded, intentional actions on behalf of the *polis* as opposed to personal actions; did they form part of the developing imperial discourse and present an effective means of civic agency; and most significantly, how did the effectiveness of informal interaction with Rome and Romans affect the internal political and social dynamics of the communities of Asia?

Colophon: Personal and Political Friendship in the Early Province

Even from the earliest period of the Roman *provincia* the line between personal and public influence was blurred. The Claros inscriptions for Polemaeus and Menippus both reveal the importance of personal relationships to their diplomatic successes. Though framed in the explicitly Roman language of

[75] E.g., Canali De Rossi's (2005, 101–3) summary of the various civic embassies complaining about Flaccus.

[76] See Chapter 5. [77] Mack 2015, 249–81.

patronage, the decrees demonstrate the extent to which face-to-face contacts underlay relationships between Greek communities and Rome. For example, Polemaeus:

> *ἐνέτυχεν | μὲν τοῖς ἡγουμένοις Ῥωμαίοις | καὶ φανεὶς ἄξιος τῆς ἐκείνων | φιλίας τὸν ἀπὸ ταύτης καρπὸν | τοῖς πολείταις περιεποίησεν | πρὸς τοὺς ἀρίστους ἄνδρας τῆι | πατρίδι συνθέμενος πατρωνεί|ας* ('met with leading Romans, and becoming known as worthy of their friendship, obtained the fruit from this for our citizens, securing patronage with the best men for the city').[78]

This clause stresses that from the civic perspective Polemaeus' individual qualities were the key driver of Roman interest in Colophon. The ambassador is praised explicitly for turning a personal relationship to the city's advantage. He served as a proxy for the worth of the whole community. Since Polemaeus was worthy of Roman friendship (*φιλία*) on an individual level, those parties were more willing to countenance a formal relationship through the medium of civic patronage with his homeland. Given this text comes directly from a civic decree, representing the official narrative of the community, the emphasis on the importance of personal connections is striking. While honorific decrees for ambassadors often draw attention to their personal prowess, the foregrounding of these relationships is rare in earlier examples.[79] Roman hegemony required ambassadors to emphasize different elements of their skill set.

Menippus' inscription is more revealing:

> *τοι|γαροῦν διὰ τὴν ἐμ πᾶσιν ἀρετὴν τοῖς μεγίστοις | Ῥωμαίων συσταθεὶς αὐτός τε πρεσβεύων ὑ|πὲρ αὐτῶν καὶ πίστεως ἀξιούμενος ἐπίσημος | γέγονε παρὰ πολλαῖς τῶν Ἑλληνίδων πόλε|ων, τῆς τε πόλεως γνησίους αὐτοὺς πεποιη|κὼς πάτρωνας χρησιμώτατος παρὰ τοῖς ἡγου|μένοις γέγονε τῶι δήμωι παρ' οἷς ἀναγκαιόταται | πᾶσιν εἰσὶν ἀνθρώποις χρεῖαι* ('Therefore, on account of his excellence in all things, recommended by the greatest Romans, he served as ambassador on behalf of them, and being worthy of their trust (sc. *fides*), became famed among many Greek cities, and he procured for the city genuine patrons, became most useful to the *demos* through the leaders, from whom were the most necessary benefits for all men').[80]

Like Polemaeus before him, Menippus was praised for his close ties to leading Romans. The decree claims that he was so valued that he was employed by them to conduct embassies on their behalf to other Greek communities. Though this recalls the use of the homonymous Menippus, ambassador of Antiochus III, by

[78] *SEG* 39.1243.2.24–31.
[79] E.g., for Hegesias of Lampsacus (*Syll.*[3] 591).
[80] *SEG* 39.1244.3.5–15.

Teos in their dealings with Rome in 193, Ferrary convincingly proposes that this involved only the communication of decisions from the Senate rather than active negotiation. Nevertheless, this demonstrates how a Greek envoy could benefit his city and the broader provincial community through his high reputation among the Romans.[81] Again, the Colophonians honoured Menippus for turning his personal reputation to the advantage of the broader community.

Both men were also praised for their entertainment of Romans visiting Colophon. Polemaeus was commended for personally paying the expenses of lodging unnamed Romans.[82] It is possible that these were *publicani* or *negotiatores*, though much more likely that they were Romans on official business. Plentiful evidence shows governors and their staff lodging with local magnates, not necessarily civic officeholders.[83] The evidence for Menippus is more concrete:

> *παραγενομένου δὲ εἰς τὴν πόλιν οὐχ ἅπαξ καὶ τοῦ | Ῥωμαίων στρατηγοῦ Κοίντου Μουκίου καὶ τοῦ ταμί|ου καὶ χιλιάρχων πάντας ὑπεδέξατο, τὰς παρὰ τῆς | πόλεως διδομένας δαπάνας ἀναπέμψας τῆι πό|λει* ('and, more than once, when the praetor of the Romans, Q. Mucius, arrived in the city with his *quaestor* and military tribunes, he received them all into his home, giving back the expenses paid out by the city').'[84]

The decree states explicitly that Menippus hosted Q. Mucius and his staff during multiple visits to Colophon. This Q. Mucius, certainly a Scaevola, could be the consul of 117 who commanded in Asia in 120/119, or the consul of 95 who commanded between 99–97. The Roberts argued that on the basis of Menippus' attested Attalid embassies the former is more likely, providing a relative date for his career of *c*.140–120.[85] The inscription also highlights that the civic treasury would ordinarily bear this cost, with Menippus returning the funds voted by the *polis*. Crucially, this lodging had an important secondary function, providing an opportunity for the host to create useful relationships on a civic and a personal level. Notwithstanding the risks inherent in a poor impression, illustrated by Verres' alleged judicial murder of Philodamus of Lampsacus and his son, the

[81] Ferrary 2009, 138–42; *pace* Robert & Robert 1989, 101. Though whether the Romans viewed it in terms of honour or convenience is another issue. Cf. the use of Rhodian ambassadors to communicate with the Hellenistic kingdoms in the *lex de provinciis praetoriis* of 100 (*RS* 12.Delphi.b.12–8); the use of Aphrodisian ambassadors by Q. Oppius (*IAph2007* 8.3) and that of Magnesian ambassadors in 29 (*I.Priene*² 13.6–8).

[82] *SEG* 39.1243.4.20–3.

[83] E.g., *IG* 5.1.1146.32–40; Cic. *Verr.* 2.1.63–84; *Att.* 5.16.3. Quass 1984, 205–6; Bérenger 2011, 179–87.

[84] *SEG* 39.1244.2.42–5. All previous commentators read χιλίαρχος as *tribunus militum* (cf. Mason 1974, s.v. χιλίαρχος) though given that Scaevola, as a praetorian governor in a peaceful region was likely unaccompanied by a legion, it is possible that this refers to his *legati*.

[85] Robert & Robert 1989, 98–9; Ferrary 2017a [1991], 161–3 contra Canali De Rossi 1991, 646–8; Eilers 2002, 125–8.

face-to-face elements of administration shared by Roman and Hellenic elite society, together with the crucial reciprocity afforded more opportunities for co-operation when based on a pre-existing personal connection.[86] Menippus' positive reputation among Romans was likely founded, at least partially, on his hospitality within Asia. Scaevola's naming here, by contrast with Polemaeus' more generic text, may indicate that Menippus did not host other commanders, suggesting that this 'honour' rotated through the members of the civic elite who could afford it.[87] Nevertheless, both inscriptions together imply the presence of the Roman commander in Colophon on a semi-regular basis. This hints at the growing weight of personal qualities and connections of individual ambassadors in the late second century. Confronted by a rotating cast of influential senators and commanders, it seems that the Colophonians, at least, recognized the critical role of skilled individuals in cultivating a strong bond with specific leaders, beyond appealing directly to the Senate.

Theophanes: Between Mytilene and Rome

Perhaps the most notable example of a provincial using his personal Roman connections to benefit his home city is Theophanes of Mytilene. A well-known intellectual, he accompanied Cn. Pompeius Magnus on his eastern campaigns after 67, of which he produced a history.[88] He is attested as a Roman citizen in 62, which Raggi identifies as unusual for Greek allies of this period, taking the name Cn. Pompeius Theophanes.[89] The ambiguity over whether individuals could hold a non-Roman citizenship alongside the *civitas Romana* has important implications for Theophanes' social status.[90] Heller has emphasized that while Greek self-identity in this period was based on language and shared culture, the Roman ideal focused more closely on participation in the citizen community.[91] After 62, the evidence places him either at Rome or in the vicinity of Pompeius, which speaks to his close attention to Roman political games.[92] Accordingly, Ferrary has argued that the mid-first century saw ambition relocated from the civic to the imperial sphere for select elite allied individuals. Direct personal relationships with Romans

[86] On Lampsacus: Steel 2004, 233–51. [87] *Pace* Robert & Robert 1989, 102.

[88] Plut. *Pomp.* 37.2–3. Pédech 1991, 74–8; Santangelo 2018, 129; Ellis-Evans 2019, 256–8. Brithagoras of Heraclea, who visited Caesar on an embassy in *c.*59 and accompanied him for twelve years while petitioning for his city's freedom, presents another contemporary example of this phenomenon (Memnon *FGrH* 434 40.3–4).

[89] Cic. *Arch.* 24. Raggi 2010, 149; Santangelo 2018, 131–3. Cf. Gold 1985, 312–13. Val. Max. 8.14.5.

[90] Cic. *Caec.* 100; *Balb.* 29–30; Nep. *Att.* 3.1: each example shows this was a matter of legal debate at Rome, irrespective of how communities in the provinces reacted. Brunt 1982; Ferrary 2005, 68–70; Fournier 2012, 85–8. Compare members of the Athenian *boule* with Roman citizenship in the mid-first century (Habicht 1997, 345).

[91] Heller 2011, 227–9.

[92] Santangelo 2018, 133–43. Compare Nicias of Cos: Herzog 1922, 190–216; Bowersock 1965, 45–6.

could secure honour and privileges beyond those offered by service within the community.[93] In this respect, Theophanes stands as a harbinger of imperial Greek elites and in subsequent decades his family continued to enjoy an elevated status: his son, Pompeius Macer, was an imperial procurator in Asia and his grandson, Q. Pompeius Macer, the earliest attested Greek senator.[94]

Though the evidence suggests that civic benefaction was no longer his sole or primary concern, he was honoured extensively at Mytilene.[95] Plutarch is explicit that Theophanes persuaded Pompeius to restore freedom to the *polis*, which it had lost following the First Mithridatic War, and it seems clear that this benefaction underpinned his honours.[96] Without evidence for specific actions on Theophanes' part, as well as his apparent absence from Mytilene, it is unlikely that he played a prominent role within the civic community. However, this does not mean that he did not press for other benefits from Rome and Romans on behalf of the city. The literary sources, understandably, focus on his role in Roman political life, but a monument at Mytilene honoured him alongside Pompeius and Potamon, the prominent ambassador from the 40s onwards. In doing so, the monument drew a link between the Roman agent responsible, the local catalyst and a contemporary who continued to defend civic independence strongly:

> *Γναίῳ Ποντη|ίῳ, Γναίω υἱω, | Μεγάλῳ, αὐτο|κράτορι, τῷ εὐ|εργέτᾳ καὶ σω|τῆρι καὶ κτιστᾳ˙ || Θέῳ Δίι [Ἐ]λε[υθε]ρίῳ φιλοπάτριδι | Θεοφάνῃ, τῷ σωτῆρι καὶ εὐεργέ|τᾳ καὶ κτιστᾳ δευ|τέρῳ τᾶς πατρίδος˙ || Ποτάμωνι | Λεσβώνακτο[ς] | τῷ εὐεργέτᾳ καὶ σωτῆρος | καὶ κτιστᾷ τᾶ[ς] | πόλιο[ς]˙* ('To Gnaeus Pompeius, son of Gnaeus, Magnus, *imperator*, benefactor and saviour and founder. || To the god Zeus Eleutherios, the country-loving Theophanes, saviour and benefactor and second founder of the city. || To Potamon, son of Lesbonax, benefactor and saviour and founder of the city').[97]

This inscription associates Theophanes with the figure of Zeus Eleutherios, suggesting that it was posthumous, and emphasizes his role in securing the city's freedom.[98] Significantly, neither Pompeius nor Potamon is granted divine status and the reference to him as *κτίστης δευτέρος*, where his two fellow honorands receive the epithet *κτίστης* without qualification (founder, preserver) is also

[93] Ferrary 1997, 204; Santangelo 2018, 144; Ellis-Evans 2019, 258.

[94] Suet. *Aug.* 56.7; Strabo 12.2.3; Tac. *Ann.* 1.72.3, 6.18.2. Syme 1982, 79–80; Buraselis 2001, 61–3. For the family's links to the Euryclids of Sparta, whose relationship with the Roman state had a similar trajectory: Bowersock 1961, 116–17. On the growing importance of dynastic relationships: Quass 1984, 212–14.

[95] *Syll.*³ 753, 755; Robert 1969, 52–3; *SEG* 42.755; *BMC Troas, Aeolis, Lesbos* #158–60; Tac. *Ann.* 6.18.5. Magie 1950, 1230; Bowersock 1965, 1–13; Santangelo 2018, 133–43.

[96] Plut. *Pomp.* 42.43.3. Gold 1985, 324.

[97] *IG* 12.2.163.

[98] Compare *BMC Troas, Aeolis, Lesbos* #158–160, Tiberian coins of Mytilene bearing the legend *Θεοφάνης Θεός*. Robert 1969a, 48–51; Santangelo 2018, 143 contra Anastasiadis 1995, 9–10.

suggestive.[99] Theophanes presents a crucial evolution in the relationship between Romans and Greeks. He was the first prominent inhabitant of Asia to leverage his personal service to a Roman commander to benefit his home city without having been active as an official ambassador on their behalf. Santangelo's persuasive argument that the bulk of Theophanes' utility to Pompeius was in a Roman political mode rather than his literary output complicates the account of his assistance. As a Roman citizen, living and operating at Rome, Theophanes, in a practical sense stood outside the Mytilenean community. Yet, as this monument reinforces, he commanded reverence and respect from his home *polis*.

The Institutionalization of Personal Relationships: The Civil Wars and Beyond

Such dual roles become increasingly visible in the 40s and 30s. Perhaps the most explicit examples are the father and son Theopompus and Artemidorus of Cnidus.[100] The literary sources emphasize that Caesar made Cnidus a *civitas libera* to gratify Theopompus, memorably dismissed by Plutarch as *μύθων συναγωγή* ('a collector of stories'). The parallels between Theopompus and Theophanes are strong: both were members of the provincial elite of Asia, both were plucked from among the literati and were connected to a powerful Roman who arranged for their *polis* to receive its freedom.[101] Theopompus' citizenship is well attested and, like Theophanes, the sources imply that he was more active at Rome than in Asia.[102] Ferrary stresses that while Theopompus and his son may have been a major factor in Cnidus' freedom and were present at the oaths for the treaty between Rome and Cnidus, they were explicitly not a part of the embassy to Caesar.[103] Mithridates of Pergamum, whose close relationship with Caesar is similarly well attested, may have played a similar role for his home city, in light of an honorific decree attesting him as *νέος κτίστης* invoking the mythical Pergamos and Philetairos, progenitor of the Attalid dynasty.[104]

More generally, evidence collected by Strubbe implies that most recipients of near-divine honours (*ἰσόθεοι τιμαί*) in the period were Roman citizens prominent in their own communities: for example, C. Iulius Hybreas at Mylasa, the father

[99] Heller 2020, 31–3.

[100] On these figures: Hirschfeld 1886, 286–90; Thériault 2003, 232–53.

[101] Plut. *Caes.* 48.1; Strabo 14.2.15; *I.Knidos* 51–2.

[102] Most evidence for the two places them explicitly in Rome, and Artemidorus plays a role in Plutarch's and Appian's assassination narratives in 44: Cic. *Att.* 13.7.1; *Phil.* 13.33; Plut. *Caes.* 65.1–4; App. *BCiv* 2.116; Cic. *QFr.* 1.2.9, 2.11.4. Theopompus was also honoured with Roman nomenclature at Delphi (*Syll.*³ 761C), Rhodes (*IG* 12.1.90), Cos (*AÉ* 1934, 91), and Syrian Laodicea (*I.Knidos* 58): see Thériault 2003, 233–6.

[103] *I.Knidos* 56.7–9. Ferrary 2005, 56–7 contra Thériault 2003, 239.

[104] *IGR* 1682.9. Note Diodorus Pasparos, named *δευτέρος κτίστης* ('second founder') at Pergamum in the 60s: *IGR* 4.293.62–3.

and son C. Iulius Apollonius and C. Iulius Epicrates at Miletus, and C. Iulius Xeno at Thyatira.[105] A key question arising here, is what made these figures worthy of (near-)divine honours? Prima facie, their successes, while significant, were no more impressive than other members of the Asian civic elites who managed to obtain benefactions from the Senate or Roman commanders. Building on Santangelo's recent argument, I argue that the close engagement of some of these men in Roman politics and society made them fundamentally different from their predecessors and contemporaries. Through their citizenship and their intimate relationships with especially powerful Romans, they began to move from being the seekers of *beneficia* to agents of benefaction. As Theophanes and Artemidorus were Roman citizens, based in Rome, providing advice to late Republican powerbrokers, they served as semi-permanent lobbyists on their homelands' behalf rather than official representatives. One plausible model, albeit impossible to demonstrate conclusively, would see these Rome-based Greeks encouraging a consistent series of benefactions over a long term through their continued influence with figures at Rome. Though Hybreas seems to have remained in Asia, he too, according to the sources developed a strong relationship with both Antonius and Octavian.[106] The evidence for Epicrates and Apollonius, by contrast, seems to place them as active participants in civic life.[107] Several of these figures, including Hybreas, Epicrates, and Xeno were the first civic ἀρχιερεῖς for the imperial cult in their *polis*, further implicating them with the regime, albeit at the local level.[108] As the rule of Augustus and his successors became more entrenched, however, the grant of divine honours for civic benefactors swiftly disappeared.[109]

By contrast, provincial figures in the following period have comparatively less success. Though C. Iulius Zoilos at Aphrodisias and Seleucus of Rhosus were both granted citizenship and served as a conduit between their home cities and Augustus, the Roman world was changing, while the civic social scene remained conservative. Both Zoilos and Seleucus had served Augustus; the dossiers at Aphrodisias and Rhosus emphasize that the two had permanently settled in their home *poleis*.[110] Their forebears, such as Theophanes, appear to have been

[105] Strubbe 2004, 320–8. Hybreas: Noè 1996, 50–64; Delrieux & Ferriès 2004, 49–71, 499–515; Epicrates and Apollonius: *Milet* 6.1.156, 159; *SEG* 44.942; Herrmann 1994, 229–34; Xeno: *TAM* 5.2.1098.1–4; Strubbe 1984–6, 299. The potential exceptions are Euthydemus at Mylasa, (e.g., Cic. *Fam.* 13.56.1; Delrieux & Ferriès 2004, 54–64) and possible ἀσιάρχης (*I.Mylasa* 151, 531; Campanile 1997, 243–4); and Asclepiades of Cyzicus (*IGR* 4.159.10–13; Robert 1950, 95–6; Strubbe 2004, 324–5). Compare, Iulius Satyrus at Chersonesus (Rostovtzeff 1917, 27–44).

[106] Delrieux & Ferriès 2004, 64–71, 509–15.

[107] Epicrates was *stephanophoros* in 40/39, prophet at Didyma from either 33/32–27/26 or 20/19, and *archiereus* of Augustus at Miletus in 6/5 (*Milet* 1.2.7). Herrmann 1994, 204–6, 221–2, 1996, 7–10.

[108] Edelmann-Singer 2016, 228–30.

[109] See discussion of *I.Kyme* 19.3–20, on the refusal of ἰσόθεοι τιμαί by L. Vaccius Labeo. Price 1984, 47–52; Strubbe 2004, 328–9; Kuhn 2017, 199–205. See the overlap with common imperial policy: Tac. *Ann.* 4.38; *SEG* 11.922.17–21; *P.London* 1912.

[110] Heller 2011, 229–31; De Chaisemartin 2017, 337–41.

engaged in the cut and thrust of Republican politics, providing avenues of communication to the 'great men' they supported and advice in times of need. By contrast neither Zoilos nor Seleucus is envisaged as providing a similar service in the future, possibly the result of the shrinking arena of political life with Augustus' growing supremacy.[111] Moreover, both men seem to have emerged from less exalted backgrounds than typical members of the elite.[112] In this respect, Zoilos and Seleucus seem to have more in common with figures like Athenodorus of Tarsus, a tutor of Augustus who, according to Strabo, was intimately involved in the government of his own *polis* without receiving Roman citizenship.[113] These men achieved local influence through their central connections, rather than vice versa. This reflects the trend visible in the eastern empire under Antonius' triumvirate, where administrative functions including tax collection were outsourced to individuals.[114] This dynamic evolved as the Principate became entrenched, becoming more focused on the civic role of individuals while concurrently encouraging the creation of a provincial elite through institutions like the *koinon* of Asia.[115]

However, this narrative does not explain every case, which Crinagoras of Mytilene neatly illustrates. A distinguished contemporary of Potamon and participant in multiple embassies to Caesar and Augustus, in 25 he visited the latter in Spain.[116] His epigrams, collected in the Palatine Anthology, stress his closeness to the Imperial family between this date and his death sometime after 11 CE.[117] No evidence for his enfranchisement survives, suggesting a long residence at Rome, familiarity and intimacy with members of the imperial house, ranging from Marcellus to Tiberius, without being accepted fully into a Roman community. By contrast with Theophanes or Potamon, Crinagoras does not appear to have been particularly feted within Mytilene, which might suggest a less active or successful role in promoting the agenda of the city.[118] Although in Crinagoras' case this could be an accident of survival, it illustrates the point that not every prominent individual mediating between Rome and their community received the

[111] *Pace* Robert 1989 [1966], 43–5. [112] Raggi 2006, 191–3; Heller 2011, 229–31.

[113] Strabo 14.5.14. Note also, Nestor of Tarsus, teacher of Marcellus and προέστη τῆς πολιτείας. Bowersock 1965, 32–6. Compare, though speculative, Grimal 1945–6, 261–73, 62–79.

[114] E.g., Anaxenor of Magnesia or Stephanus at Aphrodisias. More generally, Antonius evinced a preference for appointing trusted allies to govern territory, simplifying the process of ruling and limiting the amount of resources expended on direct administration of justice and taxation: Jordan (forthcoming a).

[115] E.g., Smith 1993, 6; Edelmann-Singer 2016, 233–5.

[116] Strabo 13.2.3; *IGR* 4.38; Gow-Page *GP* #16. Bowersock 1965, 36–7; Sherk 1969, 157; Ypsilanti 2018, 3.

[117] Gow-Page *GP* #10, 11 (Marcellus); 28 (Tiberius); 7, 12 (Antonia); 18, 25 (Cleopatra). Ypsilanti 2018, 3–4, 8–9.

[118] Parker 1991, 115. Compare too, C. Iulius Menodoros—identified by Raggi with Sextus Pompeius' freedman admiral, Mendorus/Menas, who defected to Octavian in 36—whose funeral monument in Ephesus, erected by his wife, celebrates his achievements as a Roman citizen, albeit as among the first from *provincia* Asia. *AÉ* 1993, #1479, with Raggi 2020.

same rewards. Though a broad trend pushed local magnates towards Roman citizenship and civic leadership, this was a granular and uneven process.

Summary

Across the period the *poleis* of Asia employed a variety of diplomatic strategies, to use the term loosely, in engaging with the power of Rome. From the outset, traditional embassies to the Senate or commanders in Asia were sent to deal with practical problems which attended the assertion of Roman *imperium* over the region. Some were concerned with establishing ties of patronage with individual Romans. Certain embassies from free *poleis* also solicited and received *foedera* which established the bilateral nature of their relationship with Rome. Finally, over time more personal relationships between individual Greek elites and Roman commanders predominated. These were pursued with different intensity as the broader geopolitical situation changed. After Sulla's arrangements in 85 there is limited, though growing evidence for collective embassies in response to particularly widespread problems. However, the most important implications arise from the personalization of relationships between the centre and provincial communities, on both sides. The increasing value of links such as those between Theophanes and Pompeius or Zoilos and Augustus subverted existing institutions. Civic patronage and diplomacy became less useful levers for communities, as success came to depend more on private relationships than public ones. This is not to say that these institutions fell into a sharp immediate decline, but the evidence shows that shrewd communities would employ as ambassadors those favoured by prominent Romans, and Octavian himself encouraged the citizens of Rhosus to approach him through his admiral Seleucus. Interestingly, the unchallenged supremacy of Augustus prompted a new institutionalization of relationships, fostered by a new security and stability within the empire.[119] Due to centralization of power, this took a very different form to Republican models and came to serve as the basis for imperial–provincial interaction under the Principate.

[119] Smith 1993, 8–10; Ventroux 2017, 165–6.

8
Local Displays of Imperial Documents

The Drivers of Local Display: Roman Documents in Asia

Across the period Asian *poleis* increasingly inscribed and prominently displayed Roman normative documents: that is, utterances of the Roman state or its representatives. However, key questions remain unanswered: to what degree did this reflect local choices and does this phenomenon constitute evidence of independent agency within the overarching framework of Roman hegemon? Local communities could engage meaningfully with Roman communications through their display or archiving and many extant Republican documents survive in the form of Asian copies, demonstrating the breadth of this practice. Accordingly, Ando argued for the pervasive and regular dissemination of imperial documents to provincials. This is indisputable: the evidence for the circulation of Roman documents from the late Republic onwards is substantial. However, he goes on to suggest publication was normally required by Roman authorities, citing as evidence the *lex de provinciis praetoriis*, which contains an explicit 'publication' clause.[1] Cities were to ensure that:

> *εἰς δ<έλ>τον χαλ|κῆν γράμματα ἐνκεχαραγμέ[να, εἰ δὲ μὴ ἢ ἐν λίθῳ μαρμαρίνῳ ἢ κ]αὶ ἐν λευκώματι, ὅπως ἐν ταῖς πόλεσι ἐκκέ[ηται ἐν ἱερῷ] ἢ ἀγορᾶι φανερῶς, ὅθεν δυνή|σονται ἑστακότες ἀναγινώσ[κειν ὀρθῶς]* ('the letters (from the consul to the cities of Asia), engraved on a bronze tablet, [or if not either on a marble slab or even] on a whitened board, be openly [published] in the cities, [in a sanctuary] or *agora*, in such a way that people shall be able to read (them) [properly] from ground level').[2]

However, as noted previously, this *lex* is unparalleled in the surviving material. First, the *lex* resulted from a fraught period of legislative politics at Rome during Saturninus' third tribunate. Second, it knitted together several unconnected issues

[1] Ando 2000, 81–3. Contrast Ferrary's emphasis (2009, 127–38) on local implementation of Roman decisions during the Republic with Nelis-Clément's account of the early Principate (2006, 141–8).

[2] *RS* 12.Delphi.B.24–6. Compare Colin (1924, 80) offering the same sense. Crawford et al. (1996, 19–20) take this as a standard formula, based on the Greek translation of the Latin formula *unde de plano recte legi possit*, but recognize that *leges* generally mandate publication of documents associated with the statutes, rather than the texts themselves. I avoid the debate on whether Roman laws in bronze were intended to be read, save noting that, *pace* Ando (2000, 101–3), (il)legibility does not detract from the significance of their display (Williamson 1987, 160–83; Cooley 2012, 170–1).

Imperial Power, Provincial Government, and the Emergence of Roman Asia, 133 BCE–14 CE. Bradley Jordan, Oxford University Press. © Bradley Jordan 2023. DOI: 10.1093/oso/9780198887065.003.0009

into one measure (*per saturam*) making the text's relevance to its wider audience any given point tenuous at best. Third, crucially, this clause does not mandate the publication of the *lex* at all, only of consular letters and only in Asia.[3] Consequently, the inscription of neither surviving copy, in Cnidus or Delphi, can be explained by the surviving text: other reasons must be posited for the erection of these monuments. Ando's second example is the letter of Augustus found at Miletus and Priene.[4] This letter requires that its recipients, the *koinon* and the nine cities which headed assize-districts, forward copies to other communities within their district and ensure that it 'be engraved on a stele on white stone in the most conspicuous places' (ἔν τε τῶι ἐπ̣[ι]|φανεστάτωι τόπωι ἐν στυλοπαραστάδι ἐπὶ | λίθου λευκοῦ ἐνχαραχθῆναι). Ando treats these two examples as evidence for standard practice. However, the specific requirement to inscribe the document permanently is unparalleled in magistrate's correspondence or normative documents from the Republican period, emphasizing the unusual nature of the command.[5]

This incongruity is demonstrated most clearly by two early *senatus consulta*. The first, the *senatus consultum Popillianum*, declared the decisions of Attalus III valid up to a day before his death, thereby giving them standing within Roman jurisdiction. A near-complete copy, though out of context, survives at Pergamum, plausibly taken as an assertion of that city's ἐλευθερία based on the king's testament.[6] An analogous document, the *senatus consultum Licinnianum*, seems to have reasserted this decision and has also been found at Arızlı, a modern village around 35km southeast of Synnada, as yet unidentified with an ancient community.[7] Extracts from both texts recur in a third fragment from Arızlı.[8] This document seems to distil important elements from both bills into a single format, raising questions over the date, provenance, and purpose of these inscriptions. Importantly, no obvious audience existed for these documents, so why did a community in remote Phrygia choose to inscribe them, and what impact did this have locally?

[3] Cooley 2012, 164–5; *pace* Crawford 1996, 263; Ando 2000, 82. See Chapter 1, 'The Ambitions of M'. Aquillius'.

[4] Ando 2000, 83. Ando follows the typical dating of this text to the 50s but, as argued in 'The Emergence of the *conventus iuridici*', a date in the early 20s is more plausible.

[5] Eilers 2009, 305 contra Ando 2000, 81–3. The text is ambiguous on whether the secondary recipients of the letter, including Priene, were required to inscribe it. That the Prienean *demos* decided to do so is insufficient evidence that the author intended to have every community in Asia reproduce it, though admittedly the generalizing language may support this view.

[6] *RDGE* 11 with Wörrle 2000; Merola 2001, 26. See Chapter 1, 'The Organization of a Roman Province'.

[7] *RDGE* 13, revised by Famerie 2021, 182–3. His rejection of the earlier conjecture that the Arızlı fragments referred to Mithridates V of Pontus is persuasive (178–9). Though not decisive, his subsequent reading of the presiding magistrate as [*Πό*]π̣λιος (i.e., P. Licinius Crassus Mucianus, *cos.* 131) rather than [*Γ*]ά̣ιος (i.e., C. Licinius Geta, *cos.* 116) fits the historical context better.

[8] *SEG* 28.1208.

Corcoran's observations regarding the publication of Roman official documents rom the fourth to seventh centuries CE offer a valuable comparison. In that period, *edicta* outnumber letters from magistrates or imperial *rescripta*. Based on the tendency of later emperors to state bluntly their wishes that all inhabitants of the empire be aware of and understand the law as issued, Corcoran assumes that the impetus to publish these documents was imperial, deriving from the governor or ruler directly.[9] Though he highlights the Republican origins of this tradition in the injunction contained in *leges populi Romani* and *senatus consulta* that they be published *unde de plano recte legi possit*, this formula was not generally reproduced in the Roman East during this transitional period, and the region had no existing tradition of disseminating general legislation beyond a few Seleucid *προστάγματα*.[10] In these examples, no publication clause survives: though inconclusive in itself, it is highly suggestive in lieu of an existing incentive to inscribe central legislation. Drew-Bear also notes the late date for the inscription of the Arızlı fragments, perhaps first or second century CE, which both highlights the decisions' continuing importance in the context of later changes to the Roman administration and removes their inscription from the original context.[11] The decrees' general nature divorces them from local concerns over civic privileges. Though the absence of context for the finds makes it impossible to reconstruct the way in which these two documents interacted with one another, the shared orthography would imply that they consciously did so, that is, they were inscribed at the same time for a similar purpose.

Though recognizably reproducing the same information, the wording of the documents at Pergamum and Arızlı differs. Lines 15–19 of the *senatus consultum Popillianum* read:

> *[ὅ]σα τούτων ἐγένετο πρὸ μιᾶς [ἡμέρας πρὶν ἢ | Ἄττ]αλον τελευτῆσαι, ὅπως ταῦτ[α κύρια ἦι στρατη|γο]ί τε οἱ εἰς Ἀσίαν πορευόμεν[———]ην, ἀλλὰ ἐῶσι κύρια μένειν [ἅπαντα καθῶς ἡ σύνκλη]|τος ἐπέκριν[εν]* ('Those things which have come about up to one day before the death of Attalos, so these things are legally binding, and the commanders sent out to Asia [———] but should remain legally binding, all of them, just as the Senate decreed.')[12]

By comparison the third Arızlı fragment adds [—]*τα Ἀττάλου φυλάσσηται* ('that the [—] of Attalus be protected'). Drew-Bear takes this variation as occurring in the translation of the *senatus consultum*. However, this fragment likely derives from a magistrate's or imperial letter. If so, then this change could represent an

[9] Corcoran (2018, 5–12), citing the *res gestae divi Augusti* and *senatus consultum de Cn. Pisone patre*, on which see below.

[10] Bencivenni 2014, 148–51.

[11] Drew-Bear 1978, 3, 5.

[12] *RDGE* 11.15–9.

editorial statement by the magistrate, elaborating on the text of the decree.[13] On balance, it seems preferable to view the additional clause as part of the magistrate's decision, reinforcing the extent to which local communities retained control over the creation of the text and monument in their own civic context.[14]

Why did the inhabitants of Pergamum and a small Phrygian *polis* go to the significant expense of inscribing these generic documents, which arrived with no explicit involvement on their part? For Pergamum, as the centre of the former kingdom which retained significance within the new Roman administrative schema, the display of the document may have been intended to convey continuity between the two regimes.[15] Moreover, existing elites, as a group, had a vested interest in maintaining the status quo within the *polis*. Given their access to the royal court and its participants, Pergamum and its inhabitants would have been affected by a greater proportion of regal decisions than elsewhere and naturally may have sought to emphasize the universal confirmation of Attalus' *acta*. Though the text simply brought these decisions across into a Roman framework, within which magistrates could interact with them, a simple reading of the Greek does not contradict this view.

The Arızlı copies are more difficult to explain, especially given the appearance of both decrees. It is possible that, again, the *polis* was attempting to secure specific Attalid grants, perhaps pertaining to its lands, or even its status as a community.[16] If so, it raises the question of audience. The chances that a Roman magistrate, or even their representative, would visit a small community in the vicinity of the more significant Synnada, which became a *conventus* centre during the first century BCE, are small.[17] Cicero's account of his journey through Cilicia demonstrates that he rarely visited communities outside *conventus* centres.[18] While allowing for governor's personal preferences, the proportion of time spent by Roman magistrates in small communities was likely minimal. If so, the small Phrygian *polis* cannot have been directing its publication of these documents at Rome or its representatives in any meaningful sense.

One possibility is that the display of a document dating from the earliest days of the *provincia* allowed the community to define itself. I argued previously that the three Phrygian *dioceses* of Asia and Cilicia may have been integrated into the Galatian kingdom of Amyntas between 36 and 25. By publicly erecting

[13] Drew-Bear 1978, 7; Famerie 2021, 182–4.

[14] As Corcoran (2018, 9) argues for Asia in the early fourth century CE. While the impetus for the display of Diocletian's price edict appears to have been imperial rather than local, note the wide range of variations in display, framing, and text between Aphrodisias, Stratonicea, and Aezani.

[15] E.g., Sherk 1969, 62. [16] Drew-Bear 1978, 9; *pace* Famerie 2021, 184.

[17] Thonemann 2011, 54–6; Kantor 2013, 153–5. On Synnada: Belke & Mersich 1990, 393–4. Modern Arızlı lies in a mountain pass between the two major routes east from Phrygian Apamea, the first via Synnada and Philomelium, the second via Antioch in Pisidia. Equidistant between the two, the chances that it entertained Roman governors on a regular basis must be slim.

[18] Cic. *Att.* 5.16.2, 20.1; *Fam.* 15.4.2. Hunter 1913, 81–94; Marshall 1966, 231–46.

monuments emphasizing the early establishment of a relationship—even a generic and subordinate one—with Rome, the *polis* and its neighbours drew on and memorialized a narrative which set them apart from other Galatian settlements.[19] Competition between the constituent communities of empire was crucial to the strategy of imperial rule and had roots far deeper than Roman involvement in the region. While far less significant than the disagreements over *neokoroi* and titulature of the major centres of the *provinciae* of the High Empire, these documents could have arisen from a similar phenomenon.[20] Another potential explanation, that smaller communities emulated the practice of their larger neighbours, is possible; although questions of the expense and the question of why these generic documents remain unresolved by this solution.

Though, as noted, the practical impact on Roman officials, institutions, and policy was limited, the local choice to publish these generic *senatus consulta* had important effects. First, it offered locals the chance to assert elements of self-definition and self-determination: by producing documents which appeared to define their relationship with the imperial metropole in clear and favourable terms, *poleis* could advertise to their own citizens that their position had not worsened with the permanent arrival of Roman magistrates. In this respect, as Cicero recognized, the appearance was more significant than the reality.[21] Second, by choosing to inscribe these documents, at significant expense, and place them permanently, as sizeable monuments, in public spaces alongside the political pronouncements of the *demos* and the honours decreed for local benefactors, the *poleis* placed the official utterances of the Senate on a par with the most important acts of the community itself. It normalized the format, text, and appearance of Roman documents. It granted them normative force and assimilated them with the local elite's own decisions. As Ma notes, in societies which display authoritative documents monumentally, the epigraphic medium itself can instantiate legitimacy. Even beyond this, the inscriptions themselves locate the source of their authority precisely in the institutions of the Roman state.[22] In the treatment of Roman normative documents, there are elements of previous approaches to royal letters: however, this was a very different, and difficult, learning process. By publishing and inscribing these documents, local institutions granted legitimacy to Roman norms and normative actions, but, crucially, civic elites made active and judicious choices as to which and how many Roman documents to publicize in this fashion.

The *senatus consultum de agro Pergameno* offers a different conundrum. Unlike the generic decrees discussed above, the Senate issued this response directly to a

[19] Compare Ando 2000, 94. See Chapter 2, 'The Emergence of the *conventus iuridici*'.

[20] E.g., Heller 2006, 28–51.

[21] Cic. *Att.* 6.1.15. Compare *Leg.* 3.25.

[22] Bertrand 1990, 108–15; Ma 2012, 141.

Pergamene embassy's petition on a specific issue, the boundaries of their territory vis-à-vis the surrounding *ager publicus*. Considering the success in carrying out their task, the monumental display of this text at Pergamum is unexceptional. However, further copies have been discovered at Adramyttium, Smyrna, and Ephesus. As Robert stressed, the last cannot have been directly affected by the Roman decision, as its territory cannot have bordered Pergamum's. Instead, noting that the four copies emerge from *conventus* centres, he proposed that Roman administrators sought to publicize the decision to the *provincia* at large.[23] However, despite this interpretation's popularity, there are two clear objections.[24] First, it remains unlikely that the *conventus* existed in its fully developed form when the document was produced. Second, there seems no clear motive for the Senate to insist on the publication of a specific decision on Pergamum's civic boundaries for a general provincial audience. Ferrary cogently approached this issue by positing a later date for the inscription of the decree. The greater concern with ostentatious good governance during the civil war period, he argued, provides a more plausible context for the dissemination and advertisement of a decision against the interests of the *publicani*.[25] However, this does not solve the problem. After 48, the *publicani* became a much less visible element of provincial life. Substituting Caesar for the Senate, the significance of one highly localized decision for the *provincia* writ large remains unclear. While the dictator showed clear concern for provincial well-being, the sentiment expressed in *I.Priene*[2] 13, that publication would ensure *ἵνα κοινῶς πάσηι τῆι ἐπαρχεία[ι τὸ] | δίκαιον ἑσταμένον ἧι εἰς τὸν αἰεὶ χρόνον* ('that justice be established in common for the whole province and for all time'), was a later development.[26] Finally, while the *senatus consultum de agro Pergameno* shows the Senate intervening against the *publicani*, the text did not represent the assertion of any strong principle and an explicit publication clause seems unlikely.

Inscription in the document's original context seems more reasonable. Two potential scenarios suggest themselves. First, that the *poleis* each received a copy of the *senatus consultum* and conventional treatment of Hellenistic documents led them to inscribe it. The evidence consistently demonstrates the large-scale dissemination of information by the Roman state and, upon the organization of the *provincia*, the despatch of *senatus consulta* to a wider group of communities than those immediately effected is plausible. In the preceding century, royal letters were strong normative documents which warranted record and display.[27] Roman normative documents, when received

[23] Robert 1969b, 612, n.3. [24] E.g., Mitchell 1999, 27; Kay 2014, 67.
[25] Ferrary 2009a, 71–2, with references to earlier literature. Jones 2001; Morrell 2017, esp. 237–68.
[26] *I.Priene*[2] 13.50–1. [27] Bencivenni 2014, 146–8.

by 'free' *poleis*, held a similarly significant status: though, crucially, almost exclusively in response to a petition or embassy. In the earliest days of the *provincia*, the internal drive to publicize Roman decisions may have been greater than later evidence would suggest.

The second, more plausible option would posit a hyperlocal reason to publish the *senatus consultum*. While the document appears in multiple locations, we have no way of mapping the spread of its monumentalization. Imitation may have played a role. Though, strictly, the decision pertained only to Pergamene territory, *poleis* may have seen this as articulating a general principle and sought to redeploy the decree in their own disputes with the *publicani*. A similar attitude may explain the arrival of ambassadors at Colophon to celebrate the achievements of Menippus after his successful appeal against the capital charge levelled against his fellow-citizen.[28] If so, we could posit a Roman audience, albeit a limited one, for the display.[29] The transitional period from kingdom to province, notwithstanding the general freedom granted, would have been particularly fraught with disagreements over the territorial limit of publican responsibility. In this respect, the repeated inscription of the *senatus consultum de agro Pergameno* would be aimed at asserting the support of the Senate for the territorial integrity of the free cities in a general sense: a particularly important goal in the earliest days of the new system.

A further factor may have been a desire to locate the community more solidly within an imagined Roman polity. That is, the display of this statement by the apparatus of the Roman state was intended to highlight to diverse audiences the acknowledgement of Rome's real, and now asserted, power over the former Attalid kingdom. I agree with Ando that display of normative documents generated over time a consensus of legitimacy around the Roman imperial hierarchy.[30] However, I argue here that the impetus could and often did arise from the local communities, rather than the Roman state itself. The texts were not necessarily accepted by civic actors as intended: they were adapted to the local context as appropriate. However, their publication and, especially, their inscription, nevertheless contributed to the establishment of a hegemonic discourse, generating public familiarity with the forms and language of Roman normative documents, as well as associating them with existing elements of civic authority.

[28] *SEG* 39. 1244.1.48–50.

[29] Tibiletti 1957, 138; Sherk 1966, 365; Merola 2001, 33–4. See Mitchell 1999, 27, for the decree's exemplary character.

[30] Ando 2000, esp. 131–74, 209–15, 232–9, cf. Eilers 2009, 301–4. In this case, it inverts the trend observed by Ma (1999, 241) that in the Hellenistic period, 'the ideological autarky and local identity of the *polis* were strongly affirmed . . . even under political subordination'. Conceptually, see Anderson 1991, 5–7.

Local Agency in Action: Roman Documents in Civic Spaces

A key example reinforcing how local motives often lay behind the reproduction of Roman documents is the dossier associated with Paullus Fabius Maximus' reform of Asia's calendar in 9/8, with which this study commenced. The extension of the new calendar across the whole *provincia*, irrespective of whether this was enforced, offer a crucial instance of a text which was applicable to a wide audience.[31] Indeed, the dossier appears in multiple copies scattered across the province: fragments are found at Priene, Maeonia, Phrygian Apamea, Dorylaeum, Eumenea, and Metropolis. However, like the implementation of the decision, the choice to publish the document widely was mediated by the *koinon* of Asia. Paullus himself notes that he will only: *προστάξω | δὲ χαραχθὲν <ἐν> τῇ στήλῃ τὸ ψήφισμα ἐν τῷ ναῷ ἀνατεθῆναι, προστά|ξας τὸ διάταγμα ἑκατέρως γραφέν* ('order this decree, inscribed on a stele, to be set up in the temple [of Augustus and Roma at Pergamum], having commanded that the *edictum* be written in both languages').[32] Given that the decision was taken by both the governor and *koinon* to honour Augustus, the choice to place a permanent monument to that process at the centre of the burgeoning imperial cult in Asia makes a powerful statement. However, this is as far as Paullus' instructions extend. By contrast, the *koinon*, after providing for both Paullus' *edictum* and their own decree to be monumentalized in exactly this fashion, states:

> *προνοῆσαι δὲ καὶ τοὺς καθ' ἔτος ἐκδίκους ὅπως | ἐν ταῖς ἀφηγουμέναις τῶν διοικήσεων πόλεσιν ἐν στήλαις λευ|κολίθοις ἐναραχθῇ τό τε δελτογράφημα τοῦ Μαξίμου καὶ τὸ τῆς Ἀσίας | ψήφισμα, αὗταί τε αἱ στῆλαι τεθῶσιν ἐν τοῖς Καισαρήοις* ('moreover, the *ekdikoi* for the year are to ensure that in the leading cities in each *dioikesis*, the *edictum* of Maximus and the decree of Asia are inscribed on marble steles, and these steles set up in the shrines to the Caesars').[33]

This example is particularly revealing, highlighting the extent to which non-Roman groups retained agency in the publication of ostensibly Roman documents. The enforceability of the *koinon*'s unilateral decision remains unclear. However, this command insists on the recognition of that power, assimilating the *koinon* inextricably with Paullus' original action.[34] Stern astutely notes that the *koinon*'s instructions for implementing the new schema also go beyond the proconsul's instructions, in aligning the province fully with the Julian calendar at use in Rome.[35] This stresses both that the organization was more attuned to the details of the policy than the governor and that they saw no incompatibility in introducing changes. Only one extant copy derives from a *conventus*

[31] On (non-)compliance: Magie 1950, 481; Thonemann 2015.
[32] *RDGE* 65.A.28–30.
[33] *RDGE* 65.D.62–7.
[34] Cooley 2012, 165; Ma 2012, 142–3.
[35] Stern 2012, 276–8.

centre suggesting that other communities actively wanted to demonstrate their enthusiasm for the new Princeps.[36] Finally, the Metropolis copy, consisting of Paullus' decree and the first decree of the *koinon*, was excavated *in situ* in the courtyard of the local *presbyterion* rather than a public context. Though Dreyer argues that this shows the practical impact of the changes—the *presbyteroi* needed this information to hand—it seems more plausible that this was a simple expression of hyperlocal loyalty.[37] Once again, the broad inscription and monumentalization of these Roman documents is tied to regional agents and local concerns.

That said, the community retained control over their display. Beyond the active choice to display a text, the location, size, and material of a monument had a bearing on its reception. Even where Roman documents did insist on their reproduction, for the most part they restricted their instructions to display in the *ἐπιφανέστατοι τόποι* ('the most prominent locations'). The careful ambiguity of this phrase, often employed in local honorific decrees of the second and first centuries, disguises the intense contestability and mutability of public space.[38] No single place fulfilled this criterion, as shown by the ubiquitous plural. Instead it offered the locals a further opportunity to frame the audience and interpretation of the document. Unfortunately, problems such as reuse, lack of provenance, or lack of co-ordinated excavation prevent a complete study of the space and positioning of Roman documents within Asian communities.[39] However, some hints suggest how location could be used to reinforce or shape the messaging of a Roman text.

A decree of Pergamum, responding to the conclusion of a treaty with Rome in 129, provides another intriguing example. The text states: *καθήκει καὶ | [πα]ρ' ἡμ[ῖν] ἀναγραφῆν[αι αὐτὰ ε]ἰς πίνακας | [χ]αλκοῦς δύο καὶ τε[θῆναι ἐ]ν τε τῶι ἱερῶι | [τ]ῆς Δήμητρος καὶ ἐ[ν τῶι β]ουλευτηρίωι | [παρ]ὰ τὸ ἄγαλμα τῆς [Δημοκ]ρατίας* ('and it is right that these [documents] are inscribed by us on two bronze tablets and erected both in the temple of Demeter and in the *bouleuterion* next to the statue of *Demokratia*').[40] The matter of publication is framed positively as a local choice: the words of the community obscure any suggestion of Roman commands or requests.[41] The text's display in two named locations underscores the symbolic importance of place. Neither the interior of the temple of Demeter nor the *bouleuterion* were likely to have been highly trafficked locations by most of the citizen body. The precise importance of the temple of Demeter is unclear, though Ma has suggested that it was one of the limited number of locations at which honorific statues were regularly placed.[42] The implications of the *bouleuterion*, the

[36] Magie 1950, 480–1; *pace* Heller 2014, 225.

[37] Dreyer & Engelmann 2006, 175–6, 182; Dreyer 2007, 347.

[38] Ma 2012a, 246–8; 2013a, 67–9; Chaniotis 2014, 135–6.

[39] Examples like the 'archive wall' at Aphrodisias, allowing a full landscape to be reconstructed, are exceedingly rare.

[40] *IGR* 4.1692.27–31. [41] Cooley 2012, 163. [42] Ma 2013a, 102–3.

political centre of the newly independent community, are much easier to grasp. The strong link between δημοκρατία and ideas of 'freedom' in this period are similarly well attested. The Pergamenes, in their decision to inscribe and display the treaty with Rome in these locations, were utilizing a Roman document to make a clear ideological statement of their own crafting.

Paullus' *edictum* also makes clever use of place, permanently commemorating the change of calendar, and thereby honouring Augustus, within the shrine dedicated to the Princeps and Rome. The threads drawing together the Princeps, time, the province as a whole and the divine could not have been more overt. Similarly, the choice of the *koinon* to reproduce this text, with their own decree, in temples to the deified Caesar created a dynastic element, which was entirely absent from Paullus' original text.[43] Kokkinia has recently proven how the layout of the archive wall at Aphrodisias particularly drew attention to the Augustan magnate C. Iulius Zoilos, to whose theatre the inscription was added, but otherwise documents praising individuals were removed to the edges.[44] Each of these examples reinforces the degree to which local decision-makers could coax a locally flavoured narrative from imperial texts by controlling the nature of its display.

Roman Documents in Private Contexts

Finally, a crucial subset of Roman documents appears in private, funerary contexts. These focus attention on the role of individuals and stand at odds with the communitarian aspects of civic life. Three examples in the Roman east were erected within the period of study, recorded in Table 8.1 along with two later analogous cases. Earliest is a monument for Chaeremon of Nysa, preserving the letter of L. Cassius informing the *polis* of his aid to the Roman forces in the First Mithridatic War, alongside two letters from Mithridates himself calling for his apprehension or summary execution. Unlike the other examples discussed here, this monument was demonstrably authorized by the *demos* and *boule*. However, the texts' purpose was to perpetuate knowledge of Chaeremon's deeds: the inscription subverts the language and content of Mithridates' missives, as well as those of Cassius', to memorialize a great citizen. This monument preserves Mithridatic rhetoric in a civic context, including his description of the Romans as τοὺς κοινοὺ[ς πολε]|μίους ('the common enemies').[45] The less than flattering portrayal of Nysa's hegemons in this monument directly results from the localized honorific motive.

[43] *RDGE* 65.D.64–8. Unmentioned by Laffi (1967, 66), Sherk (1969, 336–7), or Price (1984, 53–6).
[44] Kokkinia 2015–2016, 42–51.
[45] *Syll.*³ 741. Santangelo 2009, 65–6.

Later examples may not have depended on public approval. Potamon of Mytilene's huge monument, dating to the late first century, shows a marked lack of concern for the communitarian ethos of the *polis*. Though the blocks are no longer *in situ*, having been reused in the walls of a Medieval citadel, they have produced numerous documents pertaining to Potamon's activities representing the *polis*. At least seven are Roman in origin, providing an invaluable insight into the relationship between Rome and Mytilene during this period.[46] However, no evidence suggests that this was a public monument, and its aggrandizing nature better suggests a private context. Seleucus of Rhosus' dossier, discovered in that community's necropolis, may have fronted his tomb.[47] The primacy afforded him in the documents, when combined with his comparatively humble origins would again push away from a public honour. The dossier of the family of Menophilus at Aezani also likely fronted a family tomb.[48] The famous mausoleum of Opramoas at Rhodiapolis provides a final example, preserving 70 documents, thirty-eight of which involved Roman administrators.[49] Each monument appropriated Roman official documents not for administrative reasons, but to add lustre to the memory of an individual in a local context. They are transformative, taking normative documents out of their typical context and reframing them as honorific.[50] However, in doing so, they still monumentalize and bring these texts firmly into the public sphere at a local level. To serve their honorific purpose, the reader must already accept that the opinions of Roman magistrates or the Senate are authoritative and convey recognition *ipso facto*. They leverage the legitimacy of Roman power and administrative structures into a new context with localized implications for civic memory, which did not, for the most part, extend beyond the individual community. As a contrast to these private monuments, the honorific stele of the *koinon* of Asia for Menogenes at Sardis preserves twelve normative documents from non-Roman bodies. Each derived from local institutions of the *polis* or the *koinon* and the Roman citizens mentioned are explicitly framed as participants in civic or provincial life.[51] This may indicate a deliberate reaction on the part of the assembled Greek communities in Asia, an attempt to frame honours in a self-consciously and distinctively local way in opposition to private use of imperial documents.

[46] Compare Chapter 7, 'Theophanes: Between Mytilene and Rome'.

[47] Roussel 1934, 33; Eck 1995–1998, 2.372.

[48] Jones 2000, 456–7; Haensch 2009, 184–5; *pace* Wörrle 2014, 469–70. On the stemma: Wörrle 2011, 362–3.

[49] Kokkinia 2000. Compare Junia Theodora at Corinth (*SEG* 18.143), whose monument includes two decrees and a letter from the Lycian *koinon*, a decree of Patara, a letter of Myra, and a letter of Telmessos (Friesen 2013, 204–5).

[50] Eck 1995–1998, 2.372–3, providing several later examples at 369–72, 374–78.

[51] *Sardis* 7.1.8.

Table 8.1 Funerary monuments for private citizens containing Roman public documents

Date	Place	Person	Roman documents	Reference
*c.*80	Nysa	Chaeremon	One proconsular letter; Two royal letters (Mithridates)	*RDGE* 48; *RC* 73, 74
*c.*30	Rhosus, Syria	Seleucus	Three imperial letters (Augustus); One *Senatusconsultum*	*RDGE* 70
*c.*25	Mytilene	Potamon	At least four letters, three from Caesar; Two *Senatusconsulta*; One Treaty	*RDGE* 25, 26, 51, 73–78
*c.*55 CE	Aezani	Menophilus 'family'	Four letters: two proconsular, two imperial (Tiberius, in Augustus' lifetime; Nero)	*SEG* 64.1302–1306
*c.*123–153 CE	Rhodiapolis, Lycia	Opramoas	26 letters from imperial officials; 12 imperial *rescripta*	Kokkinia, *Opramoas*

Summary

The reproduction of Roman normative documents within the communities of Asia in symbolic ways played a substantial role in socializing civic elites to accept Roman power. Individuals who consciously engaged with the documents, as texts or otherwise, were exposed to the interplay between Roman and local systems of authority. Ando perceptively emphasized that these texts carried significant force and, by interacting with local frameworks of power, created a sense of legitimacy around Roman ideology and state action.[52] However, that this was intentionally cultivated by the Roman state and its representatives in the late Republican period does not follow. The limited evidence for publication clauses, when placed alongside the evidence for the *res gestae Divi Augusti* in Galatia and the *sentusconsultum de Cn. Pisone patre* in Spain and Noricum, highlight the restricted aims of the central state and the significant leeway afforded to magistrates and communities when it came to communicating directly with the inhabitants of the provinces.[53] This is not to say that the Roman state did not despatch large volumes of written correspondence and instructions to provincial communities; or, indeed, that a significant proportion of this was not displayed publicly in some impermanent media. However, the control of this documentation and the choice to

[52] Ando 2000, 73–9, 101–8.

[53] On the *Res Gestae*: Cooley 2009, 6–22; on the Spanish evidence: Eck, Caballos, & Fernández 1996, 279–88; Noricum: Bartels 2009, 1–9. If accepted, the bold suggestion of Thonemann (2012, 285–8) that *Sardis* 7.201 is a fragment of another copy of the *Res Gestae*, though significant, does not invalidate the overall point that the *Res Gestae* were not published uniformly on the basis of commands from Rome.

monumentalize it, establishing it firmly within civic memory, lay within the purview of local powerbrokers.

Beyond their textual content, the physical characteristics of these monuments are significant. Surviving documents are primarily inscribed on stone, with a few cases, exceptional in the East, of bronze documents.[54] However, as Eck stresses, the overwhelming majority of documents published in the cities of the Roman empire were produced on perishable materials, the best attested in the Greek world being painted black lettering on whitened boards.[55] This was an inexpensive and, when combined with public announcements, relatively efficient means of communicating directly with a community. Eck notes their easy reuse and presumably swift turnover—one Claudian *edictum* explicitly requires its display for thirty days—suggesting that the scale of documents under the empire necessitated judgement to be exercised over which to display, when, and for how long.[56] By contrast, to inscribe a document on stone or bronze implied permanence: the expense, time, and skills necessary to produce a monument set these texts apart from the norm.[57] This provides another strong reason not to read between the lines of texts which do not explicitly require their public inscription.[58] More importantly, within the broader traditions of civic government in Asia Minor, the inscription of Roman documents treated them in the same fashion as the utterances of the *polis* community itself or the Hellenistic monarchs of the earlier period.[59] The choice by civic leaders to memorialize Roman normative documents imbued these with a status equal to those from most significant political actors, which *poleis* were familiar with.

The widespread inscription of Roman normative documents in prominent civic spaces, then, arose primarily from the choices of civic leaders within the province. Irrespective of its rationale, such display communicated the implicit consent of the civic authorities to the content of the exhibited text. Moreover, its reproduction in the same format and spaces as pronouncements of the highest import by local authorities gave these documents legitimacy. The inscription in local contexts of imperial documents thereby instantiates the emergence of Roman hegemony in Asia. Though individuals could continue to engage with the claims of Roman

[54] The continuation of traditional practice in the Greek East of inscribing normative documents on stone rather than converting to the Roman practice of bronze is discussed extensively by Eck 2014, 139–47. See Gagarin 2008, 122, 227–31.

[55] Wilhelm 1909, 239–49; Eck 2010 [1997], 275–86. Attestations of whitened boards collected by Wilhelm at 246–7; *RS* 12.Delphi.B.24–15.

[56] Eck 2010 [1997], 282–3; Ando 2000, 90–2.

[57] Ferrary 2009a, 59–60.

[58] E.g., Sotidius Strabo does not (*pace* Mitchell 1976, 116–17) 'carefully provide for the [permanent] publication of his edict' at *I.Sagalassos* 3.5–6/29–30, but indicates only that he has arranged for their display.

[59] Note here the possibility that the Roman statutes in Greek contexts consciously resembled the format and layout of an original official translation. The observations of Decorte (2015, 246–53) point in this direction, though he admits that the number of Greek examples of Roman statutes by his definition are limited.

documents in diverse ways, there were powerful institutional reasons to accept the dominant narrative or reconfigure it into a locally acceptable alternative, such as emerges in their reproduction in private, funerary contexts. This reframing subtly altered the underlying message of the document to be interpreted within a provincial cognitive framework. Nevertheless, these inscriptions contributed to the dissemination, reproduction, and success of the hegemonic discourse. In this sense, local agents, acting for their own reasons, contributed decisively to the creation of Roman hegemony in *provincia Asia*.

Conclusions

This study starts from the premise that institutional development can be modelled as incremental, path-dependent, and socially embedded in ideal circumstances. However, the late Roman Republic was turbulent and characterized by conflict and dramatic changes in the strength of imperial administrative power. When assessed within an institutionalist framework, the Roman administration in the late Republican province of Asia developed largely in a step-by-step fashion, though punctuated by several critical junctures against a background of unintended consequences arising from Roman decisions, all embedded in a specifically Asian cultural context, in dialogue with local preferences and actors.

The development of Roman administration in *provincia Asia* from its initial establishment to the early Principate has significant implications to a wider interpretation of Roman imperialism during this period. I have focused on two specific features of Roman state power and its exercise over the diverse communities of western Asia Minor. First, the mechanics of Roman rule in the region: the institutions the Roman state introduced, when and how these were implemented, the intensity, extent, and intrusiveness of their introduction and evolution. Second, the emergence of a discourse of power which was mutually intelligible to Rome's powerbrokers and representatives, on the one hand, and inhabitants of the province—both formally free and otherwise—on the other. I emphasize the importance of the learning process on both sides, querying how local communities developed strategies to deal with imperial power and situated themselves alongside and within the evolving Roman empire. Stressing the precariousness of *poleis* during periods of imperial instability, I have shown the role of local agency in the slow evolution of a stable provincial administration. Overall, I have argued that the late Republican Roman state had a limited capacity to develop a coherent set of administrative institutions and supporting ideological bases in *provincia Asia*, forcing local elites to innovate continuously to protect their own position.

An analysis of the available evidence shows that Roman governance in *provincia Asia* did largely develop in an incremental, largely path-dependent fashion, with initial conditions—both those under the Attalids, and the decisions of M.' Aquillius from 129–126—playing an outsized role in shaping its subsequent evolution. One illustrative example is the role of the provincial governor. Throughout the period, as the holder of the *summum imperium* on the ground

Imperial Power, Provincial Government, and the Emergence of Roman Asia, 133 BCE–14 CE. Bradley Jordan, Oxford University Press. © Bradley Jordan 2023. DOI: 10.1093/oso/9780198887065.003.0010

in the province, the responsible magistrate played a critical and decisive role in managing the administrative burden within the region, mediating the relationship and jurisdictional difficulties between a patchwork of cities and non-urban areas—each with its own set of rights and responsibilities vis-à-vis the Roman hegemon—Roman citizen actors, and individual local interest-groups. Across the period, increasing demands for action by communities and individuals, both Roman and otherwise, placed growing pressure on magistrates to intervene in disputes. While an Augustan governor was more engaged within his province, his task more complex, and his relationship with central imperial institutions more subordinated than a hypothetical late second-century counterpart, it was recognizably a similar role, reached through the incremental evolution of functions across a long century. Another indicative example, that of the *koinon* of Asia, which originated as a local organization of communities celebrating common festivals for Roman governors but came to co-ordinate collective action by those same communities in dealing with the institutions of Roman governance, further underscores the point. As communities became accustomed to routinely organizing festivals in consultation with the governor under its auspices, the *koinon* came to have utility as a means to convey the collective voice of participants with more weight. In turn, this strategy was applied to embassies and groups of witnesses travelling to Rome, which implies it was perceived as a successful ploy. Certainly, the honours for Dionysus and Hierocles of Aphrodisias, Diodorus Pasparos, and others demonstrate that some representatives met with success. After the dedication of the temple of Caesar and Roma for the province at Pergamum in 27, the *koinon* came full circle to manage the province-wide operation of what would become the imperial cult but continued to act as a means for communities to collectively voice their disaffection to the governor and institutions of the Roman state. Again, there is a path-dependent logic to this development, with consecutive changes building on each other to create a more complex, institutionalized, and integrated body by the end of Augustus' life.

However, not all development was incremental. The extension of the jurisdiction of the Roman magistrate provides a crucial example. In the initial post-Attalid period most *poleis* had free status, which meant they lay beyond the governor's remit. Notwithstanding repeated breaches of this principle in practice, Roman magistrates could, in theory, only exercise jurisdiction over Roman citizens and non-civic territories. Nevertheless, we do find evidence for the Senate reaffirming the primacy of local law, as at Colophon. The pragmatic decision of Sulla in the aftermath of the First Mithridatic War to subject the cities of Asia to the governor was possible only in the context of the reconquest of the region. It made the governor the supreme arbiter of justice throughout the province, drastically expanding their workload. As Cicero opines in 59: *non sane magna varietas esse negotiorum in administranda Asia sed ea tota iuris dictione maxime sustineri* ('there is no very great variety of business in the administration of Asia: the whole province is upheld by jurisdiction').[1]

The evolution of provincial administration in Asia is also the history of unintended consequences. The collection of the *decuma* evolved in a punctuated fashion: while the Attalids collected a 'tithe' on agricultural produce, during the initial organization of the province, the *poleis* of the province were exempted by virtue of their free status. The *lex Sempronia de provincia Asia* of 122, promulgated by C. Gracchus to support his broader legislative programme, introduced a single tax-farm exploited by Roman *publicani* for the whole province. While outlining a new method of extracting regular revenues from the former *βασιλικὴ χώρα*, Gracchus did not consider the prospect of a major change in the status of territories within the province. However, Sulla's settlement fundamentally altered the underlying conditions. Through intercurrence with the *lex Sempronia*, Sulla's decision had far-reaching consequences ensuring that the *publicani* could extract vast profits from cities with minimal effort. Despite the manifest inequities and problems this created for the state, the social costs of reversing this arrangement prevented the Senate from acting. Only after the civil war with Pompeius was the victorious Caesar, taking advantage of the collapse of central institutions, able to reintroduce a less vicious and extractive regime.

Similarly, Sulla's indemnity levied on the cities of Asia provoked a major debt crisis in the region. His personal need for funds to support military action in the civil war in Italy outweighed longer-term considerations on the economic impact in Asia. Notwithstanding the attempts by Lucullus to mitigate the aftermath in 70/69, continued warfare and Roman demands provoked a related monetary crisis leading to the cessation of cistophoric coinage. In turn, the revival of this denomination a decade later, likely to meet the monetary demands of the province, required more overt Roman support.

The eruption of prolonged civil strife among the Roman political elite in 49, and the concomitant weakening of imperial institutions posed new problems for the governance and administration of Asia. The immediate needs of Roman commanders on the ground often outweighed considerations of good governance, while the concentration of political power resulted in more aggressive changes in policy. Caesar, the *tresviri*, and ultimately Augustus had different approaches to the problems of provincial governance, but structural factors ensured, for example, the continued evolution of established principles of jurisdiction in a more personalized direction, the slow standardization of the tax regime, and the emergence of a fully realized *koinon* of Asia with co-ordinating responsibility in the religious and administrative spheres.

[1] Cic. *Q.fr.* 1.1.20.

The second section argued that Roman rule dissolved existing Hellenistic discursive frameworks governing the interaction between *poleis* and the state. The comparative complexity of the Republican state, dividing responsibilities between the Senate, People, and magistrates, hindered attempts by communities to learn the new language of power. Both bodies and individual magistrates could engage in official communication with the inhabitants of Asia making lack of co-ordination a major factor, while the near-continual flux of central institutions during this period also complicated the process. The growing personalization of Roman discourse and reduction in the number of major players at Rome from the 40s onwards, however, introduced greater coherence and co-ordination, providing a more conducive environment for learning. Ultimately the reduction in the number of sources of legitimate state communication provided a firm basis for understanding. By Augustus' death in 14 CE, a new imperial framework for dialogue between the centre and provincial communities, with a common language, rules, and assumptions, was emerging.

These findings emphasize that no direct connection exists between Hellenistic and Roman imperial modes of engaging with *poleis* in Asia. Instead, the Republican interlude resulted in the complete deconstruction and slow rebuilding of an effective framework for negotiation. Despite the similarities noted by Ma, Ando, and Lenski, the two institutions evolved independently of one another. Partly, this emerged from the fact that Roman governors during this period were much more circumscribed than either Hellenistic *basileis* or their own early second-century counterparts. Moreover, if the complexity of the Republican empire fatally undermined civic attempts to engage meaningfully with the state, as compared to the monarchic empires which preceded and succeeded it, then it provides a further robust explanation for the sudden rise and collapse of civic patronage. Eilers has noted the explosion in the number of acknowledged patrons in the 90s, suggesting that *poleis* were adopting this strategy en masse after some decades of confusion under Roman rule. Equally, the resumption of a direct and coherent dialogue with an individual in the late first century rendered widespread civic patronage less useful than previously. This implies that Republican empires have inherently less control over public discourse than their monarchic counterparts. In one sense, this is an obvious point: generally, the greater the number of moving parts and sources of authority or legitimacy, the greater the variance in messaging. However, it bears stating as a to-date underemphasized point in approaches to provincialization in the eastern Mediterranean.

By contrast, the agency of *polis*-communities played a critical role the process of empire formation. In lieu of a consistent framework for engaging with the Roman state, Asian communities were forced to innovate. After the Sullan reorganization, the increasing intrusiveness of Roman jurisdiction and economic extraction added to the urgency. Evidence from civic decrees demonstrates that cities sought to establish an ongoing written dialogue with representatives of the Roman state, that is individuals, rather than its constitutive bodies. In the 90s and 80s patronage loomed large as the most common means for engaging with Romans. After the First Mithridatic War, however, as cities sought to bolster their own position vis-à-vis an increasingly dominant state, a return to Hellenistic honorific language and, more broadly, inflation of honours took place. Civic diplomacy in this period also yielded significant ground to informal relationships between locals and Roman commanders: private bonds of reciprocity came to replace public ones in some key cases. Finally, I argued that the inscription of Roman normative documents in civic contexts was driven by local concerns. Even so, it had three important effects on provincial society: it normalized Roman official discourse; it placed the communities' relationship with Rome at the centre of civic memory; and it encouraged readers to construct a mental structure of empire encompassing the individual and community. Each of these strategies aimed at promoting local agency, but each also had the effect of implicating the region more deeply in the Roman empire. Two important implications arise from these observations. First, that both the use of civic decrees to approach the representatives of the Roman state and direct diplomacy were affected by the aforementioned centralization of power at Rome. These processes encouraged a privatization of dialogue which reached its logical conclusion under the Principate: a public dialogue resulting in a personal euergetic relationship between cities and the emperor. Second, the appropriation of official documents for local uses and the absence of central planning did not undermine their central role in establishing the legitimacy of Roman rule.

These vignettes reflect Gruen's observation of the third and second centuries, that Roman power was exercised in the eastern Mediterranean though the 'structures, institutions, and attitudes' of Greek-speaking peoples. Both he and Kallet-Marx have highlighted the crucial role of provincial communities in prompting Roman action for local ends.[2] However, a neo-institutionalist approach also emphasizes the sequential, incremental impact of decisions by individual agents and groups on the development of new formal institutions. After the decisions of Aquillius established the initial conditions of Roman hegemony, this study identified three critical junctures, at which the breakdown in political institutions allowed significant innovation in provincial administration in Asia: Sulla from 85–80, Caesar from 48–44, and Augustus after Actium—though especially from 31–27—had the temporary capacity to ignore vested interests and systematically reshape the governance of Asia and the state more broadly. Consequently, I argue that the shift between Roman 'hegemony' and 'empire' in western Asia Minor happened later, and in a more punctuated fashion, than is commonly thought. Most institutions which framed provincial administration, including

[2] Gruen 1984; Kallet-Marx 1995.

the *conventus iuridici* and the provincial *koinon*, emerged only after Sulla's re-organization of the region. These did not spring fully formed from a Roman head but evolved over time and in interaction with provincial stakeholders to fill the needs of Roman magistrates. This does not deny that Roman administration was heavily contested by citizens, provincials, and magistrates on the ground across the period, or that especially after 85 it was sometimes ruthlessly imposed: the sources are quite clear that this was the case. However, such observations can function alongside the argument that at the conceptual level the Roman state—embodied in the Senate, People, and magistrates—did not implement a clear vision of provincial government. As power became increasingly centralized, the state had more motivation to act on growing concerns with good governance.

Where traditional narratives emphasize the role of the Roman state or individual magistrates in shaping the framework of Roman provincial government, I have argued that the constraints placed by institutions on human action are essential to interpreting the development of empire. If provincial institutions, such as the *koinon*, *conventus iuridici*, and tax-systems emerged incrementally and organically, this underscores the limited sense of the word *provincia* before Sulla. In this respect, late second-century Asia had more in common with contemporary Africa or early first-century Cyrenaïca than later provinces such as Pontus-Bithynia. Finally, it highlights the importance of central instability and the personal interests of governors in shaping this process of administrative change. We should not assume that individual actors pursued state interests during all or even most times during the organization of provinces. The conclusions of this study urge us not to treat decisions regarding provincial government as if they were divorced from personal and internal Roman politics.

The study revealed the limited administrative ambitions of the Roman state during the late second and early first century vis-à-vis the communities of western Asia Minor. Under Doyle's schema it pursued hegemony, not empire. Even Sulla's re-organization in the aftermath of the First Mithridatic War did not change the fact that Roman power to interfere in local affairs was not pursued to its capacity. The near-contemporary experiences of Macedonia and Achaea provide examples of Roman-led constitutional innovation, which is unparalleled in Asia, due initially to the grant of freedom to the cities of the Attalid kingdom. Though Sulla stripped most *poleis* of this freedom, fundamentally altering the power dynamic, there is little evidence of his intervention in local politics, limiting the realm of potential action for later governors. The complex structure of the *res publica*'s central institutions hindered the establishment of a common, coherent language of administration, prompting communities to pursue strategies centred on individuals within the Roman state rather than specific institutions. Through establishing ties of patronage and other less formal personal connections *poleis* were able to slowly discern the shape of the evolving Roman *imperium*. As central power became more concentrated over the course of the first century BCE, imperial discourses became more coherent, and a greater concern with the potential benefits of administration emerged. Consequently, the relationships between the communities of Asia, the Roman state, and its representatives were central to the development of the institutions of empire during the late Republic and early Principate.

Appreciating the minimalist nature of Roman government, deep into the first century, requires adjusting our notion of how the Roman political elite viewed the provinces. Even in the second century, Romans were not shy about personally profiting from empire, but this did not translate into attempts to extract substantial public profits. However, by pushing back the date at which a more extractive attitude towards administration predominated, it telescopes this into the emergence of a discourse of ethical government in the 70s and 60s. Given that institutions emerge from historically and socially contingent processes, it should be expected that each provincial administration be distinctive. In the case of Asia, the unique circumstances of its bequest to the Roman people moulded its experience, and even the multiple moments of institutional crisis did not leave a blank slate. The Roman Republic was largely unambitious: the rise of the Principate created conditions in which state legibility and uniformity were of far greater interest.

References

Adams, J.P. (1980), 'Aristonikos and the Cistophoroi', *Historia* 29(3): 302–14.
Ager, S.L. (1996), *Interstate Arbitrations in the Greek World, 337–90 B.C.*, Berkeley.
Allen, R.E. (1983), *The Attalid Kingdom: A Constitutional History*, Oxford.
Ameling, W. (1988), 'Drei Studien zu den Gerichtsbezirken der Provinz Asia in Republikanischer Zeit' *EA* 12: 9–24.
Amiotti, G. (1980), 'I greci ed il massacro degli Italici nell'88 a.C.', *Aevum* 54(1): 132–9.
Anastasiadis, V.I. (1995), 'Theophanes and Mytilene's Freedom Reconsidered', *Tekmeria* 1: 1–14.
Anderson, B.R. (1991), *Imagined Communities: Reflections on the Origin and Spread of Nationalism*, 2nd edn, London.
Ando, C. (2000), *Imperial Ideology and Provincial Loyalty in the Roman Empire*, Berkeley.
—— (2010), 'Imperial Identities', in Whitmarsh, T. (ed.), *Local Knowledge and Microidentities in the Imperial Greek World*, Cambridge, 17–45.
—— (2021), 'The Ambitions of Government: Sovereignty and Control in the Ancient Countryside', in Flower, H. (ed.), *Empire and Religion in the Roman World*, Cambridge, 71–93.
—— (forthcoming), 'Petition and Response, Order and Obey: Contemporary Models of Roman Government', in Baker, H.D., Jursa, M., Palme, B., Procházka, S. & Tost, S. (eds), *Governing Ancient Empires*, Vienna.
Aperghis, G.G. (2004), *The Seleukid Royal Economy: The Finances and Financial Administration of the Seleukid Empire*, Cambridge.
—— (2010), 'Recipients and End-users on Seleukid Coins', *BICS* 53(2): 55–84.
Arangio-Ruiz, V. (1961), 'L'iscrizione Leidense di Augusto', *BIDR* 64: 323–42.
Arrayás Morales, I. (2010), 'Diplomacy in the Greek *Poleis* of Asia Minor: Mytilene's Embassy to Tarraco', *C&M* 61: 127–49.
Ashton, R.H.J. (1994), 'The Attalid Poll-Tax', *ZPE* 104: 57–60.
—— (2013), 'The Use of the Cistophoric Weight-Standard Outside the Pergamene Kingdom', in Thonemann, P. (ed.), *Attalid Asia Minor: Money, International Relations, and the State*, Oxford, 245–71.
Ashton, R.H.J. & Kinns, P. (2004), '*Opuscula Anatolica III*', *NC* 164: 71–107.
Ashton, R.H.J., Kinns, P., & Meadows, A. (2014), '*Opuscula Anatolica IV*', *NC* 174: 1–28.
Asmis, E. (2005), 'A New Kind of Model: Cicero's Roman Constitution in *de Republica*', *AJPh* 126: 377–416.
Astin, A.E. (1985), 'Censorships in the Late Republic', *Historia* 34(2): 175–90.
Atkinson, K.M.T. (1958), 'The Governors of the Province of Asia in the Reign of Augustus', *Historia* 7: 300–30.
—— (1960), '«*Restitutio in integrum*» and «*iussum Augusti Caesaris*» in an Inscription at Leyden', *RIDA* 7: 227–72.
—— (1962), 'The "Constitutio" of Vedius Pollio at Ephesus', *RIDA* 9: 261–89.
Aubert, J.-J. (1994), *Business Managers in Ancient Rome: A Social and Economic Study of Institores, 200 B.C.–A.D. 250*, Leiden.

Austin, J.L. (1975), *How to Do Things with Words: The William James Lectures delivered at Harvard University in 1955*, 2nd edn, Oxford.
Backendorf, D. (1999), 'Ephesos als spätrepublikanischer Prägeort', in Friesinger, H., Krinzinger, F., Brandt, B., & Krierer, K.R. (eds), *100 Jahre Österreichische Forschungen in Ephesus. Akten des Symposions Wiens 1995*, Vienna, 195–201.
Badian, E. (1956), 'Q. Mucius Scaevola and the Province of Asia', *Athenaeum* 44: 104–25.
—— (1958), *Foreign Clientelae (264–70 B.C.)*, Oxford.
—— (1964), 'Notes on Provincial Governors from the Social War down to Sulla's Victory', in Badian, E. (ed.), *Studies in Greek and Roman History*, Oxford, 71–104.
—— (1965), 'M. Porcius Cato and the Annexation and Early Administration of Cyprus', *JRS* 55: 110–21.
—— (1969), 'Two Roman Non-Entities', *CQ* 19: 198–204.
—— (1972), 'Tiberius Gracchus and the Beginning of the Roman Revolution', *ANRW* 1.1: 668–731.
—— (1972a), *Publicans and Sinners: Private Enterprise in the Service of the Roman Republic*, Oxford.
—— (1984), 'Notes on Some Documents from Aphrodisias Concerning Octavian', *GRBS* 25(2): 157–70.
Baronowski, D.W. (1990), '*Sub umbra foederis aequi*', *Phoenix* 44: 345–69.
—— (1996), 'Caria and the Roman Province of Asia,' in Hermon, E. (ed.), *Pouvoir et imperium (IIIe av. J.-C.–I^e ap. J.-C.)*, Naples, 241–9.
Bartels, J. (2009), 'Der Tod des Germanicus und seine epigraphische Dokumentation: Ein neues Exemplar des *senatus consultum de Cn. Pisone patre* aus Genf', *Chiron* 39: 1–9.
Bates, T.R. (1975), 'Gramsci and the Theory of Hegemony', *J Hist Ideas* 36(2): 351–66.
Bauslaugh, R. (1990), 'Cistophoric Countermarks and the Monetary System of Eumenes II', *NC* 150: 39–66.
Belke, K. & Mersich, N. (1990), *Phrygien und Pisidien*, Vienna.
Bencivenni, A. (2010), 'Il re scrive, la città inscrive. La pubblicazione su pietra delle epistole regie nell'Asia ellenistica', *SE* 24: 149–78.
—— (2014), 'The King's Words: Hellenistic Royal Letters in Inscriptions', in Radner, K. (ed.), *State Correspondence in the Ancient World: From New Kingdom Egypt to the Roman Empire*, Oxford, 141–71.
Bérenger, A. (2011), 'Les relations du gouverneur avec les notables provinciaux: cérémonial et sociabilité', in Barrandon, N. & Kirbihler, F. (eds), *Les gouverneurs et les provinciaux sous la république romaine*, Rennes, 171–87.
Berlin, I. (1974), 'Historical Inevitability', in Gardiner, P.L. (ed.), *The Philosophy of History*, Oxford.
Bernhardt, R. (1980), 'Die *immunitas* der Freistädte', *Historia* 29(2): 190–207.
—— (1985), *Polis und römische Herrschaft in der späten Republik*, Berlin.
—— (1999), 'Entstehung, *immunitas* und *munera* der Freistädte. Ein kritischer Überblick', *MedAnt* 2: 41–68.
Bertrand, J.-M. (1978), 'Rome et la Méditerranée orientale au Ier siècle avant J.-C.', in Nicolet, C. (ed.), *Rome et la conquête du monde méditerranéen*, Paris, 789–845.
—— (1990), 'Formes de discours politiques: décrets des cités grecques et correspondance des rois hellénistiques', *CCG* 1: 101–15.
—— (1991), 'À propos d'une inscription de Kyme', in Hermon, E. (ed.), *Gouvernants et gouvernés dans l'imperium Romanum (IIIe s. av. J.-C.–Ier s. ap. J.-C.)*, Quebec, 127–35.
Bikerman, E.J. (1932), '*Bellum Antiochicum*', *Hermes* 67(1): 47–76.
—— (1938), *Institutions des Seleucides*, Paris.

—— (1939), 'La cite grecque dans les monarchies hellénistiques', *RPh* 13: 215–59.

—— (1947), 'Syria and Cilicia', *AJPh* 68(4): 353–62.

—— (1980 [1955]), 'Une question d'authenticité: Les privilèges juifs', in Bikerman, E.J. (ed.), *Studies in Jewish and Christian History*, Leiden, 2: 24–43.

Bitner, B.J. (2014), 'Augustan Procedure and Legal Documents in *RDGE* 70', *GRBS* 54: 639–64.

Bloy, D. (2012), 'Roman Patrons of Greek Communities before the Title *πάτρων*', *Historia* 61(2): 168–201.

Blümel, W. & Merkelbach, R. (2014), *Die Inschriften von Priene*, 2 vols, Bonn.

Boffo, L. (2003), 'La «libertà» delle città greche sotto i Romani (in epoca repubblicana)', *Dike* 6: 227–49.

Bonnefond-Coudry, M. (1989), *Le sénat de la république romaine de la guerre d'Hannibal à Auguste: pratiques délibératives et prise de decision*, Rome.

Börm, H. (2016), 'Hellenistische Poleis und römischer Bürgerkrieg. Stasis im griechischen Osten nach den Iden des März (44 bis 39 v. Chr.)', in Börm, H., Mattheis, M., & Wienand, J. (eds), *Civil War in Ancient Greece and Rome: Contexts of Disintegration and Reintegration*, Stuttgart, 99–125.

Böttcher, K. (1915), *Die Einnahmen der römischen Republik im letzten Jahrhundert ihren Bestehens. Ein Rekonstruktionsversuch*, Diss.—Leipzig.

Bouchon, R. (2014), 'Démophilos de Dolichè, Paul-Émile et les conséquences de la troisième guerre de Macédoine à Gonnoi', *Topoi* 19: 483–513.

Bourdieu, P. (1977), *Outline of a Theory of Practice*, Cambridge.

Bowersock, G.W. (1961), 'Eurycles of Sparta', *JRS* 51: 112–8.

—— (1965), *Augustus and the Greek World*, Oxford.

—— (1970), 'Review: *Roman Documents from the Greek East. Senatus Consulta and Epistulae to the Age of Augustus*, by Robert K. Sherk', *AJPh* 91(2): 223–8.

—— (1984), 'Review: Joyce Reynolds, *Aphrodisias and Rome*', *Gnomon* 56(1): 48–53.

Bowman, A.K. (1993), 'Imperial Pronouncements', *CR* 43(2): 406–8.

Bransbourg, G. (2021), 'Regional Currencies within an Empire. Bronze Coinages of Greece and Asia at the Time of the Roman Conquest: A Case of Partial Monetary Convergence', in Bru, H., Dumitru, A.G., & Sekunda, N. (eds), *Colonial Geopolitics and Local Cultures in the Hellenistic and Roman East (3rd century* BC*–3rd century* AD*): Géopolitique coloniale et cultures locales dans l'Orient hellénistique et romain (IIIe siècle av. J.-C.–IIIe siècle ap. J.-C.)*, Oxford, 110–24.

Braund, D.C. (1983), 'Royal Wills and Rome', *PSBR* 51: 16–57.

—— (1983a), 'Gabinius, Caesar, and the *publicani* of Judaea', *Klio* 65(1): 241–4.

—— (1989), 'Function and Dysfunction: Personal Patronage in Roman Imperialism', in Wallace-Hadrill, A. (ed.), *Patronage in Ancient Society*, London, 137–52.

Brems, E. & Ramos Pinto, S. (2013), 'Reception and Translation', in Gambier, Y. & van Doorslaer, L. (eds), *Handbook of Translation Studies*, vol. 4, Amsterdam, 142–7.

Brennan, T.C. (2000), *The Praetorship in the Roman Republic*, 2 vols, New York.

Briant, P., Brun, P. & Varinlioğlu, E. (2001), 'Une inscription inédite de Carie et la guerre d'Aristonicos', in Bresson, A. & Descat, R. (eds), *Les cités d'Asie Mineure occidentale au IIe siècle a.C.*, Bordeaux, 241–59.

Bringmann, K. (1983), 'Edikt der Triumvirn oder Senatsbeschluß? Zu einem Neufund aus Ephesos', *EA* 2: 47–76.

Broughton, T.R.S. (1934), 'Roman Landholding in Asia Minor', *TAPA* 65: 207–39.

—— (1936), 'On Two Passages of Cicero Referring to Local Taxes in Asia', *AJPh* 57(2): 173–6.

—— (1937), 'A Significant Break in the Cistophoric Coinage of Asia', *AJA* 41: 248–9.
—— (1938), 'Roman Asia', in Frank, T. (ed.), *An Economic Survey of Ancient Rome*, vol. 4, Baltimore, 499–916.
—— (1948), 'The *Elogia* of Julius Caesar's Father', *AJA* 52: 323–30.
Brun, P. (2004), 'Les cités grecques et la guerre: l'exemple de la guerre d'Aristonicos', in Couvenhes, J.-C. & Fernoux, H.–L. (eds), *Les Cités grecques et la guerre en Asie Mineure à l'époque hellénistique*, Tours, 21–54.
Brunt, P.A. (1961), 'Charges of Provincial Maladministration under the Early Principate', *Historia* 10(2): 189–227.
—— (1979), 'Laus Imperii', in Garnsey, P. & Whittaker, C.R. (eds), *Imperialism in the Ancient World*, Cambridge, 159–91.
—— (1981), 'The Revenues of Rome', *JRS* 71: 161–72.
—— (1982), 'The Legal Issue in Cicero's *Pro Balbo*', *CQ* 32(1): 136–47.
—— (1983), 'Princeps and Equites', *JRS* 73: 42–75.
—— (1988), 'The *equites* in the Late Republic', in Brunt, P.A. (ed.), *The Fall of the Roman Republic and Related Essays*, Oxford, 144–94.
—— (1988a), '*Clientela*', in Brunt, P.A. (ed.), *The Fall of the Roman Republic and Related Essays*, Oxford, 382–442.
—— (1990 [1976]), 'The Romanization of the Local Ruling Classes in the Roman Empire', in Brunt, P.A. (ed.), *Roman Imperial Themes*, Oxford, 267–81.
—— (1990a [1956]), 'Sulla and the Asian Publicans', in Brunt, P.A. (ed.), *Roman Imperial Themes*, Oxford, 1–8.
—— (1990b), 'Publicans in the Principate', in Brunt, P.A. (ed.), *Roman Imperial Themes*, Oxford, 354–432.
Bryan, A.Z. (2012), 'Judging Empire: Courts and Culture in Rome's Eastern Provinces', *Law Hist. Rev.* 30(3): 771–811.
Buckland, W.W. (1963), *A Text-Book of Roman Law from Augustus to Justinian*, 3rd edn, Cambridge.
Buckler, W.H. & Robinson, D.M. (1914), 'Greek Inscriptions from Sardis V: Decrees of the League of the Greeks in Asia and of Sardians Honouring Menogenes', *AJA* 18(3): 321–62.
Buis, E.J. (2014), 'Ancient Entanglements: The Influence of Greek Treaties and in Roman "International Law" under the Framework of Narrative Transculturation', in Duve, T. (ed.), *Entanglements in Legal History: Conceptual Approaches*, Frankfurt, 151–85.
Buraselis, K. (2000), *Kos: Between Hellenism and Rome: Studies on the Political, Institutional and Social History of Kos from ca. the Middle Second Century B.C. Until Late Antiquity*, Philadelphia.
—— (2001), 'Two Notes on Theophanes' Descendants', in Salomies, O. (ed.), *The Greek East in the Roman Context*, Athens, 61–70.
—— (2012), 'Appended Festivals: The Coordination and Combination of Traditional Civic and Ruler Cult Festivals in the Hellenistic and Roman East', in Brandt, J.R. & Iddeng, J.W. (eds), *Greek and Roman Festivals: Content, Meaning, & Practice*, Oxford, 247–66.
Burnett, A.M. (1977), 'The Authority of Coin in the Late Republic and Early Empire', *NC* 17: 37–63.
—— (2011), 'The Augustan Revolution Seen from the Mints of the Provinces', *JRS* 101: 1–30.
—— (2022), 'Overview and Some Methodological Points', in Ashton, R.H.J. & Badoud, N. (eds), *Graecia Capta? Rome et les monnayages de l'Egée aux IIe –Ier s. av. J.-C.*, Basel, 17–33.

Burnett, A.M., Amandry, M., & Ripollès Alegre, P.P. (1992), *Roman Provincial Coinage*, vol. 1, London.
Burrell, B. (2004), *Neokoroi: Greek Cities and Roman Emperors*, Leiden.
Burton, G.P. (1975), 'Proconsuls, Assizes and the Administration of Justice under the Empire', *JRS* 65: 92–106.
—— (2002), 'The Roman Imperial State (A.D. 14–235): Evidence and Reality', *Chiron* 32: 249–80.
Burton, P.J. (2009), 'Ancient International Law, the Aetolian League, and the Ritual of Surrender during the Roman Republic: A Constructivist View', *Int Hist Rev.* 31(2): 237–52.
—— (2011), *Friendship and Empire: Roman Diplomacy and Imperialism in the Middle Republic (353–146 BC)*, Cambridge.
Butcher, K. & Ponting, M. (2014), *The Metallurgy of Roman Silver Coinage: From the Reform of Nero to the Reform of Trajan*, Cambridge.
Buxton, B. & Hannah, R. (2005), '*OGIS* 458, the Augustan Calendar, and the Succession', in Deroux, C. (ed.), *Studies in Latin Literature and Roman History XII*, Brussels, 290–306.
Campanile, M.D. (1994), *I sacerdoti del koinon d'Asia (I sec. a.C,–III sec. d.C.): contributo allo studio della romanizzazione delle élites provinciali nell'Oriente greco*, Pisa.
—— (1996), 'Città d'Asia Minore tra Mithridate e Roma', *Studi Ellenistici* 8: 145–73.
—— (1997), 'Un nuovo asiarca da Milasa', *ZPE* 119: 243–4.
—— (2001), '*Provincialis molestia.* Note su Cicerone proconsole', *Studi Ellenistici* 13: 243–74.
—— (2003), 'L'infanzia della provincia d'Asia: l'origine dei "conventus iuridici" nella provincia', in Bearzot, C., Landucci, F., & Zecchini, G. (eds), *Gli stati territoriali nel mondo antico*, Milan, 271–88.
—— (2004), 'I distretti giudiziari d'Asia e la data d'istituzione del distretto ellespontico', in Laffi, U., Prontera, F., & Virgilio, B. (eds), *Artissimum memoriae vinculum: Scritti di geografia storica e di antichità in ricordo di Gioia Conta*, Florence, 129–42.
—— (2007), 'L'assemblea provinciale d'Asia in età repubblica', in Urso, G. (ed.), *Tra Oriente e Occidente: indigeni, Greci e Romani in Asia Minore*, Pisa, 129–40.
—— (2014), 'Cheremone, Pitodoro, Pitodoride', in Cassia, M., Giuffrida, C., Molè Ventura, C., & Pinzone, A. (eds), *Pignora Amicitiae: Scritti di storia antica e storiografia offerti a Mario Mazza*, vol. 1, Rome, 231–57.
Canali De Rossi, F. (1991), 'Review: *Claros I: Décrets Hellénistiques*', *Athenaeum* 69: 646–8.
—— (1992/1993), 'Morte di un ambasciatore di Alabanda', *Scienze dell'Antichità* 6/7: 35–40.
—— (1997), *Le ambascerie dal mondo greco a Roma: in età repubblicana*, Rome.
—— (2000), 'Tre epistole di magistrati romani à città d'Asia' *EA* 32: 163–81.
—— (2005), 'Flacco, Minucio Termo e il *koinòn* dei greci d'Asia', *EA* 38: 101–8.
Capdetrey, L. (2007), *Le pouvoir séleucide: territoire, administration, finances d'un royaume hellénistique, 312–129 avant J.-C.*, Rennes.
Capoccia, G. (2016), 'Critical Junctures', in Fioretos, O., Falleti, T.G., & Sheingate, A. (eds), *The Oxford Handbook of Historical Institutionalism*, Oxford, 89–106.
Capoccia, G. & Kelemen, D.R. (2007), 'The Study of Critical Junctures: Theory, Narrative and Counterfactuals in Institutional Analysis', *World Politics* 59(3): 341–69.
Carbone, L.F. (2014), 'Money and Power: The Disappearance of Autonomous Silver Issues in the Roman Province of Asia', *OMNI* 8: 10–34.
—— (2020), *Hidden Power: Late Cistophoric Production and the Organization of the* provincia Asia *(128–89 B.C.)*, New York.

—— (2020a), 'Mark Antony and the Bronze Revolution in the East', in Powell, A. & Burnett, A. (eds), *Coins of the Roman Revolution (49 BC–AD 14): Evidence Without Hindsight*, Swansea, 44–77.

—— (2022), 'The Introduction of Roman Coinages in Asia (133 BC–1st Century AD)', in Ashton, R.H.J. & Badoud, N. (eds), *Graecia Capta? Rome et les monnayages de l'Egée aux IIe –Ier s. av. J.-C.*, Basel, 233–93.

Carter, M. (2004), '*Archiereis* and Asiarchs: A Gladiatorial Perspective', *GRBS* 44: 41–68.

Chameroy, J. (2012), 'Chronologie und Verbreitung der hellenistischen Bronzeprägungen von Pergamon', *Chiron* 42: 131–81.

—— (2013), 'Review: M.-C. Marcellesi, *Pergame: de la fin du Ve au début du Ier siècle avant J.-C.: pratiques monétaires et histoire*', *Gnomon* 85(8): 711–18.

Champion, C.B. (2007), 'Empire by Invitation: Greek Political Strategies and Roman Imperial Interventions in the Second Century B.C.E.', *TAPA* 137(2): 255–75.

Chaniotis, A. (2003), 'The Perception of Imperial Power in Aphrodisias: The Epigraphic Evidence', in de Blois, L., Erdkamp, P., Hekster, O., de Kleijn, G., & Mols, S. (eds), *Representation and Perception of Roman Imperial Power: Proceedings of the Third Workshop of the International Network Impact of Empire (Roman Empire, 200 B.C.–A.D. 476)*, Amsterdam, 250–60.

—— (2013), 'Affective Epigraphy: Emotions in Public Inscriptions of the Hellenistic Age', *MedAnt* 16(2): 745–60.

—— (2014), 'Mnemopoetik: die epigraphische Konstruktion von Erinnerung in den griechischen Poleis', in Dahly, O., Hölscher, T., Muth, S., & Schneider, R. (eds), *Medien der Geschichte. Antike Griechenland und Rom*, Berlin, 132–69.

—— (2015), 'Affective Diplomacy: Emotional Scripts between Greek Communities and Roman Authorities during the Republic', in Cairns, D.L. & Fulkerson, L. (eds), *Emotions between Greece and Rome*, London, 87–103.

Chankowski, A.S. (1998), 'La procédure législative à Pergame au 1er siècle au J.–C.: à propos de la chronologie relative des décrets en l'honneur de Diodoros Pasparos', *BCH* 122: 159–99.

Chapot, V. (1904), *La province romaine proconsulaire d'Asie*, Paris.

Charbonnel, N. (1979), 'A propos de l'inscription de Kymé et des pouvoirs d'Auguste dans les provinces au lendemain du règlement de 27 av. n. è.', *RIDA* 26: 177–225.

Chin, M.J.H. (2018), '*OGIS* 332 and Civic Authority at Pergamon in the Reign of Attalos III', *ZPE* 208: 121–37.

—— (2022), 'The Career of Menogenes Son of Isidoros and Relations between Sardeis and the *koinon* of Asia under Augustus and Tiberius', *Historia* 71(4): 422–58.

Chiranky, G. (1982), 'Rome and Cotys: Two Problems', *Athenaeum* 60: 461–81.

Christol, M. (1994), 'Pline l'Ancien et la *formula* de la province de Narbonnaise', in Demougin, S. (ed.), *La mémoire perdue: À la recherche des archives oubliées, publiques et privées, de la Rome antique*, Paris, 45–63.

Coarelli, F. (2005), 'Aristonico', *Studi ellenistici* 17: 211–40.

Colin, G. (1924), 'Traduction grecque d'une loi romaine (de la fin de 101 av. J.–C.): Projets de politique orientale des démocrates et de Marius?', *BCH* 48: 58–96.

Collins, F. (1981), 'Eutropius and the Dynastic Name Eumenes of the Pergamene Pretender Aristonicus', *AncW* 4: 39–43.

Cooley, A.E. (2009), *Res Gestae Divi Augusti: Text, Translation, and Commentary*, Cambridge.

—— (2012), 'From Document to Monument: Inscribing Roman Official Documents in the Greek East', in Davies, J.K. & Wilkes, J.J. (eds), *Epigraphy and the Historical Sciences*, Oxford, 159–82.

—— (2019), 'From the Augustan Principate to the Invention of the Age of Augustus', *JRS* 109: 71–87.

Corbier, M. (2008), 'The *Lex Portorii Asiae* and Financial Administration', in Cottier, M., Crawford, M.H., & Crowther, C.V. et al. (eds), *The Customs Law of Asia*, Oxford, 202–35.

Corcoran, S. (2018), 'Less of the Same? Continuity and Change in the Official Epigraphy of the Late Empire', in Destephen, S., Dumézil, B., & Inglebert, H. (eds), *Le Prince Chrétien: de Constantin aux royautés barbares*, Paris, 3–27.

Cornwell, H. (2017), *Pax and the Politics of Peace*, Oxford.

Corvino, R. (2016), 'Circumscribing Imperium: Power and Regulation in the Republican Province', in Armstrong, J. (ed.), *Circum Mare: Themes in Ancient Warfare*, Leiden, 145–63.

Coşkun, A. (2009), 'Das Edikt des Sex. Sotidius Strabo Libuscidianus und die Fasten der Statthalter Galatiens in augusteischer und tiberischer Zeit', *Gephyra* 6: 159–64.

Cottier, M., Crawford, M.H., & Crowther, C.V., et al. (eds) (2008), *The Customs Law of Asia*, Oxford.

Cotton, H.M. (1986), 'A Note on the Organization of Tax-Farming in Asia Minor (Cic. *Fam.*, XIII, 65)', *Latomus* 45(2): 367–73.

—— (2013), 'The Evolution of the So-Called Provincial Law, or: Cicero's Letters of Recommendation and Private International Law in the Roman World', in de Kleijn, G. & Benoist, S. (eds), *Integration in Rome and in the Roman World: Proceedings of the Tenth Workshop of the International Network Impact of Empire (Lille, June 23–5 2011)*, Leiden, 43–55.

Cotton, H.M. & Yakobson, A. (2002), '*Arcanum imperii*: The Powers of Augustus', in Clark, G. & Rajak, T. (eds), *Philosophy and Power in the Graeco-Roman World: Essays in Honour of Miriam Griffin*, Oxford, 193–209.

Coudry, M. (1994), 'Sénatus-consultes et *acta senatus*: Rédaction, conservation et archivage des documents emanant du sénat, de l'époque de César à celle des Sévères', in Demougin, S. (ed.), *La mémoire perdue: A la recerche des archives oubliées, publiques et privées, de la Rome antique*, Paris, 65–102.

Coudry, M. & Kirbihler, F. (2010), 'La *lex Cornelia*, une *lex provinciae* de Sylla pour l'Asie', in Barrandon, N. & Kirbihler, F. (eds), *Administrer les provinces de la république romaine. Actes du colloque de l'Université de Nancy II, 4–5 juin 2009*, Rennes, 133–69.

Cousin, G. & Diehl, C. (1886), 'Inscriptions d'Alabanda en Carie', *BCH* 10: 299–314.

Cox, R.W. (1996), *Approaches to World Order*, Cambridge.

Crawford, M.H. (1985), *Coinage and Money under the Roman Republic*, London.

—— (ed.) (1996), *Roman Statutes*, London.

—— (2003), 'Land and People in Republican Italy', in Braund, D.C. & Gill, C. (eds), *Myth, History and Culture in Republican Rome: Studies in Honour of T.P. Wiseman*, Exeter, 56–72.

Crawford, M.H., Ferrary, J.-L., Moreau, P., & Hallof, K. (1996), 'Lex Fonteia (Cos Fragments)', in Crawford, M.H. (ed.), *Roman Statutes*, London, 497–506.

Crawford, M.H. & Reynolds, J. (1974), 'Rome and Tabae', *GRBS* 15(3): 289–93.

Crook, J.A. (1962), 'An Augustan Inscription in the Rijksmuseum at Leyden: (*S.E.G.* XVIII, no. 555)', *CCJ* 8: 23–9.

Crooks, P. & Parsons T.H. (2016), 'Empires, Bureaucracy and the Paradox of Power', in Crooks, P. & Parson, T.H. (eds), *Empires and Bureaucracy in World History: From Late Antiquity to the Twentieth Century*, Cambridge, 3–28.

Culley, G.R. (1975), 'The Restoration of Sanctuaries in Attica: *I.G.*, II^2, 1035', *Hesperia* 44(2): 207–23.

Curran, J. (2007), 'The Ambitions of Q. Labienus Parthicus', *Antichthon* 41: 33–53.

Czajkowski, K. (2016), 'Justice in Client Kingdoms: The Many Trials of Herod's Sons', *Historia* 65(4): 473–96.

—— (2019), 'The Limits of Legal Pluralism in the Roman Empire', *J legal Hist.* 40(2): 110–29.

Dahlheim, W. (1977), *Gewalt und Herrschaft. Das provinziale Herrschaftssystem der römischen Republik*, Berlin.

Dalla Rosa, A. (2014), *Cura et tutela: le origini del potere imperiale sulle province proconsolari*, Stuttgart.

—— (2015), 'L'*aureus* del 28 a.C. e i poteri triumvirali di Ottaviano', in Lucchelli, T. & Rohr Vio, F. (eds), *Viri militares. Rappresentazione e propaganda tra Repubblica e Principato*, Trieste, 171–200.

—— (2017), 'Propriété familiale, pouvoir imperial: origine et gestion du patrimonium d'Auguste en Asie Mineure', in Cavalier, L., Ferriès, M.-C., & Delrieux, F. (eds), *Auguste et l'Asie Mineure*, Bordeaux, 101–16.

—— (2018), 'Note sui primi procuratori della provincia d'Asia sotto Augusto', *Index* 46: 498–516.

Daubner, F. (2006), *Bellum Asiaticum: Der Krieg der Römer gegen Aristonikos von Pergamon und die Einrichtung der Provinz Asia*, 2nd edn, Munich.

Davenport, C. (2019), *A History of the Roman Equestrian Order*, Oxford.

Davies, J.K. (2013), 'Words, Acts, Facts', *Studi Ellenistici* 27: 413–20.

Davies, S.H. (2019), *Rome, Global Dreams, and the International Origins of an Empire*, Brill.

Debord, P. (1985), 'La Lydie du nord-est', *RÉA* 87(3/4): 345–58.

De Callataÿ, F. (1997), *L'histoire des guerres Mithridatiques vue par les monnaies*, Louvain.

—— (2011), 'More Than It Would Seem: The Use of Coinage by the Romans in Late Hellenistic Asia Minor (133–63 BC)'. *AJN* 23: 55–86.

—— (2013), 'The Coinages of the Attalids and their Neighbours: A Quantified Overview', in Thonemann, P. (ed.), *Attalid Asia Minor: Money, International Relations, and the State*, Oxford, 205–66.

—— (2016), 'The Coinages Struck for the Romans in Hellenistic Greece: A Quantified Overview (mid 2nd–mid 1st C. BCE)', in Haymann, F., Hollstein, W., & Jehne, M. (eds), *Neue Forschungen zur Münzprägungen der römischen Republik: Beiträge zum internationalen Kolloquium im Residenzschloss Dresden 19.–21. Juni 2014*, Bonn, 315–38.

De Chaisemartin, N. (2017), 'Octavien/Auguste et Aphrodisias: certitudes et perplexités', in Cavalier, L., Ferriès, M.-C., & Delrieux, F. (eds), *Auguste et l'Asie Mineure*, Bordeaux, 331–43.

Decorte, R. (2015), 'Publishing Laws: An Investigation of Layout and Epigraphic Conventions in Roman Statutes', *ZPE* 195: 243–54.

Deininger, J. (1965), *Die Provinziallandtage der römischen Kaiserzeit von Augustus bis zum Ende des dritten Jahrhunderts n. Chr.*, Munich.

De Laet, S.J. (1949), *Portorium. Étude sur l'organisation douanière chez les Romains, surtout l'époque du Haut-Empire*, Bruges.

De Libero, L. (1997), '*Ut eosdem quos populus Romanus amicos atque hostes habeant*: Die Freund-Feind-Klausel in den Beziehungen Roms zu Griechischen und Italischen Staaten', *Historia* 46(3): 270–305.

De Ligt, L. (2002), 'Tax Transfers in the Roman Empire', in de Blois, L. & Rich, J. (eds), *The Transformation of Economic Life under the Roman Empire: Proceedings of the Second Workshop of the International Network Impact of Empire (Roman Empire, c.200 B.C.–A.D. 476), Nottingham, July 4–7, 2001*, Amsterdam, 48–66.

—— (2007), 'The Problem of *ager privatus vectigalisque* in the Epigraphic Lex Agraria', *Epigraphica* 69: 87–98.
Delplace, C. (1977), 'Publicains, trafiquants et financiers dans les provinces d'Asie Mineure sous la République', *Ktema* 2: 233–52.
—— (1978), 'Le contenu social et économique du soulevement d'Aristonicos: opposition entre riches et pauvres?', *Athenaeum* 56: 20–53.
Delrieux, F. (2010), 'La crise financière des cités grecques d'Asie Mineure au Ier siècle a.C. et la lettre de Cicéron à Q. Minucius Thermus (FAM. 13.56)', in Carbon, J.-M. & van Bremen, R. (eds), *Hellenistic Karia*, Bordeaux, 505–26.
—— (2022), 'Rome et les monnayages grecs de Carie aux IIe et Ier s. av. J.-C.: De la tutelle rhodienne à l'avénement de Principat', in Ashton, R.H.J. & Badoud, N. (eds), *Graecia Capta? Rome et les monnayages de l'Egée aux IIe -Ier s. av. J.-C.*, Basel, 187–232.
Delrieux, F. & Ferriès M.-C. (2004), 'Euthydème, Hybréas et Mylasa: Une cité grecque de Carie dans les conflits romains de la fin du Ier siècle A.C.', *RÉA* 106(1/2): 49–71, 499–515.
—— (2011), 'Stratonicea de Carie et Nerva "saveur d'Asie"', *Topoi* 17(2): 421–67.
De Martino, F. (1956), '*Ager privatus vectigalisque*', in Volterra, E. (ed.), *Studi in onore di Pietro De Francisci*, Milan, 555–79.
Dench, E. (2018), *Empire and Political Cultures in the Roman World*, Cambridge.
Derow, P.S. (1991), 'Pharos and Rome', *ZPE* 88: 261–70.
Dignas, B. (2002), *Economy of the Sacred in Hellenistic and Roman Asia Minor*, Oxford.
Dmitriev, S. (1999), 'Three Notes on Attalid History', *Klio* 81(2): 397–411.
—— (2000), 'Observations on the Historical Geography of Lycaonia', *GRBS* 41(4): 349–75.
—— (2005), 'The History and Geography of the Province of Asia during its First Hundred Years and the Provincialization of Asia Minor', *Athenaeum* 93: 71–133.
—— (2005a), *City Government in Hellenistic and Roman Asia Minor*, Oxford.
—— (2017), 'The Status of Greek Cities in Roman Reception and Adaptation', *Hermes* 145(2): 195–209.
Dobesch, G. (1996), 'Caesar und Kleinasien', *Tyche* 11: 51–77.
Domingo Gygax, M. (2016), *Benefaction and Rewards in the Ancient Greek City: The Origins of Euergetism*, Cambridge.
Donnelly, J. (2006), 'Sovereign Inequalities and Hierarchy in Anarchy: American Power and International Society', *Eur. J. Int. Relat.* 12(2): 139–70.
Doyle, M.W. (1986), *Empires*, Ithaca.
Dreher, M. (1996), 'Die *lex portorii Asiae* und der Zollbezirk Asia', *EA* 26: 111–28.
Drew-Bear, T. (1972), 'Three *senatus consulta* concerning the Province of Asia', *Historia* 21(1): 75–87.
—— (1978), *Nouvelles inscriptions de Phrygie*, Zutphen.
Drew-Bear, T. & Le Rider, G. (1991), 'Monnayage cistophorique des Apaméens, des Praipénisseis et des Corpéni sous les Attalides. Questions de géographie historique', *BCH* 115(1): 361–76.
Dreyer, B. (2005), 'Rom und die griechischen Polisstaaten an der westkleinasiatischen Küste in der zweiten Hälfte des zweiten Jahrhunderts v. Chr. Hegemoniale Herrschaft und lokale Eliten im Zeitalter der Gracchen', in Coşkun, A. (ed.), *Roms auswärtige Freunde in der späten Republik und im frühen Prinzipat*, Göttingen, 55–74.
—— (2007), 'Neue Quellen zum Hellenismus: Bestand, Kontexte, Intentionen', in Weber, G. (ed.), *Kulturgeschichte des Hellenismus: Von Alexander dem Großen bis Kleopatra*, Stuttgart, 333–54.

—— (2009), 'City Elites and the Administration of the Attalid kingdom after the Peace of Apameia: Evidence, Research and Methodological Thoughts', in Mitchell, L. & Rubinstein, L. (eds), *Greek History and Epigraphy: Essays in Honour of P.J. Rhodes*, Swansea, 33–45.

—— (2015), 'Königliche Herrschaft und römische Präsenz. Römische Imperiumsträger als Nachfolger attalidischer Administration', in Baltrusch, E. & Wilker, J. (eds), *Amici – socii – clientes? Abhängige Herrschaft im Imperium Romanum*, Berlin, 199–223.

Dreyer, B. & Engelmann, H. (2003), *Inschriften von Metropolis I*, Bonn.

—— (2006), 'Augustus und Germanicus im ionischen Metropolis', *ZPE* 158: 173–82.

Driediger-Murphy, L.G. (2014), 'M. Valerius Messalla to Teos (*Syll.*[3] 601) and the Theology of Rome's War with Antiochos', *ZPE* 189: 115–20.

Drogula, F.K. (2015), *Command and Commanders in the Roman Republic and Early Empire*, Chapel Hill.

Dubouloz, J. & Pittia, S. (2009), 'La Sicile romaine, de la disparition du royaume de Hieron II à la réorganisation augustéene des provinces', *Pallas* 80: 85–126.

Eberle, L.P. (2017), 'Making Roman Subjects: Citizenship and Empire before and after Augustus', *TAPA* 147(2): 321–70.

Eberle, L.P. & Le Quéré, E. (2017), 'Landed Traders, Trading Agriculturalists? Land in the Economy of the Italian Diaspora in the Greek East', *JRS* 107: 27–59.

Eck, W. (1984), '*CIL* VI 1508 (Moretti, *IGUR* 71) und die Gestaltung senatorischer Ehrenmonumente', *Chiron* 14: 201–18.

—— (1995–8), *Die Verwaltung des Römischen Reiches in der Hohen Kaiserzeit: Ausgewählte und erweiterte Beiträge*, 2 vols, Basel.

—— (2009), 'Diplomacy as Part of the Administrative Process in the Roman Empire', in Eilers, C. (ed.), *Diplomats and Diplomacy in the Roman World*, Leiden, 193–208.

—— (2010 [1997]), 'Öffentlichkeit, Monument und Inschrift', in Eck, W. & Ameling, W. (eds), *Monument und Inschrift: Gesammelte Aufsätze zur senatorischen Repräsentation in der Kaiserzeit*, Berlin, 275–98.

—— (2014), 'Documents on Bronze: A Phenomenon of the Roman West?', in Bodel, J. & Dimitrova, N. (eds), *Ancient Documents and their Contexts: First North American Congress of Greek and Latin Epigraphy*, Leiden, 127–51.

Eck, W., Caballos, A., & Fernández, F., 1996, *Das Senatus consultum de Cn. Pisone patre*, Munich.

Eckstein, A.M., (1995), 'Glabrio and the Aetolians: A Note on *Deditio*', *TAPA* 125: 271–89.

—— (1999), 'Pharos and the Question of Roman Treaties of Alliance in the Greek East in the Third Century B.C.E.', *CP* 94(4): 395–418.

—— (2006), *Mediterranean Anarchy, Interstate War and the Rise of Rome*, Berkeley.

—— (2018), 'Rome, Empire, and the Hellenistic State System', in Ñaco del Hoyo, T. & López Sánchez, F. (eds), *War, Warlords, and Interstates Relations in the Ancient Mediterranean*, Leiden, 231–53.

Edelmann-Singer, B. (2011), 'Die Provinzen und der Kaiserkult. Zur Entstehungen und Organisation des Provinziallandtagesvon Asia', in Ebner, M. & Esch-Wermeling, E. (eds), *Kaiserkult, Wirtschaft und spectacula: zum politischen und gesellschaftlichen Umfeld der Offenbarung*, Göttingen, 81–102.

—— (2015), *Koina und Concilia: Genese, Organisation und sozioökonomische Funktion der Provinziallandtage im römischen Reich*, Stuttgart.

—— (2016), 'The Provincial Elite in the Provincial Assemblies: Eastern *koina* and their Influence on Provincial Identity', *C&M* 65: 227–39.

Edmondson, J. (2014), 'The Roman Emperor and the Local communities of the Roman Empire', in Ferrary, J.-L. & Scheid, J. (eds), *Il princeps romano: autocrate o magistrato? Fattori giuridici e fattori sociali del potere imperiale da Augusto a Commodo*, Pavia, 127–55.

Eich, A. & Eich, P. (2005), 'War and State-Building in Roman Republican Times', *SCI* 24: 1–33.

Eich, P. (2005), *Zur Metamorphose des politischen Systems in der römischen Kaiserzeit: Die Entstehung einer 'personalen Bürokratie' im langen dritten Jahrhundert*, Berlin.

Eilers, C. (1991), 'Cn. Domitius and Samos: A New Extortion Trial (*IGR* 4,968)', *ZPE* 89: 167–78.

—— (1996), 'Silanus <and> Murena (*I. Priene* 121)', *CQ* 46(1): 175–82.

—— (1999), 'M. Silanus, Stratoniceia, and the Governors of Asia under Augustus', *Tyche* 14: 77–86.

—— (2001), 'The Proconsulship of P. Cornelius Scipio (*cos.* 16 B.C.)', *CQ* 51(1): 201–5.

—— (2002), *Roman Patrons of Greek Cities*, Oxford.

—— (2005), 'Review: B. Dreyer and H. Engelmann, *Die Inschriften von Metropolis* 1', *JRS* 95: 253–4.

—— (2009), 'Inscribed Documents, Uninscribed Documents and the Place of the City in the *Imperium Romanum*', in Haensch, R. (ed.), *Selbstdarstellung und Kommunikation die Veröffentlichung staatlicher Urkunden auf Stein und Bronze in der römischen Welt*, Munich, 301–12.

Eilers, C. & Milner, N.P. (1995), 'Q. Mucius Scaevola and Oenoanda', *AS* 45: 73–89.

Elliot, J.H. (1992), 'A Europe of Composite Monarchies', *P&P* 137: 48–71.

Ellis-Evans, A. (2016), 'The Koinon of Athena Ilias and its Coinage', *AJN* 28: 105–58.

—— (2019), *The Kingdom of Priam: Lesbos and the Troad between Anatolia and the Aegean*, Oxford.

—— (2020), 'The Late Hellenistic Tetradrachms of Parion and Lampsakos', *AJN* 32: 93–126.

Engelmann, H. (1976), *Die Inschriften von Kyme*, Bonn.

Engelmann, H. & Knibbe, D. (1989), 'Das Zollgesetz der Provinz Asia: Eine neue Inschrift aus Ephesos', *EA* 14: 1–206.

Erkelenz, D. (1999), 'Cicero *pro Flacco* 55–59: Zur Finanzierung von Statthalterfesten in der Frühphase des Koinon von Asia', *Chiron* 29: 43–57.

—— (2003), *Optimo Praesidi: Untersuchungen zu den Ehrenmonumenten für Amtsträger der römischen Provinzen in Republik und Kaiserzeit*, Bonn.

Errington, R.M. (1980), 'Rom, Antiochos der Grosse und die Asylie von Teos', *ZPE* 39: 279–84.

—— (2010), 'Alabanda und Rom im 2. Jh. v. Chr.', *EA* 43: 125–30.

Erskine, A. (1994), 'The Romans as Common Benefactors', *Historia* 43(1): 70–87.

—— (1994a), 'Greek Embassies and the City of Rome', *Classics Ireland* 1: 47–53.

—— (1997), 'Greekness and Uniqueness: The Cult of the Senate in the Roman East', *Phoenix* 51(1): 25–37.

Esty, W.W. (2006), 'How to Estimate the Original Number of Dies and the Coverage of a Sample', *NC* 166: 359–64.

Famerie, É. (2009), 'Le traité d'alliance romano–cnidienne 45 av. J.–C.', *CCG* 20: 265–80.

—— (2021), 'Le sénate-consulte relatif au règlement des affaires de Phrygie (*RDGE* 13): Nouveau texte, nouveau contexte', in Buongiorno, P. & Camodeca, G. (eds), *Die senatus consulta in den epigraphischen Quellen: Texte und Bezeugungen*, Stuttgart, 171–85.

Fernoux, H.-L., (2004), *Notables et élites des cités de Bithynie aux époques hellénistique et romaine: IIIe siècle av. J.-C.-IIIe siècle ap. J.-C.: Essai d'histoire sociale*, Lyon.

—— (2011), *Le Demos et la Cité: Communautés et assemblées populaires en Asie Mineure à l'époque impériale*, Rennes.

—— (2011a), 'Les ambassades civiques des cités de la province d'Asie envoyées à Rome au Ier s. av. J.-C.: législation romaine et prérogatives des cités', in Barrandon, N. & Kirbihler, F. (eds), *Les gouverneurs et les provinciaux sous la République romaine*, Rennes, 77–99.

Ferrary, J.-L. (1977), 'Recherches sur la législation de Saturninus et de Glaucia', *MEFRA* 89 (2): 619–60.

—— (1978), 'Rome, les Balkans, la Grèce et l'Orient au IIe av. J.-C.', in Nicolet, C. (ed.), *Rome et la conquête du monde méditerranéen*, Paris, 729–88.

—— (1985), 'La lex Antonia de Termessibus', *Athenaeum* 73: 419–57.

—— (1988), *Philhellénisme et impérialisme: aspects idéologiques de la conquête romaine du monde hellénistique, de la seconde guerre de Macédoine à la guerre contre Mithridate*, Paris.

—— (1990), 'Traités et domination romaine dans le monde hellénique', in Canfora, L., Liverani, M., & Zaccagnini, C. (eds), *I trattati nel mondo antico: Forma, ideologia, funzione*, Rome, 217–35.

—— (1996), 'The *lex Antonia de Termessibus*', in Crawford, M.H. (ed.), *Roman Statutes*, London, 331–40.

—— (1997), 'De l'évergétisme hellénistique à l'évergétisme romain', *Actes du Xe Congrès International d'épigraphie grecque et latine*, Paris, 199–225.

—— (1997a), 'The Hellenistic World and Roman Political Patronage', in Cartledge, P., Garnsey, P., & Gruen, E.S. (eds), *Hellenistic Constructs: Essays in Culture, History and Historiography*, Berkeley, 105–19.

—— (1999), 'La liberté des cités et ses limites à l'époque républicaine', *MedAnt* 2(1): 69–84.

—— (2000), 'Les gouverneurs des provinces romaines d'Asie Mineure (Asie et Cilicie), depuis l'organisation de la province d'Asie jusqu'à la première guerre de Mithridate (126–88 av. J.-C.)', *Chiron* 30: 161–93.

—— (2000a), 'Les inscriptions du sanctuaire de Claros en l'honneur de Romains', *BCH* 124: 331–76.

—— (2001), 'Rome et la géographie de l'hellénisme: réflexions sur "Hellènes" et "Panhellènes" dans les inscriptions de l'époque romaine', in Salomies, O. (ed.), *The Greek East in the Roman Context: Proceedings of a Colloquium Organized by the Finnish Institute at Athens, 21 and 22 May 1999*, Helsinki, 19–35.

—— (2001a), 'À propos des pouvoirs d'Auguste', *CCG* 12(1): 101–54.

—— (2005), 'Les grecs des cités et l'obtenion de la civitas Romana', in Fröhlich, P. & Müller, C. (eds), *Citoyenneté et participation à la basse époque hellénistique*, Geneva, 51–75.

—— (2007), 'Les ambassadeurs grecs au Sénat romain', in Sot, M. (ed.), *L'audience: rituels et cadres spatiaux dans l'Antiquité et le haut Moyen Âge*, Paris, 113–22.

—— (2009), 'After the Embassy to Rome: Publication and Implementation', in Eilers, C. (ed.), *Diplomats and Diplomacy in the Roman World*, Leiden, 127–42.

—— (2009a), 'La gravure de documents publics de la Rome républicaine et ses motivations', in Haensch, R. (ed.), *Selbstdarstellung und Kommunikation die Veröffentlichung staatlicher Urkunden auf Stein und Bronze in der römischen Welt*, Munich, 59–74.

—— (2012), 'Quelques remarques à propos de Q. Mucius Scaevola (cos. 95 av. J.-C.), et en particulier de la date de son gouvernement en Asie', *Athenaeum* 100: 157–79.

—— (2017), 'Démocratie(s) des anciens' in Ferrary, J.-L. & Rousset, D. (eds), 2017, *Rome et le monde grec: choix d'écrits*, Paris, 35–53.

—— (2017a [1991]), 'Le statut des cités libres dans l'Empire romain à la lumière des inscriptions de Claros', reprinted with additional comments in Ferrary, J.-L. & Rousset, D. (eds), 2017, *Rome et le monde grec: choix d'écrits*, Paris, 161–80.

—— (2018), 'Una vita nel cuore della Repubblica. Saggio di biografia politica', in Ferrary, J.-L., Schiavone, A., & Stolfi, E. (eds), *Qvintvs Mvcius Scaevola: Opera*, Rome, 3–27.

Ferriès, M.-C. (2007), *Les Partisans d'Antoine: (des orphelins de César aux complices de Cléopâtre)*, Bordeaux.

Ferriès, M.-C. & Delrieux, F. (2011), 'Quintus Mucius Scaevola, un gouverneur modèle pour les Grecs de la province d'Asia', in Barrandon, N. & Kirbihler, F. (eds), *Les gouverneurs et les provinciaux sous la république romaine*, Rennes, 207–30.

Fioretos, O., Falleti, T.G., & Sheingate, A. (2016), 'Historical Institutionalism in Political Science', in Fioretos, O., Falleti, T.G., & Sheingate, A. (eds), *The Oxford Handbook of Historical Institutionalism*, Oxford, 3–28.

Flower, H.I. (2009), *Roman Republics*, Princeton.

—— (2018), 'Servilia's *consilium*: Rhetoric and Politics in a Family Setting', in van der Blom, H., Gray, C., & Steel, C. (eds), *Institutions and Ideology in Republican Rome: Speech, Audience, and Decision*, Cambridge, 252–64.

Foubert, L. (2016), 'The Lure of an Exotic Destination: The politics of Women's Travels in the early Roman Empire', *Hermes* 144(4): 462–87.

Foucart, P.F. (1904), *La formation de la province romaine d'Asie*, Paris.

Foucault, M. (1980), *Power/Knowledge: Selected Interviews and Other Writings 1972–1977*, New York.

—— (2000 [1979]), '*Omnes et singulatim*: Towards a Criticism of "Political Reason"', in Fabion, J.D. (ed.), *Power: Essential Works of Foucault*, vol. 3, New York, 298–325.

—— (2000a [1978]), 'Governmentality', in Fabion, J.D. (ed.), *Power: Essential Works of Foucault*, vol. 3, New York, 201–22.

Fournier, J. (2007), 'Les *syndikoi*, représentants juridiques des cités grecques sous le Haut-Empire romain', *CCG* 18: 7–36.

—— (2010), *Entre tutelle romaine et autonomie civique: l'administration judiciaire dans les provinces hellénophones de l'empire romain, 129 av. J.-C.– 235 apr. J.-C.*, Athens.

—— (2012), 'L'essor de la multi-citoyenneté dans l'Orient romain: problèmes juridiques et judiciares', in Heller, A. & Pont, A.-V. (eds), *Patrie d'origine et patries électives: les citoyennetés multiples dans le monde grec d'époque romaine*, Bordeaux, 79–98.

France, J. (2007), 'Deux questions sur la fiscalité provinciale d'après Cicéron, *Ver.* 3.12', in Dubouloz, J. & Pittia, S. (eds), *La Sicilie de Cicéron: Lectures des Verrines*, Besançon, 169–84.

Frank, T. (1927), '"Dominium in solo provinciali" and "ager publicus"', *JRS* 17: 141–61.

—— (1933), *An Economic Survey of Ancient Rome*, vol. 1, Baltimore.

—— (1937), 'The New Elogium of Julius Caesar's Father', *AJPh* 58(1): 90–3.

Frederiksen, M.W. (1965), 'The Republican Municipal Laws: Errors and Drafts', *JRS* 55: 183–98.

Freeman, P.W. (1986), 'The Province of Cilicia and its Origins', in Freeman, P.W. & Kennedy, D.L. (eds), *The Defence of the Roman and Byzantine East*, Oxford, 253–75.

French, D.H., (1991), 'C. Atinius C.f. on a coin of Ephesus', in Lightfoot, C.S. (ed.), *Recent Turkish Coin Hoards and Numismatic Studies*, Oxford, 201–3

—— (1997), 'Pre- and Early-Roman Roads of Asia Minor. The Earliest Roman Paved Roads in Asia Minor', *Arkeoloji Dergisi* 5: 179–87.

—— (2012), *Roman Roads and Milestones of Asia Minor*, vol. 3.1, London.

Friesen, S.J. (1993), *Twice Neokoros: Ephesus, Asia and the Cult of the Flavian Imperial Family*, Leiden.
—— (1999), 'Asiarchs', *ZPE* 126: 275–90.
—— (2013), 'Junia Theodora of Corinth: Gendered Inequalities in the Early Empire', in Friesen, S.J., James, S.A., & Schowalter, D.N. (eds), *Corinth in Contrast: Studies in Inequality*, Leiden, 203–26.
Frija, G. (2012), *Les prêtres des empereurs: le culte impérial civique dans la province romaine d'Asie*, Rennes.
—— (2014), 'Les Grecs et l'authorités romaines au Ier siècle av. J.-C.: réflexions sur l'évolution du language honorifique', in Dubouloz, J., Pittia, S., & Sabatini G. (eds), *L'imperium Romanum en perspective. Les savoirs d'empire dans la République romaine et leur héritage dans l'Europe médiévale et moderne*, Paris, 81–94.
—— (2016), 'Les cultes impériaux dans les cités d'Asie Mineure: des spécificités provinciales?', in Kolb, A. & Vitale, M. (eds), *Kaiserkult in den Provinzen des römischen Reiches: Organisation, Kommunikation und Repräsentation*, Berlin, 159–72.
—— (2017), 'Auguste et la concession de la citoyenneté romaine: enquête sur les Iulii en Carie', in Cavalier, L., Ferriès, M.-C., & Delrieux, F. (eds), *Auguste et l'Asie Mineure*, Bordeaux, 191–206.
—— (2017a), 'Les honneurs des cités d'Asie aux proches des gouverneurs', in Heller, A. & van Nijf, O. (eds), *The Politics of Honour in the Greek Cities of the Roman Empire*, Leiden, 272–90.
—— (2019), 'Le *koinon* d'Asie et la notion d'aristocratie provinciale', in Heller, A., Müller, C., & Suspène, A. (eds), *Philorhômaios kai philhellèn: Hommage à Jean-Louis Ferrary*, Geneva, 251–66.
Gabrielsen, V. (2000), 'The Rhodian Peraia in the Third and Second Centuries B.C.', *C&M* 51: 129–85.
Gagarin, M. (2008), *Writing Greek Law*, Cambridge.
Galani, G. (2022), 'Imprints of Roman *Imperium*: Bronze Coinages in the Republican Eastern Provinces', Diss.—Stockholm.
Gargola, D.J. (2017), 'Was there a Regular *provincia Africa* in the Second Century?' *Historia* 66(3): 331–61.
—— (2017a), *The Shape of the Roman Order: The Republic and its Spaces*, Chapel Hill.
Gauthier, P. (1985), *Les cités grecques et leurs bienfaiteurs*, Athens.
—— (2011 [1984]), 'Les cités hellénistiques: épigraphie et histoire des institutions et des régimes politiques', in Gauthier P., *Études d'histoire et d'institutions grecques. Choix d'écrits*, Geneva, 315–50.
Geertz, C. (1973), *The Interpretation of Cultures: Selected Essays*, New York.
—— (1983), *Local Knowledge: Further Essays in Interpretative Anthropology*, New York.
Genschel, P. & Zangl, B. (2008), 'Metamorphosen des Staates: vom Herrschaftsmonopolisten zum Herrschaftsmanager', *Leviathan* 36: 430–54.
Giovannini, A. (1978), *Rome et la circulation monétaire en Grèce au IIe siècle avant Jésus-Christ*, Basel.
—— (1983), *Consulare imperium*, Basel.
—— (1999), 'Les pouvoirs d'Auguste de 27 à 23 av.J.-C.: une relecture de l'ordonnance de Kymè de l'an 27 (*IK* 5, N° 17)', *ZPE* 124: 95–106.
—— (2008), 'Date et objectifs de la *lex de provinciis praetoriis* (Roman Statutes, no 12)', *Historia* 57(1): 92–107.
Giovannini, A. & Grzybek, E. (1978), 'La *lex de piratis persequendis*', *MH* 35(1): 33–47.

Girdvainyte, L. (2019), *Law and Citizenship in the Roman Greek East: The Provinces of Macedonia and Achaia (c.146 BCE–212 CE)*, Diss.—Oxford.

Glew, D.G. (1977), 'Mithridates Eupator and Rome: A Study of the Background of the First Mithridatic War', *Athenaeum* 55: 380–405.

—— (1981), 'Between the Wars: Mithridates Eupator and Rome, 85–73 B.C.', *Chiron* 11: 109–30.

Gold, B.K. (1985), 'Pompey and Theophanes of Mytilene', *AJPh* 106(3): 312–27.

Gotter, U. (2013), 'The Castrated King, or: The Everyday Monstrosity of Late Hellenistic Kingship', in Luraghi, N. (ed.), *The Splendors and Miseries of Ruling Alone: Encounters with Monarchy from Archaic Greece to the Hellenistic Mediterranean*, Stuttgart, 207–30.

Gow, A.S.F. & Page, D.L. (1963), *The Greek Anthology: The Garland of Philip and Some Contemporary Epigrams*, 2 vols, Cambridge.

Grant, M. (1946), *From Imperium to Auctoritas: A Historical Study of the Aes Coinage in the Roman Empire, 49 BC–AD 14*, Cambridge.

Gray, E. (1978), 'M'. Aquillius and the Organization of the Roman Province of Asia', in Akurgal, E. (ed.), *Proceedings of the Xth International Congress of Classical Archaeology*, Ankara, vol. 2, 965–77.

Greif, A. (2006), *Institutions and the Path to the Modern Economy: Lessons from Medieval Trade*, Cambridge.

Griffin, M.T. (1973), 'The Tribune C. Cornelius', *JRS* 63: 196–213.

—— (1989), 'Philosophy, Politics, and Politicians at Rome', in Griffin, M.T. & Barnes, J. (eds), *Philosophia Togata*, Oxford, 1–37.

Grimal, P. (1945–6), 'Auguste et Athénodore', *RÉA* 47–48: 261–73, 62–79.

Gruber, J. (1988), 'Cicero und das hellenistische Herrscherideal', *WS* 101: 243–58.

Gruen, E.S. (1982), 'Greek πίστις and Roman *fides*', *Athenaeum* 60: 50–68.

—— (1984), *The Hellenistic World and the Coming of Rome*, Berkeley.

Guerber, E. (1995), 'Cité libre ou stipendaire? A propos du statut juridique d'Éphèse a l'époque du haut empire romain', *RÉG* 108(2): 388–409.

—— (2009), *Les cités grecques dans l'empire romain: les privilèges et les titres des cités de l'orient hellénophone d'Octave Auguste à Dioclétien*, Rennes.

Habermas, J. (1979), *Communication and the Evolution of Society*, trans. T. McCarthy, Cambridge.

—— (1984), *The Theory of Communicative Action. vol. 1, Reason and the Rationalization of Society*, trans. T. McCarthy, Cambridge.

—— (1987), *The Theory of Communicative Action. vol. 2, Lifeworld and System, a Critique of Functionalist Reason*, trans. T. McCarthy, Cambridge.

Habicht, C. (1975), 'New Evidence on the Province of Asia', *JRS* 65: 64–91.

—— (1997), *Athens from Alexander to Antony*, Cambridge.

Haensch, R. (1992), 'Das Statthalterarchiv', *ZSS-Rom* 109: 209–317.

—— (1997), *Capita Provinciarum: Statthaltersitze und Provinzialverwaltung in der römischen Kaiserzeit*, Mainz.

—— (2009), 'Die Städte des griechischen Ostens', in Haensch, R. (ed.), *Selbstdarstellung und Kommunikation die Veröffentlichung staatlicher Urkunden auf Stein und Bronze in der römischen Welt*, Munich, 173–87.

Hall, A.S., Milner, N.P., & Coulton, J.J. (1996), 'The Mausoleum of Licinnia Flavilla and Flavianus Diogenes of Oinoanda: Epigraphy and Architecture', *AS* 46: 111–46.

Hall, P.A. & Taylor, R.C.R. (1996), 'Political Science and the Three New Institutionalisms', *Political Studies* 44: 936–57.

Hall, S. (1980), 'Encoding/Decoding', in Hall, S., Hobson, D., Lowe, A., & Willis, P. (eds), *Culture, Media and Language: Working Papers in Cultural Studies, 1972–79*, London, 117–27.
—— (1988), *The Hard Road to Renewal*, London.
Hall, S., Lumley, R. & McLennan, G. (2007 [1977]), 'Politics and Ideology: Gramsci', in Gray, A., Campbell, J., Erickson, M., Hanson, S. & Wood, H. (eds), *CCCS Working Papers*, Abingdon, 278–306.
Hallmannsecker, M. (2020), 'The Ionian *Koinon* and the *Koinon* of the 13 Cities at Sardis', *Chiron* 50: 1–27.
—— (2022), *Roman Ionia: Constructions of Cultural Identity in Western Asia Minor*, Cambridge.
Hantos, T. (1988), *Res publica constituta: Die Verfassung des Dictators Sulla*, Stuttgart.
Harl, K.W. (1996), *Coinage in the Roman Economy 300 BC to AD 700*, Baltimore.
Harris, W.V. (1979), *War and Imperialism in Republican Rome, 327–70 B.C.*, Oxford.
—— (2017), *Roman Power*, Cambridge.
Hassall, M., Crawford, M.H., & Reynolds, J. (1974), 'Rome and the Eastern Provinces at the End of the Second Century BC', *JRS* 64: 195–220.
Hatzfeld, J. (1919), *Les trafiquants italiens dans l'Orient hellénique*, Paris.
—— (1927), 'Inscriptions de Panamara', *BCH* 51: 57–122.
Hatzopoulos, M.B. (1996), *Macedonian Institutions under the Kings: A Historical and Epigraphic Study*, Athens.
Heberdey, R. (1929), *Termessische Studien*, Vienna.
Heil, M. (1991), 'Einige Bemerkungen zum Zollgesetz aus Ephesos', *EA* 17: 9–18.
Heller, A. (2006), *Les bêtises des grecs: Conflits et rivalités entre cités d'Asie et de Bithynie à l'époque romaine, 129 a. C.–235 p. C.*, Pessacs.
—— (2011), 'Des Grecs au service des *imperatores* romains, ou comment rester Grec tout en devenant romains', in Couvenhes, J.-C., Crouzet, S., & Péré-Nouguès, S. (eds), *Pratiques et identités culturelles des armées hellénistiques du monde méditérranéen*, Bordeaux, 227–44.
—— (2014), 'Domination subie, domination choisie: les cités d'Asie Mineure face au pouvoir romain, de la République à l'Empire', *Pallas* 96: 217–34.
—— (2016), 'Le Ier siècle av. J.-C. en Asie Mineure: *Epigraphic habit* et transition en histoire ancienne', in Müller, C. & Heintz, M. (eds), *Transitions historiques*, Paris, 69–80.
—— (2020), *L'âge d'or des bienfaiteurs: Titres honorifiques et sociétés civiques dans l'Asie Mineure d'époque romaine*, Geneva.
Heller, A. & Pont, A.-V. (eds) (2012), *Patrie d'origine et patries électives: les citoyennetés multiples dans le monde grec d'époque romaine*, Bordeaux,
Heller, A. & Suspène, A. (2019), 'C. Asinius Gallus *hagnos* à Temnos: la rhétorique civique face au pouvoir romain', in Heller, A., Müller, C., & Suspène, A. (eds), *Philorhômaios kai philhellèn: Hommage à Jean-Louis Ferrary*, Geneva, 501–20.
Heller, A. & van Nijf, O. (2017), 'Introduction: Civic Honours, from Classical to Roman Times', in Heller, A. & van Nijf, O. (eds), *The Politics of Honour in the Greek Cities of the Roman Empire*, Leiden, 1–27.
Hennig, D. (1997), 'Die Beherbergung von "Statsgästen" in der hellenistischen Polis', *Chiron* 27: 355–68.
Herrmann, P. (1989), 'Ein Tempel für Caligula in Milet?', *MDAI(I)* 39: 191–6.
—— (1989a), 'Rom und die Asylie griechischer Heiligtümer: eine Urkunde des Diktators Caesar und Sardeis', *Chiron* 19: 127–64.
—— (1994), 'Milet unter Augustus. C. Iulius Epikrates und die Anfänge des Kaiserkults', *IstMitt* 44: 203–36.

—— (1996), 'Milet unter Augustus: Erkenntnisse aus einem Inschriften-Neufund', in Strubbe, J.H.M., Tybout, R.A., & Versnel, H.S. (eds), *ENEPΓEIA: Studies on Ancient History and Epigraphy presented to H.W. Pleket*, Amsterdam, 1–18.

Herzog, R. (1922), 'Nikias und Xenophon von Kos', *HZ* 125: 188–247.

Heuss, A. (1933), *Die völkerrechtlichen Grundlagen der römischen Aussenpolitik in republikanischer Zeit*, Leipzig.

Hirschfeld, G. (1886), 'C. Iulius Theupompus of Cnidus', *JHS* 7: 286–90.

Hochard, P.E. (2021), 'Quand Aristonicos s'écrit avec un E', *Bulletin de la société française de numismatique* 76(2): 47–54.

Højte, J.M. (2006), 'From Kingdom to Province: Reshaping Pontos after the Fall of Mithridates VI', in Bekker-Nielsen, T. (ed.), *Rome and the Black Sea Region: Domination, Romanization and Resistance*, Aarhus, 15–30.

—— (2009), 'The Administrative Organisation of the Pontic Kingdom', in Højte, J.M. (ed.), *Mithridates VI and the Pontic Kingdom*, Aarhus, 95–108.

Hollander, D.B. (2007), *Money in the Late Roman Republic*, Leiden.

Horden, P. & Purcell, N. (2000), *The Corrupting Sea: A Study of Mediterranean History*, Malden.

Howgego, C.J. (1982), 'Coinage and Military Finance: The Imperial Bronze Coinage of the Augustan East', *NC* 142: 1–20.

Hoyos, D. (1973), '*Lex provinciae* and Governor's Edict', *Antichthon* 7: 47–53.

Hunter, L.W. (1913), 'Cicero's Journey to his Province of Cilicia in 51 BC', *JRS* 3: 73–97.

Hunter, V.J. (1994), *Policing Athens: Social in Attic Lawsuits, 420–320 B.C.*, Princeton.

Hurlet, F. (1993), *La dictature de Sylla: monarchie ou magistrature républicaine? Essai d'histoire constitutionelle*, Rome.

—— (2006), *Le proconsul et le prince d'Auguste à Dioclétien*, Bordeaux.

Hurlet, F. & Müller, C. (2020), 'L'Achaïe à l'époque républicaine (146–27 av. J.-C.): une province introuvable?', *Chiron*, 50: 49–100.

Iser, W. (1972), 'The Reading Process: A Phenomenological Approach', *New Lit Hist.* 3(2): 279–99.

Ish-Shalom, P. (2010), 'Political Constructivism: The Political Construction of Social Knowledge', in Bjola, C. & Kornprobst, M. (eds), *Arguing Global Governance: Agency, Lifeworld, and Shared Reasons*, New York, 231–46.

Ito, M. (2021), 'A Reconsideration of the Chronology of a Decree of Abdera (*Syll.*[3] 656) and the Introduction of the Concept of Roman Patronage to the Greeks in the Second Century BC', *JHS* 141: 136–52.

Jauss, H.R. & Benziger, E. (1970), 'Literary History as a Challenge to Literary Theory', *New Lit Hist.* 2(1): 7–37.

Jehne, M. (1987), *Der Staat des Dictators Caesar*, Cologne.

—— (2015), 'From *Patronus* to *Pater*. The Changing Role of Patronage in the Period of Transition from Pompey to Augustus', in Jehne, M. & Pina Polo, F. (eds), *Foreign* clientelae *in the Roman Empire: A Reconsideration*, Stuttgart, 297–320.

Jehne, M. & Pina Polo, F. (eds) (2015), *Foreign* clientelae *in the Roman Empire: A Reconsideration*, Stuttgart.

Jenkins, G.K., (1978), 'Hellenistic Gold Coins at Ephesos', *Anadolu* 21: 183–8.

Jones, A.H.M. (1939), '*Civitates liberae et immunes* in the East', in Calder, W.M. & Keil, J. (eds), *Anatolian Studies Presented to William Hepburn Buckler*, Manchester, 103–17.

—— (1940), *The Greek City: From Alexander to Justinian*, Oxford.

—— (1960), 'Procurators and Prefects in the Early Principate', in Jones, A.H.M., *Studies in Roman Law and Government*, Oxford, 117–25.

—— (1960a), 'I Appeal unto Caesar', in Jones, A.H.M., *Studies in Roman Law and Government*, Oxford, 53–65.
—— (1971), *The Cities of the Eastern Roman Provinces*, 2nd edn, Oxford.
Jones, C.P. (1974), 'Diodoros Pasparos and the Nikephoria of Pergamon', *Chiron* 4: 183–205.
—— (1999), 'Atticus in Ephesos', *ZPE* 124: 89–94.
—— (2000), 'Nero Speaking', *HSCP* 100: 453–62.
—— (2001), 'Memories of the Roman Republic in the Greek East', in Salomies, O. (ed.), *The Greek East in the Roman Context: Proceedings of a Colloquium Organised by the Finnish Institute at Athens, May 21 and 22 1999*, Helsinki, 11–18.
—— (2004), 'Events Surrounding the Bequest of Pergamon to Rome and the Revolt of Aristonicos: New Inscriptions from Metropolis', *JRA* 17: 469–85.
—— (2011), 'An Inscription Seen by Agathias', *ZPE* 179: 107–15.
—— (2011a), 'A Model of Euergetism for Asia Minor', *JRA* 24: 773–5.
—— (2012), 'Joys and Sorrows of Multiple Citizenship: The Case of Dio Chrysostom', in Heller, A. & Pont, A.-V. (eds), *Patrie d'origine et patries électives: les citoyennetés multiples dans le monde grec d'époque romaine*, Bordeaux, 213–19.
—— (2015), 'The Earthquake of 26 BCE in Decrees of Mytilene and Chios', *Chiron* 45: 101–22.
—— (2017), 'Strabo and the "Petty Dynasts"', in Cavalier, L., Ferriès, M.-C., & Delrieux, F. (eds), *Auguste et l'Asie Mineure*, Bordeaux, 349–56.
—— (2018), 'The Institutional History of Hierapolis', *JRA* 31: 921–7.
—— (2019), 'Messene in the Last Years of Augustus', *Chiron* 49: 23–44.
Jordan, B., (2017), 'The Consular *provinciae* of 44 BCE and the Collapse of the Restored Republic', *Hermes* 145(2): 174–94.
—— (2022), 'Political Authority and Local Agency: Cilicia Pedias and Syria between the Seleucid Empire and the Roman Republic', *Mnemosyne* 75(3): 483–513.
—— (forthcoming a), 'Negotiating the Failure of Roman Hegemony: The Experience of Allied Rulers during the Civil Wars (49–30 BCE)', in Cornwell, H. & Westall, R.W. (eds), *The Roman Civil Wars of 49–30 BCE: Analysing the Breakdown of Models*, London.
—— (forthcoming b), 'Coercion, Consent, and Republican Provincial Government: Rome and the Province of Asia', in Bellomo, M. & Zucchetti, E. (eds), *Power, Coercion, Consent. Gramsci's Hegemony and the Roman Republic*, Berlin.
Kah, D. (2012), 'Paroikoi und Neubürger in Priene', in Günther, L.-M., (ed.), *Migration und Bürgerrecht in der hellenistischen Welt*, Wiesbaden, 51–71.
Kalinowski, A. (2011), 'Review: Arjan Zuiderhoek, *The Politics of Munificence in the Roman Empire: Citizens, Elites and Benefactors in Asia Minor*', *AHB Online Reviews* 1: 148–52.
Kallet-Marx, R. (1990), 'The Trial of Rutilius Rufus', *Phoenix* 44(2): 122–39.
—— (1995), *Hegemony to Empire: The Development of the Roman Imperium in the East from 148 to 62 B.C.*, Berkeley.
—— (1995a), 'Quintus Fabius Maximus and the Dyme Affair (*Syll.*^{3} 684)', *CQ* 45(1): 129–53.
Kantor, G. (2009), 'Острова Эгейского моря и провинция Азия (The Aegean Islands and The Province of Asia)', *VDI* 2: 138–49. (French Summary: *AÉ* 2009, #1373).
—— (2010), 'SICVLVS CVM SICVLO NON EIVSDEM CIVITATIS: Litigation between Citizens of Different Communities in the *Verrines*', *CCG* 21: 187–204.
—— (2013), 'Law in Roman Phrygia: Rules and Jurisdictions', in Thonemann, P. (ed.), *Roman Phrygia: Culture and Society*, Cambridge, 143–67.
—— (2013a), '*SEG* LV 1452, ll. 32–34, and the Crime of *plagium* in the Late Republic', *ZPE* 184, 219–24.

—— (2014), 'Roman Legal Administration in the Province of Asia: Hellenistic Heritage vs. Innovation', in Dubouloz, J., Pittia, S., & Sabatini G. (eds), *L'imperium Romanum en perspective. Les savoirs d'empire dans la République romaine et leur héritage dans l'Europe médiévale et moderne*, Paris, 243–68.

—— (2017), 'Property in Land in Roman Provinces', in Kantor, G., Lambert, T., & Skoda, H. (eds), *Legalism: Property and Ownership*, Oxford, 55–74.

Katznelson, I. (1997), 'Structure and Configuration in Comparative Politics', in Lichbach, M.I. & Zuckerman, A.S. (eds), *Comparative Politics: Rationality, Culture, and Structure*, Cambridge, 81–112.

Kaufmann, F.-M. & Stauber, J. (1992), 'Poimanenon bei Eski Manyas? Zeugnisse und Lokalisierung einer kaum bekannten Stadt', in Schütte, A. (ed.), *Studien zum antiken Kleinasien II*, Bonn, 43–85.

Kay, P. (2014), *Rome's Economic Revolution*, Oxford.

Kaye, N. (2013), 'Taxation in the Greco-Roman World: The Hellenistic East', *Oxford Handbook Topics in Classical Studies*, Oxford, https://www.oxfordhandbooks.com/view/10.1093/oxfordhb/9780199935390.001.0001/oxfordhb-9780199935390-e-36, accessed 19 August 2019.

—— (2022), *The Attalids of Pergamon and Anatolia: Money, Culture, and State Power*, Cambridge.

Kearsley, R. (1986), 'Asiarchs, *Archiereis*, and the *Archierea* of Asia', *GRBS* 27(2): 183–92.

—— (1989), 'Asiarchs: Titulature and Function: A Reappraisal', *StClass* 26: 57–65.

Keaveney, A. (1982), *Sulla: The Last Republican*, London.

—— (1992), *Lucullus: A Life*, London.

—— (2005), 'Sulla the Warlord and Other Mythical Beasts', in de Blois, L., Bons, J., Kessels, T., & Schenkeveld, D.M. (eds), *The Statesman in Plutarch's Works: Proceedings of the Sixth International Conference of the International Plutarch Society, Nijmegen/Castle Hernen, May 1–5*, 2002, vol. 2, Leiden, 297–302.

Keil, J. (1911), 'Die Synodos der ökumenischen Hieroniken und Stephaniten', *JÖAI* 14: 123–34.

Kinns, P. (1987), 'Asia Minor', in Burnett, A. & Crawford, M.H. (eds), *The Coinage of the Roman World in the Late Republic*, Oxford, 105–21.

—— (1999), 'The Attic Weight Drachms of Ephesus: A Preliminary Study in Light of Recent Hoards', *NC* 159: 47–97.

—— (2006), 'A New Didrachm of Magnesia on the Maeander', *NC* 166: 41–7.

Kirbihler, F. (2007), 'Die Italiker in Kleinasien', in Meyer, M. (ed.), *Neue Zeiten - Neue Sitten. Zu Rezeption und Integration römischen und italischen Kulturguts in Kleinasien*, Vienna, 19–35.

—— (2011), 'Servilius Isauricus, proconsul d'Asie: un gouverneur populaire', in Kirbihler, F. & Barrandon, N. (eds), *Les gouverneurs et les provinciaux sous la République romaine*, Rennes, 249–72.

—— (2012), 'César, Auguste et l'Asie: continuités et évolutions de deux politiques', in Devillers, O. & Sion, K. (eds), *César sous Auguste*, Bordeaux, 125–44.

—— (2013), 'Brutus et Cassius et les impositions, spoliations et confiscations en Asie mineure durant les guerres civiles (44–42 a.C.)', in Ferriès, M.-C. & Delrieux, F. (eds), *Spolier et confisquer dans les mondes grec et romain*, Chambéry, 345–66.

—— (2016), *Des Grecs et des Italiens à Éphèse: Histoire d'une intégration croisée (133 a.C.–48 p.C.)*, Bordeaux.

—— (2017), 'Les problèmes d'une mission publique entre République et Empire: P. Vedius Pollio en Asie', in Cavalier, L., Ferriès, M.-C., & Delrieux, F. (eds), *Auguste et l'Asie Mineure*, Bordeaux, 129–52.

Kiser, E. & Kane, D. (2007), 'The Perils of Privatization: How the Characteristics of Principals Affected Tax-Farming in the Roman Republic and Empire', *Social Science History* 31(2): 191–212.

Kleiner, F.S. (1972), 'The Dated Cistophori of Ephesus', *ANSMN* 18: 17–32.

—— (1978), 'Hoard Evidence and the Late Cistophori of Pergamum', *ANSMN* 23: 77–105.

Kleiner, F.S. & Noe, S.P. (1977), *The Early Cistophoric Coinage*, New York.

Knibbe, D. (1981), 'Qvandocvmqve qvis trivm virorvm rei pvblicae constitvendae: Ein neuer Text aus Ephesos', *ZPE* 44: 1–10.

Knoepfler, D. (2010), 'Le féderalisme antique en question: renouveau et transformation des confédérations hellénistiques sous la domination de Rome', *Annuaire du Collège de France* 109: 691–706.

Kokkinia, C. (2000), *Die Opromoas-Inschrift von Rhodiapolis. Euergetismus und soziale Elite in Lykien*, Bonn.

—— (2008), 'Aphrodisias' "Rights of Liberty": Diplomatic Strategies and the Roman Governor', in Ratté, C. & Smith, R.R.R. (eds), *Aphrodisias Papers 4. New Research on the City and its Monuments*, Portsmouth, RI, 51–60.

—— (2009), 'The Role of Individuals in Inscribing Roman State Documents: Governor's Letters and Edicts', in Haensch, R. (ed.), *Selbstdarstellung und Kommunikation die Veröffentlichung staatlicher Urkunden auf Stein und Bronze in der römischen Welt*, Munich, 191–206.

—— (2015–16), 'The Design of the "Archive Wall" at Aphrodisias', *Tekmeria* 13: 9–55.

Kolb, A. & Vitale, M. (eds) (2016), *Kaiserkult in den Provinzen des römischen Reiches: Organisation, Kommunikation und Repräsentation*, Berlin.

Kondratieff, E.J. (2009), 'Reading Rome's Evolving Civic Landscape in Context: Tribunes of the Plebs and the Praetor's Tribunal', *Phoenix* 63(3/4): 322–60.

Kreiler, B. (2006), 'Der Prokonsul Lentulus, der Imperator Murena und der Proquästor Lucullus', *Tyche* 21: 73–82.

Kuhn, C.T. (2015), 'Honours for M. Appuleius in Miletus', *ZPE* 193: 189–92.

—— (2017), 'The Refusal of the Highest Honours by Members of the Urban Elite in Roman Asia Minor', in Heller, A. & van Nijf, O. (eds), *The Politics of Honour in the Greek Cities of the Roman Empire*, Leiden, 199–219.

Kunkel, W. (1962), 'Über die Leidener Augustus-Inschrift aus Kyme (zugleich ein Beitrag zur *aestimatio possessionis*', in *Studi in onore di Emilio Betti*, vol. 2, Rome, 591–620.

Kunkel, W. & Wittman, R. (1995), Staatsordnung und Staatspraxis der römischen Republik, Munich.

Labarre, G. (1996), *Les cités de Lesbos: aux époques hellénistique et impériale*, Paris.

Laffi, U. (1967), 'Le iscrizioni relative all'introduzione nel 9 a.C. del nuovo calendario della provincia d'Asia', *SCO* 16: 5–98.

—— (2006), 'L'iscrizione di Efeso sui privilegi, di insegnanti, sofisti, medici (*I. Ephesos*, 4101)', *Studi Ellenistici* 19, 453–521.

—— (2010), 'Cittadini romani di fronte ai tribunali di comunità alleate o libere dell'Oriente greco in età repubblicana', in Mantovani, D. & Pellecchi, L. (eds), *Eparcheia, autonomia e ciuitas Romana. Studi sulla giurisdizione criminale dei governatori di provincia (II sec. a. C.–II d. C.)*, Padua, 14–40.

—— (2010a), *Il trattato fra Sardi ed Efeso degli anni 90 a.C.*, Pisa.

Laignoux, R., (2017), 'Reconnaître Octavien et ses concurrents en Anatolie: les allégeances asiatiques durant les guerres civils de la fin de las République', in Cavalier, L., Ferriès, M.-C., & Delrieux, F. (eds), *Auguste et l'Asie Mineure*, Bordeaux, 211–39.

Lanfranchi, T. (2019), 'Edicts and Decrees during the Republic: A Reappraisal', *ZRG-RA* 136: 47–83.

Lehmann, G.A. (1998), *'Römischer Tod' in Kolophon/Klaros. Neue Quellen zum Status der "freien" Polisstaaten an der Westküste Kleinasiens im späten zweiten Jahrhundert v. Chr.*, Göttingen.

—— (2000), 'Polis-Autonomie und römische Herrschaft an der Westküste Kleinasiens: Kolophon/Klaros der Aufrichtung der provincia Asia', in Mooren, L. (ed.), *Politics, Administration and Society in the Hellenistic and Roman World*, Leuven, 215–38.

Lenski, N. (2017), *Constantine and the Cities: Imperial Authority and Civic Politics*, Philadelphia.

Le Rider, G. (1989), 'La politique monétaire du Royaume de Pergame après 188', *JSav* 3–4: 163–90.

—— (1990), 'Un groupe de cistophores de l'époque attalide', *BCH* 114(2): 683–701.

—— (1999), 'Sur un aspect du comportement monétaire des villes libres d'Asie Mineure occidentale au IIe siècle: leurs émissions de tétradrachmes de poids attique frappées entre 188 et c. 140', in Bresson, A. & Descat, R. (eds), *Les Cités d'Asie Mineure occidentale au IIe siècle a.C.*, Bordeaux, 37–63.

Lerouxel, F. & Pont, A.-V. (eds) (2016), *Propriétaires et citoyens dans l'Orient romain*, Bordeaux.

Leschhorn, W. (1993), *Antike Ären: Zeitrechnung, Politik und Geschichte im Schwarzmeerraum und in Kleinasien nördlich des Tauros*, Stuttgart.

Le Teuff, B. (2010), 'Les recensements dans les provinces de la République romaine: aux origines de la réforme augustéenne', in Barrandon, N. & Kirbihler, F. (eds), *Administrer les provinces de la république romaine: Actes du colloque de l'Université de Nancy II, 4–5 juin 2009*, Rennes, 195–211.

Levi, M. (1988), *Of Rule and Revenue*, Berkeley.

—— (1997), 'A Model, a Method, a Map: Rational Choice in Comparative and Historical Analysis', in Lichbach, M.I. & Zuckerman, A.S. (eds), *Comparative Politics: Rationality, Culture, and Structure*, Cambridge, 19–41.

Lewis, N. (1999), 'Imperial Largess in the Papyri', *JJP* 29: 45–50.

Liebmann-Frankfort, T. (1966), 'Valeur juridique et signification politique des testaments faits par les rois hellénistiques en faveur des Romains', *RIDA* 13: 73–94.

Linderski, J. (2007 [1999]), '*Transitus*: Official Travel Under the Sign of Obelus', in Linderski, J., *Roman Questions II: Selected Papers*, Stuttgart, 307–18.

Lintott, A.W. (1976), 'Notes on the Roman Law Inscribed at Delphi and Cnidos', *ZPE* 20: 65–82.

—— (1981), 'What was the *imperium Romanum*?', *G&R* 28(1): 53–67.

—— (1992), *Judicial Reform and Land Reform in the Roman Republic*, Cambridge.

—— (1993), *Imperium Romanum: Politics and Administration*, London.

—— (1999), *The Constitution of the Roman Republic*, Oxford.

—— (2008), *Cicero as Evidence: A Historian's Companion*, Oxford.

Lundgreen, C. (2014), 'Staatsdiskurse in Rom? Staatlichkeit als analytische Kategorie für die römische Republik', in Lundgreen, C. (ed.), *Staatlichkeit in Rom? Diskurse und Praxis (in) der römischen Republik*, Stuttgart, 15–60.

—— (2019), 'Statualità e Principato augusteo', *Politica Antica* 9: 99–139.

Ma, J. (1999), *Antiochos III and the Cities of Western Asia Minor*, Oxford.

—— (2000), 'Seleukids and Speech-Acts: Performative Utterances, Legitimacy and Negotiation in the World of the Maccabees', *SCI* 19: 71–112.

—— (2009), 'Empire, Statuses and Realities', in Parker, R., Papazarkadas, N., & Ma, J. (eds), *Interpreting the Athenian Empire*, Oxford, 125–48.

—— (2012), 'Epigraphy and the Display of Authority', in Davies, J. & Wilkes, J. (eds), *Epigraphy and the Historical Sciences*, Oxford, 133–58.

—— (2012a), 'Honorific Statues and Hellenistic History', in Smith, C. & Yarrow, L.M. (eds), *Imperialism, Cultural Politics, & Polybius*, Oxford, 230–51.

—— (2013), 'The Attalids: A Military History', in Thonemann, P. (ed.), *Attalid Asia Minor: Money, International Relations, and the State*, Oxford, 49–82.

—— (2013a), *Statues and Cities: Honorific Portraits and Civic Identity in the Hellenistic World*, Oxford.

—— (2013b), 'The History of Hellenistic Honorific Statues', in Martzavou, P. & Papazarkadas, N. (eds), *Epigraphical Approaches to the Post-Classical Polis: Fourth Century BC to Second Century AD*, Oxford, 165–80.

Mack, W. (2015), *Proxeny and Polis: Institutional Networks in the Ancient Greek World*, Oxford.

Mackil, E. (2013), *Creating a Common Polity: Religion, Economy and Politics in the Making of the Greek Koinon*, Berkeley.

Madsen, J.M. (2014), 'An Insider's View: Strabo in Amaseia on Pompey's Pontic Cities', in Bekker-Nielsen, T. (ed.), *Space, Place and Identity in Northern Anatolia*, Stuttgart, 75–86.

—— (2016), 'Who Introduced the Imperial Cult in Asia and Bithynia? The Koinon's Role in the Early Worship of Augustus', in Kolb, A. & Vitale, M. (eds), *Kaiserkult in den Provinzen des Römischen Reiches: Organisation, Kommunikation und Repräsentation*, Berlin, 21–36.

Magie, D. (1950), *Roman Rule in Asia Minor: To the End of the Third Century after Christ*, 2 vols, Princeton.

Maier, C. (2000), 'Consigning the Twentieth Century to History: Alternative Narratives for the Modern Era', *AHR* 105(3): 807–31.

Mann, M. (1984), 'The Autonomous Power of the State: Its Origins, Mechanisms and Results', *EJS* 25(2): 185–213.

—— (1986), *The Sources of Social Power: Volume 1: A History of Power from the Beginning to A.D. 1760*, Cambridge.

Mannsperger, D. (1973), 'Apollon gegen Dionysos: Numismatische Beiträge zu Octavians Rolle als Vindex Libertatis', *Gymnasium* 80(4): 381–404.

Mantovani, D. (2008), '*Leges et iura p(opuli) R(omani) restituit.* Principe e diritto in un aureo di Ottaviano', *Athenaeum* 96: 5–54.

Marcellesi, M. (2010), 'Le monnayage royale et ses interactions avec les monnayages civiques: L'exemple du royaume attalide', in Savalli-Lestrade, I. & Cogitore, I. (eds), *Des rois au prince: Pratiques du pouvoir monarchique dans l'Orient hellénistique et romain (IVe siècle avant J.-C.–IIe siècle après J.-C.)*, Grenoble, 193–206.

—— (2012), *Pergame: de la fin du Ve au début du Ier siècle avant J.-C.: pratiques monétaires et histoire*, Pisa.

Marek, C. (1988), 'Karien im ersten Mithridatischen Krieg', in Kneissl, P. & Losemann, V. (eds), *Alte Geschichte und Wissenschaftsgeschichte. Festschrift für Karl Christ zum 65. Geburtstag*, Darmstadt, 285–308.

—— (1993), *Stadt, Ära und Territorium in Pontus-Bithynia und Nord-Galatia*, Tübingen.

—— (1997), 'Teos and Abdera nach dem dritten makedonischen Krieg: Eine neue Ehreninschrift für den Demos von Teos', *Tyche* 12: 169–77.

—— (2010), *Geschichte Kleinasiens in der Antike*, Munich.

Marquardt, J. (1881), *Römische Staatsverwaltung*, 2nd edn, Leipzig.

Marshall, A.J. (1966), 'Governors on the Move', *Phoenix* 20(3): 231–46.

—— (1968), 'Pompey's Organization of Bithynia-Pontus: Two Neglected Texts', *JRS* 58: 103–9.
—— (1969), 'Romans under Chian Law', *GRBS* 10(3): 255–71.
—— (1972), 'The *lex Pompeia de Provinciis* (52 BC) and Cicero's *imperium* in 51–50 BC: Constitutional Aspects', *ANRW* 1.1: 887–921.
—— (1975), 'Flaccus and the Jews of Asia (Cicero *pro Flacco* 28.67–69)', *Phoenix* 29(2): 139–54.
—— (1980), 'The Survival and Development of International Jurisdiction in the Greek World under Roman Rule', *ANRW* 2.13: 626–61.
Martin, J. (2002), 'The Political Logic of Discourse: A Neo-Gramscian View', *Hist Eur Ideas.* 28: 21–31.
Maselli, G. (2000), *In difesa di Lucio Flacco: (Pro L. Flacco)*, Venice.
Mason, H. (1974), *Greek Terms for Roman Institutions: A Lexicon and Analysis*, Toronto.
Mastrocinque, A. (1999), *Studi sulle guerre Mitridatiche*, Stuttgart.
Mattingly, D.J. (2011), *Imperialism, Power, and Identity: Experiencing the Roman Empire*, Princeton.
Mattingly, H.B. (1923), *Coins of the Roman Empire in the British Museum, vol. 1*, London.
—— (1951), 'Review: Sutherland, C.H.V., *Coinage in Roman Imperial Policy, 31 B.C.–A.D. 68)*', *NC* 41: 136–42.
—— (1972), 'The Date of the *senatus consultum de agro Pergameno*', *AJPh* 93: 412–23.
—— (1979), 'L. Julius Caesar, Governor of Macedonia', *Chiron* 9: 147–68.
—— (1997), 'The Date and Significance of the *lex Antonia de Termessibus*', *Scholia* 6(1): 68–78.
McGing, B.C. (1980), 'Appian, Manius Aquillius, and Phrygia', *GRBS* 21(1): 35–42.
—— (1986), *The Foreign Policy of Mithridates VI Eupator King of Pontus*, Leiden.
—— (1995), 'The Ephesian Customs Law and the Third Mithridatic War', *ZPE* 109: 283–8.
Meadows, A. (2002), 'Stratonikeia in Caria: The Hellenistic City and its Coinage', *NC* 162: 79–134.
—— (2013), 'The Closed Currency System of the Attalid Kingdom', in Thonemann, P. (ed.), *Attalid Asia Minor: Money, International Relations, and the State*, Oxford, 148–206.
—— (2018), 'The Great Transformation. Civic Coin Design in the Second Century B.C.', in Iossif, P.P., de Callataÿ, F., & Veymiers, R. (eds), *Greek and Roman Coins Seen Through Their Images: Noble Issuers, Humble Users? Proceedings of the International Conference Organized by the Belgian and French Schools at Athens, 26–28 September 2012*, Liège, 297–318.
—— (2022), 'The Penetration of the *Denarius* and *Quinarius* Standards into Asia Minor in the 1st Century BC', in Ashton, R.H.J. & Badoud, N. (eds), *Graecia Capta? Rome et les monnayages de l'Egée aux IIe -Ier s. av. J.-C.*, Basel, 127–85.
Meier, C. (1966), *Res Publica Amissa: Eine Studie zu Verfassung und Geschichte der späten römischen Republik*, Wiesbaden.
Mellor, R. (1975), *Θεα Ρωμη: The Worship of the Goddess Roma in the Greek World*, Göttingen.
Merkelbach, R. (1990), 'Hat der Bithynische Erbfolgekrieg im Jahr 74 oder 73 begonnen?', *ZPE* 81: 97–100.
—— (1995), 'L. Antonius, gladiator Asiaticus, und der Brief des Q. Minucius Thermus an die Diözesen von Asia', *EA* 25: 73–6.

Merola, G.D. (1996), 'Il *Monumentum Ephesenum* e l'organizzazione territoriale delle regioni asiane', *MEFRA* 108(1): 263–97.

—— (2001), *Autonomia locale governo imperiale: fiscalità e amministrazione nelle province asiane*, Bari.

—— (2001a), 'Il sistema tributario asiano tra repubblica e principato', *MedAnt* 4: 459–72.

Metcalf, W.E. (2007), 'Regionalism in the Coinage of Asia Minor', in Elton, H. & Reger, G. (eds), *Regionalism in Hellenistic and Roman Asia Minor*, Pessac, 147–59.

—— (2009), 'A Note on the Later Republican Cistophori', *Schweizerische Numismatische Rundschau* 88: 205–10.

—— (2015), 'The *Cistophori* of Nysa' in van Alfen, P.G., Bransbourg, G., & Amandry, M. (eds), *Fides: Contributions to Numismatics in Honor of Richard B. Witschonke*, New York, 311–17.

—— (2017), *The Later Republican Cistophori*, New York.

Metzger, E. (2005), *Litigation in Roman Law*, Oxford.

Meyer, E.A. (2004), *Legitimacy and Law in the Roman World:* Tabulae *in Roman Belief and Practice*, Cambridge.

Meyer-Zwiffelhoffer, E. (2002), *Πολιτικῶς ἀρχεῖν: zum Regierungsstil der senatorischen Statthalter in den kaiserzeitlichen griechischen Provinzen*, Stuttgart.

Migeotte, L. (1984), *L'Emprunt public dans les cités grecques: Recueil des documents et analyse critique*, Paris.

—— (2014), *Les finances des cités grecques aux périodes classique et hellénistique*, Paris.

Mileta, C. (1990), 'Zur Vorgeschichte und Entstehung der Gerichtsbezirke der Provinz Asia', *Klio* 72: 427–44.

—— (1998), 'Eumenes III und die Sklaven: Neue Überlegungen zum Charakter des Aristonicosaufstandes', *Klio* 80: 47–65.

—— (2002), 'The King and his Land. Some Remarks on the Royal Area (*basilike chora*) of Hellenistic Asia Minor', in Ogden, D. (ed.), *The Hellenistic World: New Perspectives*, Swansea, 157–75.

—— (2008), *Der König und sein Land: Untersuchungen zur Herrschaft der hellenistischen Monarchen über das königliche Gebiet Kleinasiens und seine Bevölkerung*, Berlin.

—— (2008a), 'Die offenen Arme der Provinz: Überlegungen zur Funktion und Entwicklung der prorömischen Kultfeste der Provinz Asia (erstes Jahrhundert v. Chr.)', in Rüpke, J. (ed.), *Festrituale in der römischen Kaiserzeit*, Tübingen, 89–114.

Millar, F.G.B. (1992 [1977]), *The Emperor in the Roman World (31 BC–AD 337)*, 2nd edn, Bristol.

—— (2002 [1966]), 'The Emperor, the Senate and the Provinces', in Cotton, H.M. & Rogers, G.M. (eds), *Rome, the Greek World and the East*, vol. 1, Chapel Hill, 271–91.

—— (2002a [1973]), 'Triumvirate and Principate', in Cotton, H.M. & Rogers, G.M. (eds), *Rome, the Greek World and the East*, vol. 1, Chapel Hill, 241–70.

—— (2004 [1967]), 'Emperors at Work', in Cotton, H.M. & Rogers, G.M. (eds), *Rome, the Greek World and the East*, vol. 2, Chapel Hill, 3–22.

—— (2004a [1998]), 'Trajan: Government by Correspondence', in Cotton, H.M. & Rogers, G.M. (eds), *Rome, the Greek World and the East*, vol. 2, Chapel Hill, 23–46.

—— (2004b [1983]), 'Empire and City, Augustus to Julian: Obligations, Excuses and Status', in Cotton, H.M. & Rogers, G.M. (eds), *Rome, the Greek World and the East*, vol. 2, Chapel Hill, 336–70.

Mitchell, S. (1976), 'Requisitioned Transport in the Roman Empire', *JRS* 66: 106–31.

—— (1984), 'Review: Joyce Reynolds: *Aphrodisias and Rome*', *CR* 34(2): 291–7.

—— (1993), *Anatolia: Land, Men and Gods in Asia Minor*, 2 vols, Oxford.

—— (1999), 'The Administration of Roman Asia, 133 BC to AD 250', in Eck, W. & Müller-Luckner, E. (eds), *Lokale Autonomie und römische Ordnungsmacht in den kaiserzeitlichen Provinzen vom 1. bis 3. Jahrhundert*, Munich, 17–46.

—— (2000), 'Ethnicity, Acculturation and Empire in Roman and Late Roman Asia Minor', in Mitchell, S. & Greatrex, G. (eds), *Ethnicity and Culture in Late Antiquity*, London, 117–50.

—— (2005), 'The Treaty between Rome and Lycia of 46 BC (MS 2070)', in Pintaudi, R. (ed.), *Papyri Graecae Schøyen*, Florence, 165–208.

—— (2008), 'Geography, Politics, and Imperialism in the Asian Customs Law', in Cottier, M. et al. (eds), *The Customs Law of Asia*, Oxford, 165–201.

Mommsen, T. (1887), *Römishes Staatsrecht*, 3 vols, 3rd edn., Leipzig.

—— (1905 [1862]), '*Lex agraria*', in Mommsen, T. (ed.), *Gesammelte Schriften: Juristische Schriften*, Berlin, 65–145.

—— (1906 [1899]), 'Senatsbeschluss über Pergamon', in Mommsen, T. (ed.), *Gesammelte Schriften: Historische Schriften*, Berlin, 63–8.

Monson, A. (2015), 'Hellenistic Empires', in Scheidel, W. & Monson, A. (eds), *Fiscal Regimes and the Political Economy of Premodern States*, Cambridge, 169–207.

Mørkholm, O. (1982), 'Some Reflections on the Production and Use of Coinage in Ancient Greece', *Historia* 31: 290–305.

Morrell, K. (2017), *Pompey, Cato, and the Governance of the Roman Empire*, Oxford.

Morris, I. & Scheidel, W. (eds) (2009), *The Dynamics of Ancient Empires: State Power from Assyria to Byzantium*, Oxford.

Musti, D. (1998), 'I Nikephoria e il ruolo panellenico di Pergamo', *RFIC* 126: 5–40.

—— (1999), 'Nuove riflessoni sui *Nikephoria pergameni* e Diodoro Pasparo', *RFIC* 127: 325–33.

Ñaco del Hoyo, T. (2007), 'The Late Republican West: Imperial Taxation in the Making?', in Hekster, O., de Kleijn, G., & Slootjes, D. (eds), *Crises and the Roman Empire: Proceedings of the International Network Impact of Empire (Nijmegen, June 20–24, 2006)*, Leiden, 219–31.

—— (2019), 'Rethinking *stipendiarius* as Tax Terminology in the Roman Republic', *MH* 76(1): 70–87.

Ng, D.Y. (2016), 'Monuments, Memory and Status Recognition in Roman Asia Minor', in Galinsky, K. (ed.), *Memory in Ancient Rome and Early Christianity*, Oxford, 235–60.

Nichols, J. (1990), 'Patrons of Greek Cities in the Early Principate', *ZPE* 80: 81–108.

—— (2014), *Civic Patronage in the Roman Empire*, Leiden.

Nicolet, C., (1966), *L'ordre équestre a l'époque républicaine (312–43 av. J.-C.)*, Paris.

—— (1988), *L'inventaire du monde: géographie et politique aux origines de l'Empire romain*, Paris.

—— (1994), 'Dîmes de Sicile, d'Asie et d'ailleurs', in *Le Ravitaillement en blé de Rome et des centres urbains des débuts de la République jusqu'au Haut-Empire. Actes du colloque international de Naples, 14-16 Février 1991*, Rome, 215–29.

—— (2000 [1979]), 'Deux remarques sur l'organisation des sociétés de publicains à la fin de la République romaine', in Nicolet, C. & Lefebvre, S. (eds), *Censeurs et publicains: Économie et fiscalité dans le Rome antique*, Paris, 297–319.

—— (2000a [1991]), 'Le *Monumentum Ephesenum* et les dîmes d'Asie', in Nicolet, C. & Lefebvre, S. (eds), *Censeurs et publicains: Économie et fiscalité dans le Rome antique*, Paris, 353–66.

—— (2000b [1993]), 'Le *Monumentum Ephesenum* et la délimitation du *portorium* d'Asie', in Nicolet, C. & Lefebvre, S. (eds), *Censeurs et publicains: Économie et fiscalité dans le Rome antique*, Paris, 367–84.

Niebergall, A. (2011), 'Die lokalen Eliten der griechischen Städte Kleinasiens und Mithridates VI Eupator zu Beginn des ersten römisch-pontischen Krieges', *Hermes* 139 (1): 1–20.

—— (2011a), 'Lokale Eliten unter hellenistischen Herrschern. Mithridates VI. Von Pontos und die griechischen Eliten Kleinasiens und Griechenlands', in Dreyer, B. & Mittag, P.F. (eds), *Lokale Eliten und hellenistischen Könige: Zwischen Kooperation und Konfrontation*, Berlin, 55–79.

Noè, E. (1996), 'Un caso di mobilità sociale nelle tarda repubblica: il caso di Ibrea di Milasa', in Gabba, E., Desideri, P., & Roda, S. (eds), *Italia sul Baetis: Studi in memoria di Fernando Gascò*, Turin, 50–64.

North, D.C. (1995), 'Five Propositions about Institutional Change', in Knight, J. & Sened, I. (eds), *Explaining Social Institutions*, Ann Arbor, 15–26.

O'Connell, M. (2009), *Men of Empire: Power and Negotiation in Venice's Maritime State*, Baltimore.

Oliver, J.H. (1963), 'The Main Problem of the Augustus Inscription from Cyme', *GRBS* 4 (2): 115–22.

—— (1972), 'On the Hellenic Policy of Augustus and Agrippa in 27 B.C.', *AJPh* 93(1): 190–7.

Orren, K. & Skowronek, S. (1994), 'Beyond the Iconography of Order: Notes for a New Institutionalism', in Dodd, L. & Jillson, C. (eds), *The Dynamics of American Politics: Approaches and Interpretations*, Boulder, 311–30.

—— (2004), *The Search for American Political Development*, New York.

Osgood, J. (2006), *Caesar's Legacy: Civil War and the Emergence of the Roman Empire*, Cambridge.

Papazoglu, F. (1988), *Les villes de Macédoine a l'époque romaine*, Athens.

Parker, R.W. (1991), 'Potamon of Mytilene and his Family', *ZPE* 85: 115–29.

Paterson, J. (2007), 'Friends in High Places: The Creation of the Court of the Roman Emperor', in Spawforth, A.J.S. (ed.), *The Court and Court Society in Ancient Monarchies*, Cambridge, 121–56.

—— (2021), 'Hegemony in the Roman Principate: Perceptions of Power in Gramsci, Tacitus, and Luke', in Zucchetti, E. & Cimino, A.M. (eds), *Antonio Gramsci and the Ancient World*, London, 255–272.

Pawlak, M.N. (2016), 'From Independence to Dependence: The Administrative Status of the Aegean Islands from 129 BC to 294 AD', *Electrum* 23: 187–214.

Pédech, P. (1991), 'Deux Grecs face à Rome au Ier siècle av. J.-C.: Métrodore de Scepsis et Théophane de Mitylène', *REA* 93(1): 65–78.

Pelling, C.B.R. (1988), *Plutarch: Life of Antony*, Cambridge.

Peters, B.G., Pierre, J., & King, D.S. (2005), 'The Politics of Path Dependence: Political Conflict in Historical Institutionalism', *J Polit.* 67(4): 1275–300.

Pflaum, H.-G. (1968), 'La mise en place des procuratèles financières dans les provinces du haut-empire romain', *RHDFÉ* 46: 367–88.

Piejko, F. (1985), 'Review: J. et L. Robert, *Fouilles d'Amyzon en Carie, I: Exploration, monnaies et inscriptions*', *Gnomon* 57(7): 608–21.

—— (1991), 'Antiochus III and Teos Reconsidered', *Belleten Türk Tarih Kurumu* 55: 13–69.

Piérart, M. (2013), 'Penser Rome en Grec ... Penser Rome en grec', in Curty, O. (ed.), *Épigraphie romaine et historiographie antique et moderne*, Fribourg, 21–34.

Pierson, P. (1996), 'The Path to European Integration: A Historical Institutionalist Approach', *Comp. Pol. St.* 29(2): 123–63.

—— (2004), *Politics in Time: History, Institutions, and Social Analysis*, Princeton.

Pina Polo, F. (2011), *The Consul at Rome: The Civil Functions of the Consuls in the Roman Republic*, Cambridge.

—— (2013), 'Foreign Eloquence in the Roman Senate', in Steel, C. & van der Blom, H. (eds), *Community and Communication: Oratory and Politics in Republican Rome*, Oxford, 247–66.

—— (2013a), 'The Political Role of the *consules designati*', *Historia* 62(4): 420–52.

—— (2015), 'Foreign *clientelae* Revisited: A Methodological Critique', in Jehne, M. & Pina Polo, F. (eds), *Foreign* clientelae *in the Roman Empire: A Reconsideration*, Stuttgart, 19–41.

Pocock, J.G.A. (1987), 'The Concept of a Language and the *métier d'historien*: Some Considerations on Practice', in Padgen, A. (ed.), *The Languages of Political Theory in Early-Modern Europe*, Cambridge, 19–38.

—— (1987a), 'Texts as Events: Reflections on the History of Political Thought', in Sharpe, K. & Zwicker, S.N. (eds), *Politics of Discourse: The Literature and History of Seventeenth-Century England*, Berkeley, 21–34.

—— (1989 [1971]), 'Languages and Their Implications: The Transformation of the Study of Political Thought', in Pocock, J.G.A., *Politics, Language and Time: Essays on Political Thought and History*, Chicago, 3–41.

Poitras, G. & Geranio, M. (2016), 'Trading of Shares in the societates publicanorum', *Explor Econ Hist.* 61: 95–118.

Pont, A.-V. (2012), 'Aphrodisias, Presque une île: la cité et ses réseaux d'Auguste à 249/250', *Chiron* 42: 319–46.

Pottier, E. & Hauvette-Besnault, A. (1880), 'Décret des Abdéritains trouvé à Téos', *BCH* 4 (1): 47–59.

Prag, J.R.W. (2014), 'Cities and Civic Life in Late Hellenistic Roman Sicily', *CCG* 25: 165–208.

Premerstein, A. v. (1937), *Vom Werden und Wesen des Prinzipats*, Munich.

Price, S.R.F. (1979), 'The Divine Right of Emperors', *CR* 29(2): 277–9.

—— (1984), *Rituals and Power: The Roman Imperial Cult in Asia Minor*, Cambridge.

Prignitz, S. (2011), 'Ein Augustuspriester des Jahres 27 v. Chr.', *ZPE* 178: 210–14.

Pucci ben Zeev, M. (1996), *Jewish Rights in the Roman World: The Greek and Roman Documents Quoted by Flavius Josephus*, Tübingen.

Purcell, N. (1990), 'Maps, Lists, Money, Order and Power', *JRS* 80: 178–82.

—— (2001), 'The *ordo scribarum*: A Study in the Loss of Memory', *MEFRA* 113(2): 633–74.

Quass, F. (1984), 'Zum Einfluss der römischen Nobilität auf das Honoratiorenregime in den Städten des Griechischen Ostens', *Hermes* 112(2): 199–215.

—— (1993), *Die Honoratioren-schicht in den Städten des griechischen Ostens: Untersuchungen zur politischen und sozialen Entwicklung in hellenistischer und römischer Zeit*, Stuttgart.

Radt, S.L. (2002–2011), *Strabons Geographika*, Göttingen.

Rafferty, D. (2019), *Provincial Allocations in Rome, 123–52 BCE*, Stuttgart.

Raggi, A. (2001), 'Senatus consultum de Asclepiade Clazomenio sociisque', *ZPE* 135: 73–116.

—— (2006), *Seleuco di Rhosos. Cittadinanza e privilegi nell'Oriente greco in età tardo-repubblicana*, Pisa.

—— (2010), 'La scomparsa degli οἱ κατ' ἄνδρα dall'assemblea provinciale d'Asia', *ZPE* 172: 148–50.

—— (2010a), '*Praetor qui inter peregrinos et cives ius dixit* nel trattato tra Rome e Lici (46 a.C.)', in Mantovani, D. & Pellecchi, L (eds), *Eparcheia, autonomia, civitas Romana*, Pavia, 45–67.

—— (2020), '[C. Iu]lius Menodoros, il primo tribuno militare dalla provincia d'Asia', *Tyche* 35: 157–70.

Raggi, A. & Buongiorno, P. (2020), *Il senatus consultum de Plarasensibus et Aphrodisiensibus del 39 a.C.: Edizione, traduzione e commento*, Stuttgart.

Ramsay, J.T. (1999), 'Mithridates, the Banner of Ch'ih–Yu, and the Comet Coin', *HSCP* 99: 197–253.

Raßelnberg, A.L. (2007), 'Ehrung für einen Q. Mucius Scaevola in Nysa', *EA* 40: 52–4.

Rathbone, D. (2003), 'The Control and Exploitation of *ager publicus* in Italy under the Roman Republic', in Aubert, J.-J. (ed.), *Tâches publiques et entreprise privée dans le monde romain*, Geneva, 135–78.

Raubitschek, A.E. (1954), 'Epigraphical Notes on Julius Caesar', *JRS* 44: 65–75.

Rauh, N. (1986), 'Cicero's Business Friendships: Economics and Politics in the Late Roman Republic', *Aevum* 60(1): 3–30.

Rawson, E.D. (1975), 'Caesar's Heritage: Hellenistic Kings and their Roman Equals', *JRS* 65: 148–59.

—— (1994), 'Caesar: Civil War and Dictatorship', *CAH*² 9: 424–67.

Reynolds, J.M. (1982), *Aphrodisias and Rome: Documents from the Excavation of the Theatre at Aphrodisias Conducted by Professor Kenan T. Erim, Together with Some Related Texts*, London.

Rhodes, P.J. & Lewis, D.M. (1997), *The Decrees of Greek Cities*, Oxford.

Rich, J.W. (2008), 'Treaties, Allies, and the Roman Conquest of Italy', in de Souza, P. & France, P. (eds), *War and Peace in Ancient and Medieval History*, Cambridge, 51–76.

—— (2012), 'Making the Emergency Permanent: *Auctoritas, potestas* and the Evolution of the Principate of Augustus', in Riviere, Y. (ed.), *Des réformes augustéenes*, Rome, 37–121.

Rich, J.W. & Williams, J.H.C. (1999), '*Leges et Iura PR Restituit*: A New *Aureus* of Octavian and the Settlement of 28–27 BC', *NC* 159: 169–213.

Richardson, J.S. (2008), *The Language of Empire: Rome and the Idea of Empire from the Third Century BC to the Second Century AD*, Cambridge.

—— (2011), '*Fines provinciae*', in Hekster, O. & Kaizer, T. (eds), *Frontiers in the Roman World: Proceedings of the Ninth Workshop of the International Network Impact of Empire (Durham, 16–19 April 2009)*, Leiden, 1–12.

Ridley, R.T. (1975), 'Cicero and Sulla', *WS* 88: 83–108.

Rigsby, K.J. (1979), 'The Era of the Province of Asia', *Phoenix* 33(1): 39–47.

—— (1988), 'Provincia Asia', *TAPA* 118: 123–53.

—— (1996), *Asylia: Territorial Inviolability in the Hellenistic World*, Berkeley.

—— (2005), 'Agathopolis and Doulopolis', *EA* 38: 109–15.

Ritti, T. (2017), *Hierapolis di Frigia IX: Storia e istituzioni di Hierapolis*, Istanbul.

Robert, L. (1937), *Études Anatoliennes. Recherches sur les inscriptions grecques de l'Asie Mineure*, Paris.

—— (1940), *Hellenica. Recueil d'épigraphie, de numismatique et d'antiquités grecques*, vol. 1, Paris.

—— (1948), *Hellenica. Recueil d'épigraphie, de numismatique et d'antiquités grecques*, vol. 6, Paris.

—— (1949), *Hellenica. Recueil d'épigraphie, de numismatique et d'antiquités grecques*, vol. 7, Paris.

—— (1950), *Hellenica. Recueil d'épigraphie, de numismatique et d'antiquités grecques*, vol. 8, Paris.
—— (1958), 'Inscriptions grecques de Sidè en Pamphylie', *RPh* 32: 15–53.
—— (1969), 'Inscriptions', in des Gagniers, J., Devambez, P., Kahil, L., & Gionouvès, R. (eds), *Laodicée du Lycos: Le nymphée, campagnes 1961–1963*, Quebec, 247–389.
—— (1969a), 'Théophane de Mytilène a Constantinople', *CRAI* 113(1): 42–64.
—— (1969b), 'Inscriptions grecques d'Asie Mineure', *OMS* 1: 611–32.
—— (1987 [1984]), 'Un décret de Pergame', in Robert, L. (ed.), *Documents d'Asie Mineure*, Athens, 460–77.
—— (1989 [1966]), 'Inscriptions d'Aphrodisias', *OMS* 6: 1–56.
Robert, L. & Robert, J., 1989, *Claros I: Décrets Hellénistiques*, Paris.
Robinson, E.S.G. (1954), 'Cistophoroi in the Name of King Eumenes', *NC* 14: 1–8.
Robinson, W. (2001), 'Social Theory and Globalization: The Rise of a Transnational State', *Theory & Society* 30: 157–200.
Rose, C.B. (2005), 'The Parthians in Augustan Rome', *AJA* 109: 21–75.
Roselaar, S. (2010), *Public Land in the Roman Republic: A Social and Economic History of* ager publicus *in Italy, 396–89 BC*, Oxford.
Rostovtzeff, M.I. (1902), *Geschichte der Staatspacht in der Römischen Kaiserzeit bis Diokletian*, Leipzig.
—— (1910), *Studien zur Geschichte der römischen Kolonates*, Leipzig.
—— (1917), 'Caesar and the South of Russia', *JRS* 7: 27–44.
—— (1941), *Social and Economic History of the Hellenistic World*, Oxford.
Röthe, C. (1978), *Humanitas, Fides und Verwandtes in der römischen Provinzialpolitik: Untersuchungen zur politischen Funktion römischer Verhaltensnormen bei Cicero*, Berlin.
Roussel, P. (1934), 'Un Syrien au service de Rome et d'Octave', *Syria* 15(1): 33–74.
Rousset, D. (2010), *De Lycie en Cabalide: la convention entre les Lyciens et Termessos près d'Oinoanda*, Geneva.
Rowan, C. (2019), *From Caesar to Augustus: (c.49 BC–AD 14): Using Coins as Sources*, Cambridge.
Rowe, G.D. (2002), *Princes and Political Cultures: The New Tiberian Senatorial Decrees*, Ann Arbor.
—— (2008), 'The Elaboration and Diffusion of the Text of the *Monumentum Ephesenum*', in Cottier, M. et al. (eds), *The Customs Law of Asia*, Oxford, 236–50.
Rumscheid, F. (2002), 'Den Anschluß verpaßt: Priene in der (frühen) Kaiserzeit', in Berns, C., von Hesberg, H., Vandeput, L., & Waelkens, M. (eds), *Patris und Imperium. Kulturelle und politische Identität in den Städten der römsichen Provinzen Kleinasiens in der frühen Kaiserzeit. Kolloquium Köln, November 1998*, Leuven, 77–87.
Runciman, W.G. (1989), *Confessions of a Reluctant Theorist*, New York.
—— (2011), 'Empire as a Topic in Comparative Sociology', in Bang P. & Bayly, C. (eds), *Tributary Empires in Global History*, Cambridge, 99–107.
Ryan, G. (2022), *Greek Cities and Roman Governors: Placing Power in Imperial Asia Minor*, Abingdon.
Salway, B. (2000), 'Prefects, *patroni*, and Decurions: A New Perspective on the Album of Canusium', *BICS* 44(S73): 115–71.
Sánchez, P. (2007), 'La convention judiciaire dans le traité conclu entre Rome et les Lyciens (*P.Schøyen* I 25)', *Chiron* 37: 363–81.
—— (2010), '*ΕΠΙ ΡΩΜΑΙΚΩΙ ΘΑΝΑΤΩΙ* dans le décret pour Ménippos de Colophon: «pour la mort d'un Romain» ou «en vue d'un supplice romain»?', *Chiron* 40: 41–60.

Santangelo, F. (2006), 'Magnesia sul Meandro alla vigilia della prima guerra mitridatica. Nota sulla cronologia di *I.Magn.* 100b', *EA* 39: 133–8.
—— (2007), *Sulla, the Elites and the Empire: A Study of Roman Policies in Italy and the Greek East*, Leiden.
—— (2009), 'With or Without You: Some Late Hellenistic Narratives of Contemporary History', *SCI* 28: 57–78.
—— (2009a), 'What Did the Cloatii Do for Gytheum? A Note on *Syll.*³ 748', *Historia* 58 (3): 361–6.
—— (2014), 'Roman Politics in the 70s B.C.: A Story of Realignments?', *JRS* 104: 1–27.
—— (2018), 'Theophanes of Mytilene: Cicero and Pompey's Inner Circle', in van der Blom, H., Gray, C., & Steel, C. (eds), *Institutions and Ideology in Republican Rome: Speech, Audience and Decision*, Oxford, 128–46.
Sayar, M.H., Siewert, P., & Täuber, H. (1994), 'Asylie-Erklärungen des Sulla und des Lucullus für das Isis- und Sarapisheiligtum von Mopsuhestia (Ostkilikien)', *Tyche* 9: 113–30.
Scheidel, W. (2013), 'Studying the State', in Bang, P.F. & Scheidel, W. (eds), *The Oxford Handbook of the State in the Ancient Near East and Mediterranean*, Oxford, 1–57.
Schleussner, B. (1976), 'Die Gesandtschaft P. Scipio Nasicas im Jahr 133/2 v. Chr. und die Provinzialisierung des Königreichs Pergamon', *Chiron* 6: 97–112.
—— (1978), *Die Legaten der Republik. Decem legati und ständige Hilfsgesandte*, Munich.
Schuler, C. (2007), 'Ein Vertrag zwischen Rom und den Lykiern aus Tyberissos', in Schuler, C. (ed.), *Griechische Epigraphik in Lykien: Eine Zwischenblick*, Vienna, 51–79.
Schulten, A. (1892), *De conventibus civium romanorum: sive de rebus publicis civium romanorum mediis inter municipium et collegium*, Berlin.
Scott, J.C. (1990), *Domination and the Arts of Resistance: Hidden Transcripts*, New Haven.
Segre, M., (1938), 'Iscrizioni di Licia', *Clara Rhodos* 9: 179–208.
Shaw, B.D. (1981), 'The Elder Pliny's African Geography', *Historia* 30(4): 424–71.
Sherk, R.K. (1966), 'The Text of the *Senatus Consultum de Agro Pergameno*', *GRBS* 7(4): 361–9.
—— (1969), *Roman Documents from the Greek East*, Baltimore.
Sherwin-White, A.N. (1939), 'Procurator Augusti', *PBSR* 15: 11–26.
—— (1976), 'Rome, Pamphylia and Cilicia, 133–77 BC', *JRS* 66: 1–14.
—— (1982), 'The *lex repetundarum* and the Political Ideas of Gaius Gracchus', *JRS* 72: 18–31.
—— (1984), *Roman Foreign Policy in the East: 168 B.C. to A.D. 1*, London.
Sherwin-White, S.M. (1978), *Ancient Cos: An Historical Study from the Dorian Settlement to the Imperial Period*, Göttingen.
Silvestrini, M. (1996), 'Dalla «*nobilitas*» municipale all'ordine senatorio: esempi da Larino e da Venosa', *CCG* 7: 269–82.
Skoda, H. (2012), 'A Historian's Perspective on the Present Volume', in Dresch, P. & Skoda, H. (eds), *Legalism: Anthropology and History*, Oxford, 39–53.
Skramkiewicz, R. (1976), *Les gouverneurs de province à l'époque Augustéene*, 2 vols, Paris.
Smallwood, E.M. (1970), *Philonis Alexandrini Legatio ad Gaium*, 2nd edn, Leiden.
Smith, R.R.R. (1993), *The Monument of C. Iulius Zoilos*, Mainz.
Snowdon, M. (2008), 'Commemorating Freedom: *I.Metropolis* and the Restoration of Freedom', *Mouseion* 8(3): 377–93.
—— (2014), '"In the Friendship of the Romans": Melitaia, Narthakion and Greco-Roman Interstate Friendship in the Second Century BCE', *Historia* 63(4): 422–44.

Soraci, C. (2010), 'Riflessioni storico-comparative sul termine *stipendiarius*', in Cataudello, M., Greco, A., & Mariotta, G. (eds), *Strumenti e tecniche della riscossione dei tribute nel mondo antico*, Padua, 43–80.

Spagnuolo Vigorita, T. (1997), '*Lex portus Asiae*: un nuovo documento sull'appalto delle imposte', in *I rapporti contrattuali con la pubblica amministrazione nell'esperienza storico-giuridica: congresso internazionale sul tema, Torino, 17–19 ottobre 1994*, Naples, 113–90.

Stasse, B. (2009), '*Ἐπαρχεία*: le cas du *iussum Augusti* de 27ª (*I.Kyme*, 17)', *L'Antiquité Classique* 78: 161–8.

Stauber, J. (1996), *Die Bucht von Adramytteion*, Bonn.

Steel, C. (2004), 'Being Economical with the Truth: What Really Happened at Lampsacus?', in Powell, J. & Paterson, J. (eds), *Cicero the Advocate*, Oxford, 233–51.

—— (2012), 'The *lex Pompeia de provinciis* of 52 BC: A Reconsideration', *Historia* 61(1): 83–93.

—— (2014), 'The Roman Senate and the Post-Sullan *res publica*', *Historia* 63(3): 323–39.

—— (2014a), 'Rethinking Sulla: The Case of the Roman Senate', *CQ* 64(2): 657–68.

—— (2016), 'Early-Career Prosecutors: Forensic Activity and Senatorial Careers in the Late Republic', in du Plessis, P.J. (ed.), *Cicero's Law: Rethinking Roman Law of the Late Republic*, Edinburgh, 205–27.

Stern, S. (2012), *Calendars in Antiquity: Empires, States, & Societies*, Oxford.

Stoop, J. (2017), 'Between City and Empire: Awarding Statues to Romans in Greek Cities', *P&P* 235: 3–36.

Strootman, R. (2020), '"To be Magnanimous and Grateful": The Entanglement of Cities and Empires in the Hellenistic Aegean', in Domingo Gygax, M. & Zuiderhoek, A. (eds), *Benefactors and the Polis: The Public Gift in the Greek Cities from the Homeric World to Late Antiquity*, Cambridge, 137–78.

Storrs, C. (2016), 'Magistrates to Administrators, Composite Monarchy to Fiscal-Military Empire: Empire and Bureaucracy in the Spanish Monarchy, *c.*1492–1825', in Crooks, P. & Parson, T.H. (eds), *Empires and Bureaucracy in World History: From Late Antiquity to the Twentieth Century*, Cambridge, 291–317.

Strubbe, J.H.M. (1984–6), 'Gründer Kleinasiatischer Städte Fiktion und Realität', *AncSoc* 15–17: 253–304.

—— (2004), 'Cultic Honours for Benefactors in the Cities of Asia Minor', in de Ligt, L., Hemelrijk, E.A., & Singor, H.W. (eds), *Roman Rule and Civic Life: Local and Regional Perspectives: Proceedings of the Fourth Workshop of the International Network: Impact of Empire (Roman Empire, c.200 B.C.–A.D. 476): Leiden, June 25-28 June 2003*, Amsterdam, 315–30.

Stumpf, G.R. (1985), 'C. Atinius C.f., Praetor in Asia 122–121 v. Chr., auf einem Cistophor', *ZPE* 61: 186–90.

—— (1991), *Numismatische Studien zur Chronologie der römischen Statthalter in Kleinasien (122 v. Chr.– 63 n. Chr.)*, Saarbrücken.

Sumner, G.V. (1973), *The Orators in Cicero's Brutus: Prosopography and Chronology*, Toronto.

—— (1978), 'Governors of Asia in the 90s B.C.', *GRBS* 19: 147–53.

Sutherland, C.H.V. (1970), *The cistophori of Augustus*, London.

—— (1973), 'Augustan *aurei* and *denarii* Attributable to the Mint of Pergamum', *RN* 15: 129–51.

Syme, R. (1956), 'Some Friends of the Caesars', *AJPh* 77(3): 264–73.

—— (1961), 'Who was Vedius Pollio?', *JRS* 51: 23–30.

—— (1979 [1939]), 'Observations on the Province of Cilicia', *Roman Papers* 1: 120–48.
—— (1979a [1963]), 'The Greeks under Roman Rule', *Roman Papers* 2: 566–81.
—— (1982), 'Tacitus: Some Sources of his Information', *JRS* 72: 68–82.
—— (1995), *Anatolica: Studies in Strabo*, Birley, A. (ed.), Oxford.
Szaivert, W. (2008), 'Kistophoren und die Münzbilder in Pergamon', *NZ* 116–117: 29–43.
Tan, J. (2017), *Power and Public Finance at Rome, 264–49 BCE*, New York.
Täuber, H. (1991), 'Die syrische-kilikische Grenze während der Prinzipatszeit', *Tyche* 6: 201–10.
Täubler, E. (1913), *Imperium Romanum: Studien zur Entwicklungsgeschichte des römischen Reichs*, Berlin.
Thériault, G. (2001), 'Remarques sur le culte des magistrats romains en Orient', *CEA* 37: 85–95.
—— (2003), 'Évergétisme grec et administration romaine: La famille cnidienne de Gaios Ioulios Théopompos', *Phoenix* 57(3/4): 232–56.
—— (2011), 'Culte des évergètes (magistrats) romains et *agônes* en Asie Mineure', in Konuk, K. (ed.), *Stephanèphoros. De l'économie amtique à l'Asie Mineure. Hommages à Raymond Descat*, Bordeaux, 377–88.
Thomas, P.D. (2009), *The Gramscian Moment: Philosophy, Hegemony and Marxism*, Leiden.
Thompson, J.B. (1990), *Ideology and Modern Culture: Critical Social Theory in the Era of Mass Communication*, Cambridge.
Thonemann, P. (2003), 'Hellenistic Inscriptions from Lydia', *EA* 36: 95–108.
—— (2004), 'The Date of Lucullus' Quaestorship', *ZPE* 149: 80–2.
—— (2008), 'Cistophoric Geography: Toriaion and Kormasa', *NC* 168: 43–60.
—— (2010), 'The Women of Akmoneia', *JRS* 100: 163–78.
—— (2011), *The Maeander Valley: A Historical Geography from Antiquity to Byzantium*, Cambridge.
—— (2012), 'A Copy of Augustus' *Res Gestae* at Sardis?', *Historia* 61(3): 282–8.
—— (2013), 'The Attalid State, 188–133 BC', in Thonemann, P. (ed.), *Attalid Asia Minor: Money, International Relations, and the State*, Oxford, 1–47.
—— (2013a), 'Phrygia: An Anarchist History, 950 BC–AD 100', in Thonemann, P. (ed.), *Roman Phrygia: Culture and Society*, Cambridge, 1–40.
—— (2015), 'The Calendar of the Roman Province of Asia', *ZPE* 196: 123–41.
Thonemann, P. & Adak, M. (2022), *Teos and Abdera: Two Cities in Peace and War*, Oxford.
Thornton, J. (1998), '*Misos Rhomaion* o *phobos Mithridatou*? Echi storiografici di un dibattito diplomatico', *MedAnt* 1(1): 271–309.
—— (1999), 'Una città e due regine: *Eleutheria* e lotta politica a Cizico fra gli Attalidi e i Giulio Claudi', *MedAnt* 2(2): 497–538.
Tibiletti, G. (1957), 'Rome and the *ager Pergamenus*: The *acta* of 129 B.C.', *JRS* 47: 136–8.
Tilly, C. (2003), *The Politics of Collective Violence*, Cambridge.
Toher, M. (1985), 'The Date of Nicolaus' *Βίος Καίσαρος*', *GRBS* 26: 199–206.
Tröster, M. (2008), *Themes, Character, and Politics in Plutarch's Life of Lucullus: The Construction of a Roman Aristocrat*, Stuttgart.
—— (2009), 'Roman Hegemony and Non-State Violence: A Fresh Look at Pompey's Campaign against the Pirates', *G&R* 56: 14–33.
Tuchelt, K. (1979), *Frühe Denkmäler Roms in Kleinasien: Beiträge zur archäologischen Überlieferung aus der Zeit der Republik und des Augustus*, Tübingen.
Van Bremen, R. (2008), 'The Date and Context of the Kymaian Decrees for Archippe', *REA* 110(2): 357–82.

Van Nijf, O. (2001), 'Local Heroes: Athletics, Festivals and Elite Self-Fashioning in the Roman East', in Goldhill, S. (ed.), *Being Greek under Rome: Cultural Identity, the Second Sophistic and the Development of Empire*, Cambridge, 306–34.

Ventroux, O. (2017), *Pergame: Les élites d'une ancienne capitale royale à l'époque romaine*, Rennes.

Vervaet, F.J. (2004), 'The *lex Valeria* and Sulla's Empowerment as Dictator (82–79 BCE)', *CCG* 15: 37–84.

—— (2014), *The High Command in the Roman Republic: The Principle of the* summum imperium auspiciumque *from 509 to 19 BCE*, Stuttgart.

—— (2020), 'The Triumvirate *rei publicae constituendae*: Political and Constitutional Aspects', in Pina Polo, F. (ed.), *The Triumviral Period: Civil War, Political Crisis and Transformation*, Zaragoza, 23–48.

Veyne, P. (1976), *Le pain et le cirque*, Paris.

Viereck, P. (1888), *Sermo Graecus quo senatus populusque Romanus magistratusque populi Romani usque ad Tiberii Caesaris aetatem in scriptis publicis usi sunt examinatu*, Oxford.

Virgilio, B. (1994), 'La città ellenistica e i suoi «benefattori»: Pergamo e Diodoro Pasparos', *Athenaeum* 82(2): 299–314.

—— (2013), 'Forme e linguaggi della comunicazione fra re ellenistici e città', *Studi Ellenistici* 27: 243–61.

Vitale, M, (2012), *Eparchie und Koinon in Kleinasien von der ausgehenden Republik bis ins 3. Jh. n. Chr.*, Bonn.

—— (2014), 'Il sommo sacerozio federale del culto imperiale nell'oriente romano: Un riesame generale della documentazione epigrafica e numismatica', *MedAnt* 17(1): 287–308.

Walker, D.R. (1976), *The Metrology of the Roman Silver Coinage*, Oxford.

Wallace, C. (2014), '*Ager Publicus* in the Greek East: *I. Priene* 111 and Other Examples of Resistance to the *publicani*', *Historia* 63(1): 38–78.

Walser, A.V. (2021), 'Das sogenannte *Senatus Consultum Popillianum*', in Buongiorno, P. & Camodeca, G. (eds), *Die senatus consulta in den epigraphischen Quellen: Texte und Bezeugungen*, Stuttgart, 147–69.

Wankerl, V. (2009), *Appello ad Principem: Urteilsstil und Urteilstechnik in kaiserlichen Berufungsentscheidungen (Augustus bis Caracalla)*, Munich.

Watson, A. (1983), 'Roman Slave Law and Romanist Ideology', *Phoenix* 37(1): 53–65.

Weber, M. (1978), *Economy and Society: An Outline of Interpretative Sociology*, New York.

Wehrli, C. (1978), '«*Ῥωμαῖοι οἱ κοινοὶ εὐεργέται πάντων*» («Les Romains, communs bienfaiteurs de tous») dans les inscriptions grecques de l'époque republicaine', *SicGymn* 31: 479–96.

Welch, K. (1990), 'The *Praefectura Urbis* of 45 BC and the Ambitions of L. Cornelius Balbus', *Antichthon* 24: 53–69.

Welles, C.B. (1934), *Royal Correspondence in the Hellenistic Period: A Study in Greek Epigraphy*, New Haven.

Wendt, A. (1999), *Social Theory of International Politics*, Cambridge.

Wilamowitz-Moellendorf, U. von (1902), *Griechisches Lesebuch*, Berlin.

Wilhelm, A. (1909), *Beiträge zur griechischen Inschriftenkunde*, Vienna.

Williamson, C. (1987), 'Monuments of Bronze: Roman Legal Documents on Bronze Tablets', *CA* 6(1): 160–83.

—— (2005), *The Laws of the Roman People: Public Law in the Expansion and Decline of the Roman Republic*, Ann Arbor.

Willrich, H. (1899), 'Alabanda und Rom zur Zeit des ersten Krieges gegen Mithradates', *Hermes* 34: 305–11.

Winterling, A. (2014), '"Staat" in der griechisch-römsichen Republik', in Lundgreen, C. (ed.), *Staatlichkeit in Rom? Diskurse und Praxis (in) der römischen Republik*, Stuttgart, 249–56.

Wörrle, M. (1988), *Stadt und Fest im kaiserzeitlichen Kleinasien: Studien zu einer agonistischen Stiftung aus Oinoanda*, Munich.

—— (2000), 'Pergamon um 133 v. Chr.', *Chiron* 30: 543–76.

—— (2009), 'Neue Inschriftenfunde aus Aizanoi V: Aizanoi und Rom I', *Chiron* 39: 409–44.

—— (2011), 'Neue Inschriftenfunde aus Aizanoi VI: Aizanoi und Rom II', *Chiron* 41: 357–76.

—— (2014), 'Neue Inschriftenfunde aus Aizanoi VII: Aizanoi und Rom III. Der julisch-claudische Kaiserkult in Aizanoi', *Chiron* 44: 439–512.

Worth, O. (2011), 'Recasting Gramsci in International Politics', *Rev Int Stud.* 37(1): 373–92.

Woytek, B. (2016), 'The Denarii *RRC* 445/3, Signed by the Consuls Lentulus and Marcellus (49 BC): A Die Study', in Haymann, F., Hollstein, W., & Jehne, M. (eds), *Neue Forschungen zur Münzprägungen der römischen Republik: Beiträge zum internationalen Kolloquium im Residenzschloss Dresden 19.–21. Juni 2014*, Bonn, 173–214.

—— (2019), 'Inschriften und Legenden auf Münzen des Augustus im Kontext. Eine numismatisch-epigraphische Studie', *Chiron* 49: 383–440.

Yakobson, A. (2009), 'Public Opinion, Foreign Policy and "Just War" in the Late Republic', in Eilers, C. (ed.), *Diplomats and Diplomacy in the Roman World*, Leiden, 45–72.

Yarrow, L.M. (2006), *Historiography at the End of the Republic: Provincial Perspectives on Roman Rule*, Oxford.

—— (2012), '*Decem Legati*: A Flexible Institution, Rigidly Perceived', in Smith C. & Yarrow, L.M. (eds), *Imperialism, Cultural Politics, & Polybius*, Oxford, 168–83.

Ypsilanti, M. (2018), *The Epigrams of Crinagoras of Mytilene: Introduction, Text, Commentary*, Oxford.

Zack, A. (2001), *Studien zum 'römischen Völkerrecht': Kriegsklärung, Kriegsbeschluss, Beeidung und Ratifikation zwischenstaatlicher Verträge, internationaler Freundschaftund und Feindschaft während der römischen Republik bis zum Beginn das Prinzipats*, Göttingen.

Zarecki, J. (2012), 'The Cypriot Exemption from *evocatio* and the Character of Cicero's Proconsulship', *G&R* 59(1): 46–55.

Zuiderhoek, A. (2004), 'Review: C. Eilers, *Roman Patrons of Greek Cities*', *JRS* 94: 264–6.

—— (2008), 'On the Political Sociology of the Imperial Greek City', *GRBS* 48: 417–45.

—— (2009), *The Politics of Munificence in the Roman Empire: Citizens, Elites and Benefactors in Asia Minor*, Cambridge.

—— (2017), *The Ancient City*, Cambridge.

De Zulueta, F. (1953), *The Institutes of Gaius*, 2 vols, Oxford.

Zoumbaki, S. (2018), 'Sulla, the Army, the Officers and the *poleis* of Greece: A Reassessment of Warlordism in the First Phase of the Mithridatic Wars', in Ñaco del Hoyo, T. & López Sánchez, F. (eds), *War, Warlords, and Interstates Relations in the Ancient Mediterranean*, Leiden, 351–79.

Index

For the benefit of digital users, indexed terms that span two pages (e.g., 52–53) may, on occasion, appear on only one of those pages.